Italian Yearbook of Human Rights 2020

P.I.E. Peter Lang

Bruxelles · Bern · Berlin · New York · Oxford · Wien

Translator from the Italian version:
Rosemary Burnham

The Yearbook is edited by the
University of Padova
Human Rights Centre "Antonio Papisca",
via Martiri della Libertà 2,
35137 Padova

tel. +39 049.8271817

centro.dirittiumani@unipd.it
www.italianhumanrightsyearbook.eu

Italian Yearbook of Human Rights 2020

Italian Yearbook of Human Rights
Vol. 11

UNIVERSITÀ DEGLI STUDI DI PADOVA

HUMAN RIGHTS CENTRE "ANTONIO PAPISCA"

United Nations Educational, Scientific and Cultural Organization*

UNESCO Chair "Human Rights, Democracy and Peace", University of Padova

REGIONE DEL VENETO

ARCHIVIO PACE DIRITTI UMANI peace human rights

* The authors are responsible for the choice and presentation of information contained in this publication as well as for the opinions expressed therein, which are not necessarily those of UNESCO and do not commit the Organization

First Italian edition: *Annuario italiano dei diritti umani 2020*, Padova, Padova University Press, 2020.

ISSN 2294-8848
ISBN 978-2-8076-1795-7
ePDF 978-2-8076-1796-4
ePub 978-2-8076-1797-1
Mobi 978-2-8076-1798-8
DOI 10.3726/b17905
D/2021/5678/06

Bibliographic information published by "Die Deutsche Nationalbibliothek"
"Die Deutsche Nationalbibliothek" lists this publication in the "Deutsche Nationalbibliografie"; detailed bibliographic data is available in the Internet at http://dnb.d-nb.de.

Contents

PART III Italy in Dialogue with International Human Rights Institutions

PART IV National and International Case-Law

List of Acronyms

C.l.: Constitutional Law (legge costituzionale)
CAT: Convention against Torture and Other Cruel, Inhuman or Degrading Treatment or Punishment
CDFUE: Charter of Fundamental Rights of the European Union
CEDAW: Convention on the Elimination of All Forms of Discrimination against Women
CIDU: Inter-Ministerial Committee for Human Rights (*Comitato interministeriale dei diritti umani*)
CJEU: Court of Justice of the European Union
CM: Committee of Ministers of the Council of Europe
CoE: Council of Europe
CPED: International Convention for the Protection of All Persons from Enforced Disappearance
CPR: Repatriation Centre (*Centro di permanenza per i rimpatri*)
CPT: European Committee for the Prevention of Torture and Inhuman or Degrading Treatment or Punishment
CRC: Convention on the Rights of the Child
CRPD: Convention on the Rights of Persons with Disabilities
D.p.c.m.: Decree of the President of the Council of Ministers (decreto del Presidente del Congilio dei Ministri)
DPO: Department for Equal Opportunities of the Presidency of the Council of Ministers
D.p.r.: Decree of the President of the Republic (decreto del Presidente della Repubblica)

ECHR:	European Convention for the Protection of Human Rights and Fundamental Freedoms
ECOSOC:	United Nations Economic and Social Council
ECRI:	European Commission against Racism and Intolerance
ECtHR:	European Court of Human Rights
ESC-R:	European Social Charter (Revised)
FAO:	Food and Agriculture Organisation of the United Nations
FRA:	Fundamental Rights Agency of the European Union
FRONTEX:	European Border and Coast Guard Agency
GRECO:	Group of States against Corruption (Council of Europe)
GRETA:	Group of Experts on Action against Trafficking in Human Beings (Council of Europe)
ICC:	International Criminal Court
ICCPR:	International Covenant on Civil and Political Rights
ICERD:	International Convention on the Elimination of All Forms of Racial Discrimination
ICESCR:	International Covenant on Economic, Social and Cultural Rights
ICRMW:	International Convention on the Protection of the Rights of all Migrant Workers and Their Families
ILO:	International Labour Organisation
IOM:	International Organisation for Migration
L.:	Law
L.d.:	Law Decree (decreto-legge)
Lgs.d.:	Legislative Decree (decreto legislativo)
NATO:	North Atlantic Treaty Organisation
ODIHR:	Office for Democratic Institutions and Human Rights (OSCE)
OHCHR:	Office of the High Commissioner of the United Nations for Human Rights
OPCAT:	Optional Protocol to the Convention against Torture

OSCE: Organisation for Security and Cooperation in Europe
P.l.: Provincial Law
PACE: Parliamentary Assembly of the Council of Europe
R.l.: Regional Law
TAR: Administrative Regional Court (Tribunale Amministrativo Regionale)
TFUE: Treaty on the Functioning of the European Union
TUE: Treaty on European Union
UNAR: Office for the Promotion of Equal Treatment and the Fight against Racial Discrimination (*Ufficio per la promozione della parità di trattamento e la rimozione delle discriminazioni fondate sulla razza e sull'origine etnica*)
UNDP: United Nations Development Programme
UNEP: United Nations Environmental Programme
UNESCO: United Nations Educational, Scientific and Cultural Organisation
UNGA: United Nations General Assembly
UNHCR: United Nations High Commission for Refugees
UNICEF: United Nations Children's Fund
UPR: Universal Periodic Review
WHO: World Health Organisation

Italy and Human Rights in 2019: Back on Track?

One year ago, the Introduction of the *Yearbook 2019* spoke of Italy's stagnation, immobilisation and regressive attitude on human rights. It was a difficult moment for conducting human rights dialogue between the State and the international community. Two distinguishing features stood out during that time: friction between Italy and its international peers and a suggested strategic change in attitude on human rights issues; both in policy and tone, the country moved closer to the ideas of openly critical and hostile governments regarding international monitoring, protection and guarantee of rights. This implied change in strategic position appeared both within the European setting (where in general, "human rights" issues tend to be technical and not politicised) and in a global setting (where there is a greater political polarisation of these issues). Italian "sovereignism" (meant here as a principally rhetorical trend to disengage from long-standing international allies and to assertively and with authority declare national interests) finds its place in immigration policies. Government action and initiatives have developed around this topic, bringing to the forefront the role of international NGOs, managing public order and protecting the groups most at risk of discrimination and hate speech and the rights of private stakeholders to personal freedom – including migrants held in reception centres.

Some communications sent by the Special Procedures of the Human Rights Council tackled these problems in 2019. Similar concerns were expressed by the Committees on the Rights of the Child and on Enforced Disappearances, both of which evaluated Italy's reports this year. Once again, we saw similar considerations in the in-depth evaluation reports of many monitoring bodies of the Council of Europe – European Committee of Social Rights, CPT, GREVIO, GRETA, ECRI, and GRECO, highlighting consistent problems in the Italian system for human rights protection. Even the Commissioner for Human Rights of the Council of Europe, in a letter to the Government and in other institutional reports, drew attention to some grave issues concerning Italy: the treatment of migrants and asylum seekers, the ongoing practices disregarding the rights of

Roma communities, and even the insufficient efforts made in combatting intolerance and corruption in public life.

As anticipated in the Introduction of the *Yearbook 2019*, the tipping point of these complex dynamics came in November 2019 in the form of the discussion of Italy's Universal Periodic Review (UPR). Italy's UPR coincided with a significant political change in the structure of its Government, with the Democratic Party (*Partito Democratico*) replacing the League (*Lega*) to form a majority parliament with the 5 Star Movement (*Movimento 5 Stelle*) (whose coalition had been in government since the 2018 elections). As widely-discussed in this *Yearbook*, the interactive dialogue concerning Italy caused great interest at an international level, evident from the high number of State delegations discussing and sending recommendations to Italy. More detailed analysis on this issue can be found in the *in-depth study*, however, there seems to be a new-found harmony, in substance but also more importantly in the "form" of institutional communications, between the Italian Government and international human rights bodies, supported by international legal organisations and procedures. However, one problem remains unresolved for Italy: there is a lack of willingness to provide information in response to the international community's questions, when there are objective difficulties and structural delays in implementing specific requests. These issues are not usually recognised for what they really are: systemic and structural problems, which may require a specialised intervention of international institutions in order to overcome them. Let us consider (among others) the issue of a national human rights institution: its creation has now been "imminent" for years. Or we could consider the criminalisation of torture, which only took place in 2019 thanks to an intervention by the Court of Cassation which clarified some potential lacunae in the text of the Italian Criminal Code adopted in 2017. Moreover, a similar discussion has just been opened on the crime of forced disappearances, which Italy considers to be fully covered by the crime of aggravated kidnapping, while the Committee on Enforced Disappearances (not without good reason) urges the State to recognise that the particular nature and gravity of the crime should foresee a separate law.

A comprehensive and transparent analysis of the data released by the UPR process and many other international human rights bodies should be sufficient to identify the long-standing points of vulnerability and imbalance of the State-system. It could piece together the main complaints formulated by bodies in which they can monitor, prevent and verify violations of human rights, starting from the numerous bodies working within the framework of the Council of Europe, and can tackle them systematically. This would disentangle them from any possible influence from the ever-changing, fleeting political whim. A reading of the *Italian Agenda of Human Rights* (which follows this *Introduction*) could also be of assistance; in it the Editorial Committee strives to unite diagnosis, prognosis and treatment.

In this recent phase of the relationship between Italy and human rights policy, what is still not clear is the direction in which to march. We need a "compass" to help us to overcome the prophetic and *à la carte* attitude so far seen; rather, we need clear lines, trustworthiness and commitment. Above all, since the fight for fundamental rights is critical for everyone, especially those most vulnerable, more precarious and least integrated of our society, life and essential goods must be absolutely guaranteed and not given or taken away on some unforeseeable whim or for some arbitrary reason. These issues include minimum welfare support, residence permits for migrants, access to essential services (such as housing or school) and the recognition of citizenship to young people born in Italy, or who have spent their school career in the country. All fundamental issues that individuals and families are fighting for, including immigrants, persons with disabilities, children and Roma communities, are the same that suffer from complicated and destabilising changes and shifts at all institutional levels. The fundamental rights of the most precarious people in society are precarious in their very nature.

These words were written as Italy, Europe and the entire world were being encompassed beset by a health emergency caused by the Covid-19 virus. Innumerable voices – which cannot be included in this 2019 edition of the Yearbook – have raised concerns on the dramatic impact that the global crisis is having on the world's population, and therefore raising questions on State obligations on human rights. The right to health for billions of individuals is at risk, but the knock-on, snowballing consequences of this emergency hit the whole social and economic organisation of our communities. There are also clear, predictable political consequences to this issue. In light of the new, dramatic situation, States have been forced to prioritise different measures, to impose new obligations on citizens, to rethink the meaning of individual freedom, and even to reimagine its own role and that of international organisations – establishing a new balance between public institutions, civil society and the market. A new political paradigm could emerge; fast-tracked by the health crisis, but that has already shown to be necessary from tackling numerous other pandemic-like challenges. The long-term effects of these previous challenges have so far been covered up: for example, the environmental and energy crisis linked to human-caused climate change. It is important that our "human rights compass" is central to this new paradigm. After the Covid-19 pandemic, we will not be going back to the conditions that caused this crisis (as the dangerous "great again" catchphrase puts it), but rather we must try something unprecedented. And what if systematic human rights-based policies were to fit that "unprecedented" description?

Italian Agenda of Human Rights 2020

Like every year, the Research and Editing Committee of the *Italian Yearbook of Human Rights* at the University of Padova Human Rights Centre "Antonio Papisca", offers the updated version of the *Italian Agenda of Human Rights*, built on the basis of analysing the recommendations received from Italy in the international sphere and of the most critical aspects identified in the various editions of the same yearbook

The Agenda should be used as a guiding tool for the main initiatives to be carried out in the country, on the legal, infrastructural and policy-writing levels, in order to strengthen the national system to promote and protect human rights and sharpen the country's contribution to the international community's commitment to human rights.

This version of the Agenda offers a vision of the country's human rights situation across 2019. However, it is impossible not to mention the situation in which we find ourselves in 2020. These first months of 2020 have seen Italy and the world struck by the devastating global pandemic caused by COVID-19 which is distinguished by its extraordinary contagion rate.

The Research and Editing Committee must postpone all in-depth comments and analysis on this issue to the 2021 Agenda. That edition will have to tackle the almost permanent state of health emergency that has and (presumably) will define the social life of Italy and so many other States. The 2020 Agenda will therefore seem somewhat "lacking".

The Research and Editing Committee has taken advantage of this moment of transition to review the points and sub-points collected over the past decade, respecting, however, the work that has been done in these years in presenting this tool. With respect to the 2019 Agenda, the Committee has not deleted any points or sub-points: some, however, have been amended in light of recent developments, which are discussed in depth in this edition of the Yearbook. One example is point 7, on the definition of the crime of torture within the Italian Criminal Code, on which the Court of Cassation clarified its interpretation in judg. 47079/ 2019 (see, Part IV, Human Rights in Italian Case-law, XIII, B).

Some points and sub-points have been added. These concern the ratification of further international legal instruments, including the Treaty on the Prohibition of Nuclear Weapons, the ILO Violence and Harassment Convention, the "Kampala Amendments" to the Rome Statute of the International Criminal Court and the European Charter of Regional and Minority Languages (point 1). Regarding domestic legislation, Italy has been urged to approve a law against homotransphobia (on which there are already consolidated bills being discussed). In the "adoption of policies" section of the Agenda, other than updating the list of Nation Action Plans on human rights awaiting adoption, and updating those which have now expired or have no information on their implementation or impact (points 20, 21 and 22), the Research and Editing Committee has added one new point on the need to implement initiatives to combat hate speech (point 24). Within the "Initiatives in Specific Areas", other points have been added to the Agenda 2020; this particularly concerns the rights of migrants, refugees and asylum seekers: point 34, on re-establishing flexible forms to recognise international protection which take into account the intersectionality of discrimination and other human rights violations that migrants may be exposed to. Overall, the 2020 Agenda presents 38 points and 34 sub-points.

Italian Agenda of Human Rights 2020

Normative level	1) Ratify the following legal instruments at the United Nations and the Council of Europe: a. International Convention on the Protection of the Rights of All Migrant Workers and Members of their Families; b. Additional Protocol to the Convention on Cybercrime, Concerning the Criminalisation of Acts of a Racist and Xenophobic Nature Committed through Computer Systems c. Treaty on the Prohibition of Nuclear Weapons; d. Amendments to the Rome Statute of the International Criminal Court ("Kampala Amendments"); e. ILO Violence and Harassment Convention (C190); f. Protocol No. 12 to the European Convention on Human Rights; g. Protocol No. 15 to the European Convention on Human Rights;

Italian Agenda of Human Rights 2020

	h. Protocol No. 16 to the European Convention on Human Rights; i. European Convention on Nationality; j. Additional Protocol to the Criminal Law Convention on Corruption. k. European Charter for Regional or Minority Languages.
	2) Deposit the instruments of ratification for the following legal instruments for which Parliament has already adopted the relative ratification and implementation laws: a. Convention on Human Rights and Biomedicine (Oviedo Convention); b. Additional Protocol to the Convention on Human Rights and Biomedicine Concerning Transplantation of Organs and Tissues of Human Origin.
	3) Promote the awareness and application of the Declaration on the Right to Peace adopted by the Human Rights Council on 1 July 2016 before the UN General Assembly.
	4) Accept article 25 of the European Social Charter (revised), on the right of workers to protection of their claims in the event of insolvency of their employer.
	5) Withdraw the declaration that excludes the application for Italy of Chapter C of the European Convention on the Participation of Foreigners in Public Life at Local Level and, accordingly, provide for the introduction of active and passive voting rights in local elections for foreigners who have been residing in Italy for a certain number of years.
	6) Include hate motivation as an aggravating factor, currently covered by article 604-*ter* of the Criminal Code, in article 61 of the Criminal Code on common aggravating factors, since this is then applied to all crimes (except those punished by life sentences).
	7) Bring the crime of torture, introduced under article 613-*bis* of the Criminal Code, in line with article 1 of the UN Convention Against Torture making sure the interpretation given by the Court of Cassation in judgment 8 July 2019, No. 47079 is effectively followed by relevant case-law.

Italian Agenda of Human Rights 2020

	8) Expressly recognise representative non-governmental organisations within Italian jurisdiction as having scope on issues regulated by the European Social Charter (revised) and the right to present collective complaints pursuant to the 1995 Protocol.
	9) Complete the parliamentary procedure to adopt a law against homotransphobia to combat discrimination and violence based on sexual orientation and gender identity.
	10) Complete the adoption process of parliamentary bill No. 925 on defamation in light of the of United Nations, Council of Europe and OSCE standards.
	11) Continue efforts to reform the system for the prevention and repression of corruption in both the public and private sector, with special reference to the most recent recommendations made by GRECO on the following subjects: indictment for corruption, transparency in party financing, and preventing corruption in Members of the Chamber of Deputies and magistrates.
Infrastructural level	12) Complete the system of independent national human rights institutions in line with the Paris principles adopted by the United Nations and: a. Establish the National Human Rights Commission; b. Establish the National Ombudsperson.
	13) Ensure the existence of a permanent parliamentary Human Rights Commission, in one or both Chambers.
	14) Assign all Ministries an ad hoc human rights office.
	15) Assign all necessary personnel and financial resources to the independent human rights authorities working in the human rights sector and ensure that the competent personnel is elected in a timely and regular manner.

Italian Agenda of Human Rights 2020

Implementation of international obligations and commitments	16) Complete the legislative process for the implementation of the Statute of the International Criminal Court as concerns substantive law.
	17) Increase the timeliness and full execution of European Court of Human Rights rulings, including paying out compensation awarded, and improve Italy's capacity to conform to the standards defined by the same Court.
	18) Address as a matter of urgency the issue of the excessive duration of legal proceedings, including those initiated to seek remedy for their excessive duration.
Adoption of policies	19) Hold an annual debate on human rights in Parliament
	20) Adopt the following national action plans, providing them with suitable tools for monitoring and assessment: a. National Action Plan on the Human Rights Situation within Detention Structures; b. National Programme on Education for Democratic Citizenship and Education and Training on Human Rights; c. Integrated Action Plan for Combatting and Preventing cyberbullying; d. National Strategy for Gender Equality.
	21) Update the following national action plans upon expiry: a. National Strategy for Preventing and Combating Discrimination on Grounds of Gender Identity and Sexual Orientation (last reference period: 2013–2015); b. National Action Plan against Racism, Xenophobia and Intolerance (last reference period: 2013–2015); c. National Action Plan against Trafficking in and Serious Exploitation of Human Beings (2016–2018); d. National Strategic Plan on Male Violence against Women (2017–2020).

Italian Agenda of Human Rights 2020

	22) Implement and provide information on the impact of the following national action plans: a. National Strategy for the inclusion of Roma, Sinti and Travellers – 2012–2020; b. National Action Plan on Business and Human Rights (2016–2021); c. National Action Plan on "Women, Peace and Security" (2016–2019); d. Fourth National Action Plan for the protection of the rights and of the development of children and adolescents (2016–2017); e. National Strategic Plan on Male Violence against Women (2017–2020); f. Second two-year Action Programme for the promotion of the rights and the integration of persons with disabilities (2018–2020); g. National Plan for the Prevention and Fight against Abuse and Sexual Exploitation of Children (2015–2017).
	23) Formally extend the remit of UNAR to include all forms of discrimination, including those based on language, religion, nation of origin, disabilities, sexual orientation and gender identity.
	24) Implement initiatives to combat hate speech and incitement to hatred.
	25) Ensure sufficient public social spending in the various categories (health, disability, family support, unemployment, social housing and combating social exclusion).
	26) Strengthen efforts to resolve the problem of overcrowding in prisons, making further progress on the structural measures and deflation mechanisms introduced.

Italian Agenda of Human Rights 2020

Initiatives in specific areas	
Women's rights	27) Promote actual equality between men and women in all aspects of public and private life, specifically through the adoption of policies and actions directed at: a. Reducing the deficit in the number of women represented in the highest decision-making roles in political bodies, including Parliament and Regional Councils, public administration including the Diplomatic Service and in the private sector; b. Reducing the salary gap between men and women; c. Fostering a more balanced sharing of family duties between men and women, both in running the home and in care-giving duties; d. Eliminating stereotypical attitudes on the roles and responsibilities of women and men in the family, in society and in the workplace; e. Encouraging plans for the integration of foreign women; f. Tackling and resolving the phenomenon of resignations without a justified reason ("blank resignation letters") for pregnant women and working mothers.
Children's rights	28) Adopt a general legislative measure which enshrines the right of children to be listened to in court, in administrative bodies, in the institutions, at school and in the family on every issue which concerns them directly and establish suitable mechanisms and procedures to this end, to ensure that the participation of children actually takes place.
	29) Amend the criminal code so as to explicitly forbid and criminalise the recruitment and the deployment, by either the armed forces or armed groups, of young people under the age of 18 in the course of armed conflicts.
	30) Adopt legislation prohibiting and criminalising the sale of light and small calibre arms to countries which deploy child soldiers.

Italian Agenda of Human Rights 2020

Citizenship rights; rights of migrants, refugees and asylum seekers	31) Address migratory flows as a structural phenomenon, the systematic planning for which must be assigned to instruments of an ordinary nature (rather than to emergency measures linked to a purely security- oriented viewpoint) and to multi- level governance with the involvement of the relevant ministries, regions, local administrations and civil society.
	32) Respect the principle of non- refoulement, the right of asylum seekers to an individual examination of their case, as well as immediate access to asylum procedures and other forms of national and international protection, including where there are bilateral agreements for return or for cooperation in management of migratory flows.
	33) Implement initiatives that aim to overcome the rigid nature of the Dublin III regulations, in order to meet both the expectations of those seeking international protection and the needs of those communities in Europe who are particularly exposed to the impact of potential asylum seekers.
	34) Re-establish flexible forms to recognise international protection which take into account the intersectionality of discrimination and other human rights violations that migrants may be exposed to.
	35) Maintain the working spaces for non-governmental organisations involved in search and rescue operations at sea, as required by existing international standards.
	36) Support the activities of the "Roundtable on the Legal Status of Roma", established on 30 January 2013 as part of the National Strategy for Inclusion of the members of these communities, with the objective of finding solutions to the situation of statelessness of large numbers of Roma and Sinti originally from the former Yugoslavia, and of their children born in Italy (the so-called *de facto* stateless people).

Italian Agenda of Human Rights 2020

	37) Develop a more expeditious identification system, in order to reduce as far as possible the period that migrants are detained while waiting for the identification procedures to be completed, ensuring complete respect of the rights of people detained in repatriation centres.
	38) Re-examine laws on citizenship in the light of the principle of *ius humanae dignitatis*, continuing in the direction to simplify the process for acquiring citizenship status pursuant to article 33 of l.d. 21 June 2013, No. 69 and establishing a form of acquisition of citizenship based on *ius culturae*.

Structure of the Yearbook 2020

Just as in previous editions, the *Italian Yearbook of Human Rights 2020* aims at presenting a snapshot of the human rights situation in Italy, both from a legislative and "infrastructural" point of view, and from that of the practical implementation of policies and initiatives to promote and protect them. This version of the Yearbook looks specifically at the calendar year 2019. The level of detail and background analysis provided in the various sections allows for crosscutting and targeted readings, which can also be developed by consulting the analytical indexes.

Information presented in the first three parts of the Yearbook come from public documents, which are normally consultable via the official webpage for each body examined. For Part IV, the databases of the specific courts cited were used (for Italian case-law, most data were taken from the Giuffrè *"De Iure"* database).

Part I of the *Yearbook* illustrates the main developments in Italy's incorporation of international and regional standards into its domestic legislation. The overview starts from the international level (United Nations) and moves on to the regional level, comprising legislation drawn up by the Council of Europe and the European Union, before presenting domestic legislation that transposes international obligations into national and regional laws.

Part II illustrates the human rights infrastructure in Italy and is divided into three chapters. The first describes the structure, functions and activities of State bodies (Parliament, Government, the judiciary, independent authorities) and also presents the activities of civil society organisations and academic institutions operating at State level. The second chapter considers the sub-national level of the Italian legal order and illustrates the variegated local and regional human rights infrastructure and the relative coordinating bodies. The third chapter is devoted to the "peace human rights" infrastructure and to initiatives developed in this area by the Region of Veneto. The specific focus on this Region is explained by the pioneering commitment shown by Veneto, dating back to its 1998 r.l. 18, in promoting a culture of human rights, peace and international solidarity.

Part III deals with Italy's position with reference to the international and regional bodies and mechanisms for monitoring the implementation of human rights. It includes the assessments and recommendations that these bodies have addressed to Italy following specific missions to the State and periodic monitoring activities. The role of Italy within these organisations and the contribution of its diplomatic representatives for the promotion of human rights at regional and global level are highlighted. This Part is subdivided into five chapters. The first focuses on the United Nations system; in particular on the activities of the General Assembly, the Human Rights Council, the Treaty Bodies and the specialist Agencies. The second chapter is devoted to the Council of Europe, while the third to the European Union. These two chapters complement the information presented in Part I (concerning legislation) and in Part IV (concerning case-law), relative to Council of Europe and EU activities in 2019. The fourth chapter deals with the Organisation for Security and Cooperation in Europe (OSCE) and its bodies for the promotion of the human dimension of security. The fifth and final chapter is on international humanitarian and criminal law. In this chapter, in addition to providing updates on Italy's level of conformity, there is a list of all international peace missions to which Italian troops contributed in 2019.

Finally, *Part IV* presents a selection of domestic and international case-law concerning Italy over the year in question. In the three chapters, the cases are subdivided according to the subject to which the judgment refers. The chapters respectively deal with the internal case-law (mainly of the Constitutional Court, the Court of Cassation and the State Council), the case-law of the European Court of Human Rights and the case-law of the Court of Justice of the European Union, the latter with reference to the cases directly concerning Italy. A targeted reading of the case-law is also possible by using the index of case-law cited at the end of the book.

Across these four parts, the Yearbook pays particular attention to the link between the analysis of the main recommendations directed at Italy on human rights and the implementation of the Sustainable Development Goals (SDGs) of the UN Agenda 2030.

The part of the Introduction which aims at giving the reader an in-depth look at some specific aspects of the country's human rights behavior concerns, this year, Italy's third cycle of the UPR at the UN Human Rights Council, which took place on 14 November 2019. This *in-depth study* was written by Pietro de Perini and Andrea Cofelice.

In-Depth Study – Italy and Human Rights in the Third Universal Periodic Review at the United Nations (2010–2019)*

On 4 November 2019, Italy underwent its third cycle of the UPR at the United Nations Human Rights Council. As the Introduction of the previous year's *Yearbook* highlighted, the then-imminent evaluation would be seen as a "litmus test" to understand the state of health of human rights in Italy, both in the facts and the perception of the international community.

Other than representing a scrutinising update starting 10 years ago, the third UPR cycle represents the first real opportunity for the international community to carry out a comprehensive overview of Italy's human rights behaviour during this controversial phase, already marked by the gradual slide into "stagnation" concerning the capacity of the Italian system to put new laws on fundamental issues into place (see *Yearbook 2018*, pp. 15–19). Especially in the period between summer 2018 and 2019, it was characterised by the legitimised forms of human rights compressions 'by omission' (see *Yearbook 2019*, pp. 18–23), provoking, incidentally, a compact wave of international concern for Italy's detour from its traditional commitment on these matters.

This in-depth study considers these reflections as a starting point, with the dual objective of presenting and discussing what came out of the interactive dialogue which characterised Italy's third UPR and, at the same time, evaluating the result of this review more comprehensively, considering the recommendations received and the Italian Government's responses from 2010 to the present day.

---

* Andrea Cofelice, Pietro de Perini

I Peer Participation and Recommendations: A Record UPR

Italy's third UPR was record-breaking in two interesting ways. The first concerned the large overall attraction that the review produced in Geneva. The number of delegations who signed up for the 'interactive dialogue' to present the Italian authorities with comments, concerns and recommendations – 121 in total – marked one of the highest participations overall since the activation of this monitoring mechanism in 2008. The number was exceeded by countries such as China, whose third UPR attracted 150 delegations, and Turkey which received inputs from 122 delegations. The number 121 also represents a visible increase country-wise, although this was consistent with a larger trend in overall participation that exposes the growing appreciation for UPR procedures by member states. 51 delegations (plus 13 which could not be heard during the time allocated) participated in the first UPR of Italy in 2010, and 92 in 2014.

This large participation can, in fact, be assessed in two opposing ways. One that is generally voiced by the representatives of the Ministry for Foreign Affairs, considering this as an indicator of the effectiveness of the dialogue and cooperation mechanism set up by the UPR and giving weight to the open and cooperative attitude of the Italian delegation in tackling the various phases of the monitoring cycle. The second assessment of the large participation of delegations is that it serves as an indicator of growing concern by the international community about the country in question.

This latter perception could be confirmed by another Italian "record" in its third UPR; the number of recommendations received by Italy as a whole (306) is an exponential increase from 157 received in the first cycle in 2010 (then summarised into 92 recommendation by the troika) and a substantial increase from 186 received in the second cycle (2014). What do these recommendations say about Italy's human rights commitment? How many of the issues raised in this review are new challenges for the country to address and how many highlight recurrent problems?

During the interactive dialogue, Manlio Di Stefano (Undersecretary of State for Foreign Affairs and International Cooperation and head of the Italian Delegation in Geneva) was called in front of the Human Rights Council to report on the main initiatives of Italy to promote human rights, both internationally and domestically. In his presentation, he emphasised that Italy had successfully implemented 153 out of the 176 recommen-

Tab. 1:

	Human rights issues	**III Cycle (November 2019)**		**II Cycle (October 2014)**		**I Cycle (February 2010)**	
		N	%	*N*	%	*N*	%
1	Racial Discrimination	47	*15.4*	33	*17.7*	25	*15.9*
2	National Human Rights Institutions	46	*15.0*	25	*13.4*	16	*10.2*
3	Migrants and Asylum Seekers	43	*14.1*	20	*10.8*	24	*15.3*
4	Women's Rights, Gender Equality and Violence Against Women	32	*10.5*	18	*9.7*	2	*1.3*
5	Economic and Social Rights	16	*5.2*	5	*2.7*	2	*1.3*
6	Human Trafficking	15	*4.9*	8	*4.3*	9	*5.7*
7	Torture and Rights of Detained Persons	15	*4.9*	6	*3.2*	5	*3.2*
8	Sexual Orientation and Gender Identity	14	*4.6*	5	*2.7*	4	*2.5*
9	Minorities	13	*4.2*	16	*8.6*	19	*12.1*
10	International Instruments	12	*3.9*	23	*12.4*	18	*11.5*
11	Children's Rights	11	*3.6*	9	*4.8*	10	*6.4*
12	Persons with Disabilities	11	*3.6*	3	*1.6*	0	*0.0*
13	Right to Education and Human Rights Education	8	*2.6*	1	*0.5*	4	*2.5*
14	Civil rights and the rule of law	6	*2.0*	3	*1.6*	4	*2.5*
15	Other	4	*1.3*	2	*1.1*	1	*0.6*
16	Human Rights Defenders	3	*1.0*	0	*0.0*	0	*0.0*
17	Development Cooperation	2	*0.7*	4	*2.2*	2	*1.3*
18	Freedom of Expression	2	*0.7*	3	*1.6*	7	*4.5*
19	Modern forms of Slavery	2	*0.7*	0	*0.0*	0	*0.0*
20	Arms Trade	2	*0.7*	0	*0.0*	0	*0.0*
21	Cooperation with the United Nations (UPR, Independent Committee of Experts…)	1	*0.3*	2	*1.1*	2	*1.3*
22	Freedom of Religion	1	*0.3*	0	*0.0*	3	*1.9*
	TOTAL	306	*100*	186	*100*	157	*100*

dations accepted during the second UPR cycle (that is 87 %), while the remaining recommendations concerning the setting up of an independent national human rights institution were being implemented. It is worth noting that this statement remained totally unchecked by other delegations.

Of the 306 recommendations that Italy received, 22 concerned different human rights issues. However, over half of these recommendations concern only four thematic areas, namely: racial discrimination (15.4 %); national human rights institutions (15 %); rights of migrants, refugees and asylum seekers (14.1 %); women's rights, gender equality, violence against women (10.5 %).

Tab. 1 shows a diachronic analysis of the recommendations received by Italy in its three UPR cycles (2010, 2014 and 2019), disaggregated by thematic areas. This allows us to identify the main trends of the recommendations, as well as structural and/or contingent critical issues affecting the national human rights protection system as perceived by Italy's 'peers' within the international community.

First and foremost, what clearly emerges from the data above is that in all UPR cycles the most frequent recommendations addressed to Italy (both in absolute terms and as a percentage of the total number of recommendations received) deal with racial discrimination and the rights of migrants, refugees and asylum seekers. Therefore, in spite of the fact that during its 2019 review Italy was under the spotlight for the 'security decrees' adopted by the Conte I cabinet, in the international community's view these issues are not contingent, but rather represent the main structural challenges to the national human rights protection system. At least over the past ten years, indeed, Italy has been constantly called upon to take further and more incisive actions primarily to counter the spread of hate speech in the public sphere, administrative forms of discrimination, the violation of the principle of non-refoulement, as well as to improve living conditions in reception centres for migrants.

In addition to this stable 'stock' of human rights issues, a growing 'flow' of recommendations deals with the establishment of independent national human rights institutions, in line with the Paris Principles. The lack of these institutions in Italy, an issue that was discussed deeply in the previous edition of the *Yearbook* (see, in particular, *Yearbook 2017*, pp. 17–22), has become a consistent case of great concern by the international community: the number of recommendations on this issue has almost tripled over the past ten years, from 16 in 2010 (10 % of the total recommendations received in the first UPR cycle) to 46 in 2019 (15 %).

Unlike international expert-based mechanisms (such as UN treaty bodies) that tend to discuss human rights national reports years after their initial submission, in general the UPR procedure has proven to be more flexible and 'responsive' towards new and emerging challenges, including issues which appear to be relevant to human rights but have not yet found universal recognition in binding treaties. This is particularly evident in Italy's case; as already discussed above, between 2018 and 2019, several Human Rights Council Special Procedures had sent urgent communications to Italy expressing concern over the negative impact of government decrees on a number of human rights-related issues, including discrimination based on sexual orientation, the rights of minorities (particularly Roma, Sinti and Caminanti communities), the regression on women's rights, and the criminalisation of solidarity (see *Yearbook 2019*, pp. 192–203). These concerns are largely reflected in the 2019 UPR cycle, both in terms of a spectacular increase in the number of recommendations concerning issues that, in previous cycles, were perceived as 'marginal' for Italy, such as women's rights (from 2 recommendations in 2010 to 32 in 2019) or the promotion of economic and social rights (from 2 recommendations in 2010 to 16 in 2019)- also in terms of the emergence of brand-new issues, such as the need to better protect human rights defenders (especially by countering the criminalisation of NGOs carrying out search and rescue missions in the Mediterranean) and to combat contemporary forms of slavery, particularly in the agricultural sector. It is worth stressing that the protection of human rights defenders appears also among Italy's 2018 voluntary commitments in its candidacy to the Human Rights Council for the period 2019–2022 (A/73/72).

These concerns reflect the perceptions of the Government delegations which participated in the "interactive dialogue" with Italy. It is worth noting that these perceptions are enriched and enhanced by the research and advocacy work of the numerous civil society groups. Most of these national and international organisations actively contribute to the various evaluation mechanisms of Italy, participating in the pre-session organised by the UPR working group and contributing to the report compiled by the Office of the High Commissioner of Human Rights (OHCHR) that collects and summarises the recommendations of various stakeholders. Specifically, Italy's third UPR benefited from receiving 16 joint submissions involving over two hundred national and international civil society organisations.

II Acceptance Rate and Non-acceptance Strategies

Italy's overall acceptance rate of UPR recommendations stands at 87 % for the first cycle, 94 % for the second cycle and 95 % for the third cycle (an average of 92 % over all three cycles): these figures are significantly higher than the global mean registered during the first 31 UPR sessions (74 %). The (few) recommendations 'noted' (i.e. 'not-accepted') by Italy for each of its three review cycles, respectively, 12 in 2010, 9 in 2014 and 12 in 2019, are reported in Tab. 2 below.

At least three interesting observations can be drawn from the table. Firstly, almost two-thirds of the noted recommendations deal with the rights of migrants, refugees and asylum seekers, which has proven itself to be a highly sensitive issue. On the one hand, Italy has systematically rejected, with no exception, all the requests to ratify the International Convention on the protection of the rights of all migrant workers and members of their families, formulated by all regional groups; also, encouragements to decriminalise irregular entry and stay in Italy, repeal discriminatory laws against irregular migrants, provide humanitarian protection for all migrants, and put an end to the practice of collective expulsion (among others) have been declined on the grounds that Italy's laws and practice are considered as fully consistent with international and European standards. The remaining third of the noted recommendations refer to eight different human rights-related issues, including the protection of minorities (especially Roma and Sinti communities), the prohibition of all corporal punishment of children, the adoption of a national integrated human rights plan in accordance with the Vienna Declaration and Programme of Action, and so on.

Secondly, these rejections are almost distributed evenly among four out of the five regional groupings existing within the UN. Italy noted recommendations formulated by 15 African states, 14 Asian states, 14 Latin American and Caribbean states (GRULAC), as well as 11 states belonging to the Western European and other states group (WEOG, Italy's own regional group). On the contrary, Italy noted just 3 recommendations originating from the Eastern European group (EEG); according to the

Tab. 2:

UPR Cycle	Recommendation	Recommending State	Regional Group	Issue	Strategy
I	Become a party to remaining human rights instruments and consider withdrawing its reservations, in particular to International Covenant on Civil and Political Rights	Pakistan	Asian	International Instruments	Already implemented/guaranteed
I	Consider ratification of the International Convention on the Protection of the Rights of All Migrant Workers and Members of Their Families (ICRMW)	Algeria, Azerbaijan, Chile, Egypt, Iran, Mexico, The Philippines	Asian, EEG, African, GRULAC	International Instruments	Already implemented/guaranteed + Tied hands
I	Incorporate the crime of torture into domestic law	The Netherlands, Czech Republic, New Zealand	WEOG, EEG	Torture	Already implemented/guaranteed
I	Establish its national human rights institution in accordance with the Paris Principles before the end of 2010	Denmark	WEOG	National Human Rights Institutions	Tied hands
I	Develop a national integrated human rights plan in accordance with the Vienna Declaration and Programme of Action	Iran	Asian	Other	Already implemented/guaranteed

Tab. 2 Continued

UPR Cycle	Recommendation	Recommending State	Regional Group	Issue	Strategy
I	Incorporate in its legislation the 1996 Supreme Court judgement that corporal punishment was not a legitimate method of discipline in the home, and criminalise corporal punishment in all cases, including in education	Spain	WEOG	Children's Rights	Already implemented/guaranteed
I	Strengthen the independence of the judiciary	Iran	Asian	Diritti civili e stato di diritto	Already implemented/guaranteed
I	Protect the Roma and the Sinti as national minorities, and to ensure that they are not the object of discrimination	United States, Cuba	WEOG, GRULAC	Minorities	Already implemented/guaranteed
I	Take all measures necessary to ensure the rights of the Roma people under article 27 of the International Covenant on Civil and Political Rights, specifically by amending the 1999 Act, which lays down this creation of connection with a specific territory	Denmark	WEOG	Minorities	Public explanation
I	Take appropriate legislative measures to decriminalise irregular entry and stay in Italy	Brazil, Mexico	GRULAC	Migrants and Asylum Seekers	Public explanation

I	Take appropriate legislative measures to exclude undocumented stay in Italy as an aggravating circumstance for the purposes of sentencing following a criminal conviction	Brazil	GRULAC	Migrants and Asylum Seekers	Public explanation
I	Repeal all discriminatory laws against irregular migrants	Pakistan	Asian	Migrants and Asylum Seekers	Public motivation
II	Study the possibility of acceding to the International Convention on the Protection of the Rights of All Migrant Workers and Members of Their Families (ICRMW)	Egypt	African	International Instruments	Already implemented/guaranteed
II	Consider ratifying ICRMW	Chile, Indonesia	Asian	International Instruments	Already implemented/guaranteed
II	Ratify ICRMW	Ghana, Sierra Leone, Uruguay, Peru, Iran	African, GRULAC, Asian	International Instruments	Already implemented/guaranteed
II	Ratify ICRMW	Senegal	African	International Instruments	Already implemented/guaranteed
II	Complete the ratification process of ICRMW	Turkey	WEOG	International Instruments	Already implemented/guaranteed

Tab. 2 Continued

UPR Cycle	Recommendation	Recommending State	Regional Group	Issue	Strategy
II	Strengthen the legal framework to take better account of migrants and migrant workers, in particular by ratifying ICRMW	Algeria	African	International Instruments	Already implemented/guaranteed
II	Enact legislation to enshrine the 1996 Supreme Court ruling in legislation and explicitly prohibit all corporal punishment of children in the home	Liechtenstein	WEOG	Children's Rights	Already implemented/guaranteed
II	Explicitly prohibit all corporal punishment of children	Sweden	WEOG	Children's Rights	Already implemented/guaranteed
II	Suspend summary returns to Greece	Sweden	WEOG	Migrants and Asylum Seekers	Public explanation
III	Ratify the International Convention on the Protection of the Rights of All Migrant Workers and Members of Their Families	Uganda, Uruguay, Senegal, Sierra Leone, Sri Lanka, Azerbaijan, Bangladesh, Egypt, Seychelles	African, GRULAC, EEG, Asian	International Instruments	Already implemented/guaranteed

III	Raise domestic awareness on the International Convention on the Protection of the Rights of All Migrant Workers and Members of Their Families	Indonesia	Asian	International Instruments	Public explanation
III	Sign and ratify the Treaty on the Prohibition of Nuclear Weapons	Ecuador	GRULAC	International Instruments	Public explanation
III	Consider revising the framework regulating the control of firearms, given the correlation between their use and feminicides	Peru	GRULAC	Women's Rights	Public explanation
III	Investigate all allegations of ill-treatment and excessive use of force against asylum seekers and migrants	Pakistan	Asian	Migrants and Asylum Seekers	Already implemented/guaranteed
III	Implement the principles of non-refoulement and relevant minimum standards, relating to the rights of migrants and asylum seekers	Kenya	African	Migrants and Asylum Seekers	Already implemented/guaranteed
III	Observe the principle of non-refoulement and provide humanitarian protection for all migrants	Thailand	Asian	Migrants and Asylum Seekers	Already implemented/guaranteed

Tab. 2 Continued

UPR Cycle	Recommendation	Recommending State	Regional Group	Issue	Strategy
III	Guarantee the individual assessment of the situation of each migrant in order to put an end to the practice of collective expulsion	Burkina Faso	African	Migrants and Asylum Seekers	Already implemented/guaranteed
III	Endorse the Global Compact for Safe, Orderly and Regular Migration	Colombia	GRULAC	Migrants and Asylum Seekers	Tied hands
III	Take measures to avoid collective expulsions of migrants	Argentina	GRULAC	Migrants and Asylum Seekers	Already implemented/guaranteed
III	Review Law No. 132 of 2018 on the detention of asylum seekers to align it with international refugee law and human rights law	South Africa	African	Migrants and Asylum Seekers	Public explanation
III	Extend the provision of paid paternity leave and promote the equitable distribution of parental responsibilities between women and men	Iceland	WEOG	Sexual Orientation and Gender Identity	Confrontational attitude

UPR-Info database (an NGO established to raise awareness of the UPR process), this group's 'recommending attitude' is however significantly lower than the global mean (UPR-Info 2020).

Finally, Italy has almost always adopted a non-confrontational approach in rejecting the recommendations received. In this respect, three main strategies can be identified. The most recurrent response (65 % of the cases) consists in considering the recommended action or the right to be protected as already implemented or guaranteed. Illustrative examples are represented by the comments on the numerous recommendations inviting Italy to ratify the International Convention on the protection of the rights of all migrant workers and members of their families, which generally end with the following: 'However, the Italian legal framework already guarantees the rights of regular and irregular migrants'. Similarly, when during the third UPR cycle Italy was invited by Kenya and other states to put an end to the practice of collective expulsion, Italy replied that: 'The principle of non-refoulement is established by Italian law and is fully implemented in the practice. Rights of migrants and asylum seekers are recognized and respected in full compliance with national, EU and international law' (A/HRC/43/4/Add.1).

In other cases (23 %), Italy has made the effort to publicly explain the reason why specific recommendations have been noted. For example, following its third review, Italy took steps to respond to concerns expressed by Peru about its firearms control policy and the correlation between their use and the high rate feminicides, indicating detailed statistical data showing that such correlation simply does not exist and listing the steps that can be taken when cases of domestic violence and stalking are reported (A/HRC/43/4/Add.1).

At times, Italy also resorted to a 'tied hands' strategy, invoking (alleged) institutional or financial impediments that prevent the government from taking action. One example refers to the setting up of national human rights institutions, as recommended by Denmark in the 2010 review. The Government committed to submit a bill to Parliament, 'as soon as the required budgetary resources are made available' (A/HRC/14/4/Add.1). Another example, based on the separation of the power principle, refers to the signature of the UN Global Compact for safe, orderly and regular migration, as recommended by Colombia in 2019. According to the Government, Italy was not in a position to accept this recommendation since 'an assessment by the Italian Parliament on whether to join the Compact is still ongoing' (A/HRC/43/4/Add.1).

In one single case concerning a recommendation by Iceland on a sexual orientation and gender identity related issue (third UPR cycle), Italy decided to adopt a more confrontational approach by declaring that it would simply ignore it ("taking note").

In summary, Italy's acceptance rate of the recommendations received is higher than the global mean. Moreover, negative responses to recommendations essentially focus on a single main issue (i.e. the rights of migrants, refugees and asylum seekers) and, as shown by data broken down by region, do not seem to be as significantly affected by 'political motivations' as, for example by the level of friendship and alliances among states. Finally, Italy generally tends to adopt non-confrontational approaches when rejecting the recommendations received.

Conclusions

This analysis of Italy's UPR behaviour and recommendations across the various monitoring cycles has confirmed a certain degree of immobility for the country's action on human rights: the issues highlighted in the recommendations and the reasons given to "reject" them have been reiterated over the last ten years, showing little overall change on a content level and on a formal level.

These findings have both positive and negative implications for the overall assessment of the country's behaviour and performance vis-à-vis human rights. On a more negative note, the findings confirm that Italy's phase of stagnation is not over. If Italy aims to effectively comply with the international human rights agenda's priorities – an agenda which, also due to the flexibility and responsiveness of the UPR mechanism, is particularly dynamic – it has to solve its long-standing problems at home, especially those highlighted in the context of migration policies, the treatment of Roma minorities, the protection of women's and children's rights and the long-promised development of a dedicated national infrastructure. The latter, namely the creation of an independent national human rights commission consistent with the Paris Principles, would constitute a significant step towards this achievement and help Italy to be more consistent with the goals of the 2030 Sustainable Development Agenda, especially with Goal 16 (Promote peaceful and inclusive societies for sustainable development, provide access to justice for all and build effective, accountable and inclusive institutions at all levels).

In this immobility, we can also find positive implications. The cooperative way in which Italy's UPR was conducted in Geneva and welcomed domestically suggest that, after all, the phase of regression that marked the country with regards its commitment to human rights (which in some moments between 2018 and 2019 were marred by the previous Government's attempt to delegitimise international organisations and machinery for human rights monitoring) have not left permanent traces or stains. This phase attracted much attention and concern from the international community, particularly on Italy's genuine commitment to promoting and protecting human rights, and is the basis for the large number of recommendations received in 2019.

However, when observed alongside recommendations from the first and second UPR monitoring cycles, these recommendations show that the tones and themes of discussion in the third cycle were not exacerbated by the shadows of delegitimisation by these recent and controversial developments – although, there was a significant concentration on topics which previous cycles only marginally touched upon. The role conception and international perception of Italy has thus remained unaltered overall.

It is now high time to bring Italy's commitment to promoting and protecting human rights into domestic and international issues in line with its institutional reputation, starting with taking concrete steps to overcome the numerous and recurring problems that this analysis of all three UPR cycles has highlighted.

Part I

The Reception of International Rules On Human Rights In Italy

International Human Rights Law*

The first Part of the *Yearbook* is divided into two chapters. The first is devoted to updates concerning the major international human rights instruments that Italy has ratified, as well as to the identification of both international instruments signed, but not ratified, by the country and those adopted in 2019 that have not been subjected to any initiative of acceptance yet.

This summary is particularly relevant from the implementation point of view of the Agenda 2030 for Sustainable Development, more than 90 % of which is deeply rooted in the numerous international instruments that constitute international human rights law. From this perspective, as in previous editions, there are no differences in Italy's status of acceptance of international human rights treaties.

More specifically, many of the commitments set out in the International Convention on the Protection of the Rights of All Migrant Workers and Members of Their Families (the only core treaty which Italy has neither signed nor ratified) refer to targets in the Agenda 2030.

Italy's lack of ratifying the International Convention on the Protection of the Rights of All Migrant Workers and Members of Their Families – the only core human rights treaty that Italy has not signed and ratified – has knock-on consequences on the country's commitment to fulfil many of the Agenda 2030 targets, particularly Goal 3 (Good Health and Well-being), 4 (Quality Education), 8 (Decent Work and Economic Growth), 10 (Reduced Inequalities) and 16 (Peace, Justice and Strong Institutions).

The framework of Italy's international obligations takes into consideration the universal conventions adopted within the system of the United Nations, the conventions of the Council of Europe, and also the European Union treaties and secondary law. Accordingly, the information provided is preliminary to the presentation of the national normative apparatus –

---

* Andrea Cofelice, Pietro de Perini, Ino Kehrer

the Constitution, national and regional laws – which is the subject of the following chapter.

I International Human Rights Law

In 2019, Italy did not file new instruments of ratification.

II Legal Instruments on Disarmament and Non-proliferation

In 2019, Italy did not file new instruments of ratification.

III Legal Instruments of the Council of Europe

In 2019, there were no new signatures or ratifications of the Council's primary human rights conventions or protocols to which Italy had not previously adhered. However, Italy ratified a series of instruments on other topics which have some implication on the enjoyment of human rights: Council of Europe Convention on the Manipulation of Sports Competitions (adopted 18 September 2014, ratified 11 June 2019); Second Additional Protocol to the European Convention on Mutual Assistance in Criminal Matters (adopted 8 November 2001, ratified 30 August 2019); and the Third and Fourth Additional Protocol to the European Convention on Extradition (adopted respectively 10 and 20 November 2010, both ratified 30 August 2019).

IV European Union Law

A Treaties

As envisaged by the Treaty of Lisbon, since 1 December 2009, the EU legal framework has consisted of two fundamental instruments: the Treaty on the European Union (TEU) and the Treaty on the Functioning of the European Union (TFEU). Article 6 TEU attributes the status of primary law to the Charter of Fundamental Rights of the EU, and also refers specifically to the rights guaranteed by the European Convention for the Protection of Human Rights and Fundamental Freedoms (ECHR) and those deriving from the constitutional traditions common to the Member States, which are part of EU law as general principles.

Furthermore, in the Preamble of the TEU, explicit reference is made to the 1989 Community Charter of Fundamental Social Rights of Workers and the 1961 European Social Charter of the Council of Europe (revised in 1996). Both these instruments are also mentioned in the TFEU in the context of Title X on Social Policy (article 151).

B EU Law in 2019

In 2019, the European Parliament (EP) and the Council of the EU adopted directives, regulations and decisions with particular relevance for human rights. For its part, the European Commission presented significant communications and legislative proposals.

In 2019, the following directives were adopted: on accessibility requirements for products and services (2019/882 of 17 April 2019); on the work/life balance for parents and caregivers which repeals Council Directive 2010/18/EU (2019/1158 of 20 June 2019); on transparent and foreseeable conditions of work in the European Union (2019/1152 of 20 June 2019); for the protection of persons reporting violations of EU law (2019/1937 of 23 October 2019). Regarding environmental protection, the following directives were adopted: on promoting clean and low-energy consumption road vehicles (2019/1161 of 20 June 2019); on reducing the impact of certain plastic products on the environment (2019/904 of 5 June 2019); and on port reception facilities for the delivery of waste from ships, which amends Directive 2010/65/EU and repeals Council Directive 2000/59/EC (2019/883 of 17 April 2019). On the protection of the health and life of workers, directives on the protection of workers against the risk of exposure to carcinogenic or mutagenic agents at work which amends Council Directive 2004/37/EC (2019/130 of 16 January 2019 and 2019/983 of 5 June 2019) and on the fifth list of indicative occupational exposure limit values in implementation of Council Directive 98/24/EC and which amends Commission Directive 2000/39/EC (2019/1831 of 24 October 2019) were adopted. Regarding crime prevention and investigation through the use and exchange of data, the approved directives concern the exchange of a third country's citizens' data and the

European Criminal Records Information System (ECRIS). This which amends the Council Framework Decision 2009/315/JHA and replaces Council Decision 2009/316/JHA (2019/884 of the EP and the Council of 17 April 2019) facilitating the use of financial and other information for the prevention, detection, investigation or prosecution of certain criminal offences, and repealing Council Decision 2000/642/JHA (2019/1153 of 20 June 2019).

Various regulations in the field of human rights were adopted in 2019: Regulation 2019/126 of 16 January 2019, establishing the European Agency for Safety and Health at Work (EU-OSHA) which repeals and replaces Regulation (EC) No. 2062/94; Regulation 2019/1149 of 20 June 2019, establishing the European Labour Authority, amending Regulations (EC) No. 883/2004 No. 492/2011, and (EU) 2016/589 and repealing Decision (EU) 2016/344; Regulation 2019/127 of 16 January 2019, establishing the European Foundation for the Improvement of Living and Working Conditions (Eurofound) and repealing Regulation (EEC) No. 1365/75; Regulation 2019/125 of 16 January 2019, concerning trade of certain goods which could be used for capital punishment, torture or other cruel, inhuman or degrading treatment or punishment; Regulation 2019/788 of 17 April 2019 on the European citizens' initiative; Regulation 2019/1111 of 25 June 2019, on jurisdiction, the recognition and enforcement of decisions in matrimonial matters and the matters of parental responsibility, and on international child abduction; Regulation 2019/2089 of 27 November 2019 amending Regulation (EU) 2016/1011 regarding EU Climate Transition Benchmarks, EU Paris-aligned Benchmarks and sustainability-related disclosures for benchmarks; Regulation 2019/1896 of 13 November 2019 on the European Border and Coast Guard and repealing Regulations (EU) Nos. 1052/2013 and 2016/1624. Various regulations emerge from the withdrawal of the United Kingdom from the European Union, including: Regulation 2019/500 of 25 March 2019 establishing contingency measures in the field of social security coordination.

Furthermore, some decisions were adopted that are particularly relevant: The Commission approved the registration of various proposed citizens' initiatives, including: Commission Decision 2019/719 of 30 April 2019 on the proposal entitled "A fast, fair and effective solution to climate change"; Decision 2019/569 of 3 April 2019 on the proposal entitled "Respect for the rule of law within the European Union" aiming at "Creation of an objective and impartial evaluation mechanism to verify the application of the European Union's values by all the Member States"; with the Decision 2019/1564 of 4 September 2019, the proposal entitled "Stop corruption in Europe at its root, by cutting off funds to countries with inefficient judiciary after deadline"; Decision 2019/434 of 27 February 2019 on the proposal entitled "Europe CARES – Inclusive Quality Education for Children with Disabilities" and the Decision of 12 March 2019 on the proposal "Housing for all". The Commission Decision 2019/236 of 7 February 2019 lays out internal rules concerning the provision of information to data subjects and the restriction of certain rights in the context of the processing of personal data by the European Commission for the purposes of internal security of the Union institutions; Commission Decision 2019/154 of 30 January 2019 establishes internal rules concerning the restriction of the right of access of data subject right to their medical files; Decision of the Bureau of the European Parliament of 3 April 2019 lays out the implementation of the rules on the restriction of certain data subject rights in relation to the transfer of personal data by the EP to national authorities in the context of criminal or financial investigations; Decision 2019/420 of the EP and of the Council of 13 March 2019 amending Decision No. 1313/2013/EU on a Union Civil Protection Mechanism; Council Decision 2019/1181 of 8 July 2019 lays out guidelines for the employment policies of the Member States; Council Decision 2019/97 of 21 January 2019 supports the Biological and Toxin Weapons Convention in the framework of the EU Strategy against Proliferation of Weapons of Mass Destruction; Council Decision 2019/2191 of 19 December 2019 supports a global reporting mechanism on illicit conventional arms and their ammunition to reduce the risk of their diversion and illicit transfer.

Concerning Communications adopted by the Commission during 2019: on strengthening the Rule of Law within the Union; State of play and possible next steps (COM/2019/163 of 3 April 2019); on data protection rules as a trust-enabler in the EU and beyond: taking stock (COM/2019/374 of 24 July 2019); on the implementation of Directive 2013/48/EU of the EP and of the Council, of 22 October 2013 on the right of access to a lawyer in criminal proceedings and in European arrest warrant proceedings, and on the right to have a third person informed upon deprivation of liberty and to communicate with third persons and with consular authorities while deprived of liberty (COM/2019/560 of 26 September 2019);

Progress report on the Implementation of the European Agenda on Migration (COM/2019/481 of 16 October 2019); on the implementation of national Roma integration strategies until 2020, (COM/2019/ 406 of 5 September 2019); nineteenth progress report towards an effective and genuine Security Union (COM/2019/353 of 24 July 2019); on the activities and consultations of the Anti-Torture Coordination Group referred to in article 31 of Regulation (EU) 2019/125 concerning trade in certain goods which could be used for capital punishment, torture or other cruel, inhuman or degrading treatment or punishment (COM/2019/449 of 7 October 2019); on a draft Regulation of the EP laying down the regulations and general conditions governing the performance of the Ombudsman's duties (Statute of the European Ombudsman) and repealing Decision 94/262/CECA, EC, Euratom (COM/2019/553/final/3 of 18 November 2019); on the implementation of Directive 2003/86/EC on the right to family reunification (COM/2019/162 of 29 March 2019); on the ex post evaluation of the 2017 European Capitals of Culture (Paphos and Aarhus) (COM/2019/266 11 June 2019).

From the adoption of l. 24 December 2012, No. 234, the adaptation of the Italian legal system in line with the European system is achieved through two legislative instruments: the European Law and the Law of European delegation. While the former contains regulations for the direct implementation of EU law aimed at remedying cases of incorrect transposition of EU legislation, the latter contains the delegation provisions required for the transposition of directives and other Union acts.

On 12 December 2019, the draft of the European Delegation Law 2019 was approved (the final version was approved by the Council of Ministers on 23 January 2020). The law foresees the implementation of 33 European directives into Italian Law, including: Directive 2018/1673 of 23 October 2018 on combating money laundering by criminal law; Directive 2018/1808 of 14 November 2018, establishing the amendment of Directive 2010/13/EU on the coordination of certain provisions laid down by law, regulation or administrative action in Member States concerning the provision of audiovisual media services (Audiovisual Media Services Directive) in view of changing market realities, which guarantees the protection of minors, greater accessibility for persons with disabilities and measures to combat incitement to hatred and violence; Directive 2019/883 of 17 April 2019 on port reception facilities for the delivery of waste from ships, amending Directive 2010/65/EU and repealing Directive 2000/59/EC; Directive 2019/884 of 17 April 2019, which amends the Council Framework Decision 2009/315/JHA concerning the exchange of a third country's citizens' data and the European Criminal Records Information System (ECRIS) and replaces Council Decision 2009/316/GAI; Directive (EU) 2019/1152 of 20 June 2019 on transparent and predictable working conditions in the European Union; Directive 2019/1158 of 20 June 2019 on work-life balance for parents and caregivers and repealing Council Directive 2010/18/EU; Directive (EU) 2019/1153 of the EP and the Council of 20 June 2019 laying down rules facilitating the use of financial and other information for the prevention, detection, investigation or prosecution of certain criminal offences, and repealing Council Decision 2000/642/JHA; Directive 2019/1937 of 23 October 2019 regarding the protection of people who report breaches of European Union law.

Italian Law*

I Constitution of the Italian Republic

"The Republic recognises and guarantees the inviolable rights of the persons, both as an individual and in the social group where the human personality is expressed. The Republic expects that the fundamental duties of political, economic and social solidarity be fulfilled" (article 2).

"All citizens have equal social dignity and are equal before the law, without distinction of sex, race, language, religion, political opinion, personal and social conditions.

"It is the duty of the Republic to remove those obstacles of an economic or social nature which constrain the freedom and equality of citizens, thereby impeding the full development of the human person and the effective participation of all workers in the political, economic and social organisation of the Country" (article 3).

"The Italian legal system conforms to the generally recognised principles of international law. The legal status of foreigners is regulated by law in conformity with international provisions and treaties. A foreigner who, in his home Country, is denied the actual exercise of the democratic freedoms guaranteed by the Italian Constitution shall be entitled to the right of asylum under the conditions established by law. A foreigner may not be extradited for a political offence" (article 10).

"Italy rejects war as an instrument of aggression against the freedom of other peoples and as a means for the settlement of international disputes. Italy agrees, on conditions of equality with other States, to the limitations of sovereignty that may be necessary to a world order ensuring peace and justice among the Nations. Italy promotes and encourages international organisations furthering such ends" (article 11, on conditions of equality with other States, to the limitations of sovereignty that may be necessary

---

* Pietro de Perini, Ino Kehrer

to a world order ensuring peace and justice among the Nations. Italy promotes and encourages international organisations furthering such ends.).

The whole of Fundamental Principles and Part I of the Constitution (articles 1–54) is devoted to the fundamental rights and duties of citizens, which are grouped into four areas: civil relations, ethical and social relations, economic relations and political relations.

II National Legislation

During 2019, the Parliament and the Government adopted a total of 181 legislative acts (laws, decree-laws, legislative decrees) that are directly and indirectly related to the protection of internationally recognised human rights. Below the legislative acts are listed on the basis of the following typologies, based on this *Yearbook*'s categorisation of human rights instruments:

a) general human rights legislative acts;
b) legislative acts concerning specific human rights subjects;
c) legislative acts concerning the protection of human rights of particular groups

A General Human Rights Legislative Acts

L. 4 October 2019, No. 118 (Ratifying and carrying out the Memorandum of Understanding between The Italian Republic and the Council of Europe at the Office of the Council of Europe in Venice and its legal status, signed in Strasbourg 14 June 2017).

L. 8 August 2019, No. 77 (Conversion into law, with amendments, of law-decree 14 June 2019, No. 53, regarding urgent provisions on public order and security).

L. 20 May 2019, No. 41 (Conversion into law, with amendments, of law-decree 25 March 2019, No. 22, regarding urgent measures to guarantee security, financial stability and market integrity and protecting the health and freedom of residency of Italian and UK citizens, in case of the recession of the UK from the European Union).

L. 28 March 2019, No. 26 (Conversion into law, with amendments, of law-decree 28 January 2019, No. 4, regarding urgent provisions for basic and retirement income).

B Legislative Acts Concerning Specific Human Rights Subjects

Crime, criminal procedure, judicial system

L. 21 May 2019, No. 43 (Amending article 416-*ter* of the Criminal Code on the exchange of votes between politicians and the mafia).

L. 26 April 2019, No. 36 (Amending the Criminal Code and other provisions on self-defence).

L. 12 April 2019, No. 33 (Inapplicability of shortened procedures for crimes punishable by life sentences).

L. 9 January 2019, No. 3 (Measures on combating crime against public administration and the statute of limitations and on transparency in political parties and movements).

Lgs.d. 7 March 2019, No. 24 (Implementing Directive (EU) 2016/1919 of the EP and the Council, of 26 October 2016, on legal aid for suspects and accused persons in criminal proceedings and for requested persons in European arrest warrant proceedings).

D.p.r. 10 April 2019, No. 89 (Regulation concerning the structure and composition of the Office employed by the National Ombudsperson for the Rights of Persons Detained or Deprived of their Liberty).

L.d. 30 December 2019, No. 161 (Urgent amendments to legislation on the interception of conversations and communications).

Lgs.d. 4 October 2019, No. 125 (Amending and integrating legislative decrees 25 May 2017, No. 90 and No. 92, concerning the implementation of Directive (EU) 2015/849, and the implementation of Directive (EU) 2018/843 amending Directive (EU) 2015/849 on the prevention of the use of financial systems for money laundering or financing terrorism and amending Directives 2009/138/EC and 2013/36/EU).

L. 12 April 2019, No. 31 (Provisions on class action).

Extradition

L. 19 July 2019, No. 66 (Ratifying and implementing of the Convention on Extradition between Member States, with annex, Dublin, 27 September 1996).

L. 24 July 2019, No. 88 (Ratifying and implementing the following Protocols: a) Second Additional Protocol to the European convention on mutual legal assistance in criminal matters, Strasbourg, 8 November 2001; b) Third Additional Protocol to the European convention on extradition,

Strasbourg, 10 November 2010; c) Fourth Additional Protocol to the European convention on extradition, Vienna, 20 September 2012).

L. 17 January 2019, No. 10 (Ratifying and implementing Additional Bilateral Agreement between the Italian Republic and Bosnia-Herzegovina to the European Convention of Extradition of 13 December 1957, aiming to expand and facilitate its implementation, Rome, 19 June 2015).

L. 16 January 2019, No. 9 (Ratifying and implementing the following Treaties: a) Additional Bilateral Agreement between the Italian Republic and the Macedonian Republic to the European Convention of Extradition of 13 December 1957 aiming to expand and facilitate its implementation, Skopje, 25 July 2016; b) Additional Bilateral Agreement between the Italian Republic and the Macedonian Republic to the European Convention on Mutual Assistance in Criminal Matters of 20 April 1959 aiming to expand and facilitate its implementation, Skopje, 25 July 2016).

L. 24 July 2019, No. 90 (Ratifying and implementing the following Treaties: a) Treaty of mutual legal assistance in criminal matters between the Italian Republic and the Republic of Kazakhstan, Astana, 22 January 2015; b) Treaty of extradition between the Italian Republic and the Republic of Kazakhstan, Astana, 22 January 2015).

L. 24 July 2019, No. 91 (Ratifying and implementing the following Treaties: a) Treaty of extradition between the government of the Italian Republic and the government of the Republic of Kenya, Milan, 8 September 2015; b) Treaty of mutual legal assistance in criminal matters between the government of the Italian Republic and the government of the Republic of Kenya, Milan, 8 September 2015).

L. 24 July 2019, No. 87 (Ratifying and implementing the following Agreements: a) Agreement between the Italian Republic and the Republic of Serbia aiming to facilitate the application of the European Convention of Extradition of 13 December 1957, Belgrade, 9 February 2017; b) Agreement between the Italian Republic and the Republic of Serbia aiming to facilitate the application of the European Convention on Mutual Assistance in Criminal Matters of 20 April 1959, Belgrade, 9 February 2017).

L. 25 November 2019, No. 152 (Ratifying and implementing the following Treaties: a) Treaty of extradition between the government of the Italian Republic and the government of the Republic of Ecuador, Quito, 25 November 2015; b) Treaty of mutual legal assistance in criminal matters between the government of the Italian Republic and the government of the Republic of Ecuador, Quito, 25 November 2015).

L. 25 November 2019, No. 151 (Ratifying and implementing the Treaty of extradition between the government of the Italian Republic and the government of the Republic of Uruguay, Montevideo, 11 May 2017).

L. 25 November 2019, No. 150 (Ratifying and implementing the following Treaties: a) Treaty of extradition between the government of the Italian Republic and the government of the Republic of Costa Rica, Rome, 27 May 2016; b) Treaty of mutual legal assistance in criminal matters between the government of the Italian Republic and the government of the Republic of Costa Rica, Rome, 27 May 2016).

L. 18 November 2019, No. 146 (Ratifying and implementing the following Treaties: a) Treaty of extradition between the government of the Italian Republic and the government of the Federal Republic of Nigeria, Rome, 8 November 2016; b) Agreement of mutual legal assistance in criminal matters between the government of the Italian Republic and the government of the Federal Republic of Nigeria, Rome, 8 November 2016; c) Agreement on the Transfer of Sentenced Persons between the government of the Italian Republic and the government of the Federal Republic of Nigeria, Rome, 8 November 2016).

L. 18 November 2019, No. 147 (Ratifying and implementing the Treaty on the transfer of sentenced persons or persons under security measures between the Italian Republic and the Republic of Argentina, Buenos Aires, 8 May 2017).

Education, sport

L. 20 August 2019, No. 92 (Introducing Civil Education to the school curriculum).

Lgs.d. 7 August 2019, No. 96 (Integrative and corrective provisions to legislative decree 13 April 2017, No. 66, concerning: "Regulations promoting the inclusion of students with disabilities, pursuant to article 1, paragraphs 180 and 181, letter c of l. 13 July 2015, No. 107").

L. 3 May 2019, No. 39 (Ratifying and implementing the Council of Europe Convention on the Manipulation of Sports Competitions, Magglingen, 18 September 2014).

Health

D.p.r. 23 August 2019, No. 131 (Implementation Regulations of Commission Directive 2012/39/EU of 26 November 2012 amending Directive 2006/17/EC as regards certain technical requirements for the testing of human tissues and cells).

Lgs.d. 14 May 2019, No. 52 (Implementing the delegation for the reorganisation and reformation of regulations on clinical experimentation of medicine for human use, pursuant to article 1, paragraphs 1 and 2, of law 11 January 2018, No. 3).

L. 25 June 2019, No. 60 (Conversion into law, with amendments, of law-decree 30 April 2019, No. 35, concerning emergency measures for the Calabria Region health service and other urgent health measures).

D. Ministry of Health, 10 December 2019, No. 168 (Regulations regarding national databases for registering advance provisions of treatment choices).

L. 12 December 2019, No. 141 (Conversion into law, with amendments, of law-decree 14 October 2019, No. 111, concerning urgent measures respecting the obligations provided for by Directive 2008/50/EC on ambient air quality and extending the deadline of article 48, paragraphs 11 and 13, of law-decree 17 October 2016, No. 189, converted, with amendments, from law 15 December 2016, No. 229).

Work

L. 2 November 2019, No. 128 (Conversion into law, with amendments, of law decree 3 September 2019, No. 101, concerning urgent provisions for job protection and for resolving corporate crises).

L. 19 June 2019, No. 56 (Interventions for concrete steps in public administration to prevent absenteeism).

C Legislative Acts Concerning the Protection of the Human Rights of Particular Groups

Minors

D. Ministry of Transport and Infrastructure 2 October 2019, No. 122 (Regulations for implementing article 172 of the new highway code concerning provisions against the abandonment of children under four years old).

Victims of crime

L. 19 July 2019, No. 69 (Amending the Criminal Code, Criminal Proceedings Code and other provisions for protecting domestic and gender-based violence victims).

III Municipal, Provincial and Regional Statutes

The so-called peace human rights norm has been included in the statutes of numerous Italian Municipalities, Provinces and Regions since 1991. Its inclusion followed the adoption of l. June 8, 1990, No. 142 (Arrangement of local autonomies), and was originally contained in article 1 of the Veneto Regional Law of 30 March 1988, No. 18 (now updated by L. 55/1999) on "Regional interventions for the promotion of a culture of peace".

The standard text reads:

> "The Municipality … (the Province … the Region …), in accordance with constitutional principles and international norms that recognise the innate rights of human persons, sanction the rejection of war as a means of resolving international disputes and promote cooperation between the peoples, peacefully recognises a fundamental right of the person and of the peoples.
>
> For this reason, the Municipality … (the Province … the Region …) promotes the culture of peace and human rights through cultural initiatives and research, education, cooperation and information that tend to transform the City into a land of peace.
>
> The Municipality … (the Province … the Region …) will take direct initiatives and will favour those of cultural and scholastic institutions, associations, voluntary groups and international cooperation".
>
> There are also numerous statutes of local and regional authorities that contain a specific reference to international human rights norms and principles, in particular: the UN Charter, the Universal Declaration of Human Rights, the International Covenant on Civil and Political Rights, the International Covenant on Social and Cultural Economic Rights, the International Convention on the Rights of the Child, and the Charter of Fundamental Rights of the EU (see *Yearbook 2011*, pp. 55–58).

In 2019, no changes were made to the Regional Statutes with reference to the "peace human rights" norm. There are 15 Italian Regions that contain this standard within its statutory law in its standard formulation or in alternative formulations (Abruzzo, Apulia, Basilicata, Calabria, Campania, Emilia-Romagna, Lazio, Liguria, Lombardy, Marche, Molise, Piedmont, Tuscany, Umbria and Veneto). Most of these Statutes make reference to the Universal Declaration of Human Rights and other international human rights instruments.

IV Regional Laws

This section lists the laws on: human rights, equal opportunities, development cooperation, fair trade, immigration, Ombudspersons and the protection of children's rights, the rights of persons deprived of their liberty, minorities' rights, workers' rights, the rights of persons with disabilities, solidarity, social advancement, family assistance, citizenship and legality education, and the fight against bullying adopted by the Councils of the Italian Regions and Autonomous Provinces in 2019. The laws are divided according to topics and listed for each authority in chronological order.

If the subject of the act spans more than one category, the categories will be briefly listed beside it.

Peace, human rights, development cooperation, fair trade

R.l. Campania 4 December 2019, No. 23 (Regional interventions for sustainable development cooperation and international solidarity).

R.l. Emilia-Romagna 1 August 2019, No. 16 (Supporting emergency microcredit).

R.l. Friuli-Venezia Giulia 7 November 2019, No. 18 (Amending regional law 30 October 2000, No. 19 (Interventions for the promotion of international development cooperation and partnership, at a regional and local level)).

R.l. Lazio 17 July 2019, No. 12 (Regional interventions for international sustainable development cooperation, promoting a culture of peace and human rights).

Equal opportunities, gender

R.l. Emilia-Romagna 1 August 2019, No. 15 (Regional laws against sex- and gender-based violence and discrimination).

Ombudspersons, children's Ombudspersons, National Guarantor

R.l. Abruzzo 4 July 2019, No. 16 (Amending regional law 2 August 2018, No. 24 (Establishing an Ombudsperson for Children and Adolescents)).

R.l. Aosta Valley 27 March 2019, No. 3 (Provisions on an Ombudsperson for Children and Adolescents. Amending regional law 28 August 2001, No. 17 (Framework on the functioning of the Office of the Ombudsperson. Repealing regional law 2 March 1992, No. 5 (Establishment of the Ombudsman)).

Persons with disabilities

R.l. Abruzzo 23 July 2019, No. 21 (Contribution to the Regional Council of Abruzzo and Provincial Sections of the National Association for the Deaf and further provisions).

R.l. Apulia 28 March 2019, No. 9 (Amending regional law 19 December 2008, No. 39 (Contribution to support solidarity activities undertaken by associations to protect and represent invalids)).

R.l. Calabria 31 May 2019, No. 17 (Intervention for assistance for blind and handicapped persons).

R.l. Calabria 25 June 2019, No. 26 – see below *Workers' rights*

R.l. Lombardy 29 October 2019, No. 17 (Provisions for persons with specific learning disorders and early identification of signs and symptoms).

R.l. Piedmont 12 February 2019, No. 3 (Promoting policies on rights of persons with disabilities).

R.l. Tuscany 1 October 2019, No. 61 (Provisions on the Single Committee on assessing conditions of disability. Amending R.l. 60/2017).

Minority rights

R.l. Calabria 25 November 2019, No. 41 (Integrating and promoting the Romanì minority and amending regional law 19 April 1995, No. 19).

R.l. Friuli-Venezia Giulia 13 November 2019, No. 20 (Provisions for the protection and promotion of minority Slovenian, Friulian and German languages of Friuli-Venezia Giulia. Amending regional laws 26/2007, 29/2007, 20/2009, 13/2000 and 26/2014).

Workers' rights

R.l. Calabria 25 June 2019, No. 26 (Amending R.l. 14/1984 (Provisions for persons who have been mutilated or rendered invalid both in society and at work)).

R.l. Lazio 29 November 2019, No. 26 (Measures supporting socially-useful workers: job stability and pension contributions for voluntarily leaving the regional database).

R.l. Lazio, 12 April 2019, No. 4 (Provisions for the protection and security of digital workers).

R.l. Lazio 14 August 2019, No. 18 (Provisions to eliminate irregular work and exploitation of agricultural workers).

R.l. Molise 9 December 2019, No.16 (Provisions on active work and professional training policies and the correct functioning of the regional system for work-related services).

R.l. Sardinia 26 June 2019, No. 9 (Measures favouring employees at risk of collective dismissal. Amending regional law No. 48 of 2018 (Financial Stability law 2019)).

Solidarity, social promotion, family assistance

R.l. Abruzzo 23 August 2019, No. 32 (Regulations for economic support for micro- and small commercial and artisan businesses working in the Abruzzo Region to build public or private works related to the reconstruction after the 2009 and 2016/2017 earthquakes).

R.l. Abruzzo 10 December 2019, No. 42 (Interventions for families with a person affected by grave oncological illnesses or undergone transplants).

R.l. Aosta Valley, 27 March 2019, No. 2 (Further measures for preventing and combatting compulsive gambling. Amending regional law 15 June 2015, No. 14 (Provisions on preventing, combatting and treating pathological gambling. Amending regional law 29 March 2010, No. 11 (Regional policies and initiatives for promoting legality and security))).

R.l. Aosta Valley, 16 July 2019, No. 10 (Amending regional law 15 June 2015, No. 14 (Provisions on preventing, combatting and treating pathological gambling. Amending regional law 29 March 2010, No. 11 (Regional policies and initiatives for promoting legality and security))).

R.l. Basilicata 10 December 2019, No. 28 (Establishing a Regional Day to combat pathological gambling).

R.l. Calabria 16 October 2019, No. 35 (Regulations for promoting reading in pre-school children).

R.l. Emilia-Romagna 29 November 2019, No. 28 (Regional measures to prevent, eliminate and resolve over-indebtedness).

R.l. Lombardy 22 October 2019, No. 16 (Establishing a Lombardy civil volunteering service – Repealing R.l. 2/2006 and R.l. 33/2014).

R.l. Marche 28 January 2019, No. 1 (Promoting healthy and active ageing).

R.l. Marche 1 April 2019, No. 7 (Provisions to guarantee good care for late-stage and end-of-life treatment and access to palliative care in the Marche Region).

R.l. Piedmont 9 April 2019, No. 16 (Establishing the "Family Factor" for tax benefits).

R.l. Piedmont 9 April 2019, No. 17 (Promoting and valuing active ageing).

R.l. Piedmont 9 April 2019, No. 18 (Provisions supporting mortgages on a first house).

R.l. Apulia 30 April 2019, No. 16 (Promoting and valuing active ageing and good health).

R.l. Apulia 17 June 2019, No. 21 (Amending and integrating regional law 13 December 2013, No. 43 (Combatting pathological gambling)).

R.l. Apulia 5 July 2019, No. 31 (Promoting a culture of social living).

R.l. Sardinia 11 January 2019, No. 2 (Provisions on gambling disorders).

R.l. Sardinia 18 January 2019, No. 5 (Provisions on recognising, diagnosing and treating fibromyalgia).

R.l. Sicily 8 May 2019, No. 6 (Regulations on youth politics. Establishing a Regional Youth Forum and a Regional Observatory of the youth policies).

R.l. Sicily, 28 December 2019, No. 27 (Provisions for the protection and support of women with endometriosis).

R.l. Tuscany 17 July 2019, No. 45 (Provisions for the protection of basic human needs. Amending R.l. 41/2005 and R.l. 29/2009).

R.l. Umbria 11 April 2019, No. 2 (Framework for community cooperation).

R.l. Veneto 24 January 2019, No. 5 (Establishing the "Memorial Day for the Vajont Dam disaster" and recognising "Vajont Memorial").

R.l. Veneto 10 September 2019, No. 38 (Regulations on preventing and treating pathological gambling disorders).

R.l. Veneto 23 December 2019, No. 52 (Amending and integrating regional law 10 August 2012, No. 29 (Regulations to support single-parent families and separated or divorced parents in difficult situations)).

Education for citizenship and legality, fight against bullying

R.l. Calabria 25 June 2019, No. 24 (Amending article 16 of regional law 26 April 2018, No. 9 (Regional interventions for preventing and combatting the 'ndrangheta mafia and promoting legalist, responsible economics and transparency)).

R.l. Tuscany 4 June 2019, No. 28 (Forms of inter-institutional collaboration on job security, environment, health and the culture of legality).

R.l. Tuscany 26 November 2019, No. 71 (Provisions on preventing and combatting bullying and cyberbullying).

Part II

The Human Rights Infrastructure In Italy

National Bodies with Jurisdiction over Human Rights*

International human rights law requires States to set up structures that are adequately specialised in promoting and protecting fundamental rights. In this regard, a distinction shall be made between strictly governmental bodies and independent structures directly emanating from civil society. The latter in particular, through different channels from those classically used by governmental powers, aims to participate in policy-making and to promote and develop a human rights culture, as well as to prevent violations.

In this Part, the composition, mandate and activities of the following institutions will be illustrated:

- *Parliamentary Bodies*: The Special Commission for the Promotion and Protection of Human Rights of the Italian Senate; the Permanent Committee on Human Rights instituted within the Foreign Affairs Commission (III) of the Italian Chamber of Deputies; and the Parliamentary Commission for Children and Adolescents.
- *Governmental bodies*: Bodies established within the Prime Minister's Office: Department for Equal Opportunities; Commission for International Adoptions; National Committee on Bioethics. Bodies established within the Ministry of Foreign Affairs: Inter-Ministerial Committee for Human Rights; National Commission for UNESCO. Bodies established within the Ministry of Labour and Social Policy: National Observatory for Children and Adolescents; National Observatory Monitoring the Condition of Persons with Disabilities; and other departments and bureaus of the Ministry of Justice which work specifically on human rights matters.
- *The Constitutional Court*
- *Judicial Authorities*: The Court of Cassation, acting as the supreme judge of legitimacy.
- *Independent Authorities*: The Communications Regulatory Authority; the Data Protection Authority; the Committee Guaranteeing the Implementation of the

---

* Andrea Cofelice, Fabia Mellina Bares

Law on Strikes Affecting Essential Public Services; the National Ombudsperson for Children and Adolescents; and the National Ombudsperson for the Rights of Persons in Prison or Deprived of Liberty

Italy's national human rights infrastructure is completed by academic institutions promoting not only research, but also education and training in human rights issues, and by several non-governmental organisations, some of which work across a network.

I Parliamentary Bodies

A Senate of the Republic: Special Commission for the Protection and Promotion of Human Rights

The Senate's Special Commission for the Protection and Promotion of Human Rights was first set up during the 14th legislature (motion 20, 1 August 2001) and is the fruit of long-term experience by the Committee against Capital Punishment (1996–2001). Since the Commission is not permanent, it must be instituted formally at the beginning of each legislature and the Senate did so during the 15th legislature (motion 20, 12 July 2006), the 16th legislature (motion 13, 26 June 2008) and the 17th legislature (motion 7, 26 March 2013). In the latter motion, the Senate decided to commence the proceedings for the establishment of a permanent human rights commission.

The Commission has the task of studying, observing and taking initiatives on issues concerning the protection and promotion of internationally recognised human rights. To this end, it can establish relations with institutions of other countries and with international bodies; carry out missions in or outside Italy, in particular with foreign Parliaments, in order to establish agreements fostering human rights or to facilitate other forms of collaboration; it can carry out informational procedures and formulate proposals and Assembly reports; and provide its advisory opinions on proposed legislation as well as on matters deferred to other Commissions.

The Commission is made up of 25 members, present in proportion to the size of the parliamentary groups to which they belong. Among these members, the Commission elects the bureau, made up of the Chair, two Vice Chairs and two Secretaries.

In 2019, the Commission consisted as follows: *President*: Stefania Pucciarelli; *Vice president*: Alberto Airola (up to July 2019), Giorgio Fede (from July 2019), Paola Binetti; *Segretaries*: Elena Botto (up to July 2019), Orietta Vanin (from July 2019), Monica Cirinnà; *Members*: Emma Bonino, Marzia Casolati, Stefania Gabriella Anastasia Craxi, William De Vecchis, Daniela Donno (up to July 2019), Elena Fattori (from October 2019), Valeria Fedeli, Gabriella Giammanco, Barbara Guidolin, Vanna Iori, Alessandra Maiorino, Gaspare Antonio Marinello, Barbara Masini, Assuntela Messina, Michela Montevecchi, Cesare Pianasso, Isabella Rauti, Mariarosaria Rossi, Loredana Russo, and Julia Unterberger.

In 2019, the Commission held twenty hearings for the survey on the levels and mechanisms in force in Italy and internationally for the protection of human rights:

- 22 January: Federica Giannotta, advocacy coordinator and Italian programmes manager, and Paolo Ferrara, Communications manager, of *Fondazione Terre des Hommes Italy NGO*, on child marriages.
- 5 February: Giusy D'Alconzo, advocacy and Italian programmes office, and Giulia Di Cristo, international programmes office, of *Save the Children*, on child marriages.
- 5 March: Yuri Guaiana, *Associazione All Out*, on the situation of LGBTI persons in Chechnya.
- 12 March: Antonella Napoli, president of the association *Italians for Darfur*, on the 2019 annual report.
- 2 April: Riccardo Noury, spokesperson for *Amnesty International Italy*, on the situation of LGBTI persons in Chechnya.
- 9 April: Katia Anedda, president, and Francesca Carnicelli, lawyer, of the association *Prigionieri del Silenzio NGO*, on the situation of Italians imprisoned in foreign countries.
- 16 April: Mauro Palma, president of the National Ombudsperson for the rights of persons detained or deprived of their liberty, on the situation of incarcerated mothers.
- 14 May: Mauro Palma, president of the National Ombudsperson for the rights of persons detained or deprived of their liberty, on the situation of incarcerated mothers.
- 13 June: Nadia Murad, Nobel Peace Prize 2018, on the condition of the Yazidi people.
- 18 June: Giovanna Longo, president; Gustavo Imbellone, member of the board; Maria Grazia Piletti, secretary; Matteo Massimi, lawyer of the Rome

District Court, for the association *A Roma, Insieme – Leda Colombini*, on the situation of incarcerated mothers.

- 25 June: Giorgia Butera, president of *Mete NGO*, on child marriage.
- 9 July: Carlo Stasolla, president of *Associazione 21 Luglio*, on child marriage.
- 23 July: Vittorio Ferraresi, Undersecretary of State for Justice, on the situation of incarcerated mothers.
- 8 October: Vincenzo Falabella, president of the *Italian Federation for Overcoming Handicap* (*Federazione Italiana per il Superamento dell'Handicap – FISH NGO*), on the rights of persons with disabilities.
- 7 November: Elena Bonetti, Minister for Equal Opportunities and the Family, on gender equality.
- 12 November: Roberto Speziale, president of the *National Association of Families of Persons with Intellectual and/or Relational Disabilities* (*ANFFAS*), on the rights of persons with disabilities.
- 19 November: Laurence Hart, director of the Coordination Office for the Mediterranean and Gilda Violato, expert on trafficking and disembarkation of the IOM, on trafficking.
- 20 November: Manlio Di Stefano, Undersecretary of State for Foreign Affairs, on the UPR of Italy at the UN Human Rights Council.
- 26 November: Guido Trincheri, president of *Unione Famiglie Handicappati* (*U.F.Ha. NGO*), on the rights of persons with disabilities.
- 3 December: Amb. Giorgio Novello, on the rights of persons with disabilities.

Furthermore, in July 2019, there were two resolutions examining the condition of Italians incarcerated in foreign countries (doc. XXIV-*ter* No. 1) and on reviewing the matter of child and forced marriages (doc. XXIV-*ter* No. 2).

B Chamber of Deputies: Permanent Committee on Human Rights

The international protection of human rights is one of the focal points of the activities performed by the Commission for Foreign and European Union Affairs (Third Commission) of the Chamber of Deputies. As from the 10th legislature (1987–1992), the Commission set up within it the Permanent Committee on Human Rights, which, especially through hearings, ensures that Parliament is kept continually informed and up-to-date with regard to the status of international human rights. The Committee also has the task of following the course of individual human rights measures, performing preliminary tasks pertinent to the activities of the Commission. The Committee for the current legislature (18th) was set up on 5 December 2018.

In 2019, the Committee was composed of: *President*: Iolanda Di Stasio; *vice president*: Maurizio Lupi; *Secretary*: Ivan Scalfarotto (up to September 2019); *Members*: Michaela Biancofiore, Simone Billi, Laura Boldrini, Mario Alejandro Borghese, Pino Cabras, Emilio Carelli, Maria Rosaria Carfagna, Edmondo Cirielli, Andrea Colletti, Vito Comencini, Sabrina De Carlo, Andrea De Maria (up to September 2019), Chiara Ehm Yana, Mirella Emiliozzi, Piero Fassino, Paolo Formentini, Lia Quartapelle Procopio, Valentino Valentini.

In 2019, as part of the fact-finding mission on Italy's commitment to promoting and protecting human rights and combatting discrimination within the international community, the Commission held the following hearings:

- 29 January: Roanna Tay, Italian coordinator at the OHCHR; Claude Cahn, coordinator of the EU relations office of the OHCHR; Maria Belen Rodriguez de Alba Freiria, coordinator of the minorities protection department of the OHCHR; and Tania Gueorguieva Naydenova, coordinator of the anti-discriminations office of the OHCHR.
- 6 March: Fabrizio Petri, president of the Inter-Ministerial Committee on Human Rights.
- 2 April: Peter Pierre Krähenbühl, general commissioner of the United Nations Relief and Works Agency for Palestine Refugees in the Near East (UNRWA).
- 8 May: Minetu Larabas Sueidat, secretary general of Saharawi women; Gianfranco Fattorini, representative of American Association of Jurists at the UN Human Rights Council; Michael O'Flaherty, Director of FRA.
- 13 May: Yannick Cocard and Claudia Carnevale, representatives of *Americans for Democracy and Human Rights in Bahrain*.
- 11 June: Elio Pacilio, president of *Green Cross Italia*.
- 12 June: Gerald Steinberg, founder and president of the NGO *Monitor*.
- 13 June: Nadia Murad, Nobel Peace Prize 2018 and Activist for the Yazidi people.
- 31 July: Fabrizio Petri, president of the Inter-Ministerial Committee on Human Rights.
- 16 October: Rosario Maria Gianluca Valastro, vice president of the Italian Red Cross.

- 17 October: Nino Santomartino, vice president of the *Federation of Christian Organizations for International Volunteer Service* (FOCSIV); Luis Ventura Ferandéz, Representative of the Brazilian *Indigenous Missionary Council* (CIMI); Varney da Silva Tavares Kanamary, Josè Luiz Cassupà and Zenilda Maria De Aracùjo, Representatives of indigenous Amazonian populations.
- 6 November: Peter Maurer, president of the International Committee of the Red Cross.
- 7 November: Leslie Piquemal, representative of the *Cairo Institute for Human Rights Studies*; Ahmed Mefreh, Executive Director of the *Committee for Justice*; and Muhammad AL Kashef, lawyer of Egyptian human rights.
- 21 November: Alessandro Giannì, director of campaigns for *Greenpeace Italy*, and Martina Borghi, Head of forest campaigns for *Greenpeace Italy*.
- 4 December: Benjamin Blanchard, director general of the NGO *SOS Chrétiens d'Orient*, and Sebastiano Caputo, President of *SOS Chrétiens d'Orient*

C Bicameral Bodies: Parliamentary Commission for Children and Adolescents

The Parliamentary Commission for Children and Adolescents was set up by l. 23 December 1997, No. 451, although its name and responsibilities were modified by l. 3 August 2009, No. 112.

Essentially, the Commission is entrusted with a supervisory and policymaking role related to the enforcement of international obligations and domestic law on children's rights. It may also present to the two Houses of Parliament observations and proposals concerning the effects and limitations of current legislation and the possible need to amend it to ensure compliance with international law concerning the rights of the child.

The Commission is composed of 20 senators and 20 representatives appointed, respectively, by the Chair of the Senate and the Chair of the Italian Chamber of Deputies, proportionately to the total number of members in the various parliamentary groups. In 2019, the Commission was composed as follows: *President*: Licia Ronzulli; *Vice president* Caterina Bini, Simone Pillon; *Secretaries*: Grazia D'Angelo, Veronica Giannone; *Members from the Chamber of Deputies*: Maria Teresa Bellucci, Rossana Boldi, Fabiola Bologna, Vittoria Casa, Laura Cavandoli, Rosa Maria Di Giorgi, Ketty Fogliani (up to August 2019), Claudia Gobbato, Carmela Grippa, Anna Macina, Patrizia Marrocco, Ubaldo Pagano, Patrizia Prestipino,

Michela Rostan, Rossano Sasso (from August 2019), Paolo Siani, Maria Spena, Gilda Sportiello, Giuseppina Versace, Leda Volpi; *Members from the Senate*: Luisa Angrisani, Stefano Bertacco, Paola Binetti, Paola Boldrini, Lello Ciampolillo, Barbara Floridia, Francesco Maria Giro, Lucio Malan, Maria Laura Mantovani (from October 2019), Raffaela Fiormaria Marin, Susy Matrisciano, Raffaele Mautone, Edoardo Patriarca (up to July 2019), Maria Saponara, Liliana Segre, Pierpaolo Sileri (up to October 2019), and Julia Unterberger.

In 2019, the Commission conducted two fact-finding surveys.

As part of the fact-finding mission on forms of violence between minors and harm to children and adolescents, the Commission conducted the following hearings:

- 23 January: Filomena Albano, president of the National Ombudsperson for Children and Adolescents.
- 13 February: Nunzia Ciardi, director of the Postal Police and Communications Service.
- 20 June: Alberto Villani, president of the Italian Pediatrics Society; Carla Berardi, coordinator of the *Cultural Association of Pediatricians*; Luigi Nigri, national vice president of the Italian Medical Federation of Pediatricians.
- 26 June: Annamaria Nicolò, child neuro-psychiatrist and president of the Italian Psychoanalytical Society; Tonino Cantelmi, psychiatrist and professor of psychopathology at the Pontifical *Gregorian University* of Rome; Luigi Janiri, Professor of psychiatry at the Catholic University of the Sacred Heart or Catholic University of Milan.
- 18 July: Federico Bianchi di Castelbianco, psychologist and director of the Institute of orthophonology in Rome; Magda Di Renzo, psychologist and evolutionary development psychotherapist.
- 23 July: Marco Bussetti, Minister for Education, University and Research.
- 15 October: Gianluca Guida, director of the Penal Institute of minors of Nisida; Don Gennaro Pagano, Director of the *Diocesan Regina Pacis Educational Centre Foundation*
- 27 November: Enrico Parano, head of the Institute of Biomedical Research and Innovation of the National Research Council (Catania headquarters); Vito Pavone, director of the Specialisation School of Orthopedics and Traumatology of the University of Catania.
- 11 December: Monica Micheli, vice president, and Marianna Giordano, regional representative for Campania, for the Italian Coordination of the Services against child maltreatment and abuse.

As part of the fact-finding mission on bullying and cyberbullying, the Commission conducted the following hearings:

- 6 February: Filomena Albano, president of the National Ombudsperson for Children and Adolescents.
- 27 February: Fosca Nomis, head of institutional relations, and Brunella Greco, expert on new technology, for *Save the Children*; Giuseppe Magno, Board member, and Salvatore Ciro Conte, head of the school-education sector for *Blue Telephone Association* ("*Telefono azzurro*").
- 7 March: Annamaria Nicolò, President, and Elena Bozzola, secretary advisor, for the *Italian Psychoanalytical Society*; Giuseppe Bersani, associate professor of psychiatry at La Sapienza University of Rome; Alberto Maria Gambino, President of the *Science and Life* association ("*Scienza e Vita*").
- 13 March: Pietro Guidani, President, Laura di Raimondo, director, and Marzia Minozzi, head of regulations and normatives, for *"Asso-telecommunications"* ("*Assotelecomunicazioni*"); Paolo Di Bartolomei, head of relations with national and international institutions, and Carlo De Martino, head of digital communications and CSV projects, for the company *Tim*; Paolo Pinzoni, head of relations with national institutions for company *Vodafone Italy*; and Sabina Strazzullo, head of institutional relations for the company *Wind Tre*.
- 14 March: Federico Bianchi di Castelbianco, director of the Institute of Orthophonology in Rome, Flavia Ferrazzoli, psychotherapist at the same institute, and Benedetta Emanuela Palladino, Researcher at the Department of Education Sciences at the University of Florence.
- 21 March: Michele Petrucci, president of the *Regional Communications Committee of Lazio*; Federica Celestini Campanari, president, and Elisa Onorati, Process Supervisor, for the Italian movement of associations for volunteering; Laura Lecchi, President, and Chiara Morelli, Vice president, of the *"Chromosome 2.0"* ("*Cromosoma 2.0*") association.
- 27 March: Giancarlo Blangiardo, president of the *Italian National Institute of Statistics* accompanied by Patrizia Cacioli, director of the Central Directorate for Communications, Vittoria Buratta, director of the *Central Directorate of Social Statistics and Population Censor*, Giuseppina Muratore of the *Central Directorate of Social Statistics and Population Censor* and Elisabetta Segre of the *Bureau*.
- 28 March: Carlo Bolognini, President of the *National Centre against Cyberbullying* (*CNAC*).
- 3 April: Leonardo Bellini and Maria Cappello, from the Office of Institutional Advocacy and Campaigns of the Italian Committee of UNICEF; Elisabetta Scala, vice president, and Gianluca Amico, head of the *Italian Parents Movement* (MOIGE).

- 4 April: Maria Carla Gatto, president of the Milan Juvenile Court.
- 10 April: Alida Montaldi, president of the Rome Juvenile Court.
- 11 April: Claudio Cecchella, president of the National Observatory on the rights of the family.
- 17 April: Luigi De Vecchis, president of *Huawei Technologies Co. Ltd.* for Italy; Martina Colasante, policy analyst, and Diego Ciulli, manager government affairs and public policy, for *Google LLC Italy and Greece*; Laura Bononcini, public policy director of *Facebook, Inc* for Southern Europe.
- 18 April: Maria Rita Parsi, psychologist and psychotherapist; Dario Bacchini, ordinary professor of Developmental Psychology and Education at the University of Naples "Federico II".
- 15 May: Caterina Flick, professor of Criminal Corporate Law and Cybercrime and Privacy; Maria Sabina Lembo, professor of Criminal Law and Procedure.
- 13 June: Luciana Delfini and Maurizio Mensi, experts in judicial subjects.
- 23 July: Marco Bussetti, Minister for Education, University and Research.
- 30 July: Alfonso Bonafede, Minister of Justice; and Alessandra Locatelli, Minister for Family and Disabilities.

On 29 October, the Commission approved the final document on the fact-finding investigation into bullying and cyberbullying (doc. XVII-*bis*, No. 1): the paper is made up of eight parts, summarising the content of the numerous hearings and providing insight into both the forms of bullying and cyberbullying and how widespread the issue is. It identifies three action paths to combat the problem: prevention measures, protection measures and repressive interventions, alongside proposals for amendments to the current legal framework.

Finally, in 2019, the Commission initiated an investigation into two issues connected to ritual circumcision of children and to foster families and community placement within families of children.

Concerning the issue of ritual circumcision of children, the Commission conducted the following hearings:

- 25 July: Nicola Capozza, president of the Italian Society of Urology and head of the department of Urologic Surgery of the Bambino Gesù Children's Hospital in Rome; Simona La Placa, doctor at the *'P. Giaccone'* Polyclinic of Palermo and secretary of the national working group for migrant children of the Italian Society of Pediatrics; Mario Lima, professor of Pediatric Surgery at the University of Bologna and president of the Italian Society of Pediatric Surgery.

– 23 October: Noemi Di Segni, president of the Union of Italian Jewish Communities; Riccardo Shmuel Di Segni, director of the Italian Rabbinical College and chief rabbi of Rome; Yahya Sergio Yahe Pallavicini, president of the Italian Islamic Religious Community.

D Parliamentary Acts Concerning Human Rights

The bills on human rights presented in Parliament are organised into 12 categories. These refer to the main legal instruments adopted by the UN on human rights, disarmament and international humanitarian and criminal law (see Part I, International Human Rights Law, I and II; Part III, The United Nations System, V, and Humanitarian and criminal law), as well as to the SDGs, adopted by the UN in 2015. To codify the bills, 52 descriptors were used within the classification system for parliamentary documents, TESEO (*TEsauro SEnato per l'Organizzazione dei documenti parlamentari*) as shown in the table below.

List of Acronyms of Italian Parliamentary Groups employed in the following tables

ALA-PRI: *Alleanza Liberal Popolare-Partito Repubblicano Italiano* ("Liberal-Popular Alliance-Italian Republican Party")

Aut(SVP-UV-PATT-UPT)-PSI: *Per le Autonomie-Partito Socialista Italiano* ("In Support of Autonomies-Italian Socialist Party")

FI-PdL: *Forza Italia-Il Popolo delle Libertà* ("The People of Freedom")

FL(Id-PL), *Federazione della Libertà* ("Federation of Freedom")

Lega: *Lega Nord* ("Northern League")

M5S: *Movimento 5 Stelle* ("Five Star Movement")

MDP-LeU: *Articolo 1 – Movimento Democratico e Progressista – Liberi e Uguali* ("Article 1 – Progressive and Democratic Movement – Free and Equal")

Mixed: *Gruppo Misto* ("Mixed Group")

NcI; *Noi con l'Italia* ("We together with Italy")

PD: *Partito Democratico* ("Democratic Party")

PLI: *Partito Liberale Italiano* ("Italian Liberal Party")

SC-ALA CLP-MAIE; *Scelta Civica-Alleanza Liberal Popolare per la Costituente Liberale e Popolare- Movimento Associativo Italiani all'Estero* ("Civic Choice-

Liberal-Popular Alliance for the Liberal-Popular Costituent-Associative Movement of Italians Living Abroad")

SI-SEL-POS: *Sinistra Italiana-Sinistra Ecologia e Libertà-Possibile* ("Italian Left-Left, Environment and Freedom-Possible")

For each proposal listed below, there is indicated: the person who originally proposed or first signed the bill, its assigned code (particularly the letter "C" if the bill was presented in the Chamber of Deputies and "S" if the bill was presented in the Senate), the name of the bill, the date of presentation and the date of its latest updates.

Category	**International reference instrument**	**SDGs**	**Descriptor (TESEO)**
1) Racism	International Convention on the Elimination of All Forms of Racial Discrimination	-	Racism
2) Civil and political rights	International Covenant on Civil and Political Rights	16-Peace, Justice and Strong Institutions	Civil and political rights Freedom of Correspondence Right to housing Freedom of press Religious freedoms Protection of Privacy (personal or sensitive data, privacy, personal computer systems) Freedom of Association Freedom of Thought Freedom of Assembly Freedom of the Individual

Category	**International reference instrument**	**SDGs**	**Descriptor (TESEO)**
3) Economic, social and cultural rights (including bioethics and environmental rights)	International Covenant on Economic, Social and Cultural Rights	1-No Poverty 3-Good Health and Well-being 4-Quality Education 6-Clean Water and Sanitation 8-Decent Work and Economic Growth 10-Reduced Inequalities 13-Climate Action 15-Life on Land 17-Partnerships for the Goals	Social Security Protection of workers Freedom of teaching Protection of health Human Life
4) Women's Rights	Elimination of All Forms of Discrimination against Women	5-Gender Equality	Women Equality (discrimination, equality balance) Gender relations Equality between the sexes (equal opportunities) Sexual Offences (sexual harassment, abuse within the family, sexual violence) Violence and Threats (domestic and family violence)
5) Torture, Prison Conditions, Rights of Detained Persons	Convention against Torture	-	Prison Systems Inmates (mothers in prison) Work of inmates Mistreatment and torture (torture, mutilation) abuse

Category	**International reference instrument**	**SDGs**	**Descriptor (TESEO)**
6) Children's Rights	Convention on the Rights of the Child	-	Minors Sexual Crimes (sexual harassment, abuse within the family, sexual violence, corruption of minors, exploitation and sexual abuse, paedophilia)
7) Migrants, Refugees, Asylum Seekers, Minorities	The International Convention on the Protection of the Rights of All Migrant Workers and Members of Their Families	-	Foreign nationals' rights Migrant workers Immigration Religious and ethnic minorities Citizenship
8) Persons with Disabilities	Convention on the Rights of Persons with Disabilities	-	People with disabilities
9) Enforced Disappearances	The International Convention for the Protection of All Persons from Enforced Disappearance	-	Political or racial persecution
10) National Human Rights Institutions	A/RES/48/134 (Paris Principles)	16-Peace, Justice and Strong Institutions	Independent supervisory and guarantee authorities

Category	**International reference instrument**	**SDGs**	**Descriptor (TESEO)**
11) Ratification of International Instruments	see *Part I, International Human Rights Law, I and II; Part III, The United Nations System, V*	-	Rights and duties of the person Non-traditional fundamental rights Traditional human rights Rights of man Crimes against fundamental rights Non-governmental organizations (NGOs) Right to self-determination of peoples Treaty ratification
12) Disarmament, international humanitarian law and criminal law	see *Part I, International Human Rights Law, I and II; Part III, The United Nations System, V*		Disarmament International crimes War (cyber warfare) War crimes, crimes against humanity, genocide Peace Prisoners of war War zones, military operation zones International tribunals

In 2019, a total of 217 initiatives were presented in parliament concerning human rights (compared to 232 in 2018). Just as in 2018, more than half of these fit into three main categories: economic, social and cultural rights (52), women's rights (39) and children's rights (36). Around a third are then distributed in four other categories: civil and political rights (26), national institutions and ratification of international instruments (19), the rights of persons with disabilities (19) and the rights of migrants, refugees, asylum seekers and minorities (13). The remaining categories make up just over 5 % of the law proposals presented: torture and prison conditions (6), disarmament and international humanitarian law and criminal law (5), and racism (3). There were no initiatives presented regarding forced disappearances.

Bills presented in Parliament in 2019

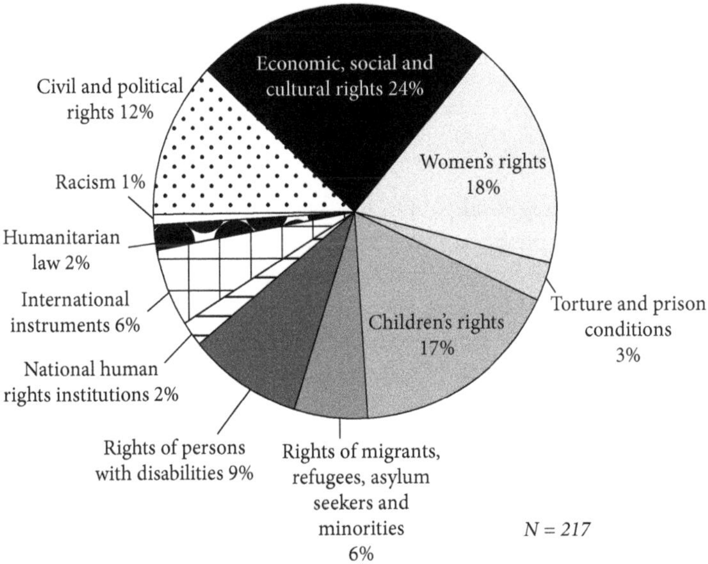

Around 90 % of initiatives are presented through parliamentary processes. There were, however, 19 initiatives presented through government initiatives, concerning:

- *Economic, social and cultural rights*: provisions to combat violence at sporting events (bills C.1603-*ter* and S. 1439); provisions on security for health and social-health professionals at work (bill C.2117); urgent amendments to legislation on the interception of conversations and communications (bill C.2324);
- *Economic, social and cultural rights:* urgent provisions on basic and retirement income (bills S. 1018, S. 1018-B and C.1637); urgent provisions for job protection and for resolving corporate crises (bills S. 1476 and C.2203);
- *Women's rights*: amendments to the Criminal Code, the Criminal Procedures Code and other provisions on the protection of victims of gender-based and domestic violence (bill S. 1200);
- *Ratification of the following international instruments*: Council of Europe Convention on the Manipulation of Sports Competitions (C.1638);

Amendment to the Montreal Protocol on Substances that Deplete the Ozone Layer (S. 1220); Additional Protocol to the Convention on the Transfer of Sentenced Persons (S. 1239); Convention relating to extradition between the Member States of the European Union (C.1797 and S. 1307); Second Additional Protocol to the European Convention on Mutual Assistance in Criminal Matters, and Third and Fourth Additional Protocol to the European Convention on Extradition (C.1798 and S. 1308); Protocol on Pollutant Release and Transfer Registers (C.1862); Protocol amending the Convention for the Protection of Individuals with regard to Automatic Processing of Personal Data (S. 1384).

There were six regional proposals, five of which concerning work on digital platforms (presented by the regional councils of Piedmont-bill C.1592; Umbria-bill S. 1198; Emilia Romagna-bills S. 1393 and C.1957; and Marche-bill C.2114) and one concerning provisions on the prevention and surveillance in infant schools and nurseries, as well as in social-assistance structures for the elderly, minors and persons with disabilities in situations of distress (regional council of Veneto, bill C.1568).

Finally, two proposals were presented by the CNEL on women's rights ("Amending article 46 of the Code of Equal Opportunities, of which legislative decree 11 April 2006, No. 198, concerning the reporting on staff situations", bills C.1925 and S. 1353) and two were made through public initiative on economic, social and cultural rights: teaching citizenship education as a stand-alone graded subject in the school curriculum at all levels (bill C.1485); draft law on the *Rodotà Commission* on common, social and sovereign goods (bill C.2237).

One bill was rejected by parliamentary initiative ("establishing a Parliamentary Enquiry Commission on the situation of security and the state of degradation of cities and their outskirts": bill C.1604); 11 were approved by one branch of Parliament and only seven of the 217 bills presented in the field of human rights (3 %) were definitely approved by Parliament.

Out of these, only one bill was made through parliamentary initiative: "Introducing Civil Education to the school curriculum" (l. 20 August 2019, No. 92). Other cases were government initiatives:

– Conversion into law, with amendments, of law-decree 28 January 2019, No. 4, concerning urgent provisions on basic and retirement income (l. 28 March 2019, No. 26);

- Ratifying and implementing the Council of Europe Convention on the Manipulation of Sports Competitions, Magglingen 18 September 2014 (l. 3 May 2019, No. 39);
- Ratifying and implementing the Convention on Extradition between Member States, with annex, Dublin, 27 September 1996 (l. 19 July 2019, No. 66);
- Amending the Criminal Code, the Criminal Procedures Code and other provisions on the protection of victims of gender-based and domestic violence (l. 19 July 2019, No. 69);
- Ratifying and implementing the following protocols: a) Second Additional Protocol to the European convention on mutual legal assistance in criminal matters, opened in Strasbourg, 8 November 2001; b) Third Additional Protocol to the European convention on extradition, opened in Strasbourg, 10 November 2010; c) Fourth Additional Protocol to the European convention on extradition, opened in Vienna, 20 September 2012 (l. 24 July 2019, No. 88);
- Conversion into law, with amendments, of the law-decree 3 September 2019, No. 101, concerning urgent provisions for job protection and for resolving corporate crises (l. 2 November 2019, No. 128).

Racism

Even though the UPR of the UN Human Rights Council urged Italy to combat all forms of racism, racial discrimination, xenophobia and hate speech through recent recommendations (see Part III, The United Nations System, II, B), only about 1 % of the bills present in parliament in 2019 concerned the subject, as follows:

1. **S.1058** – *Sen. Loredana De Petris (Mixed, Free and Equal) and others*
   Amending law 20 July 2000, No. 211, concerning the extension of the "Giorno della Memoria" day of remembrance in honour of all victims of ethnic, sexual and religious persecution who were deported to the Nazi extermination camps.
   12 February 2019: Presented to the Senate
   13 May 2019: Assigned (examination not yet begun)
2. **S.1455** – *Sen. Valeria Fedeli (PD) and others*
   Measures to combat inciting hate online.
   5 August 2019: Presented to the Senate
   18 November 2019: Assigned (examination not yet begun)
3. **C.2262** – *Hon. Marco Marin (FI) and others*
   Introducing article 594-*bis* of the Criminal Code, concerning the crime of racial, ethnic, nationalist or religious abuse at sporting events.
   20 November 2019: Presented to the Chamber of Deputies
   27 February 2020: Assigned (examination not yet begun)

Political and civil rights

Of the 25 bills concerning civil and political rights, the promotion of which is outlined in the targets of Goal 16 (Promote peaceful and inclusive societies for sustainable development, provide access to justice for all and build effective, accountable and inclusive institutions at all levels), almost half (13) concern combatting various forms of violence, that is: violence against health and education workers (4); maltreatment and abuse in nurseries, infant schools and social-assistance structures for minors, the elderly and persons with disabilities (3); violence at sporting events (2); psychological coercion and violence (2); male genital mutilation (1); personal security in the outskirts of cities (1).

Around a quarter of bills concern the protection of privacy and personal data, above all regarding new technologies (7); the remaining 20 % of the bills are divided as follows: communication freedom and confidentiality (2); freedom of expression (1); protecting whistle-blowers (1); combatting gender-based and sexual-orientation based discrimination (1).

Bills concerning civil and political rights

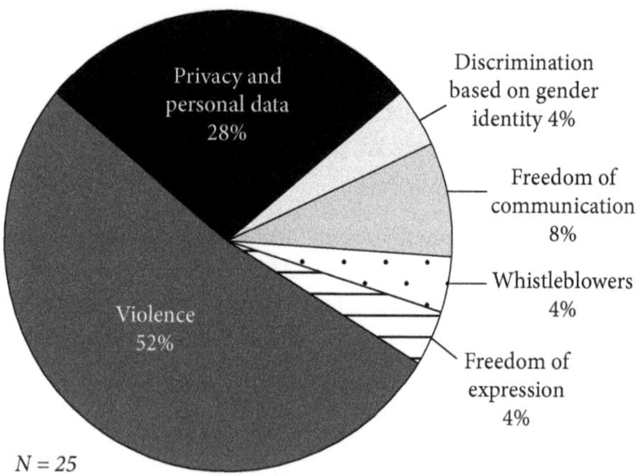

Economic, social and cultural rights (including bioethics and environmental rights)

Economic, social and cultural rights were not only the highest presented category of bills in 2019 (52) but also the category that showed greatest relevance to pursuing the SDGs. Over 80 % of the legislation proposed in this category directly refers to three main areas:

- *employment related rights*: right to work, health and safety in the workplace, protection of legal and retributive conditions of employees working on online platforms, provisions on domestic work, life-work balance, and protection from being fired illegally (Goal 8: Promote sustained, inclusive and sustainable economic growth, full and productive employment and decent work for all);
- *health and bioethics:* (Goal 3: Ensure healthy lives and promote well-being for all at all ages).
- *education*, referring particularly to the various educational courses in primary and secondary schools: civil education, civil harmony education, "Citizenship and Constitution", emotional education, culture of security, and health education (Goal 4: Ensure inclusive and equitable quality education and promote lifelong learning opportunities for all).

10 % of the bills aim to promote social security, primarily through funds, fiscal incentives, benefits and pension incomes (Goal 1: End poverty in all its forms everywhere; Goal 10: Reduce Inequality within and among countries);

The remaining 5 % aim to protect environmental rights (Goal 13: Take urgent action to combat climate change and its impacts; Goal 15: Protect, restore and promote sustainable use of terrestrial ecosystems, sustainably manage forests, combat desertification, and halt and reverse land degradation and halt biodiversity loss), safeguarding common goods, as well as introducing the right to happiness into the Constitution.

Bills concerning economic, social and cultural rights

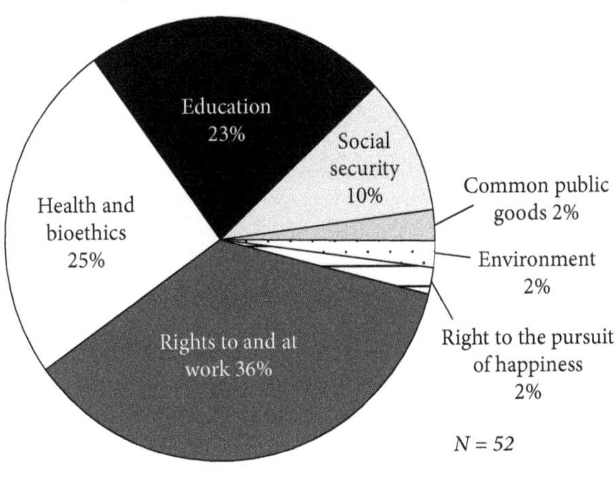

Women's rights

The main theme tackled by the legislator on bills concerning the protection of women's rights was the combatting all forms of violence (incitement of hate, stalking, domestic violence and so on).

In line with Goal 5 (Achieve gender equality and empower all women and girls), around a third of bills regarding the promotion of gender equality and equal opportunities for men and women. They focus on overcoming the gender pay gap and on equal representation in the following areas: administrative bodies, oversight bodies for companies listed on regulated financial markets, the judiciary, institutional bodies, and professional sport.

Six bills concern the participation of women in the workforce; two concern social security (in the form of pension incomes and income support); finally, one project establishes gender budgeting within territorial bodies.

Bills concerning women's rights

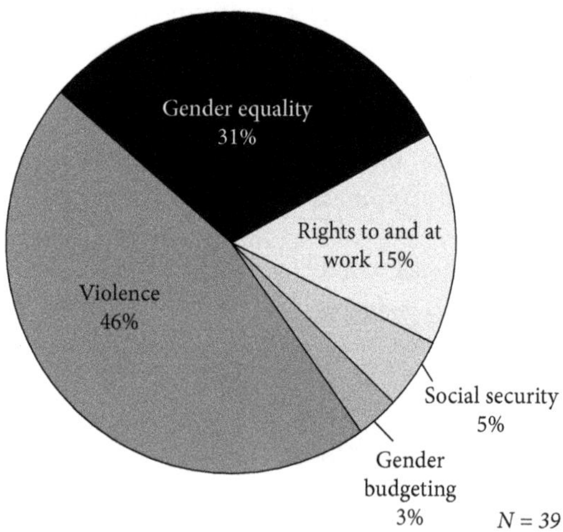

Torture, prison conditions and the rights of detained persons

Particularly noteworthy is bill C.2286, presented in December 2019, which aims at amending provisions of the Criminal Code concerning the crime of torture.

1. **S.1046** – *Sen. Valeria Valente (PD) and others*
   Provisions to prevent suicide in prison.

7 February 2019: Presented to the Senate
19 March 2019: Assigned (examination not yet begun)

2. **C.1611** – *Hon. Jole Santelli (FI)*
Amending law 26 July 1975, No. 354, and other provisions concerning the way minors access prison institutes to visit incarcerated parents.
19 February 2019: Presented to the Chamber of Deputies
To be assigned
3. **C.1780** – *Hon. Edmondo Cirielli (FDI) and others*
Amending the Criminal Code and other provisions on postponing punishment for pregnant women or mothers with children under 3 years, suspending the exercise of parental responsibility following enforcement orders for detentive punishment as well as a ban on children entering prison institutes.
16 April 2019: Presented to the Chamber of Deputies
17 September 2019: Assigned (examination not yet begun)
4. **C.1951** – *Hon. Vincenza Bruno Bossio (PD)*
Amending articles 4-*bis* of law 26 July 1975, No. 354, and 2 of law-decree 13 May 1991, No. 152, converted, with amendments, from law 12 July 1991, No. 203, concerning revisions of regulations on the ban of prison benefits for detainees who do not cooperate with judicial authorities.
2 July 2019: Presented to the Chamber of Deputies
25 September 2019: Assigned (examination not yet begun)
5. **C.2286** – *Hon. Anna Bilotti (M5S)*
Introducing articles 583-*quater*.1, 583-*quater*.2 and 583-*quater*.3 and repealing articles 613-*bis* and 613-*ter* of the Criminal Code, concerning the crime of torture, as well as establishing a fund to compensate victims.
3 December 2019: Presented to the Chamber of Deputies
To be assigned
6. **C.2298** – *Hon. Paolo Siani (PD) and others*
Amending the Criminal Code, the Criminal Procedures Code and law 21 April 2011, No. 62, concerning the protection of the relationship between incarcerated mothers and children.
11 December 2019: Presented to the Chamber of Deputies
4 February 2020: Assigned (examination not yet begun)

Rights of the child

The most common subject in this field (totalling around a third of all bills presented) was the protection of the rights of the child in fostering and adoption procedures: six bills aimed at establishing a Parliamentary Enquiry Commission on child fostering and on foster families.

The remaining two thirds of bills concerning: combatting bullying; combatting violence against children (including sexual exploitation, paedophilia and pedopornography); civil rights (particularly to the removal or retention (domestically and abroad) of minors and to the juvenile justice legal system); right to health; protection of minors related to communication (particularly internet); social security (funds and tax deductions); right to education; reinforcement of the powers of the bicameral parliamentary commission for children and adolescents.

Bills concerning children's rights

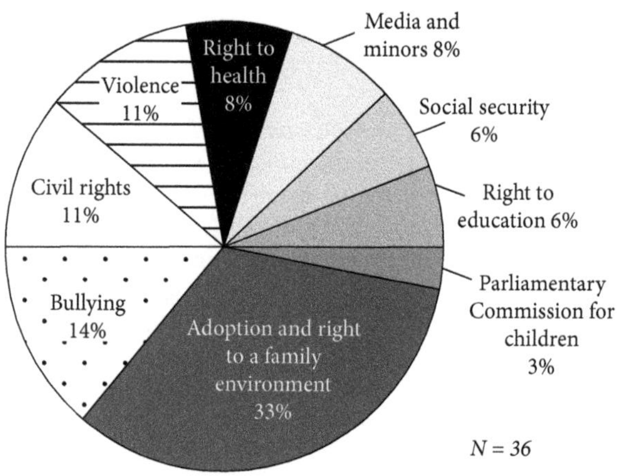

N = 36

Migrants, refugees, asylum seekers, minorities

Out of the 13 bills presented in this area, three propose amendments to law 5 February 1992, No. 91, concerning acquiring Italian citizenship; three concerned the establishment of a Parliamentary Enquiry Commission on shipwrecks and the loss of human life of migrants in the Mediterranean Sea; and finally, two regarded the establishment of Parliamentary Commission on Italian mobility across the world.

1. **C.1546** – *Hon. Graziano Delrio (PD) and others*
   Establishing a parliamentary enquiry commission on shipwrecks and the loss of life of migrants in the Mediterranean Sea.
   29 January 2019: Presented to the Chamber of Deputies
   11 March 2019: Assigned (examination not yet begun)
2. **S.1029** – *Sen. Andrea Marcucci (PD) and others*
   Establishing a parliamentary enquiry commission on the death of migrants in the Mediterranean Sea.
   29 January 2019: Presented to the Senate

5 March 2019: Assigned (examination not yet begun)

3. **C.1569** – *Hon. Riccardo Magi (Mixed, +Democratic Central-Europe)*
Establishing a parliamentary enquiry commission on the shipwrecked migrant ships in the Mediterranean Sea and the implementation of cooperation agreements between the Italian Republic and Libya.
5 February 2019: Presented to the Chamber of Deputies
18 April 2019: Assigned (examination not yet begun)
4. **C.1760** – *Hon. Paolo Ficara (M5S)*
Amending article 12 of the consolidated text on provisions concerning immigration and regulations on the condition of foreign citizens, of which legislative decree 25 July 1998, No. 286, regarding the destination of confiscated goods during police operations preventing and cracking down on illegal immigration.
9 April 2019: Presented to the Chamber of Deputies
To be assigned
5. **S.1418** – *Sen. Fabrizio Ortis (M5S) and others*
Establishing an intercultural defence advisor.
17 July 2019: Presented to the Senate
4 February 2020: Currently under examination by the Commission
6. **C.2142** – *Hon. Stefania Prestigiacomo (FI) and others*
Amending article 9 of law 5 February 1992, No. 91, on granting citizenship for sporting merit.
4 October 2019: Presented to the Chamber of Deputies
To be assigned
7. **C.2159** – *Hon. Massimo Ungaro (IV)*
Establishing a parliamentary commission on emigration and the mobility of Italians in the world.
9 October 2019: Presented to the Chamber of Deputies
To be assigned
8. **C.2212** – *Hon. Giuditta Pini (PD)*
Repealing Chapters I, II and III of Title I of law-decree 4 October 2018, No. 113, converted, with amendments, from law 1 December 2018, No. 132, and of articles 1, 2, 3 and 3-*bis* of law-decree 14 June 2019, No. 53, converted, with amendments, from law 8 August 2019, No. 77, concerning international protection, immigration, acquiring and revoking citizenship, public order and security.
24 October 2019: Presented to the Chamber of Deputies
22 December 2019: Assigned (examination not yet begun)
9. **C.2239** – *Hon. Angela Schiro' (PD) and others*
Establishing a parliamentary commission on emigration and the mobility of Italians in the world.
6 November 2019: Presented to the Chamber of Deputies
27 January 2020: Assigned (examination not yet begun)

10. **S.1621** – *Sen. Francesco Verducci (PD) and others*
Amending law 5 February 1992, No. 91, and other provisions concerning citizenship.
20 November 2019: Presented to the Senate
18 February 2020: Assigned (examination not yet begun)
11. **S.1622** – *Sen. Francesco Verducci (PD) and others*
Amending law-decree 4 October 2018, No. 113, converted, with amendments, from law 1 December 2018, No. 132, concerning international protection, immigration, public security, as well as measures for the correct functioning of the Ministry of the Interior and the organisation and functioning of the National Agency for the administration and the destination of assets seized and confiscated from organized crime. Amending decree-law 14 June 2019, No. 53, converted, with amendments, from law 8 August 2019, No. 77, concerning urgent provisions on public order and security. Amendments to law-decree 20 February 2017, No. 14, converted, with amendments, from law 18 April 2017, No. 48, concerning urgent provisions on the security of cities.
20 November 2019: Presented to the Senate
To be assigned
12. **C.2269** – *Hon. Elisa Siragusa (M5S) and others*
Amending law 5 February 1992, No. 91, on citizenship.
25 November 2019: Presented to the Chamber of Deputies
To be assigned
13. **S.1629** – *Sen. Nicola Calandrini (FdI) and others*
Amending article 20 of law-decree 25 June 2008, No. 112, converted, with amendments, from law 6 August 2018, No. 133, on paying foreign citizens a social allowance.
26 November 2019: Presented to the Senate
23 January 2020: Assigned (examination not yet begun)

Rights of persons with disabilities

Around half of the 19 bills presented concern social security (in the form of parental leave, financial benefits, healthcare and homecare); four bills aim to promote independent life of persons with disabilities (particularly quality of life, equal opportunities, and emotional assistance); two promote the right to health; one regards the right to sport; one aims to encourage job insertion; and finally, one bill concerns the right to play for children with disabilities.

Bills concerning persons with disabilities

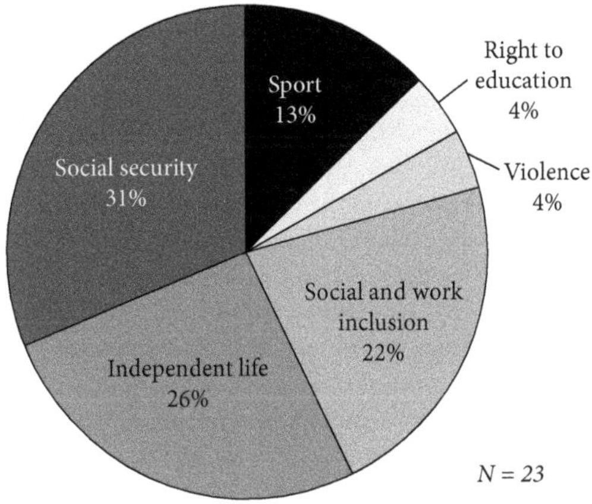

1. **C.1547** – *Hon. Debora Serracchiani (PD) and others*
   Provisions on recognising full treatment and social inclusion of persons affected by epilepsy.
   29 January 2019: Presented to the Chamber of Deputies
   15 May 2019: Assigned (examination not yet begun)
2. **C.1584** – *Hon. Rosa Menga (M5S)*
   Amending article 33 of law 5 February 1992, No. 104, on the right to choose workplace for workers assisting family members with disabilities.
   7 February 2019: Presented to the Chamber of Deputies
   To be assigned
3. **C.1594** – *Hon. Debora Serracchiani (PD) and others*
   Introducing support teaching assistants for teachers with disabilities.
   13 February 2019: Presented to the Chamber of Deputies
   12 June 2019: Assigned (examination not yet begun)
4. **S.1068** – *Sen. Antonio De Poli (FI-BP) and others*
   Amending the consolidated text on income taxes set out in the Presidential Decree 22 December 1986, No. 917, on supporting assistance to persons with disabilities and to elderly persons who are not self-sufficient.
   14 February 2019: Presented to the Senate
   25 March 2019: Assigned (examination not yet begun)
5. **S.1092** – *Sen. Raffaella Fiormaria Marin (L-SP-PSd'Az) and others*
   Amending Presidential Decree 26 October 1972, No. 633, on VAT incentives for the acquisition of motor vehicles by persons with disabilities.
   22 February 2019: Presented to the Senate
   15 May 2019: Assigned (examination not yet begun)
6. **S.1117** – *Sen. Raffaella Fiormaria Marin (L-SP-PSd'Az) and others*

Provisions on the quality of life for non-self-sufficient people.
4 March 2019: Presented to the Senate
28 May 2019: Assigned (examination not yet begun)

7. **C.1695** – *Hon. Augusta Montaruli (FDI)*
Recognising Italian Sign Language and provision for the protection of deaf people and their children, social and cultural integration and full participation in public life.
21 March 2019: Presented to the Chamber of Deputies
5 July 2019: Assigned (examination not yet begun)
8. **C.1721** – *Hon. Giuseppina Versace (FI) and others*
Provisions concerning the recruitment of Paralympic athletes with physical and sensory disabilities in military and state corps sports groups.
1 April 2019: Presented to the Chamber of Deputies
2 October 2019: Assigned (examination not yet begun)
9. **S.1219** – *Sen. Paola Binetti (FI-BP) and others*
Provisions for persons with epilepsy.
4 April 2019: Presented to the Senate
11 February 2020: Currently under examination by the Commission
10. **C.1796** – *Hon. Massimiliano Panizzut (League) and others*
Amendments to Table A attached to Presidential Decree 26 October 1972, No. 633, to reduce additional VAT concerning vehicles for persons with disabilities.
18 April 2019: Presented to the Chamber of Deputies
10 July 2019: Assigned (examination not yet begun)
11. **S.1267** – *Sen. Iunio Valerio Romano (M5S) and others*
Amending article 33 of law 5 February 1992, No. 104, concerning assistance, social integration and rights of persons with disabilities.
8 May 2019: Presented to the Senate
19 June 2019: Assigned (examination not yet begun)
12. **S.1274** – *Sen. Daniela Donno (M5S) and others*
Provisions concerning equal opportunities for treatment for people with colour-blindness and delegates the Government for legal reorganisation and reforms.
9 May 2019: Presented to the Senate
11 June 2019: Assigned (examination not yet begun)
13. **C.1841** – *Hon. Luca Rizzo Nervo (PD) and others*
Provisions concerning the organisation and functioning of residential and semi-residential family structures for the elderly and adults with physical or psychological disabilities.
9 May 2019: Presented to the Chamber of Deputies
8 October 2019: Assigned (examination not yet begun)

14. **C.1876** – *Hon. Leonardo Salvatore Penna (M5S)*
    Provisions on the emotional, affectionate, physical, and sexual assistance for persons with disabilities.
    30 May 2019: Presented to the Chamber of Deputies
    To be assigned
15. **C.1935** – *Hon. Lisa Noja (PD) and others*
    Amending Table A attached to Presidential Decree 26 October 1972, No. 633, to law 9 April 1986, No. 97, and to article 8 of law 27 December 1997, No. 449, concerning tax incentives related to electric cars and hybrid engines used by persons with disabilities, as well as provisions concerning disabled parking badges.
    26 June 2019: Presented to the Chamber of Deputies
    21 October 2019: Assigned (examination not yet begun)
16. **C.1959** – *Hon. Antonino Minardo (FI)*
    Retirement benefits and incentives for workers assisting family members with serious disabilities.
    5 July 2019: Presented to the Chamber of Deputies
    14 October 2019: Assigned (examination not yet begun)
17. **S.1468** – *Sen. Gianmauro Dell'Olio (M5S) and others*
    Amending Presidential Decree 26 October 1972, No. 633, concerning tax incentives related to the acquisition of motor vehicles by persons with disabilities.
    6 August 2019: Presented to the Senate
    To be assigned
18. **S.1461** – *Sen. Simona Nunzia Nocerino (M5S) and others*
    Provisions for recognising and supporting family caregivers.
    7 August 2019: Presented to the Senate
    18 February 2020: Currently under examination by the Commission
19. **C.2318** – *Hon. Maria Teresa Bellucci (FDI) and others*
    Delegating the Government on the subject of building children's parks that are accessible for children with disabilities.
    23 December 2019: Presented to the Chamber of Deputies
    27 February 2020: Assigned (examination not yet begun)

Forced Disappearances

In 2019, no bills were presented in this area.

National Human Rights Institutions

In 2019, four bills were presented on the creation of national human rights institutions in Italy (Goal 16: promote peaceful and inclusive societies for sustainable development, provide access to justice for all and build effective, accountable and inclusive institutions at all levels), with particular reference to the National Authority for Human Rights (S. 1065), to the

Ombudsperson for persons with disabilities (S. 1035 and C.1884) and to the Ombudsperson for combatting discrimination (C.1794, the only one being examined by the Committee). Furthermore, one bill contains provisions on the Ombudsperson on the Rights of Detained Persons concerning access of the Ombudsperson to detainees subjected to the special prison regime set out in article 41-*bis* (S. 1550).

Overall, 14 bills have been presented in this area from the beginning of the XVIII legislature (23 March 2018), of which:

- four on the Commission/National Authority for Human Rights (S. 1065, C.855, S. 593 and S. 654);
- three on the Ombudspersons for the Rights of the Family (S. 183, S. 108 and S. 129)
- two on the National Ombudsperson (C.1415 and C.145)
- two on the Ombudsperson for Persons with Disabilities (S. 1035 and C.1884)
- one on the Ombudsperson for Combatting Discrimination (C.1794)
- one on the National Ombudsperson on the Protection of the Rights of Victims of Intentional Violent Crime (C.500)
- one on the Ombudsperson for the Rights of Detained Persons (S. 1550).

Of these bills, only two are currently in the discussion phase in the commission: bill C.855 "Establishing a national Commission for the promotion and protection of fundamental human rights" and bill C.1794 "Establishing a National Ombudsperson for combatting discrimination".

1. **S.1550**–18th Legislature
   Sen. Franco Mirabelli (PD) and others
   Provisions on the Ombudsperson for the Rights of Detained Persons.
   11 October 2019: Presented to the Senate
   12 February 2020: Assigned (examination not yet begun)
2. **C.1884** – 18th Legislature
   Hon. Andrea De Maria (PD)
   Establishing an Ombudsperson for Persons with Disabilities.
   3 June 2019: Presented to the Chamber of Deputies
   28 November 2019: Assigned (examination not yet begun)
3. **C.1794** – 18th Legislature
   Hon. Giuseppe Brescia (M5S) and others
   Establishing a National Ombudsperson for combatting discrimination and amending legislative decree 9 July 2003, No. 215.
   18 April 2019: Presented to the Chamber of Deputies
   11 December 2019: Currently under examination by the Commission

4. **S.1065** – 18th Legislature
   *Sen. Ma*uro Antonio Donato Laus (PD)
   Establishing a National Authority for human rights.
   13 February 2019: Presented to the Senate
   9 Dece*mber 2019: Assigned (examination not yet begun)*
5. **S.1035** – 18th Legislature
   *Sen. Ma*ria Rizzotti (FI-BP)
   Establishing an Ombudsperson for Persons with Disabilities.
   31 January 2019: Presented to the Senate
   5 Mar*ch 2019: Assigned (examination not yet begun)*
6. **C.1415** – 18th Legislature
   *Hon. Fran*cesco Silvestri (M5S)
   Establishing a national Ombudsperson.
   5 December 2018: Presented to the Chamber of Deputies
   To be ass*igned*
7. **S.654** – 18th Legislature
   Sen. Valeria Fedeli (PD) and others
   Establishing a National Commission for the promotion and protection of fundamental human rights.
   12 July 2018: Presented to the Senate
   4 October *2018: Assigned (examination not yet begun)*
8. **S.593** – 18th Legislature
   *Sen. Nic*ola Morra (M5S)
   Establishing an independent National Commission for the promotion and protection of fundamental human rights and freedoms.
   5 July 2*018: Presented to the Senate*
   To be assigned
9. **C.855** – 18th Legislature
   Hon. Lia Quartapelle Procopio (PD) and others
   Establishing a National Commission for the promotion and protection of fundamental human rights.
   3 July 2018: Presented to the Chamber of Deputies
   11 December 2019: Currently under examination by the Commission
10. **C.500** – 18th Legislature
    Hon. Walter Rizzetto (FDI) and others
    Establishing a National Ombudsperson for the Protection of the Rights of Victims of Intentional Violent Crime.
    11 April 2018: Presented to the Chamber of Deputies
    25 July 2019: Assigned (examination not yet begun)
11. **S.183** – 18th Legislature
    Sen. Maria Rizzotti (FI-BP) and others
    Framework for family services to protect and support families, maternity, infancy and adolescents and the establishing a national Commissioner for family policies.

28 March 2018: Presented to the Senate
26 Ju*ne 2018: Assigned (examination not yet begun)*

12. **C.145** – 18th Legislature
Hon. Paolo Russo (FI)
Establishing a National Ombudsperson.
23 March 2018: Presented to the Chamber of Deputies
26 J*une 2018: Assigned (examination not yet begun)*
13. **S.108** – 18th Legislature
*Sen. Ant*onio De Poli (FI-BP) and others
Establishing a National Ombudsperson for the rights of the family.
23 March 2018: Presented to the Senate
21 Jun*e 2018: Assigned (examination not yet begun)*
14. **S.129** – 18th Legislature
*Sen. Anton*io De Poli (FI-BP)
Provisions on the protection of the rights of the family, establishing a National Ombudsperson for the rights of the family.
23 March 2018: Presented to the Senate
21 June 2018: Assigned (examination not yet begun)

Ratification of international instruments

Fourteen bills promote the ratification and implementation of the following international instruments:

- Council of Europe Convention on the Manipulation of Sports Competitions, Magglingen, 18 September 2014 (C.1638);
- Amendment to the Montreal Protocol on Substances that Deplete the Ozone Layer, adopted in Kigali, 15 October 2016 (S. 1220);
- Additional Protocol to the Convention on the Transfer of Sentenced Persons, Strasbourg, 18 December 1997; Protocol amending the Additional Protocol to the Convention on the Transfer of Sentenced Persons, Strasbourg, 22 November 2017 (S. 1239);
- Convention on Extradition between Member States, with Annex, Dublin, 27 September 1996 (C.1797 and S. 1307);
- Second Additional Protocol to the European Convention on Mutual Assistance in Criminal Matters; Third and Fourth Additional Protocol to the European Convention on Extradition (C.1798 and S. 1308);
- Protocol on Pollutant Release and Transfer Registers, Kiev, 21 May 2003 (C.1862);

Protocol amending the Convention for the Protection of Individuals with regard to Automatic Processing of Personal Data, Strasbourg, 10 October 2018 (S. 1384);

Additional Protocol to the *Convention on Cybercrime*, concerning the criminalisation of acts of a racist and xenophobic nature committed through computer systems, Strasbourg, 28 January 2003 (S. 1524);

Framework Convention on the Value of Cultural Heritage for Society, Faro, 27 October 2005 (C.2165);

Convention of the International Labour Organization No. 190 on Violence and Harassment Convention (C.2207 and S. 1598);

Chapter C of the Council of Europe Convention on the Participation of Foreigners in Public Life at Local Level, Strasbourg 5 February 1992 (C.2226).

Disarmament, international humanitarian and criminal law

1. **S.1049** – *Sen. Gianluca Ferrara (M5S) and others*
   Amending law 9 July 1990, No. 185, on importing, exporting and transporting materials for weapons.
   7 February 2019: Presented to the Senate
   17 December 2019: Remitted to Parliament
2. **S.1126** – *Sen. Roberto Rampi (PD) and others*
   Provisions to combat international violations of human rights.
   6 March 2019: Presented to the Senate
   15 May 2019: Assigned (examination not yet begun)
3. **S.1255** – *Sen. Luca Ciriani (FdI)*
   Amending article 604-*bis* of the Criminal Code on denying, grossly minimising or defending the Foibe massacres.
   29 April 2019: Presented to the Senate
   4 June 2019: Assigned (examination not yet begun)
4. **C.1922** – *Hon. Roberto Cataldi (M5S)*
   Amending article 19-*bis* of decree-law 12 September 2014, No. 132, converted, with amendments, from law 10 November 2014, No. 162, on the waivers on the untraceable nature of sums of money belonging to diplomatic representatives in cases of claims deriving from war crimes or crimes against humanity.
   19 June 2019: Presented to the Chamber of Deputies
   15 October 2019: Assigned (examination not yet begun)
5. **S.1471** – *Sen. Tommaso Nannicini (PD) and others*
   Establishing the National Day of Wounded Humanity.
   7 August 2019: Presented to the Senate
   To be assigned

II Prime Minister's Office (Presidency)

The organisation of the Prime Minister's Office is regulated by the decree of the Prime Minister of 1 October 2012. The Prime Minister's Office has a number of departments and offices (the so-called general structures), which the Prime Minister draws on for guidance and coordination functions regarding specific political and institutional fields. Of particular importance for human rights is the Department for Equal Opportunities.

A number of committees and commissions with specific tasks of economic and social relevance operate within the ambit of the Prime Minister's Office. These include the Commission for International Adoptions and the National Committee on Bioethics.

A Department for Equal Opportunities: UNAR and Observatory for the Fight against Paedophilia and Child Pornography

The Department for Equal Opportunities, established under the auspices of the Prime Minister's Office, plans and coordinates legislative, administrative and research initiatives in all areas pertaining to equal opportunities policies. From June 2018 to September 2019, its management was entrusted to Undersecretary of State to the Prime Minister's Office Vincenzo Spadafora. In September 2019, Elena Bonetti was named Minister for Equal Opportunities and the Family.

The Department was instituted by Prime Ministerial Decree 28 October 1997, No. 405, subsequently amended by various decrees (the most recent being ministerial decree 8 April 2019). It comprises three offices: the Office of General Affairs, International Affairs and Social Measures; the Office for Measures to Promote Equality and Equal Opportunities; and the National Anti-Racial Discrimination Office (UNAR).

UNAR was established by lgs.d. 9 July 2003, No. 215, in compliance with the European Community directive 2000/43/CE. Its mission is to guarantee observance of the principle of equal treatment of individuals, to monitor the efficacy of current instruments against discrimination and to help to stamp out forms of discrimination based on race or ethnic origin, while analysing their diversified impact on gender and their connection with other forms of racism of a cultural and religious nature.

In 2019, the work of the *Permanent Consultation Table for the Promotion of Rights and the Protection of LGBT people* carried on. The Table is the working tool for dialogue and confrontation with associations in the sector, working to promote LGBT rights and combatting discrimination based on sexual orientation and gender identity.

The UNAR is the national focal point for implementing the *National Inclusion Strategy for Roma, Sinti and Caminanti (2012–2020)*: in 2019, work was done that focussed on four main issues, which led to the creation of four Consultation Tables and Working Groups: home, health, education and work.

In addition to the three abovementioned offices, the following collegial bodies also have their secretariat within the Department for Equal Opportunities: the Inter-Ministerial Commission for support to victims of trafficking, violence and severe exploitation (as per Presidential Decree 14 May 2007, No. 102); the Committee for Prevention and Combating Female Genital Mutilation; the Committee to Evaluate the Legitimacy to Act on Behalf of People with Disabilities; the Committee for Equal Opportunities for Men and Women; and the Observatory for the Fight against Paedophilia and Child Pornography.

The Observatory for the Fight against Paedophilia and Child Pornography was established in accordance with l. 3 August 1998, No. 269, as amended by l. 6 February 2006, No. 38, with the task of acquiring and monitoring data and information relating to activities carried out by all Government bodies to prevent and stamp out the sexual abuse and exploitation of minors. A further significant task of the Observatory is to prepare the National Plan for preventing and combating sexual abuse and exploitation of minors.

B Commission for International Adoptions

Article 6 of the Hague Convention on the Protection of Minors and Cooperation in Respect of Intercountry Adoption, which was adopted on 29 May 1993 and came into force on 1 May 1995, requires State Parties to establish a central authority to ensure that adoptions of foreign children adhere to the principles established by the Convention itself. To comply with this requirement, via l. 31 December 1998, No. 476, Italy instituted the Commission for International Adoptions, which operates through the Prime Minister's Office. The Commission is Italy's central authority for the implementation of the Hague Convention.

The Commission is comprised of a Chair, nominated by the Prime Minister (from September 2019: Elena Bonetti, Minister for Equal Opportunities and the Family), a vice-chair (in 2019 Laura Laera, magistrate) and the following members: three representatives of the Prime Minister's Office; a representative of the Ministry of Foreign Affairs; a representative of the Ministry of Education; a representative of the Ministry for Labour and Social Policy; one from the Ministry of the Interior; two from the Ministry of Justice; one from the Ministry of Health; one from the Ministry of Economy; four from the Unified Conference between State and Region; three from family associations; and experts.

According to the data provided by the Commission, in 2019, 969 international adoption procedures were concluded (-14 % compared to the previous year, with 1130 adoptions). The biggest falls in adoptions came from China (46 adoptions in 2019 compared to 84 in 2018), Russian Federation (126 adoptions in 2019 compared to 152 in 2018), Belarus (72 adoptions in 2019 compared to 91 in 2018) and Vietnam (37 adoptions in 2019 compared to 54 in 2018).

Despite this general decrease of minors arriving from almost every country, some countries go against this trend: for example, Colombia (which goes from 128 adoptions in 2018 to 161 in 2019) and Peru (from 24 adoptions in 2018 to 44 in 2019).

C National Committee on Bioethics

The National Committee on Bioethics performs an advisory role vis-à-vis the Government, Parliament and other institutions, with a view to providing guidelines on legislative and administrative instruments designed to define the criteria to use in medical and biological practice in order to protect human rights. It also has a role in informing the public and in raising awareness with regard to ethical problems arising in connection with progress in scientific research and in technological applications in the life sciences and in healthcare.

The Committee was established by the Prime Ministerial decree 28 March 1990. It is made up of the following bodies: President (Lorenzo d'Avack, professor in Philosophy of Law); Vice President (Riccardo Di Segni, Chief Rabbi of Rome; Laura Palazzani, professor in Philosophy of Law; Mariapia Garavaglia, former Minister of Health); Office of the President (made up of the Chair and the Vice Chairs); and Assembly.

One of the tasks of the Committee is to produce studies and make recommendations that can also be used for legislative purposes. The Committee's documents offer in-depth focus and reflection on ethical and legal issues that arise as knowledge in the field of the life sciences advances. According to their nature and purpose, the documents are classified as: *opinions* (approved in the Committee's assembly on the basis of inquiries conducted by working groups); *motions* (urgent documents approved with a two-thirds majority of those present in the assembly); *responses* (documents in which the Committee makes recommendations on issues about which opinion has been sought by other bodies or by physical persons).

In 2019, two opinions (Mental health and psychiatric assistance in prison, 22 March; Bioethical reflections on medically assisted suicide, 18 July) and a motion (Against nicotine addiction and smoking, 27 September) were approved.

Furthermore, the following working groups were formed:

- Futile medical care or unreasonable lengthening of treatment for small children;
- Use of animals for profit;
- Treatment and vulnerability;
- Protocols, guidelines and clinical judgment: bioethical observations;
- Definition of the role of bioethicist;
- Precision medicine;
- Hate speech;
- Artificial intelligence and health.

III Ministry of Foreign Affairs and International Cooperation

The Ministry of Foreign Affairs has a number of directorate-generals and offices that deal specifically with human rights, disarmament and cooperation. Up until September 2019, responsibility for issues dealt with in the United Nations ambit were entrusted to Undersecretary of State Manlio Di Stefano.

Particularly noteworthy is Office II-Human rights advocacy and international humanitarian law, Council of Europe, which falls within the directorate-general for Political Affairs and Security. Other offices in the same directorate are: Office I-The United Nations system and the institutional reform process, peacekeeping operations and preventive diplomacy; Office V-Disarmament, arms control and nuclear, biological and chemical non-proliferation, Office of the national authority for the banning of chemical weapons; Office VI-Organisation for Security and Cooperation in Europe. The theme of human rights also relates across the board to the directorate-general for Global Affairs (Office IV-Energy, environmental protection and sustainable global development policies), the directorate-general for the European Union (Office III-European space of freedom, security and justice, the free movement of people and migratory flows towards the European Union) and the directorate-general for Development Cooperation (Office I – Development of cooperation policies within the European Union; Office II – Multilateral development cooperation; Office VI – Emergency and humanitarian aid; Office VIII – Planning and monitoring of the cooperation budget; gender issues, the rights of children and people with disabilities).

A Inter-Ministerial Committee for Human Rights (CIDU)

The Inter-Ministerial Committee for Human Rights (CIDU) was established by decree of the Minister of Foreign Affairs on 15 February 1978, No. 519. Its composition was updated by Prime Ministerial decree 11 May 2007. Over 2012–2013, the CIDU was involved in a restructuring process; initially phased out as a result of the spending review, it was re-established on 5 September 2013. It maintained its functional competences because it was regarded as indispensable, both for its advice and its strategic guidance regarding the promotion and protection of human rights and in ensuring correct compliance with the obligations that Italy assumed following the signature and ratification of conventions and international agreements in this field.

The CIDU is chaired by a functionary of the diplomatic service appointed by the Minister of Foreign Affairs: Fabrizio Petri in 2019. Committee members include representatives of the Prime Minister's Office, of various Ministries and of many different institutions such as the Association of Italian Municipalities (ANCI); the Conference of Presidents of the Regions and Autonomous Provinces; the Union of Italian Provinces (UPI); the National Commission for UNESCO; the Italian Committee for UNICEF; the Italian Society for International Organisation (SIOI); as well as three eminent personalities in the field of human rights.

The CIDU has the following tasks: to promote measures necessary for ensuring full compliance with international obligations assumed by Italy; to facilitate the implementation of international conventions in Italy; to draft the reports Italy is required to submit to the pertinent international organisations; and to maintain and develop appropriate relations with civil society organisations engaged in promoting and protecting human rights.

In 2019, the CIDU carried out the following activities:

- discussion of the V-VI joint periodic report on the UN Convention on the Rights of the Child;
- discussion of the I periodic report on the UN Convention for the Protection of All Persons from Enforced Disappearance;
- presentation of Italy's report on the third UPR of the UN Human Rights Council;
- implementation of the Third National Action Plan on Women, Peace and Security (2016–2019);
- implementation of the first National Action Plan on "Business and Human Rights" (2016–2021);
- convention: *The situation of childhood and adolescence in Italy: recommendations from the UN Committee on the Rights of the Child*, organised in collaboration with the Italian UNICEF Committee, on the occasion of the thirtieth anniversary of the adoption of the UN Convention on the Rights of the Child;
- celebrating *Human Rights Day*, in collaboration with the University of Padova Human Rights Centre "Antonio Papisca" and the UNESCO Chair "Human Rights, Democracy and Peace".

B Italian National Commission for UNESCO

The Commission was established by inter-ministerial decree on 11 February 1950, at the Ministry of Foreign Affairs, two years after Italy entered the Organisation, and pursuant to article 7 of the UNESCO Charter.

Members of the Commission include representatives from Parliament, the Prime Minister's Office, various Ministries, public and private agencies, local authorities and civil society.

> The Commission's mission is to promote the implementation of UNESCO programmes in Italy; to spread the ideals of the Organisation, especially among the younger generations; to disseminate information on its principles, goals and activities, thus stimulating action by institutions, civil society and the world of culture, education and science. The Commission also advises the Government regarding its dealings with UNESCO.

In 2019, as nominated by the Ministry of Foreign Affairs, the president of the Commission was Franco Bernabè, while the post of Secretary General was held by Enrico Vicenti.

In 2019, the National Commission carried out many activities (seminars, conferences, meetings in schools, competitions, exhibitions, workshops, and shows) in various Italian cities, especially regarding the different UN International Days, including International Mother Language Day (21 February), World Poetry Day (21 March), World Book and Copyright Day (23 April) and International Jazz Day (30 April).

IV Ministry of Labour and Social Policies

Many departments and offices within the Ministry of Labour and Social Policies deal specifically with human rights.

The following are particularly noteworthy:

- *Directorate-general for Inclusion and Social Policies.* Functions: promoting policies to combat poverty, social exclusion and severe marginalisation; promoting and monitoring policies for children and adolescents, and the protection of minors; coordination policies for the social inclusion, protection and promotion of the rights and opportunities of persons with disabilities; managing the National Fund for Social Policies, the National Fund for the Non Self-Sufficient, the National Fund for Childhood and Adolescence and other funds for financing social policies and monitoring transferred resources; study, research and investigations concerning social policies; participation in all the pertinent internationally significant activities, and managing relations with the European Union, the Council of Europe, the International Labour Organisation, the United Nations and the Organisation for Economic Cooperation and Development.

- *Directorate-General for the third sector and corporate social responsibility.* Functions: promoting and supporting the activities carried out by third sector subjects, especially initiatives relating to social promotion and voluntary associations, in order to facilitate the growth of an active society welfare to support policies of social inclusion and integration; promotion, development and coordination of policies, initiatives and activities to support the spread of corporate social responsibility.
- *Directorate-General for immigration and integration policies.* Functions: planning migratory flows, and managing and monitoring entry quotas of foreign workers as well as bilateral cooperation agreements with countries of origin; coordinating policies for social and job integration of foreign immigrants and initiatives designed to prevent and combat discrimination, xenophobia and racism; developing international cooperation for activities to prevent and study social and employment emergencies, and for initiatives regarding work-related migratory flows.

In 2012, the Directorate-General for immigration and integration policies took over the functions of the Committee for Foreign Minors, which was abolished in accordance with the decree on the so-called spending review (article 12, para. 20 of l.d. 95/2012, converted into law, with amendments, in l. 135/2012). Consequently, the Directorate-General is now responsible for monitoring the presence of foreign minors temporarily present on Italian territory, whether they be unaccompanied minors present on Italian territory or admitted minors.

As regards unaccompanied minors, the Directorate-General may adopt two kinds of measures. The first is "no repatriation", which amounts to activating the procedures for integrating the person into Italy; the second is "assisted repatriation", designed to reunite the child with his or her family in their country of origin. As regards the first option, responsibility for managing and monitoring the measures is placed in the hands of local authorities. The most frequent choice made for unaccompanied minors in Italy is to place them in residential care facilities for children.

As regards admitted minors, the Directorate-General makes decisions, following due appraisal and according to predetermined criteria, at the request of organisations, associations or Italian families, regarding the temporary admission of children into the framework of humanitarian programmes. The Committee then makes decisions on temporary fostering and repatriation. It keeps a register of minors already admitted into the framework of humanitarian programmes and defines criteria for assessing requests for the admission of temporarily admitted minors.

By 31 December 2019, 6,054 unaccompanied foreign minors were registered with the Commission – that is, around four thousand fewer than on 31 December 2018. The majority of these were boys, around 94.8 % of the total. The main countries of origin were Albania (27.7 %), Egypt (8.8 %), Pakistan (8.3 %) and Bangladesh (8 %): together, these four represent just over half of all unaccompanied minors in Italy (52.8 %). The region with the highest number of minors (about 19 % of the total) in reception centres is still Sicily, in line with a trend which has consolidated over many years, followed by: Lombardy (13.6 %), Friuli Venezia Giulia (11 %) and Emilia Romagna (10 %).

A National Observatory for Children and Adolescents

The Observatory performs a role of coordination among central administrations, local and regional bodies, associations, professional groups and non-governmental organisations dedicated to children's issues.

It was instituted by l. 23 December 1997, No. 451, and is currently regulated by the decree of the President of the Republic (d.p.r.) 14 May 2007, No. 103, which assigns joint chairmanship by the Ministry of Labour and Social Policies and the Undersecretary of State to the Prime Minister's Office mandated with family policies. It is made up of representatives from national and local public administrations, associations and professional orders, voluntary and third sector organisations as well as experts in the field of children's rights.

Presidential decree 103/2007 assigns the Observatory the task of preparing three documents about the condition of childhood and adolescence in Italy:

- The *National Plan of Action and of Measures to Safeguard the Rights and Development of Children and Adolescents*. Drawn up every two years, the plan contains the fundamental strategic guidelines and concrete commitments that the Government intends to pursue in order to develop a satisfactory policy for children and adolescents in Italy. The last National Plan (the 4th) adopted by the Observatory refers to the years 2016/2017.
- The *Report on the Condition of Children and Adolescents in Italy*. It aims to provide an updated picture of the aspects that characterise the condition of children and adolescents in Italy and of the social services system and measures for promoting and protecting the rights of children and adolescents. In

October 2017, the Observatory published the Report on the Condition of Childhood and Adolescence in Italy 2012–2015.

- The *Periodic Report of the Government to the UN Committee on the Rights of the Child regarding the application of the 1989 International Convention on the Rights of the Child*, pursuant to article 44 of the Convention. The latest report (combined 5th and 6th reports) was discussed in Italy in 2019.

In carrying out its functions, the National Observatory uses the National Centre of Documentation and Analysis for Children and Adolescents, which performs documentation, analysis, research, monitoring and training tasks.

More specifically, the National Centre of Documentation deals with:

- collecting and disseminating regional, national, European, and international norms and regulations, as well as statistical data and scientific studies;
- creating, based on information coming from the Regions, an annually-updated map of public, private and private social services (including assistance and health services), and resources for children at the national, regional and local level;
- analysing the situation of childhood and adolescence in Italy, including the conditions of foreign minors;
- preparing an outline, based on National Observatory directives, of the biennial report on the condition of children in Italy, and of the Government report to the United Nations Committee on the Rights of the Child on the domestic implementation of the Convention on the Rights of the Child;
- formulating proposals, also at the request of local authorities, for the creation of pilot projects designed to improve children's living conditions as well as to assist mothers during the prenatal period.

B National Observatory Monitoring the Conditions of Persons with Disabilities

The Observatory is an advisory body offering technical and scientific support in defining national policies regarding disabilities.

It was established by l. 3 March 2009, No. 18, at the Ministry of Labour, Health and Social Policies. It is chaired by the Ministry of Labour and includes a maximum of 40 members. Members are appointed by ministerial decree and represent central administrations involved in defining and implementing disability-related policies; regional and local authorities; social security institutions; the National Statistics Institute; trade unions; and most representative associations and organisations of persons with disabilities, joined by a maximum of five experts of proven experience in the field of disabilities. Within the Observatory there is also a technical-scientific committee, with the purpose of analysis and scientific direction in relation to the activities and tasks of the organism. In 2019, the coordinator of this committee was Giampiero Griffo.

The Observatory's tasks include the following: to promote the implementation of the United Nations Convention on the Rights of Persons with Disabilities and to prepare, together with CIDU, the national report for the monitoring procedure established by that Convention; to prepare a biennial Plan of Action on disability implementing national and international laws; promotes the realisation of studies and research that can help to identify priority areas in which to direct actions and actions for the promotion of the rights of persons with disabilities.

In 2019, the Observatory carried out three meetings and, in July, adopted the action plan for the next three years. The plan is divided into nine thematic areas and 13 working groups. The cultural approach is to tackle the issue of disability on the basis of the human rights enshrined in the relevant UN Convention (non-discrimination, equal opportunities) and to identify some key innovative issues (work, combatting segregation, right to an adult life, freedom, civil rights and participation, and international cooperation) other than the traditional issues (accessibility, health, education, social policy, and work).

V Ministry of Justice

Within the Ministry of Justice there are various departments and bureaus specifically involved with human rights. The most relevant are:

- *Office II*: (Directorate-General for litigation and human rights – Department of legal affairs): it is actively involved in examining cases pending before the European Court of Human Rights. In addition, it is responsible for drafting the reports requested by international human rights bodies, mainly by the Council of Europe and UN bodies and committees.
- *Department for Juvenile Justice and Community*: the office deals with promoting and protecting the rights of unaccompanied foreign minors and of persons at risk of social exclusion.

VI Judicial Authorities

The judiciary, that is to say the various justice authorities – ordinary, administrative and auditing – constituting judicial power, is the fundamental guarantee of rights and legality in a state that respects the principles of democracy, the division of powers and the rule of law. The Italian courts – the Constitutional Court, which delivers judgments regarding the constitutionality of laws; the Supreme Court, which is the court of last resort; the penal and civil tribunals and trial courts; and those concerned with administrative, audit and military matters – deal in a contentious manner with cases which often affect human rights in the most various ways and according to the most disparate perspectives. Access to a judge to obtain a ruling on a right that a plaintiff claims has been breached is a fundamental human right, linked to which are the many other procedural rights that distinguish a fair trial.

Other than adjudicating on individual cases, the judicial system builds and develops the applicable legislation, via its own case-law. In recent years, Italian case-law on human rights has been strongly influenced by case-law deriving from the international courts, particularly the European Court of Human Rights and the European Court of Justice. The interaction between the national judicial bodies and international courts with jurisdiction on human rights highlights the universal nature of fundamental rights. Dialogue with international courts and with other States' courts (applying the same standards on human rights) is not just relevant to a State's Supreme Courts, but all judges who can draw from discussions in foreign and international courts to ensure access of fundamental rights, in full respect of the Constitution and of relevant legislation.

Part IV of this Yearbook is specifically devoted to a summary presentation of cases in the Italian courts on which rulings were delivered in 2019 (with particular reference to the judgments of the Constitutional Court and the Supreme Court), and of case-law elaborated by the European Court of Human Rights or the Court of Justice of the European Union which directly concerns Italy, either because the Italian State was the "defendant" or because the intervention of the European judge regarded pleas presented by Italian citizens or related to Italian legal norms.

VII Independent Authorities

In this section, the five independent authorities that relate more pertinently to human rights are described: the Communications Regulatory Authority (AGCOM); the Data Protection Authority; the Committee Guaranteeing the Implementation of the Law on Strikes Affecting Essential Public Services; the National Ombudsperson for Children and Adolescents; and National Ombudsperson for the Rights of Persons in Prison or Deprived of Liberty.

A Communications Regulatory Authority (AGCOM)

AGCOM was set up by l. 31 July 1997, No. 249. It has a dual mandate: to ensure correct competition among market actors and to guarantee the fundamental freedoms of citizens in the area of communications, particularly in regards to the protection of minors.

The composition of the Authority is disciplined by decree 6 December 2011, No. 201 (the so-called Save Italy decree), and its conversion into law (22 December 2011, No. 214). In 2019, the Authority was made up as follows: *Chair*: Angelo Marcello Cardani; members of the *Services and Products Commission*: Antonio Martusciello and Francesco Posteraro; and members of the *Commission for Infrastructure and Networks*: Antonio Nicita and Mario Morcellini. The Council consists of the Chair and Commissioners.

According to the annual report on work programmes and activities in 2019 (reference period: May 2018–April 2019), the Authority focussed on carrying out surveillance activities on protecting minors, on promotional communications about paid games and on combatting hate speech.

Regarding child protection, an intervention by the Authority in the exercise of specific regulatory power was particularly significant. Moreover, lgs.d. 7 December 2017, No. 203, containing "Reform of legislative provisions concerning child protection in the cinema and audio-visual sector, pursuant to article 33 of law 14 November 2016, No. 220", gave AGCOM the scope to regulate the classification of film and audio work for the internet and videogames (article 10) within a child protection framework. After a public consultation on the regulation framework on classifying the aforementioned film and audio work, the Authority definitely approved the regulation (Resolution No. 74/19/CONS of 6 March 2019), establishing a dedicated co-regulatory technical table to define the guidelines on the perquisites on classifying web content and videogames.

Furthermore, the Authority has substantially increased sanctions for violation of duties regarding broadcasting programming, focussing on user protection, especially children. The sanction procedures are also based on alerts from the Postal and Communications Police and the Guardia di Finanza (Finance division of the police). There have been 121 sanction procedures initiated in total (in the audio-visual commercial communication sector, following a violation of the child protection regulations) and concluded, of which 101 concluded with enforcing the foreseen sanctions and 20 with archiving measures with no further actions.

This reference period entered into force with l.d. 12 July 2018, No. 87, (Urgent provisions for dignity of workers and businesses, converted with amendments to l. 9 August 2018). This law established a general ban on any form of promotional communication concerning paid gaming. The sanction applied (responsibility of the Authority) seems highly dissuasive: for non-compliance with this ban, an administrative fine of the sum of 20 % of the value of the sponsored advertisement/publicity communication (in any case, no less than €50,000) has been set. Following a public consultation, the Authority approved (with deliberation No. 132/19/CONS of 18 April 2019) the law's implementation guidelines. These guidelines assume that the rationale behind the provision is to protect the consumer, apart from information communication and *business to business* communication. In 2019, several complaints were received for alleged violations of the decree, coming predominantly from consumer rights associations, in almost all cases in reference to contracts in progress which were stipulated before the ban came into force.

Finally, following the growing rise in hate speech and discrimination against categories or groups of people based on their economic-social status, their nationality or ethnicity, their sexual orientation or their religious beliefs in informative or entertainment programmes, the Authority adopted the *Regulation concerning provisions for the respect of human dignity and the principle of non-discrimination in combatting hate speech*, contained within deliberation 157/19/CONS of 15 May 2019. Before the adoption of the regulation, a public consultation was held, in which associations from the sector, civil society and commercial representatives all participated. Through this regulation, the Authority aims to provide a definite legal framework to combat hate speech, following the principles of Italian and international law on this issue which focuses on combatting all forms of discrimination based on constructing and spreading stereotypes, as well as uncontextualized generalisations of single reported episodes which are harmful to the dignity of a person. The regulation establishes the principles and provisions which media service broadcasters and providers must adhere to in order to respect human dignity and the principle of non-discrimination and to combat hate speech. This applies to all service broadcasters providing information or entertainment programmes which are subject to Italian jurisdiction. Furthermore, the Authority aims at promoting the creation of codes of conduct and co-regulation on online video-sharing platforms and extending these same obligations to those platforms.

B Data Protection Authority

The Data Protection Authority was instituted by l. 31 December 1996, No. 675, later substituted by lgs.d. 30 June 2003, No. 196 (Personal data protection code), with the aim to ensure protection of the fundamental rights and freedoms and respect for the dignity of persons, in the processing of personal data.

The Data Protection Authority is a collegial body made up of four members elected by Parliament, who remain in office for a seven-year non-renewable mandate. The current body is made up of Antonello Soro (Chair), Augusta Iannini (Vice Chair), Giovanna Bianchi Clerici and Licia Califano.

In 2019, the Authority issued 215 provisions to protect the fundamental rights of individuals with regard to the processing and circulation of personal data, with particular reference to the following issues (among others): freedom of the press; right to education, work, health and scientific research; rights of minors; handling of sensitive data; and internet and social media.

C Commission Guaranteeing the Implementation of the Law on Strikes Affecting Essential Public Services

The Commission was instituted by l. 12 June 1990, No. 146, and subsequent amendments. It is comprised of five members designated by the Chairs of the Chamber of Deputies and the Senate, among experts in matters of constitutional law, labour law and industrial relations, and was instated by decree of the President of the Republic. In 2019, the members of the Commission were: Giuseppe Santoro Passarelli (Chair), Lauralba Bellardi, Alessandro Bellavista, Domenico Carrieri and Orsola Razzolini.

Some of the main tasks of the Commission are:

- assessing the capacity of essential services to guarantee protection of both the right to strike and the enjoyment of constitutionally guaranteed human rights;
- requesting that those calling the strike delay the date of abstention from work if the Commission intends to attempt conciliation, or if it finds that the abstention violates legal and/or contractual obligations for strikes in essential public services;
- pointing out to those calling the strike any violations of norms concerning advance notice or any other requirements relative to the phase preceding collective abstention;
- notifying the appropriate authority which can order strikers back to work of situations where the strike or collective abstention could give rise to an imminent, probable risk of infringing constitutionally protected human rights;
- taking note of behaviour by administrations or enterprises which provide essential public services in clear violation of the law;
- assessing behaviour of both parties and if any non-compliance or violation of legal or contractual obligations relative to essential services emerges, inflicting penalties pursuant to article 4 of l. 146/1990 as amended by article 3 of l. 83/2000, ordering the employer to apply the disciplinary actions.

The annual report on the activity carried out in 2018 was presented in June 2019. According to the data contained in the report, in 2018, there was a decrease in strikes compared to the previous year: the overall number of strikes called was 2,109 (2,448 in 2017). Following the interventions by the Commission, the strike action that took place almost halved (1,389, compared to 1,616 in the previous year).

The majority of strike actions were called in full compliance with the law, agreements and regulations: emblematic of the acceptance of these rules by industrial stakeholders. Of the 2,109 calls for strike, the Commission intervened with only 312 preventative actions as the strikes were deemed illegitimate. Furthermore, this led to adjustments in over 94 % of cases; there have only been ten behaviour evaluation proceedings opened by the Commission and concluded with the imposition of sanctions.

There are still high levels of unrest in the following sectors: environmental hygiene (411 calls for strike) local public transport (302), air transport (221), cleaning and multi-services (176), local autonomies and regions (143), national health service (112) and railway transport (112).

Furthermore, in 2018, there were 9 national general strikes (compared to 13 in 2017) all organised by trade unions with insignificant levels of participation.

D National Ombudsperson for Children and Adolescents

The National Ombudsperson for Children and Adolescents was established with l. 12 July 2011, No. 112 to ensure the full implementation and protection of children's rights at a national level, pursuant to the International Convention of the Rights of the Child 1989.

It is a single presiding organ, and the holder of the post is appointed by the Presidents of the Chamber of Deputies and of the Senate, who choose a figure of unquestioned morality, independence and professional competence in the field of children's rights. The term of office lasts four years. It has autonomous powers, administrative independence and the organisation is not tied to a hierarchical chain. To achieve its general aims of promoting and protecting the rights and best interests of minors, the National Ombudsperson carries out diverse tasks; its stakeholders include the Parliament and Government (who collaborate greatly with the Ombudsperson) both at a national level (Ministries, Parliamentary Commission for Children and Adolescents, Regional and Autonomous Province Ombudsperson, non-profit organisations, universities and others) and at an international level (European Network of Ombudspersons for Children, Ad hoc Committee for the Rights of the Child (CAHENF) and others), which allow intervention on the issue and carry out a role to guide public institutions and make them more aware of pressing issues. From March 2016 onwards, Filomena Albano has held the post of Ombudsperson.

The Ombudsperson has, amongst others, the following responsibilities:

- to promote the implementation of the UN Convention on the Rights of the Child, and of other pertinent international and European instruments, and to ensure appropriate forms of collaboration with all the national and international bodies and organisations engaged in promoting and protecting children and adolescents;

- to express opinions on legislative initiatives concerning the protection of the rights of children and adolescents, and the report that the Government presents periodically to the UN Committee on the Rights of the Child;
- to inform the Government, Regions and other local or territorial bodies involved, in relation to their respective responsibilities, of all appropriate measures to ensure full promotion and protection of the rights of children and adolescents;
- to inform judicial authorities and bodies concerned of problem cases or risks of minors' rights being infringed, as well as serious cases of neglect of minors, so that they can be taken into care by the appropriate authorities;
- to enhance knowledge of the rights of children and adolescents, organising, to this end, awareness-raising activities, studies, and research.

Article 6 of l. 112 also allows anyone to address the Ombudsperson to report violation of rights or the risk thereof. Finally, Article 3 states that the Ombudsperson is to establish appropriate forms of cooperation with the regional Ombudspersons or similar figures. The National Conference for the Rights of Children and Adolescents was set up for this purpose; coordinated by the National Ombudsperson, it brings together all the other Ombudspersons, where these have been established (see this Part, Sub-national Human Rights Structures, IV).

In April 2020, the Ombudsperson presented the report to Parliament on the actions undertaken in 2019. She sent the *Report 2016–2020* to summarise the work achieved by the office by the end of her mandate. The main points concerned the family, the right to school, peer relationships, minors who break the law, drugs, HIV and car safety and the right to inclusion.

In 2019, Ombudsperson continued the examination of bills regarding children. It formulated five written opinions on proposals and bills for discussion in the Chambers (on video surveillance in nursery schools, child fostering, preventing and combatting forced marriages, preventing and combatting bullying, framework for granting residence permits and converting residence permits upon becoming an adult); one written opinion based on prime ministerial decree on the new competences of the Ministry of Employment and Social Policy following the closure of the Committee for Foreign Minors; one written opinion based on the decree of the Minister for Economic and Financial Affairs on providing support measures for orphans of domestic crime; an opinion, expressed at the Standing Committee, based on the multidisciplinary protocol on determining age set out by the Ministry of Health; and a note with written observations on bills regarding the establishment of a National Commission for promoting and protecting fundamental human rights.

Throughout the year, four hearings in the Parliamentary Commission for Children and Adolescents were held (one as part of the fact-finding investigation into bullying and cyberbullying, one as part of the fact-finding investigation into forms of violence among minors and harm to children and adolescents, one to present the Annual Report and one as part of the explanatory procedure on the general outline of the National Ombudsperson's activities, particularly on minors "outside the family" setting); a hearing in the Committee on Constitutional Affairs of the Senate (as part of discussions on bills regarding video surveillance in nursery and infant schools); two hearings in the Senate Judiciary Committee (one as part of discussions on bills proposals on forced child marriages and one as part of discussions on bills on child fostering); and a hearing in the Chamber Judiciary Committee (as part of discussions on bill proposals on preventing and combatting forced marriage).

The year also saw many recommendations and requests in various areas concerning minors. Furthermore, hearing days with institutional representatives, experts and associations were organised in order to improve the child protection system.

Many of these also presented an opportunity to speak directly with children and adolescents, thus guaranteeing their right to be heard, enshrined in article 12 of the Convention on the Rights of the Child. Among the many initiatives, there was: a working group created within the National Council of Associations which organised three meetings on the subject of "protecting orphans of domestic crime"; 18 children involved in the Council of the Ombudsperson who, over 26 meetings, took an in-depth look at the following issues: the UN Convention on the Rights of the Child; active participation in the democratic life of the State, sex and relationships education, legality, taking HIV tests without parental consent, unaccompanied minors' journeys, bullying and cyberbullying, and rights of children in hospital. Thousands of children were also involved in projects within primary and secondary schools across Italy.

Over the year, the Ombudsperson visited 13 communities in the Municipality of Rome as part of a listening and participation project for unaccompanied foreign minors (in collaboration with the UN High Commissioner for Refugees).

There were also numerous training courses both inside and outside of the office (National Association of Italian Municipalities; National Social Work Foundation; State police; Prison system employees; teachers and educators; coordinators of the Regional Offices for Education). Two training courses took place for future volunteer tutors for unaccompanied foreign minors (with the support of the European Asylum Support Office – EASO) – one in Abruzzo (a region with no territorial Ombudsperson) and one as part of the Memorandum of Understanding with the Tuscany Ombudsperson for Children and Adolescents. There were also many activities to support the Basilicata Ombudsperson for Children and Adolescents in organising a training course (again with the support of the EASO).

Furthermore, as part of the monitoring programme for voluntary protection of unaccompanied foreign minors, implementing article 11 of law 47 of 2017, numerous help points have been opened in municipality buildings and other locations for minors; agreements were signed for implementing local operational plans, information tables and campaigns and thematic seminars.

Across 2019, the Ombudsperson participated in various roundtables, seminars and conferences on the rights of minors, as well as creating publications and translations of important documents, comments and recommendations. The office promoted initiatives, events and sent out a communication to celebrate the 30th anniversary of the UN Convention on the Rights of the Child.

E National Ombudsperson for the Rights of Persons in Prison or Deprived of Liberty

This Ombudsperson was established by Article 7 of l.d. 23 December 2013, No. 146, converted with amendments by l. 21 February 2014, No. 10. It is collegial and consists of the Chair and two members chosen from independent people who are competent in areas relating to the protection of human rights. Members are nominated, following a decision of the Council of Ministers, by a Presidential Decree, having heard the competent parliamentary commissions, with a five-year mandate which may not be extended.

Since 2016, the National Ombudsperson for the Rights of Persons in Prison or Deprived of Liberty has been Mauro Palma, alongside the other members Daniela De Robert and Emilia Rossi.

> The Ombudsperson is tasked with ensuring that custody of persons in prison and persons subject to other types of limitations on personal freedom is carried out in accordance with the rules and principles set out in the Constitution, in international conventions on human rights, and national laws. As an independent state monitoring body, it has the faculty to visit penitentiary institutions and other structures used to host persons subject to measures restricting their personal freedom (police stations, immigration centres, secure residencies which have been recently reopened after the closure of secure psychiatric hospitals and hospital wings where compulsory health treatment is carried out) without requiring authorisation. The aim of these visits is to highlight any critical issues and, collaborating with competent authorities, find solutions to resolve them. Furthermore, at the institutions it controls, part of the National Ombudsperson's role is to resolve hostile situations or any situation which originates from complaints from incarcerated persons, reserving legal complaints to the judiciary authorities which need the intervention of a supervisory magistrate. After every visit, the Ombudsperson drafts a report of the observations and recommendations and forwards the report to the authorities.
>
> The Ombudsperson has been identified as an independent national monitoring mechanism required under the Optional Protocol to the Convention against Torture (OPCAT), which Italy ratified in 2012. The National Ombudsperson is also tasked with coordinating the network of local ombudspersons, promoting their solidity as an institution through the recognition of sufficient guarantees of independence and autonomy vis-à-vis the local government which appointed them (see, in this Part, Sub-national Human Rights Structures, V). Finally, the Ombudsperson monitors procedures relating to forced repatriations pursuant to the system provided for in article 8, para. 6, of EU Directive No. 115 of 2008.

In 2019, the Ombudsperson conducted 74 visits for a total of 100 places visited across the national territory, monitoring the rights of persons deprived of liberty in prison, health and migratory process conditions; the reports have been published online.

For the same period, with regard to monitoring activities of forced repatriation, 46 operations were monitored, mostly destined for Tunisia (14), Nigeria (8) and Egypt (7).

Furthermore, in 2019, the Ombudsperson spoke at various meetings and hearings on the year's situation in front of the competent Parliamentary Commissions. He spoke to the Extraordinary Human Rights Commission of the Senate on the relationship between detainees and their children and as part of the fact-finding investigation into the levels and mechanisms of protection of rights in Italy and internationally, and in front of the Antimafia Parliamentary Committee on the special prison regime under article 41-*bis* of the Prison Administration Act.

As part of the dialogue with the legislative body (in line with powers attributed by article 19 letter C of the OPCAT on National Preventive Mechanisms [NPMs], on 5 July 2019) the National Ombudsperson sent Parliament his own compulsory opinion on l.d. 53/2019 concerning "*Urgent provisions on public order and security*", better known as "*Security Decree bis*".

In April 2019, the Ombudsperson was heard in front of the UN Committee on Enforced Disappearances (CED) in Geneva, established by International Convention for the Protection of All Persons from Enforced Disappearance.

The production of the technical-themed writing is highly salient, such as the norms and regulations. The *Standards for the deprivation of freedom of migrants* volume, which contains the national standards for administrative detention, written by the National Ombudsperson and the collection of the recommendations directed towards the various Ombudspersons following visits carried out at repatriation centres, in hotspots, during forced repatriations operations and in places where de facto people's freedom is restricted, with the "Ubaldo Diciotti" ship.

In September, the National Ombudsperson published the second edition of the *"Da dove"* ("From where") series entitled "*The Impossible Crime*" ("*Il reato impossibile*"). It talks about the crime of plagiarism (article 603 of the Criminal Code), which was declared illegitimate by the Constitutional Court with a 1981 judgment. It revisits the trial which resulted in the conviction of Aldo Braibanti.

VIII Non-Governmental Organisations

In Italy, numerous non-governmental organisations are active in promoting and protecting human rights. Some that are organised in networks at national and international levels have gained consultative status with international organisations and actively participate in their programmes.

As of 31 December 2019, 119 Italian non-governmental organisations hold consultative status with the United Nations Economic and Social Council, six of which have general status; 95 have special status and 18 have roster status. There are 197 non-governmental organisations with headquarters or representative offices in Italy enjoying participatory status with the Council of Europe dealing specifically with human rights.

In addition, some of the most important international non-governmental organisations have local branches in Italy. These include Amnesty International, the International Federation on Human Rights, Save the Children, Médecins sans Frontières and ActionAid.

Non-governmental organisations play an important role in monitoring the level of compliance with and protection of human rights in Italy. In 2019, the following monitoring reports were published and are particularly noteworthy:

- Antigone Association: *XV National Report on Detention Conditions – Prison according to the Constitution*. According to data published within this report, as of 30 April 2019 there were 60,439 detainees in Italian prisons, around 10,000 more than the official number of beds available. This gives an official overcrowding rate of over 120 %. Women make up around 4.4 % of the total, with 2,659 inmates; 33.6 % of detainees (equivalent to 20,324 inmates) are foreign nationals.

As of 31 December 2018, there were 17,614 working prisoners, of which 6,373 foreign nationals and 809 women. This is the first drop (even if slight) after a constant rise since the early 1990s, when the number of prisoners participating in work programmes began to progressively increase. The number of prisoners participating in professionalising courses is also in decline.

On the contrary, during the 2018 academic year, 20,357 detainees signed up for educational courses – a rise of over 2,000 compared to the previous year.

Finally, regarding the number of suicides (the most dramatic indicator of prison well-being), Antigone shows that, in the last ten years, the suicide rate (deaths per 10,000 people) has gone up from 8.3 in 2008 to 10.4 in 2018 (the rate in the non-incarcerated population is 0.6 %). In absolute figures, this means going from 46 deaths in 2008 to 61 deaths in 2018.

- Working Group for the UN Convention on the Rights of the Child (CRC): *X Update Report on Monitoring the UN Convention on the rights of children and adolescents in Italy*. To mark the 30th anniversary of the UN Convention on the

Rights of the Child, the CRC group gave its analysis on the implementation of the rights of minors in Italy, in light of the concluding observations of the UN Committee on the Rights of the Child towards Italy in February 2019. Furthermore, the report introduces specific references to the themes of the SDGs to propose a current reading of the rights of children and adolescents and to underline the close connection between the Agenda 2030 Goals and guaranteeing the rights of minors.

– Italian Alliance for Sustainable Development (*Alleanza Italiana per lo Sviluppo Sostenibile* -ASviS): *Report 2019*. The report analyses Italy's progress in achieving the SDGs of the Agenda 2030. According to the report, Italy has improved on some issues (health, gender equality, economic and working conditions, innovation, inequality, city conditions, sustainable models of production and consumption, quality of governance and international cooperation), worsened in others (poverty, economic and employment conditions, urban conditions, the condition of the sea and the terrestrial ecosystem) and has remained stable on educating on and combatting climate change. There are some alarming delays in essential sectors in moving towards a more sustainable economic, social and environmental model and there is still grave discrimination within the State. Italy is therefore still a long way from implementing the Agenda 2030 and the Paris Agreement for Climate Change.

To reverse the trend, the ASviS recommended the Prime Minister to: send individual ministers a policy document that explicitly mentions their responsibilities in achieving the SDGs; strengthen the role of the Benessere Italia steering committee, instituted at the Chigi Palace; and support the introduction of an ex-ante assessment of the expected impact of laws on the SDGs. Furthermore, the ASviS recommended that the government support the proposed "declaration of an environmental and climate emergency", which has already been approved in some regions and several cities; update the National Sustainable Development Strategy and present a report on the state of progress in its implementation; transform the Inter-Ministerial Committee for Economic Planning into the Inter-Ministerial Committee for Sustainable Development in order to gear public investment policy towards achievement of the SDGs; identify policies to achieve the 21 targets that Italy committed to reach by the end of 2020; draw up an annual law on sustainable development, designed to introduce systemic regulatory changes; and implement a comprehensive information and communication plan on the issue of sustainable development aimed at the entire population.

- *Leone Moressa* Foundation: *IX report on immigration economics – Global Citizenship of the Millennial Generation*. The report tackles the themes of the value of immigration, the profile of migrants in Italy, the declining Italian population, the 'brain drain' or 'youth drain' and its cost to the country and the gap between young people from Italy and their European counterparts.

According to the report, in the last few years, the number of foreign nationals in Italy has remained stable: there are 5.2 million foreigner nationals residing in Italy (8.7 % of the total population). The net migration (the difference between the number of immigrants and emigrants) remained positive (+245,000) but the reasons for immigrants arriving seem to have changed: prevalently for family reunifications, followed by immigration for humanitarian reasons. There are few arrivals into Italy for work reasons.

There is a slightly higher percentage of foreign women (52 %) present in Italy than men. Immigrants arrive mainly from Eastern Europe (45 % of the total). Romania represents 23 % of the total of foreign nationals in Italy, followed by Albania (8.4 %) and Morocco (8 %); the majority of immigrants have been in Italy for more than 10 years. Last year, there were 2.5 million foreign workers in Italy (10.6 % of the total of employees) and wealth produced by foreign workers was €139 billion (9 % of GDP); in order, the sectors in which foreign nationals are employed are: agriculture, construction and commerce, hotels and restaurants.

The economic contribution of immigration was produced by over 700 thousand business owners born in a foreign country, and from a fiscal point of view, 2.3 million contributors who paid in 13.9 billion social security and pension contributions.

In the last few years, there has been a decline in the Italian population: there is an ageing population, fewer births and an increase in young people emigrating abroad. At the same time, for the last ten years, the doors for legal immigration for foreign nationals have been closed under the illusion that unemployed Italians can do manual labour jobs, forgetting that the over 5 million foreigners currently residing in Italy represent a vital energy for the country. There are fewer births – 1.32 per woman – and an increase in elderly people. According to ISTAT estimations, this means that by 2038, the over 65 population will make up a third of the population – this will cause an economic imbalance: more unemployed people and more retired people.

Within almost ten years, 500 thousand Italians (of which 250 thousand young people form 15–34 years) have married abroad, to a cost of €16 billion: this is the added value that young people could have contributed if they were employed in Italy. Among the reasons for leaving, there is the lack of employment in Italy. The unemployment rate for people from 25–29 years is the third highest in Europe after Greece and Spain. In this age range, the NEET rate (not in employment, education or training) is 30.9 % higher than the European average (17.1 %). Much more concerning is the level of education of Italian youths – which is decidedly low. In this age bracket, only 27.6 % have a university degree, which is 12 points lower than the EU average.

– FOCSIV – Volunteers across the world: *Land grabbing report 2019 – Lords of the Land*. Land grabbing is the issue of wide-scale acquisition, through buying or renting land at low cost or expropriating lands of local populations for large (often single crop) agricultural cultivations in order to exploit natural resources. The report contains a series of information and data on this issue and highlights some cases of abuse suffered by the poorest communities who are losing the right to their lands and livelihood.

These issues concern over 1800 contracts between big businesses and States investment, to exploit land, to cultivate large-scale single crops, create plantations, extract minerals, and build infrastructure and industrial zones. All this adds up to a surface area of over 70 million hectares (source: *Land Matrix*), two and a half times the size of Italy. However, indigenous populations, shepherd communities and small farmers currently live on these lands, communities that take care of the natural resources and look after a huge range of invaluable biodiversity, necessary for the life of the whole planet. In many cases, land grabbing degrades the earth, water, natural resources and life of local populations. Case studies laid out in the report from Congo, Mali, Ethiopia, Madagascar, and the Peruvian Amazon show the damage caused to the environment due to the dumping of toxic waste, pollution, reduction of biodiversity, toxic material spills, pollution, reduction of biodiversity, and soil degradation. Socially, land grabbing can cause expulsion of communities, violence and the murder of human rights defenders.

Using the data in the report, FOCSIV lays out some recommendations for the Italian Government and Parliament:

- proactively participate in negotiations on the binding UN treaty on Business and Human Rights and strengthen the National Plan on business and human rights;
- reconsider extending, implementing and applying the UN Declaration on the Rights of Peasants both in Italy and in developing countries;
- work with the European Commission to remove articles of commercial and investment treaties which contain Investor-State Dispute Settlement (*ISDS*) provisions;
- make a commitment within the Italian Agency for Development Cooperation (AICS) and the Deposits and Loans Fund (CDP) to support agriculture in developing countries by creating two specific programmes: one supporting human rights defenders and one supporting victims of abuse to accede to a fair trial to fulfil their own rights;
- make a commitment within the AICS to adopt an Action Plan to implement the UN Guiding Principles on Business and Human Rights on operations carried out by Italian companies using public funds.
- *Sbilanciamoci!* Campaign: ("Let's flip it!") *2019 Report- How to use public expenditure for human rights, peace and the environment.* The Report contains 101 detailed proposals by the 47 countries registered with the *Sbilanciamoci!* campaign, starting from a detailed analysis of the quality of public spending in Italy. It aims to save and bring in more money, cut excessive or wasteful spending and allocate the money for more correct usage. It identified seven key areas: finance; work and wages; culture and knowledge; environment and sustainable development; welfare and rights; peace, cooperation and disarmament; and fair trade.
- Amnesty International: *Laws Designed to Silence: The Global Crackdown on Civil Society Organisations.* The report states that in the last ten years, a worrying trend has emerged across the world of Governments introducing laws designed to interfere with the right to freedom of association and to block the work of civil society organisations and their members.

According to the report, 50 States have adopted anti-NGO laws. These are legislative provisions that impose institutional barriers on these organisations, rendering it more difficult to work, raise money, plan interventions, carry out advocacy work or create publicity campaigns.

Amnesty International addresses a series of recommendations to Governments across the world to guarantee the full enjoyment of the right to defend human rights, including the fundamental right to freedom of association without discrimination. The report calls for the explicit and public recognition by States of civil society organisations and human rights defenders and their work and urges them to repeal all laws and regulations that place unnecessary burdens upon them.

Finally, at the end of 2016, in the initiative of *Un Ponte Per…*, the network "In defence of – for human rights and those who defend them" (*In Difesa Di – per i diritti umani e chi li difende*) was established. It is made up of over thirty Italian organisations and associations that are active in the field of human rights, environmental rights, international solidarity, peace and disarmament, workers' rights, the freedom of press and the state of rights. The aim of the network is to promote campaigns and initiatives that protect human rights defenders, to raise awareness of these subjects among public opinion, and to ask Italian institutions (Government, Parliament and local institutions) to commit to developing protective instruments and mechanisms for human rights defenders.

In 2019 the network continued establishing its territorial groups, aiming to develop shelter cities for human rights defenders who need to temporarily leave their own countries. There are currently around ten cities and municipalities (among which Padova, Trent and Turin) that have adopted measures to temporarily host and aid activists and movements from around the world.

In October 2019, *In Difesa di…* hosted its first national assembly, with an aim to strengthen its network of associations, movements and stakeholders, to offer these the opportunity to use the tools available to protect human rights defenders and to decide on strategies and methods of future work.

IX Teaching and Research on Human Rights in Italian Universities

In the Italian academic world, there has been an increase in research and training regarding human rights. The subject is now present in many different modules and in the curricula of many university and post-university courses, such as transdisciplinary research programmes. In the following pages, there is a mapping of the institutions and university research centres that work specifically in human rights related subjects, from three-year (Bachelor's) and two-year specialisation (Master's) degree programmes to one-year Master's programmes and PhDs that were activated or published in 2019. The courses and structures highlighted contain "human rights" in their name, or other equivalent expressions such as "rights of people", "rights of man", or "fundamental rights". This mapping shows how widespread the teaching of human rights and its various dimensions has become in the academic environment.

University Institutions and Research Centres

University	Name	Founding year
University of Padova	University Human Rights Centre	1982
University of Salento	Inter-University Centre on Bioethics and Human Rights	1992
41 European universities in partnership	European Inter-University Centre for Human Rights and Democratisation (EIUC)	2002
University of Ca' Foscari, Venice	Human Rights Research Centre (CESTUDIR)	2012
University of Nuoro	Research Centre on the rights of persons and peoples	2016

Source: elaboration by the 2020 Yearbook research and editorial committee.

Bachelor's Degree Courses

University	Name	Scientific Area
University of Padova	Political science, international relations, human rights	L-36: Political science and International Relations
Aldo Moro University of Bari	Immigration law, human rights and interculturality	L-14: Legal services

Source: elaboration by the 2020 Yearbook research and editorial committee.

Master's Degree Courses

University	Name	Scientific Area
University of Bergamo	Human Rights and the Ethics of International Cooperation	LM-81: Cooperation development sciences
University of Bologna	International Cooperation on Human Rights and Intercultural Heritage	LM-81: Cooperation development sciences
University of Padova	Human rights and multi-level governance	LM-52: International Relations
University of Perugia	European judicial integration and human rights	LM-90: European Studies

Source: elaboration by the 2020 Yearbook research and editorial committee.

Teachings

In 2019, a total of 153 human rights courses were taught in 43 universities. Around 60 % of these were delivered via degree courses in the field of political and social sciences (94 modules), while over one third related to the area of law (53 modules); 2 modules in the area of history, philosophy, pedagogy and psychology and 4 in the area of economics and statistics.

As in the years between 2010 and 2018, in 2019, the university with the greatest number of human rights teachings was Padova (18 modules), followed by Bari (10), Turin (9), Rome Tre (9), Florence (6), Milan (6) and Perugia (6). Of the 153 courses available, 45 were taught in English – 10 of which were at the University of Padova, 5 at Trent, 4 at Florence, 3 at Milan, 3 at Rome Tre, 3 at Bologna, as well as two at each of the following universities: Catania, Macerata, Turin; and 1 at each of the following: Bari, Ferrara, Genoa, Modena and Reggio Emilia, Palermo, Pavia, Perugia, "La Sapienza" Rome, Tor Vergata Rome and Siena.

University	Area	Degree Course	Teaching	Lecturer/Professor
Aldo Moro University of Bari	Law	5-Year Degree in Law	International Protection of Human Rights	Andrea Cannone
		BA in Law: Immigration, Human Rights and Interculturality	Philosophy of Human Rights and Intercultural procedures	Michele Indelicato
			International Law and Human Rights	Giuseppina Pizzolante
			Legal Comparison, Democracy and Protection of Fundamental Rights	Pamela Martino
	Political and social science	BA in Political Science, International Relations and European Studies	International Protection of Human Rights	Egeria Nalin
		MA in International Relations and European Studies	International Protection of Human Rights	Egeria Nalin
			Legal Philosophy, Human Rights and Religion in the Middle and Far East	Gianfranco Longo
			Human Rights and Geopolitics of Religions	Roberta Santoro
			Migrations, borders and Human rights	Giuseppe Campesi

University of Bologna	Political and social science	MA in Local and Global Development	Human Rights and Political Institutions	Raffaella Gherardi
		MA in International Cooperation on Human Rights and Intercultural Heritage	Political Power Beyond State Boundaries: Migration, Development and Human Rights	Annalisa Furia
			Public Law and Protection of Fundamental Rights	Caterina Drigo
			Human rights and Children's rights	Annalisa Furia
		MA in International Studies and Diplomacy	International Human Rights Protection (seminar)	Marco Balboni
University of Calabria	Political and social science	MA in Cooperation and Development	Theory of fundamental rights	Paolo Stancati
		MA in Political Science	History of Human Rights and the Culture of Peace	Antonella Salomoni
	Law	5-Year Degree in Law	Human Rights Theory	Helzel Paola Barbara
University of Catania	Political and social science	MA in Global Politics and Euro-Mediterranean Relations	International Human Rights Law	Daniela Fisichella, Calogero Alfio Pettinato
			Human Rights: a Historical Approach	Giorgia Agata Costanzo

University	Area	Degree Course	Teaching	Lecturer/Professor
University of Camerino	Economics and Statistics	BA in Social Sciences for Non-profit Organisations and International Cooperation	International Protection of Human Rights	Agostina Latino
	Law	MA in Migration Management and	History of Human Rights	Carlotta Latini
		Integration Policy with the European	Human Rights and Data Protection	Antonio Magni
		Union	Constitutional Protection of Migrants' Rights	Tatiana Guarnier
University of Cassino and Southern Lazio	Law	5-Year Degree in Law	Fundamental Rights	Marco Plutino
University of Enna "Kore"	Law	BA in Strategic and Security Studies	General Theory of Human Rights	Lucia Corso
			Citizenship and Migrants' Rights	Daniele Anselmo
University of Ferrara	Law	5-Year Degree in Law	Human Rights and Humanitarian Law in Armed Conflicts	Francesco Salerno
			International Human Rights	Serena Forlati
University of Florence	Law	BA in Science of Law Services	Legal Systems and Protection of Rights	Caterina Silvestri, Leonardo Suraci

			Welfare State and Rights	Emilio Santoro, Erik Longo, Marco Rizzuti
		5-Year Degree in Law	History and politics of globalisation and human rights	Lucia Re
	Political and Social Science	MA in International Relations and European Studies	International Human Rights Law	Luisa Vierucci
	Economics and Statistics	BA in Economic Development, International Social-Health Cooperation and Conflict Management	Human Rights and Armed Conflicts	Antonio Bultrini
		MA in Economics and Development	Politics of Globalisation and Human Rights	Lucia Re
University of Foggia	Law	BA in Investigative Science	Constitutional law – Fundamental Rights	Daniele Sebastiano Coduti
			Comparative Public Law – Fundamental Rights	Francesca Rosa
University of Genoa	Law	5-Year Degree in Law	Rights to Freedom and Social Rights	Simona Rodriguez
			Tribunal Justice and Fundamental Rights	Michele Marcheselli

University	Area	Degree Course	Teaching	Lecturer/Professor
	Political and social science	MA in Public Administration and Policies	Fundamental Rights and Liberties	Lorenzo Cuocolo
		MA in International studies and Cooperation	Protection of Human Rights	Pierangelo Celle
			Human Rights Law	Mattia Costa
University of L'Aquila	Economics and Statistics	BA in Economics	Theory of Interpretation and Fundamental Rights	Francesca Caroccia
Link Campus University	Political and Social Science	MA in Strategic Studies and Diplomatic Science	International Organizations and Human Rights	
		BA in Political Science and International Relations	Theory and Practise of Human Rights	
University of Macerata	Political and Social Science	BA in Political Science and International Relations	Philosophy of Human Rights	Natascia Mattucci
		MA in Theory, Culture and Techniques for Social Work	Social and Citizenship-related Rights	Angela Cossiri
	Law	MA in International Politics	Human Rights and Differences	Ines Corti
		MA in Global Politics and	International Human Rights	Laura Salvadego
		International Relations	Human Rights and Constitutional Adjudication	Benedetta Barbisan

University of Messina	Political and social science	MA in International Relations and Development Aid	International Organisations and Human Rights	Carmela Panella
Sacro Cuore (Sacred Heart) Catholic University	Political and social science	BA in Politics and International Relations	International Protection of Human Rights	Monica Spatti
	Law	5-Year Degree in Law	Human Rights	Pasquale De Sena
University of Milan	Political and social science	BA in International Studies and European Institutions	International Protection of Human Rights	Ilaria Viarengo
		BA in Administration and Management	Theory of Equality and Rights	Alessandra Facchi, Beatrice Magni
		BA in Politics	Theory of Justice and Human Rights	Nicola Riva
		BA in Social Science for Globalisation	Fundamental Rights (Jean Monnet course)	Davide Galliani
	Law	5-Year Degree in Law and MA in	EU Law on Business and Human Rights	Angelica Bonfanti
		Sustainable Development	Sociology of Human Rights and the Ombudsman	Alessandra Raffi, Marco A. Quiroz Vitale

University	Area	Degree Course	Teaching	Lecturer/Professor
University of Milan-Bicocca	Political and social science	MA in Sociology	Citizenship: Rights, Conflicts, Gender	Marina Calloni
		MA in Planning and Managing Social Policy and Social Services	Cooperation and Human Rights Protection	Gabriella Citroni
	Law	5-Year Degree in Law	International Protection of Human Rights	Gabriella Citroni
			Sociology of Fundamental Rights	Massimiliano Verga
			European Constitutional Law (Fundamental Rights)	Palmina Tanzarella
University of Modena and Reggio	Law	5-Year Degree in Law	Theory and Practice of Human Rights	Thomas Casadei
Emilia			Comparative Human Rights Law	Silvia Angela Sonelli
University of Molise	Political and social science	BA in Media Studies	Human Rights and Globalisation	Lorenzo Scillitani
University of Campania	Law	BA in Legal Services	Constitutional Law and Protection of Human Rights	Maria Pia Iadicicco
	Political and social science	MA in International Relations and	Human Rights and International Courts	Antonella Silvia Angioi

		MA in Political Science	International and European Protection of Human Rights	Antonella Silvia Angioi
Federico II University of Naples	Political and social science	MA in Social Services and Policy	International Protection of Human and Social Rights	Adriano Maffeo
University of Naples "L'Orientale"	Political and social science	MA in International Studies	Protection of Human Rights in the European Union	Giuseppe Cataldi
University of	Political and social	BA in Politics,	Human Rights	Elena Pariotti
Padova	science	International Relations and	Public Policy and Human Rights	Paola Degani
		Human Rights	Society, Religion and Human Rights	Andrea Maria Maccarini
			Economic Development and Human Rights	Mario Pomini
			International Protection of Human Rights	Paolo De Stefani
		MA in Government and Public Policies	Citizenship and Fundamental Rights	Costanza Margiotta Broglio Massucci
		MA in Human Rights and Multi-Level Governance	European Union Law and Human Rights	Paolo Piva
			Human Rights and International Justice	Costanza Margiotta Broglio Massucci

University	Area	Degree Course	Teaching	Lecturer/Professor
			International Law of Human Rights	Paolo De Stefani
			Women's Human Rights	Paola Degani
			Culture, Society and Human Rights	Andrea Maria Maccarini
			Economic Globalisation and Human Rights	Roberto Antonietti
			Human Rights Governance	Pietro de Perini/Petra Roter
			Human Rights Practice	Sara Pennicino
			Refugee Human Rights Protection	Antoine Pierre Georges Meyer
			Religions and Human Rights	Giuseppe Giordan
	History, Philosophy, Pedagogy and Psychology	BA in Social and Workplace Psychology	Human Rights and Inclusion	Laura Nota
	Law	5-Year Degree in Law	Public Ethics and Human Rights	Umberto Vincenti
University of Palermo	Law	5-Year Degree in Law	Human Rights	Bruno Celano
			Human Rights	Marco Brigaglia

			International Protection of Human Rights	Alfredo Terrasi
	Political and social science	BA in Cooperation, Development and Migration	Human Rights: Theory and Policies	Serena Marcenò
University of Parma	Law	5-Year Degree in Law	Constitutional Protection of Rights	Paola Torretta
	Political and social science	MA in International and European Relations	International Protection of Fundamental Rights	Laura Pineschi
University of Pavia	Law	5-Year Degree in Law	Constitutional Justice and Fundamental Rights	Francesco Rigano
	Political and social science	MA in Economic Development and International Relations	Human Rights and International Justice	Carola Ricci
University of Perugia	Political and social science	MA in International Relations	Sustainable Development, Global Trade and Social Rights	Stefano Giubboni
		Degree in Social Services	Public Law Institutions and Fundamental Rights	Alessandra Valastro
	Law	MA in European Judicial Integration and Human Rights	Protection of Human Rights in the European Judicial Space	Simone Vezzani
			Legal Culture, Fundamental Rights and Migration Processes	Maria Chiara Locchi

University	Area	Degree Course	Teaching	Lecturer/Professor
			Fundamental Human Rights and Civil Procedure	Chiara Cariglia
			Human Rights Philosophy and Sociology	Stefano Anastasia
University of Pisa	Political and social science	Degree in Social Services	Constitutional Law and Human Rights	Saulle Panizza
Guido Carli Free International University of Social Studies – LUISS	Law	5-Year Degree in Law	International Protection of Human Rights	Pietro Pustorino
Maria SS. Assunta Libera University – LUMSA	Political and social science	Degree in International and Political Science	Fundamental Freedoms and Rights	Marco Olivetti
		MA in International Relations	International Law and Protection of Human Rights	Roberta Greco
Roma Tre University	Political and social science	BA in Political Science for Cooperation and Development	International Organisation and Protection of Human Rights	Cristiana Carletti
		MA in International Studies	Theory of Human Rights	Francesco Maiolo

			Global Economy and Labour Rights	Maria Giovannone
	Law	5-Year Degree in Law	European Constitutions and Human Rights	Mauro Palma
			Constitutional Rights and Freedoms	Elisabetta Frontoni
			International Human Rights Law	Giuseppe Palmisano
			Protection of Personal Data and Fundamental Rights – Legal Privacy Clinic	Carlo Colapietro
			Welfare, Social Rights and Territory	Carlo Colapietro
			Prisoners' Rights and the Constitution – Legal Advice Service in Prisons	Silvia Talini
La Sapienza University of Rome	Political and social science	MA in Development and International	Human Rights and Bioethics	Luca Marini
		Cooperation	European Union Law and Human Rights	Alessandra Mignolli
		MA in International Relations	International Human Rights Law	Luigino Manca

University	Area	Degree Course	Teaching	Lecturer/Professor
			European Constitutionalism and Fundamental Rights	Roberto Nania
Tor Vergata University of Rome	Political and social science	BA in Global Governance	Fundamental rights	Andrea Buratti
University of Salento	Political and social science	MA in Geopolitical and International Studies	Theory and Practice of Human Rights	Attilio Pisanò
University of	Law	5-Year Degree in	Human Rights	Alfredo d'Attorre
Salerno		Law	Human Rights and Biolaw	Anna Malomo
			Rights of the Person	Maria Antonietta Urcioli
			International Protection of Human Rights	Michele Nino
University of Siena	Political and social science	MA in International Studies	International Protection of Human Rights	Federico Lenzerini
		MA in Public and Cultural Diplomacy	Rule of Law and Human Rights	Federico Lenzerini
University of Turin	Political and social science	MA in Sociology	Theories of Human Rights	Valentina Pazé
			Citizenship, Social Rights, Justice	Franco Prina, Valeria Ferraris

			Infant Culture and Children's Rights	Roberta Bosisio
		MA in Area & Global Studies for International Cooperation	Fundamental rights in Latin America	Mia Caielli
		MA in International Studies	Human Rights and Immigration	Alessandra Algostino
			History of Human Rights	Franco Motta
			Fundamental Rights in Europe	Joerg Luther
		MA in Social Policy and Services	Citizenship, Social Rights, Justice	Franco Prina, Valeria Ferraris
			Vulnerable People and the Protection of Rights	Maurizio Riverditi, Joelle Long
University of Trent	Political and social science	BA in International Studies	International Relations and Human Rights	Alessia Donà
		MA in European and International Studies	Human rights and natural re-sources under international law	Marco Pertile
			Democratising Security: Human Rights, Democracy and the Rule of Law in the Age of Uncertainty	Michele Nicoletti
			Labour Rights in the Global Economy	Matteo Borzaga

University	Area	Degree Course	Teaching	Lecturer/Professor
		MA in Security, Intelligence and Strategic Studies	Conflict, Human Rights and Natural Resources	Marco Pertile
	Law	BA in Comparative, European and International Legal Studies	International and Supranational Protection of Fundamental Rights	Roberto Toniatti
University of Udine	Law	5-Year Degree in Law	Theory of Human Rights	Giovanni Turco
Carlo Bo University of Urbino	Political and social science	MA in Management of Policy, Social Services and	Fundamental Rights: History, Theory and Politics	Giuseppe Giliberti
		Intercultural Mediation	Equal Opportunity Rights	Athanasia Andriopoulou
Ca' Foscari University of Venice	Political and social science	MA in Work, Social Citizenship and	Fundamental Rights and Privacy	Roberto Senigaglia
		Interculturality	Human Rights and Immigration	Giuseppe Pascale
University of Verona	Political and social science	MA in Social Services in Challenging	Social and Citizenship-related Rights.	Giorgia Anna Parini
		Environments	Protection of Fundamental Rights	Stefano Catalano

Source: elaboration by the 2020 Yearbook research and editorial committee based on data from the prospectuses of each university.

Doctoral programmes (academic year 2019–2020)		
University	**Name**	**Area of scientific discipline**
University of Camerino, School of Advanced Studies	Legal and Social Sciences-Curriculum Fundamental Rights in the Global Society	M-STO/02; M-STO/04; M-DEA/01; M-FIL/03; M-FIL/06; IUS/04; IUS/08; IUS/09; IUS/13 – IUS/21 SECS-P/01; SECS P/02; SECS-P/04; SPS/01; SPS/02; SPS/04; SPS/06; SPS/07; SPS/11; SPS/12
University of Florence	Theory and History of Law – Theory of Human Rights and Society, Genealogy and Perspectives of Legal Thought	IUS/18, IUS/19, IUS/20
University of Padova, Western Sydney University (Australia), University of Zagreb (Croatia), Panteion University of Athens (Greece)	Joint Ph.D Degree in Human Rights, Society, and Multi-level Governance	IUS/13: IUS/20; IUS/21; SPS/04; SPS/08; SECS-P/01
University of Palermo	International Doctorate in Human Rights: Evolution, Protection and Limits	IUS/01, IUS/09, IUS/12, IUS/20, SPS/02, IUS/13, IUS/19, IUS/10, SPS/09, SECS-P/01, IUS/08
Sant'Anna School of Advanced Studies of Pisa	Human Rights and Global Politics: Legal, Philosophical and Economic Challenges	SPS/01, SPS/06, IUS/13, IUS/03, IUS/14, SPS/04, SECS-P/02, SECS-P/06, SECS-P/08
La Sapienza University of Rome	Private Autonomy, Business, Labour and Protection of Human Rights: an International and European Perspective	IUS/07, IUS/12, IUS/04, IUS/05, IUS/02, IUS/01, IUS/19, IUS/13, IUS/14, IUS/15,

Doctoral programmes (academic year 2019–2020)		
University of Macerata	Global Studies: Justice, Rights, Politics	IUS/21, M-FIL/03, SPS/01, SPS/04, SPS/09, IUS/13, SPS/03, IUS/03, SECS-P/06, SECS-P/08
Federico II University of Naples	Human Rights. Theory, History and Practice	IUS/08, IUS/09, IUS/16, IUS/17, IUS/18, IUS/19, IUS/20
Aldo Moro University of Bari	Legal Principles and Institutions between Global Markets and Fundamental Rights	IUS/03, IUS/04, IUS/07, IUS/15, IUS/01, IUS/08, IUS/09, IUS/10, IUS/12, IUS/21, IUS/13, IUS/14, IUS/17
University of Campania	Internationalisation of Legal Systems and Fundamental Rights	IUS/01, IUS/07, IUS/04, IUS/08, IUS/09, IUS/10, IUS/13, IUS/15, IUS/16, IUS/17, IUS/20, IUS/21

Source: elaboration by the *2020 Yearbook* research and editorial committee.

Master's degree programmes – postgraduate

University	Name	Level
University of Bologna	Human Rights, Migration and Intercultural Inclusion	I
	Constitutional Justice and Human Rights	I
	Democracy and Human Rights for South East Europe	II
University of Ferrara	Protections and Rights of Minors	I
European Inter-University Centre for Human Rights and Democratisation (EIUC, 41 European partner universities)	European Master's degree in human rights and democratisation	I
Sant'Anna School of Advanced Studies of Pisa	Human rights and conflict management	I

Master's degree programmes – postgraduate

University of Siena	Global governance, inter-cultural relations and peace-process management	I
Aldo Moro University of Bari	Peace ethics, rights and protection of the person in productive educational and economic contexts	I
La Sapienza University of Rome	"Maria Rita Saulle" International protection of human rights	II
Italian Society for International Organisation (SIOI)	International relations and international protection of human rights	-
University of Genoa	Fundamental Rights and Safeguards	II

Source: elaboration by the *2020 Yearbook* research and editorial committee.

Sub-national Human Rights Structures*

I Peace Human Rights Offices in Municipalities, Provinces and Regions

At the sub-national level, especially by virtue of the inclusion of the "peace human rights norm" in thousands of municipal, provincial and regional statutes and of the adoption of dedicated regional laws on this topic (see Part I, Italian Law, III, IV), Italy has a number of local consultancies, offices, departments, bureaux and centres for human rights, peace, equal opportunity, development cooperation, fair trade and international solidarity. From a subsidiary point of view, these structures contribute to implementing the Agenda 2030 for sustainable development, with particular reference to Goals 5 (Gender Equality), 11 (Sustainable Cities and Communities) and 16 (Peace, Justice and Strong Institutions).

II Ombudspersons in the Italian Regions and Provinces

The Ombudsperson is a guarantee body with pervading investigative powers and the power to publish its own conclusions, assigned the task to protect citizens from the ineffectiveness of public administration, to improve public administration, as well as ensuring and fostering the good performance and impartiality of administrative initiatives according to the principles of legality, transparency, efficiency, effectiveness and equity.

In comparison to all other European Countries, a law establishing the national Ombudsperson has never been approved in Italy. The State instead has a regional (or autonomous province) level arrangement, which results in discrepancies in services across the country (see, in this Part, Sub-national Human Rights Structures, III).

---

* Pietro de Perini, Fabia Mellina Bares

In 2019, there were 18 incumbent Ombudspersons for the regions or Autonomous Provinces (and guarantors which meet the criteria for Ombudspersons): Abruzzo, Aosta Valley, Basilicata, Campania, Emilia-Romagna, Friuli Venezia Giulia, Lazio, Liguria, Lombardy, Marche (Guarantor for the Rights of the Person, formerly known as Ombudsman), Molise (Guarantor for the Rights of the Person), Piedmont, Sardinia, Tuscany, Umbria and Veneto (Guarantor for the Rights of the Person), as well as the Autonomous Provinces of Bolzano and Trent. No Ombudsperson was appointed in Calabria and Apulia in 2019. No legislative provision has been made for the role by the regions of Sicily and Trentino-Alto Adige (where, however, the region has delegated full responsibility in their respective territories to the Ombudspersons of the Autonomous Provinces).

The role of Ombudsperson was strengthened by the approval of legislative decree 97/2016 (Reviewing and simplifying provisions for preventing correction, for publicity and for transparency), the so-called Italian Freedom of Information Act (F.O.I.A.), on general civil access, as well as law 24/2017 (Provisions on the safety of treatments and the person being assisted, as well as on the professional responsibility of health care) within which article 2 gives the Regions the power to entrust the task of *Guarantor for the right to health* to Regional Ombudspersons.

Alongside other guarantor figures working for the rights of children and detainees at a regional level, the regional Ombudspersons contribute to Italy's efforts to build worldwide secure institutions for peace, justice and human rights, pursuant to Goal 16 of the Agenda 2030, particularly Target 16.10 (ensure public access to information and protect fundamental freedoms, in accordance with national legislation and international agreements).

In March 2019, the Venice Commission of the Council of Europe published a set of principles for the protection and promotion of the institution of Ombudsperson (the so-called Venice Principles, CDL-AD(2019)005), reiterating its role in protecting the rights of citizens (see Part III, Council of Europe, IX). The document states that the Ombudspersons are important for democracy as they are able to independently act against cases of misconduct and alleged violations of human rights and carry out a crucial role before Governments and Parliaments which have to accept such criticism. As they interface between administration and citizens, the Ombudspersons are often the first and last recourse to remedy human rights violations.

III National Coordinating Body of Ombudspersons

The National Coordinating Body of Regional and Autonomous Provinces Ombudspersons is an associative body working to harmonise and enhance the institutional role of the Ombudsperson in Italy by promoting initiatives (often in collaboration with other institutions) to spread awareness on their competences on specific issues, and for sharing and discussing best practices.

The Coordinating Body is made up of the incumbent Ombudspersons in the Regions and the Autonomous Provinces. It operates the office of a collectively elected Ombudsperson, made up of a Chair and two vice chairs. In 2019, the role of Chair of the Coordinating Body was covered by Andrea Nobili, Ombudsperson of Marche Region, assisted by Vice Chair Enrico Formento Dojot, Ombudsperson of the Aosta Valley, and Vice Chair Daniela Longo, Ombudsperson of the Province of Trent (succeeded by Sandro Vannini, Ombudsperson of Tuscany).

The Coordinating Body has its headquarters in Rome at the Network of the Presidents of the Legislative Assemblies of the Regions and the Autonomous Provinces. It has regular meetings held in Rome, and further meetings are held in rotation in various Italian cities, in which issues relating to development and problems with the smooth functioning of the Ombudsperson in Italy are discussed.

At the international and European level, the National Coordinating Body of Ombudspersons cooperates with the European Ombudsman Institute (EOI) and the International Ombudsman Institute (IOI). The National Coordinating Body can intervene in issues regarding the mandate of the European Ombudsman at the State central offices. Furthermore, the National Coordinating Body represents the National Italian Ombudsperson at the European Ombudsman and works with the Network of Ombudspersons/European Ombudsman, of which all Italian Ombudspersons are a member (often through a functionary).

The presentation of the third periodic report of the Italian National Coordinating Body to Parliament was due to take place by mid-2020. The year's meetings were themed around the issue of the Ombudsperson for the right to health and examining specific cases in the area of the right to access to documents.

Furthermore, a large part of 2019 was dedicated to writing the *Guidelines for Regions and Autonomous Provinces of Trent and Bolzano on the Guarantee Bodies framework,* approved on 26 September 2019 by the Plenary Assembly of the Network of Chairpersons of the Legislative Assembly of the Regions and Autonomous Provinces.

Following the demand for greater uniformity of regional laws shared with Guarantee Bodies and taking advantage of the work of the ad hoc technical group formed of Ombudspersons and public advocates, the Coordinating Body made the first step to harmonising the regional legal system which over the years has become drastically varied across the country. These steps must also respect the individual choices of each administration.

Therefore, the document is the result of a series of meetings held across the first months of 2019. The aim was to write the Guidelines so that the legislative assemblies will be able to ensure better uniformity in their laws and to value their regional Guarantee Bodies and any future nominations. The lack of a precise legal framework to refer to has caused the regions to continue with great discrepancies across various services and caused complications in defining each Guarantee Body. The document is made up of two parts (divided into paragraphs) regarding institutional aspects (Nature of the Guarantee Body and statutory arrangements: autonomy, independence and impartiality of the body; requirements of nomination; incompatibility and ineligibility; election process; length, limitation, withdrawal and prorogation of the office; remuneration) and functional aspects (Programming of activities; functions, interventions and powers of the Guarantee Body; relationships with national, regional and local authorities; relationships with other bodies and associations; treatment of personal data), which are necessary to carry out the role of the various established figures.

IV Network of Ombudspersons for Children and Adolescents

Since the 1980s, the role of Public Guardian of Children and Adolescents has existed within the regions, autonomous provinces and municipalities. The role was then renamed Ombudsperson, with the same aim of monitoring the implementation of the International Convention on the Rights of the Child and other international instruments (as well as domestic laws) on children's rights and their application within the Italian system.

In 2019, there were 19 Ombudspersons for Children and Adolescents for the Regions or Autonomous Provinces (Apulia, Basilicata, Calabria, Campania, Emilia-Romagna, Lazio, Lombardy, Piedmont, Sardinia, Sicily, Tuscany and the Autonomous Provinces of Trent and of Bolzano); others have competences in other fields, such as the ombudsperson and/or public advocate of the rights of persons with restricted personal freedom (Aosta Valley, Friuli-Venezia Giulia, Liguria, Marche, Molise and Veneto).

With the approval of law 12 July 2011, No. 112, the role of National Ombudsperson for Children and Adolescents was introduced (see this Part, National Bodies with Jurisdiction over Human Rights, VII, D), and with it, the formal establishment of the Network of Ombudspersons for Children and Adolescents, made up of Ombudspersons from the regions and the autonomous provinces (or similar figures) (article 3). The law stated that the Ombudsperson would "guarantee suitable forms of collaboration" with the territorial Ombudspersons, given the "numerous requirements for the Ombudsperson to be independent, autonomous and exclusively competent on issues about children and adolescents". To this end, the Network of Ombudspersons was established, with the aim of promoting "common lines of action for all regional Ombudspersons" (to be adopted unanimously) and of "exchanging data and information on the situation of minors" (article 3, para. 6 and 7, of the instituting law). The Network is chaired by the National Ombudsperson and is equipped with an internal regulation system that establishes its function and reiterates the important role that the Provincial and Regional Ombudspersons carry out. Moreover, it underlines that the Regional and Provincial Ombudspersons are not outlying offices of the National Ombudsperson, but are working offices established by regional or provincial laws in their own right, with their own requirements for the nomination, powers held and competences. The Network meets at least twice a year upon the convocation of the National Ombudsperson or on the majority request of the territorial Ombudspersons (article 7 of the Prime Ministerial Decree 20 July 2012, No. 168). The National Ombudsperson has expressed the need to clearly define the role and competencies of territorial Ombudspersons in order to avoid overlapping competencies or duplicating measures carried out by the National Authority. (2019 Report of the National Ombudsperson in Parliament).

Law 7 April 2017, No. 47 (Provisions for protection measures for unaccompanied foreign minors) gave the Territorial Ombudspersons specific competences (article 11), establishing the stipulation of specific Memoranda of Understanding with the Presidents of Juvenile Courts. It aims at creating a list of private citizens (selected and adequately trained by the Regional Ombudspersons for Children and Adolescents and those of the Autonomous Provinces of Trent and Bolzano) to become guardians of unaccompanied minors. This had already been a topic of discussion and reflection within the Network before this law had entered into force.

In 2019, the Network met in June and December, convocated by the National Ombudsperson to discuss the theme of common interests. This included discussions on: the awareness campaign for the thirtieth anniversary of the International Convention on the Rights of the Child; comments addressed to Italy by the UN Committee on the Rights of the Child (February 2019); measures to end educational poverty; monitoring measures (pursuant to article 11 of law 47/2017); and initiatives aimed at raising the level of participation and involvement of children.

Just as the National Coordinating Body of Ombudspersons, the Network of Ombudspersons for Children and Adolescents also spent the first 6 months of 2019 working on the writing of the Guidelines (see, in this Part, Sub-national Human Rights Structures, III).

V Network of Territorial Ombudspersons for Persons Detained or Deprived of Their Liberty

Since 2003, regions, provinces and municipalities with prison institutions or any place where persons are deprived of their liberty for legal, administrative or health reasons have established Ombudspersons for persons detained. In most cases, this is an ad hoc figure, whereas in others, this role is given to Ombudspersons or to other figures with various competences (Ombudspersons on the rights of persons or similar). Currently, there are 13 regional Ombudspersons in office, in addition to those of the Autonomous Provinces of Trent, 3 Provinces, one metropolitan area and 43 Municipalities.

Other than the various competences recognised at the territorial level by regional laws or other constituent decrees, national laws recognise that territorial Ombudspersons are able to access prevention and penal institutes and juvenile criminal institutes (article 67(1)-lett. L-*bis*, l. 26 July 1975,

No. 354), police force security cameras (article 67-*bis*) in the repatriation centre for foreigners deprived of their residency documents within national borders (article 19(3), l.d. 17 February 2017, No. 13, as amended by conversion law 13 April 2017, No. 46). In the prison sector, complaints made by detained persons are directed to the territorial Ombudsperson (article 35, l. 26 July 1975, No. 354), in order to ensure confidentiality of their correspondence (article 18-*ter*(2)). Just like national Ombudspersons, the Ombudspersons for Persons Detained or Deprived of their Liberty can carry out interviews requested by a prisoner (article 18(2)).

Since 2008, the various Ombudspersons for Persons Deprived of their Liberty named by national territorial bodies met in a national network (from 2018: Network of territorial Ombudspersons for Persons Detained or Deprived of their Liberty, with offices at the Conference of Presidents of the legislative assemblies of Regions and Autonomous Provinces). Since its institution, national Ombudsperson have been invited to participate in the meetings (see, in this Part, 1.7.5). Pursuant to l.d. 23 December 2013, No. 146, article 7, the Ombudsperson for persons detained or deprived of their liberty promotes and fosters collaborative relationships with territorial Ombudspersons.

With note verbale No. 1105, dated 25 April 2014 addressed to the UN Subcommittee on Prevention of Torture, the Permanent Representative of Italy to the United Nations described the NPM, pursuant to the Optional Protocol to the Convention Against Torture (OPCAT, in force since 3 May 2013), as coordinated by the Ombudsperson for the rights of persons detained or denied of their liberty and the regional and local Ombudspersons.

Therefore, the Italian NPM is made up of the National Ombudsperson, coordinating a network community of Ombudspersons to build a coherent system in different local systems with a wide mandate to fulfil all areas set out by the OPCAT.

Other than ordinary and monitoring work of detainment places and the civil defence of the people deprived of their liberty, 2019 saw the application of legislative decrees 123/2018 and 124/2018, implementing delegation law Orlando, reviewing the Prison Administration Act and regulating the autonomous Juvenile legal system. As the first experience of coworking between the Regions and the Italian Fines Fund (*Cassa delle ammende*) for measures aimed at the reinsertion of prisoners into society, this is especially important, above all to highlight the role of territorial bodies in criminal enforcement policies. Finally, it must be noted that there has been a shift in the interventions and activities of the Ombudsperson for the rights of persons detained or denied of their liberty from prison to administrative detention, compulsory health treatment, health management and implementing security measures in new residences for those unable or unwilling to take full responsibility for their actions at the time of the crime.

The Network of territorial Ombudspersons for Persons Detained or Deprived of their Liberty, just like National Coordinating Body of Ombudspersons and Network of Ombudspersons for Children and Adolescents, took part in writing the Guidelines in the first six months of 2019 (see, in this Part, Sub-national Human Rights Structures, III).

VI National Coordinating Body of Local Authorities for Peace and Human Rights

Founded on 12 October 1986, the National Coordinating Body of Local Authorities for Peace and Human Rights is the largest Italian network of municipalities, provinces and regions involved in promoting peace and human rights; it is a unique experience in Europe and worldwide. The Coordinating Body is chaired by Andrea Ferrari and directed by Flavio Lotti.

Among the many activities to take place in 2019, the following are particularly significant within framework of the commitment of the Coordinating Body to support the increase of human rights education, and of citizenship and peace:

- *Massive Online Open Course* (*MOOC*) for teachers of all levels and ages "Teaching Human Rights", on the *Eduopen* platform in collaboration with the University of Padova Human Rights Centre and the Department of Political Sciences, Law and International Studies, the Specialisation School "Educating for meeting and solidarity" (EIS) of the University Lumsa, and the Network of Schools for Peace and the Peace Round Table. This MOOC was the first in Italy on this subject. It aimed at teaching educators and professionals who are aware of the importance of the culture of human rights, encompassing the awareness and understanding of the meaning, values, laws and principles of human rights and their protection mechanisms.

- Citizenship educational programme for the years 2019–2021 “I care” (*“Io ho cura”*). The programme was promoted within initiatives of the Network of Schools for Peace, in collaboration with the Universities of Rome, Padova and Verona. It aims to develop students’ ability to care for themselves, for others, for the community, for the environment and for the world, placing the students at the forefront through the “Service Learning” experience; valuing teachers’ work as professionals in educational care, and involving them in training/research/action programmes; and integrating the curriculum with various educational topics (human rights, sustainability, solidarity, peace, the Constitution, legality, health, glocal citizenship and so on) within subject areas. Students from all the schools involved in the programme contribute to planning these training courses alongside their teachers – the programme will culminate in the organisation of a Plenary Meeting and the latest Perugia-Assisi March.
- The research and action course “Citizenship 2030”, promoted within the initiatives of the Network of Schools for Peace using widespread collective intelligence, inside and outside schools, to tackle new educational challenges for the present day and a fast-changing future with the view of implementing the UN Agenda 2030 for sustainable development.

VII Archives and Other Regional Projects for the Promotion of a Culture of Peace and Human Rights

Besides the “Pace Diritti Umani – Peace Human Rights” Archive of the Region of Veneto, established by r.l. 18/1988 and managed by the University of Padova Human Rights Centre (see this Part, Region of Veneto, IV), there are other more recent archives and similar projects set up by Italian Regions and Autonomous Provinces to foster the promotion and dissemination of a culture of human rights and peace.

The “Peace and Human Rights” project in the Region of Emilia-Romagna was set up by the Regional Council in collaboration with the Department for Social Policies, Immigration, Youth Projects and International Cooperation and the Regional Governments Management Control and Statistics Systems Department. The project has been managed by the Europe Direct Centre of the Legislative Assembly of Emilia-Romagna since 2013 and follows the principles laid out in r.l. 24 June 2002, No. 12 (Regional interventions for cooperation with developing countries and countries in transition, international solidarity and the promotion of a culture of peace). It aims to support activities described in the law.

The commitment of the Legislative Assembly is illustrated in the page "Peace and Rights" ("*Pace e Diritti*") of the Europe Direct Centre of Emilia-Romagna, which also provides citizens with a repository of documents and videos on the topic (www.assemblea.emr.it/europedirect/pace-e-rights).

In 2019, the commitment of the regional legislative assembly of Emilia-Romagna for the defence and promotion of human rights continued through supporting and organising numerous events and initiatives at the Europe Direct Centre. Particularly noteworthy was the educational project "Rights are born" ("*Diritti si nasce*"), the launch of #PACEeDIRITTI ("#PEACEandRIGHTS"), a database aimed at broadcasting news articles on human rights and peace in Emilia-Romagna via social network and the XVI edition of the "René Cassin" graduation prize on the subject of fundamental rights and human development for professional training.

The "*Forum Trentino per la pace e i diritti umani*" ("*Trentino for Peace and Human Rights Forum*") standing body was established in 1991 at the behest of the Provincial Council of Trent with p.l. 10 June 1991, No. 11 (Promoting and disseminating the culture of peace). Website: http://www.forumpace.it/.

The annual theme approved during the 2019 Forum Assembly was "What rights?" ("*Quali diritti?*"). It is aimed at refocusing attention on the rights set out in the Universal Declaration of Human Rights and on the significant changes these have gone through over time, from first generation rights (civil and political rights), to second generation rights (social, economic and cultural rights) and finally to third generation rights (solidarity rights). The Forum continued this theme by announcing a call for proposals for civil society associations to create a shared calendar of interconnected actions and events aimed at strengthening and creating positive synergy among the various actors working in the Trentino territory.

Region of Veneto*

The Region of Veneto has been operating organically for the promotion of human rights, the culture of peace and international cooperation since 1988, the year when the first regional law on such issues was adopted in Italy (r.l. 30 March 1988, No. 18). In 1999, r.l. 18/1988 was replaced by the current r.l. 16 December 1999, No. 55, on "Regional measures for the promotion of human rights, a culture of peace, development cooperation and solidarity and then with the current r.l. 21 June 2018, No. 21 (Regional intervention for the promotion of human rights and sustainable development cooperation)".

With r.l. 24 December 2013, No. 37, the Region established the post of *Regional Ombudsperson for the Rights of the Person* which integrates the functions of the Ombudsperson, of the Ombudsperson for Children and Adolescents (both created in 1988 and working for the implementation of the aforementioned r.l. 37/2013), as well as those of promotion and protection of the rights of persons deprived of their liberty.

In the context of the Regional Government, issues concerning human rights pertain to the Councillor on Social Services, programme implementation and relations with the Regional Council, a post currently held by Manuela Lanzarin. Measures and activities concerning international relations and development cooperation are overseen directly by the Regional Governor, Luca Zaia.

Article 2 of the new r.l. 21/2018 commits the Veneto region to promoting and sustaining the following within the territory:

a) cultural, informative, awareness, research, training and education initiatives regarding human rights, fundamental freedoms and sustainable development cooperation;
b) collecting, sorting and disseminating studies, research, publications, multimedia and documents produced in regional, national and international head-

* Pietro de Perini, Fabia Mellina Bares

quarters, in relation to other databases, on the topic of promoting and human rights and sustainable development cooperation;

c) database of human rights and sustainable development coordination organisations working in Veneto;
d) participating [...] in projects on development cooperation, in the field of the application of public development cooperation [...] including participating in the cooperation programmes of the European Union.

To this end, the law institutes the Regional Table on human rights and sustainable development cooperation (article 5) with advisory status on the regional programming and on consultancy concerning regional institutions. It promotes and supports the Venice Foundation for Research on Peace (article 8) and the work of the European Commission for Democracy through Law (*Venice Commission*) of the Council of Europe (article 7). The regional infrastructure for peace and human rights also includes the Commission for achieving equality between men and women, the Regional Observatory on Immigration, and the Peace Human Rights Archive (established by law 18/1988).

Regional law 23 April 2013, No. 5 (Regional Intervention to prevent and combat violence against women) established a Regional Coordination Table for Preventing and Combating Violence against Women within the Regional Government. In implementing this law, in 2019, the Region has financed specific autonomous projects for women within anti-violence centres and refuge shelters. These so-called violence escape routes are specific independent projects for women (either alone or with children) victims of violence who are housed within these structures. The overall regional allocation was divided among 22 anti-violence centres and 21 shelters.

Concerning public resources for "Funds for policies on rights and equal opportunities" from the Veneto Region, in 2019, they were directed towards: financing the establishment of the new anti-violence centres and shelter houses; support the activities of pre-existing anti-violence centres and shelter houses; and issue educational vouchers for courses on equal dignity, recognising and respecting women's rights for primary and secondary schools in Veneto, aiming to raise awareness on, prevent and combat violence against women in the region.

By way of r.l. 28 December 1998, No. 33, the Region promotes and financially supports the European Master's degree Programme in Human Rights and Democratisation (E.MA), located in Venice. With the adoption of r.l. 22 January 2010, No. 6, the Region has recognised the social and cultural value of fair trade, proclaiming its support for the organisations which operate in this sector.

I Department for International Relations, Communications and SISTAR

The Department is in charge (among other things) of implementing r.l. 21/2018. In 2019, Diego Vecchiato was the coordinator of the structure.

> The Department is responsible for various international initiatives undertaken by the Region, including: managing international relations; signing Memoranda of Intesa between national and foreign institutions; participating in international bodies and initiatives; participating in the European Grouping of Territorial Cooperation *"Euregio Senza Confini"*; programming and/or managing regional interventions on international solidarity; fair trade and human rights; culture of peace; promoting equal opportunities; and protecting linguistic minorities. It houses the Regional Veneto Committee for UNICEF.

In 2019, among the various activities to promote human rights, the Department granted vouchers for educational courses for the year in question. Like the previous year, in 2019, the Region allocated an overall fund of €70,000 for 100 vouchers to create educational courses in schools across the region (35 in secondary middle schools, 30 in secondary high schools and 35 in primary schools) on the following themes: sustainable development and Agenda 2030, women's rights and gender-related issues, bullying and cyber-bullying, environmental protection, right to food, non-discrimination and social and cultural integration and children's rights. The vouchers were introduced by the Region in 2014 to create opportunities for meetings and exchanging ideas between schools and associations in the region on human rights issues.

II Regional Table on Human Rights and Sustainable Development Cooperation

The Regional Table was established pursuant to article 5 of r.l. 21/2018. It is responsible for consulting on regional programmes and bodies on human rights, development cooperation and fair-trade issues.

With regional government decree 956 of 12 July 2019, the Regional Table approved the 2019 Annual Implementation Plan for interventions on promoting human rights and sustainable development cooperation. To support the regional actions laid out in the 2019 Plan, the resources available in the estimated Regional budget 2019–2021 add up to €500,000 for development cooperation initiatives, €130,000 for initiatives supporting fair trade and €105,000 for actions aimed at promoting human rights and a culture of peace. The final sum establishes (pursuant to r.l. 21/2018) supporting Venice for Peace Research Foundation and the activities of the University of Padova Human Rights Centre to manage the Peace Human Rights Regional Archive, as well as assigning 100 vouchers for educational courses in schools of all levels in the region.

III Venice for Peace Research Foundation

The Foundation was established by r.l. 18/1988 and reconfirmed first by r.l. 55/1999 and then by r.l. 21/2018. The Foundation aims, as its main objective, to carry out research. This is in collaboration with national and international institutions on issues related to security, development and peace.

In 2019, the Foundation, other than continuing to promote the project *Blind Spots* (see *Yearbook 2016*, p. 119), created a Research Group on "the defence of heritage and identities/cultural diversity in armed conflicts". It contributed to organising two conferences: the first at the IUAV University of Venice on the theme of "Europe, one hundred years on from the First World War: what perspectives?" (24–25 March); the second was at the Ca' Foscari University of Venice on the "Protection of cultural heritage in cases of armed conflict – twenty years on from the second Protocol of the Hague Convention of 1954" (27 May). Furthermore, the Foundation edited and published the seventh volume of its series, entitled *Post-Genocide Redress in Rwanda. An international-law perspective* series (edited by S. Pinton).

IV Human Rights Authority

The Human Rights Authority of Veneto was established by regional law 24 December 2013, No. 37. The first and current Human Rights

Authority is Mirella Gallinaro, who was appointed in 2015 and re-elected for her second three-year mandate in 2018.

> Regionally, the Human Rights Authority carries out the role of ensuring the rights of physical and legal persons towards public administration and public service management via non-judicial promotion, protection and mediation procedures; furthermore, it carries out the role of promoting, protecting and facilitating the pursuit of the rights of children and adolescents and of the rights of persons deprived of their personal liberty.
> Regarding the role of the Human Rights Authority, the Ombudsperson receives complaint reports from individuals and associated subjects, reporting mismanagement or abuse by public administration who have offices in the region (including individuals who have approached public administration without getting any results, or have obtained unsatisfactory results), carrying out guidance, mediation, solicitation and recommendation activities for administration bodies; furthermore, it rules on complaint reports to review bans (either explicit or implied) or to postpone access to administrative documents under article 24 of law No. 241 of 1990 as well as review requests to restrict civic access under legislative decree No. 33 of 2013, amended and integrated by legislative decree No. 97 of 2016. All complaint reports are concluded with a motivated response.

In 2019, there were 393 complaint reports presented (formally 394 due to a registration error) of which 108 were review requests. The remaining complaint reports concerned construction, welfare, administrative fines, personal services, taxes and levies, region and environment, urban planning, and one request on exercising substitute power pursuant to article 30 para. 10 of regional law 23 April 2004, No. 11 and successive amendments. It should be noted that in Veneto, in comparison to other regions, the regional legislator has not given the Human Rights Authority the role of "Ombudsperson for the right to health" pursuant to article 2(1) of law 24/2017 (Provisions on safety of treatments and assisted persons, as well as on professional responsibility of health professional workers).

> To carry out the role of promoting and protecting minors in the public sector, pursuant to its establishing law, the Human Rights Authority: carries out training programmes for people who are suitable for carrying out protection and care activities, providing consultations, updating and upkeeping the relative regional list and making these lists available to the competent authorities; promote consultancy, mediation, facilitation and accompanying programmes,

> in collaboration with regional structures, local bodies, institutions and services working with children in the region, the ordinary and juvenile courts, preventing difficult situations for children and encouraging the best treatment of situations that require judicial, social, health or educational interventions; sets up forms of institutional listening with regards to social and health services, schools, reception communities and other public or private institutions; brings attention to cases of violations of children's rights, as well as issues that may occur when carrying out protection procedures. Institutional listening has been extended to families and minors, collecting reports on mediation, consultation and guidance, and reporting these to the competent administration and, if necessary, to the judicial authorities. Furthermore, it supports the monitoring of the assistance for children in contexts outside their own family; in collaboration with other specific regional institutions (universities and judicial authorities), it carries out monitoring activities, research and cultural promotion on the situation of children and adolescents in Veneto and holds initiatives to promote the participation of children and adolescents in the life of the community, in collaboration with local institutions, schools, youth organisations and civil society bodies.

In 2019, institutional listening activities got 193 requests concerning both private individuals and public services and institutions. The Office carried out training programmes for people willing to undertake roles to protect minors, manage data banks, and carry out consultation and support activities. In 2019, there were 422 requests for volunteer tutors by the judicial authorities.

In 2019, furthermore, the Human Rights Authority of Veneto continued to participate in various projects (going on from 2018) and organised new initiatives. In some cases, it was a partner in exclusively local initiatives, in others, it was involved in developing or implementing at a local/regional level of comprehensive projects (national; international/national). In particular:

- *C.re.s.c.e.r.e. project* longitudinal study promoted and carried out by the Zancan Foundation of Padova aiming at understanding the changes of a sample of children and families residing in 84 Municipalities of the Padova province and the city of Rovigo.
- *Terreferme project* promoted by CNCA and UNICEF Italy, aiming at facilitating the placement of unaccompanied minors coming from the emergency immigration structures in Palermo in foster families in the Veneto and Lombardy Regions (who have signed up to the family reception network of the CNCA. In Veneto, in April-May 2019, a new training course took place (the second since the beginning of the project) addressed at families available to support

and welcome unaccompanied minors and public and private social workers dealing with the welfare and reception system.

- *National Project "Monitoring the voluntary protection of unaccompanied foreign minors"* aimed at promoting the voluntary protection of those minors across Italy, monitoring the implementation of provisions of l. 7 April 2017, No. 47 (Provisions on protection measures for unaccompanied foreign minors). The project belongs to the Ombudsperson for Children and Adolescents and is financed through the Asylum, Migration and Integration Fund (AMIF) (European funds), managed by the Ministry of the Interior. The Human Rights Authority of Veneto joined the project in August 2019, entering into an agreement with the Ombudsperson for Children and Adolescents "Agreement for technical and working collaboration on monitoring, evaluating and supporting the system and local practices of voluntary protection".
- *N.A. Ve Project (Anti-trafficking Network Veneto)* aiming at implementing and consolidating an integrated system to assist victims of human trafficking and/or grave exploitation. The Human Rights Authority in Veneto has participated since September 2017. In 2019, phase two of the project concluded (*N.A. Ve 2*: 01/12/2017–28/02/2019) and phase three began (*N.A. Ve 3*), supported by the Region of Veneto. The partnership with the Municipality of Venice (lead partner) to carry out interventions under r.l. 41/1997 (Decision of the Regional Council 19 June 2019, No. 849) has been renewed.

At the same time, various participation activities continued at coordination meetings for the Ombudsperson for minors in diverse regions and conferences at a national level (States-general of children and adolescents – 14 and 15 November 2019 in Naples; Convention on the Rights of Children and Adolescents celebrating the 30th anniversary of the UN Convention – Rome 21 November 2019) and at a regional level (Conference on the rights of children in parental separation – Venice 7 June 2019 and Conference on gender-based violence – Bassano 22 March 2019).

To fulfil the role of protecting the rights of detainees in prison institutions, in structures managed by Juvenile Justice Centres (juvenile penal institutes and first reception centres), in Immigration detention, in health structures (when dealing with compulsory medical treatment) and also of people deprived of all of personal freedoms, the Ombudsperson carries out a non-judicial role and works with mediation, persuasion, facilitation, orientation, solicitation and recommendation tools, undertaking all initiatives aimed at ensuring the services inherent to the right to health, to improving the quality of life, to education, to professional training, to social and work re-insertion are effectively carried out.

In 2019, the Human Rights Authority managed complaint reports by detainees or by their partners, organised a conference through various forms of participation and promotion of rights and participation in coordinating tables, and finally monitored two prison structures.

> It is noteworthy that in Belluno, Rovigo, Venice and Verona, there are Municipal Ombudspersons effectively present within the region – the office is constantly working in cooperation, alongside a Regional Coordinating body which meets every three months. Managing these complaint reports, therefore, is entrusted to institutions working in Municipalities where a guarantor has not been re-elected (even when foreseen) (Vicenza), or no guarantor has been envisaged within the Municipality (Padova, Treviso).

In 2019, the complaint reports from imprisoned persons or their families concerned health services, work conditions, education/training, prison life, affectivity and information requests.

There were 53 open cases: 11 C.R. of Padova, 9 C.C. Padova, 1 ICATT Padova, 0 C.C Rovigo; 18 C.C. Treviso; 2 C.C. Venice and 0 C.R. Venice; 4 C.C. Vicenza, 2 C.C. Verona. 1 C.C. Belluno; 2 alternative measures. In 19 cases, the complaint reports were received via interview, in 29 cases via written communication, and in 5 cases via telephone interviews.

> Among the Authority's many competencies, it is also able to check whether health, education, professional training and social and work re-insertion services have been made available for inmates. To implement this duty, in 2019, the Authority undertook three unannounced visits: on 27 February and 5 November to Vicenza Correctional Facility; on 6 March to Treviso Correctional Facility. At the end of these visits, written reports were sent to the respective directors of the institutes and to the PRAP.

On 29 November 2019, the conference *"The Complexities of the Prison System: working with men who are violent against women"* was organised in collaboration with the Veneto Prison Health Services and the Superintendency of the Triveneto Prison Administration (PRAP). The conference was the second part of a series of "reflections" on the complexities of the prison system – the first constituted an event organised with the Veneto Prison Health Services: *"The Complexities of the Prison System: mental health challenges in the system"*, in December 2018. This was followed by a series of training meetings organised for prison staff in accordance with the PRAP and the University of Padova.

Furthermore, the following institutions are also active: the Permanent Inter-institutional Observatory for healthcare in prison; the Inter-institutional Technical Body on managing patients under REMS security measures; the Permanent Committee on Reparative Justice and Criminal Mediation – "handshake" project; the Regional Coordinating Body to prevent and combat violence against women; the Regional Bioethics Committee; and the meetings of the Regional Labour Department for the Italian Fines Fund (*Cassa delle Ammende*).

In 2019, the Memorandum of Understanding for the "Procedures for implementing forms of reception for children in prison with their mothers" was set up once again, and has already seen its first monitoring board. It has been promoted by the Director of the I.C.A.M. at the Women's House of Detention of Venice; the president of the Interdisciplinary Office of External Criminal Execution of Venice; the Venice Chief of Police; and the Municipality of Venice, and, acknowledged by the president of the Venice Juvenile Court; and the Procurator of the Republic at the Venice Juvenile Court. The Protocol aims at ensuring the rights of children who are placed in prisons with their mothers until they are six years old, and those who at six years (or before, if necessary) are placed in alternative care. It also aims at guaranteeing all necessary measures for their physical and mental well-being and their growth. It outlines intervention strategies that are to be carried out by the institutions supporting the needs of children placed with their mothers at the Venice Female Prison Institution.

Finally, the Authority is a member of the National Coordinating body of Ombudspersons for the Regions and Autonomous Provinces, of the National Conference for ensuring the Rights of Children, and of the Network of territorial Ombudspersons for Persons Detained or Deprived of their Liberty; furthermore, it has participated in relevant meetings and initiatives across the year (see, in this Part, Sub-national Human Rights Structures, III, IV, and V).

V Regional Commission for Equal Opportunities between Men and Women

The Commission was established by r.l. 30 December 1987, No. 62, and it is the regional consultative body on gender policies for the actual implementation of the principles of equality and equal opportunities enshrined in the Constitution and Regional Statute. The Commission was established at the Veneto Regional Council and is chaired by Elena Traverso.

> The main task of the Commission is to investigate and research the condition of women in Veneto, with particular reference to issues involving employment, labour and professional training and to disseminate information on these areas. At the same time, the Commission respects its commitment to being present on the ground and to developing new synergies with all the actors and forces involved to promote and support the realisation of equal opportunities in the social, political and economic life of the population of Veneto. It may offer opinions on the current state of implementation of laws and on bills, as well as drawing up proposals of its own. The Veneto Equal Opportunities Commission carries out its mission in contact with other Commissions at the local, regional and national level and maintains a constant exchange with all women's organisations in the region.

Among the activities and the awareness initiatives promoted and supported by the Commission during 2019, the following are noteworthy:

- the start of the training course "Gender Innovation and Communication" within the project "Veneto in action" of the Region of Veneto (May 2019);
- the "Pink Run" ("Corsa Rosa"), a solidarity walk for women, promoted by UISP, Legnago, 24 March;
- the project – "Pink October – breast tumour prevention month", promoted by the Rovigo Province and the Equals Opportunity Commission of the Rovigo Province, in collaboration with the National Association of Women affected by breast cancer of Rovigo;
- the series of events organised by the Verona Province and the Municipality of San Giovanni Lupatoto for the International Day for the Elimination of Violence against Women (November).

VI Regional Observatory on Immigration

The Observatory is a service offered by the Region of Veneto – Immigration flows office – and is managed by Veneto Lavoro. It was established under the three-year immigration initiative programme of 2007–2009 and was subsequently reconfirmed in each successive three-year plan under article 3 of r.l. 9/1990 (Interventions in the immigration sector).

> The Observatory is a technical and scientific tool aimed at monitoring, analysing and spreading information and data on migration flows and integration both regionally and nationally. To achieve this aim, the Observatory: ensures collaboration with other regional observatories concerned with immigration in several respects; guarantees the smooth running and constant update of databanks; monitors the various dynamics of immigration, in-depth studies of various themes and issues, children's living situations and social/school insertion, education and training; ensures updated specialist laws and proposes initiatives to improve the understanding and correct application of those laws.

The most recent annual report by the Regional Observatory on Immigration was published in October 2019. It is the fifteenth report, with data up to the start of 2019. As in previous reports, it analyses data and trends on crucial aspects for Italy and Veneto on migration flows, such as demographic information, work and unemployment, the situation of young foreign nationals in the regional school system, the issue of unaccompanied minors and asylum seekers, and the economic integration of immigrants.

In general, the statistics presented in the report show that there were 501,085 foreign nations residing in Veneto on 1 January 2019, 9.5 % of the national total. There was a slight increase of just over 13,000 from last year (487,893, which still corresponded to 9.5 % of the national total). Nationally, Veneto was the fourth region in Italy for the number of foreign nationals residing in the region (after Lombardy, Lazio and Emilia-Romagna). The percentage of the foreign nations compared to the overall regional population was 10.2 %, placing Veneto at sixth place after Emilia-Romagna, Lombardy, Lazio, Tuscany and Umbria. The provinces with the highest percentage of foreign nationals compared to the population on 1 January 2019 were Verona (110,029, 11.9 % of the population), Padova (97,085, 10.4 % of the population) and Treviso (93,074, 10.5 % of the population). The number of foreign nationals obtaining Italian citizenship (registered at municipality record office) – after the record number of 2016 (29,313) – almost halved in 2018 (15,536, 13.8 %) of the total issued nationally (around 112,000, which was also much lower than the previous years). The main countries of origin for the foreign nations residing in Veneto on 1 January 2019 were Romania (25.3 %), Morocco (9.1 %), China (7.1 %), Albania (6.7 %) and the Republic of Moldova (6.7 %). Of the main national groups registered in Veneto, the highest numbers of residence permits issued on 1 January 2018 were Morocco (51,653), China (39,801), Albania (35,963) and the Republic of Moldova (33,553).

VII Regional Archive "Pace Diritti Umani – Peace Human Rights"

The Regional Archive was created pursuant to r.l. 18/1988 and reconfirmed by the subsequent r.l. 55/1999. The Archive is managed by the University of Padova Human Rights Centre. It is one of the main instruments through which the Region of Veneto promotes the culture of human rights, peace, development cooperation and solidarity in Italy and abroad.

The Archive works to collect, elaborate and publish documents, thematic databases and informational resources on topics regarding regional law, particularly through the regular updating of the portal "*Archivio Pace Diritti Umani*" (http://unipd-centrodirittiumani.it/en/), available in Italian and English, and the distribution of knowledge on human rights through multimedia tools and social networks. In addition, it oversees publication of books, teaching aids, in-depth studies and multimedia and offers technical and scientific support to the actors most closely involved in the promotion and practice of the culture of peace, especially as concerns initiatives promoted by teachers, education staff, schools and civil society organisations. In 2019, the Archive published and distributed 16 editions of the "peace human rights" newsletter in Italian and in English to its established mailing list.

In 2019, the Archive updated the databases available on its website, notably the Italian translations of the database of international legal instruments on human rights, humanitarian law, criminal law and refugee law; the associations and NGOs active in the field of human rights and development cooperation in Veneto; and the collection of national and international documents and publications for persons with disabilities. In addition to its usual activities of updating, providing in-depth studies and information, the Archive contributed to promoting the scientific journal of the University of Padova Human Rights Centre, *Peace Human Rights Governance* (*PHRG*). The Archive also contributed to the publication and promotion of the 2019 edition of the *Italian Yearbook of Human Rights* in Italian and in English and the institutional presentation of this publication in Rome at the Ministry of Foreign Affairs and International Cooperation (16 December).

Furthermore, in 2019, the Archive collaborated with national and international organisations and experts in organising a series of initiatives at the University of Padova, especially multimedia and documentary aspects.

The following initiatives are noteworthy: the technical and multimedia support in promoting the training course for educators "Gender and Women, Peace and Security" (March-May) and the 1st Massive Open Online Course (MOOC) on human rights for school teachers of all levels "Teaching human rights" (October-December) in collaboration with the National Coordinating Body of Local Bodies for Peace and Human Rights and the Schools for Peace Network (see, in this part, 2.6); promoting the "Human Rights and Inclusion" general course of the University of Padova for the academic year 2019/2020; facilitating the organisation of the international seminars "A fresh sight on the Convention on the Rights of the Child, and beyond" (Master Class with Ton Liefard, 27 February) and "Current trends and challenges in the work of the CRC: states' reporting, civil society inputs and communications" (Master Class with Ann Skelton, 21 March), of the International Conference "On women's rights: between violence and exploitation" (12–13 November), of the event "1989–2019: 30th Anniversary of the UN Convention on the Rights of the Child" (20 November) and of the training seminar for planning civic education for headteachers and teachers of schools of all levels on the subject "Everyone has the right to be happy" (10 December 2019).

PART III

Italy in Dialogue With International Human Rights Institutions

The United Nations System*

I General Assembly

The General Assembly, which is the main deliberative body of the United Nations, is comprised of six Committees, each of which is made up of all 193 United Nations Member States. Human rights issues are handled mainly within the Third Committee (the Social, Humanitarian and Cultural Committee). The responsibilities of this Committee include issues such as torture and other cruel, inhuman and degrading treatment or punishment; the advancement of women; the rights of refugees and displaced persons; the promotion and protection of the rights of children; the rights of indigenous peoples; the elimination of racism, racial discrimination, xenophobia and related intolerance; the right of peoples to self-determination; and social development.

> In December 2019, the 74th session of the GA adopted 62 resolutions on human rights (43 of which by consensus), that had already been discussed and approved by the Third Committee in October and November. The resolutions concerned a wide range of issues, from the rights of migrants to digital privacy, from protection against discrimination on the basis of sexual orientation and gender identity to specific country situations.

In 2019, Italy's Permanent Representative to the United Nations in New York was Ambassador Mariangela Zappia; the Deputy Permanent Representative was Ambassador Stefano Stefanile; First Counsellor Simona De Martino and First Secretary Ilario Schettino were responsible for following the activities of the Third Committee.

---

* Andrea Cofelice

A Resolutions on Human Rights – Italy's Voting Behaviour

As in the past, in 2019, Italy's action in support of human rights prioritised the following thematic areas: promotion of the rule of law and strengthening of democracy; the fight against torture, xenophobia, racism and all forms of discrimination, with specific attention to religious discrimination and intolerance; the rights and protection of children; the abolition of the death penalty; and combating violence against women and female genital mutilation.

Specifically, Italy presented the Resolution *Strengthening the United Nations crime prevention and criminal justice programme, in particular its technical cooperation capacity*, approved by consensus by the General Assembly (A/RES/74/177). Regarding the SDGs, this resolution comes under the scope of Goal 16: Promote peaceful and inclusive societies for sustainable development, provide access to justice for all and build effective, accountable and inclusive institutions at all levels.

Furthermore, Italy sponsored 32 resolutions and was asked to pass an open vote on 19 resolutions (9 votes in favour, 6 against and 4 abstentions), the outcome of which is shown below.

Subject	Resolution	Main sponsor of the Resolution	Information regarding Italy	Outcome of the Plenary Session
Social Development	A/RES/74/119 Cooperatives in social development	Mongolia	Co-sponsor of the Resolution	Adopted by consensus
	A/RES/74/120 Promoting social integration through social inclusion	Peru	Co-sponsor of the Resolution	Adopted by consensus
	A/RES/74/121 Policies and programmes involving youth	Portugal, Cape Verde and Kazakhstan	Co-sponsor of the Resolution	Adopted by consensus
	A/RES/74/122 Implementation of the outcome of the World Summit for Social Development and of the 24th special session of the General Assembly	Palestine	Voted in favour	186 in favour, 2 against, no abstention
	A/RES/74/123 Persons with albinism	Malawi and Tanzania	Co-sponsor of the Resolution	Adopted by consensus
	A/RES/74/125 Follow-up to the Second World Assembly on Ageing	Palestine	Co-sponsor of the Resolution	Adopted by consensus
Advancement of women	A/RES/74/126 Improvement of the situation of women and girls in rural areas	Mongolia	Co-sponsor of the Resolution	Adopted by consensus

Subject	Resolution	Main sponsor of the Resolution	Information regarding Italy	Outcome of the Plenary Session
Report of the United Nations High	A/RES/74/130 Office of the United Nations High Commissioner for Refugees	Denmark	Co-sponsor of the Resolution Voted in favour	179 in favour, 2 against, 5 abstentions
Commissioner for Refugees, questions relating to refugees, returnees and displaced persons and humanitarian questions	A/RES/74/131 Assistance to refugees, returnees and displaced persons in Africa	Kenya	Co-sponsor of the Resolution	Adopted by consensus
Report of the Human Rights Council	A/RES/73/132 Report of the Human Rights Council	Lesotho	Abstention	120 in favour, 4 against, 59 abstentions
Promotion and protection of children's rights	A/RES/74/133 Rights of the child	Finland and Uruguay	Co-sponsor of the Resolution	Adopted by consensus
Elimination of racism, racial discrimination, xenophobia and related intolerance	A/RES/74/136 Combating glorification of Nazism, neo-Nazism and other practices that contribute to fuelling contemporary forms of racism, racial discrimination, xenophobia and related intolerance	Russian Federation	Abstention	133 in favour, 2 against, 52 abstentions

	A/RES/74/137 A global call for concrete action for the elimination of racism, racial discrimination, xenophobia and related intolerance and the comprehensive implementation of and follow-up to the Durban Declaration and Programme of Action	Palestine	Abstention	135 in favour, 9 against, 43 abstentions
The right to self-determination	A/RES/74/138 Use of mercenaries as a means of violating human rights and impeding the exercise of the right of peoples to self-determination	Cuba	Voted against	130 in favour, 52 against, 7 abstentions
	A/RES/74/139 The right of the Palestinian people to self-determination	Egypt	Co-sponsor of the Resolution Voted in favour	167 in favour, 5 against, 11 abstentions
Promotion and protection of human rights	A/RES/74/141 The human rights to safe drinking water and sanitation	Germany and Spain	Co-sponsor of the Resolution	Adopted by consensus
	A/RES/74/142 International Equal Pay Day	Australia, Canada, Germany, Iceland, New Zealand, Panama, South Africa and Switzerland	Co-sponsor of the Resolution	Adopted by consensus

Subject	Resolution	Main sponsor of the Resolution	Information regarding Italy	Outcome of the Plenary Session
Implementation of human rights instruments	A/RES/74/143 Torture and other cruel, inhuman or degrading treatment or punishment	Denmark	Co-sponsor of the Resolution	Adopted by consensus
	A/RES/74/144 Implementation of the Convention on the Rights of Persons with Disabilities and the Optional Protocol thereto: accessibility	Mexico and New Zealand	Co-sponsor of the Resolution	Adopted by consensus
Human rights questions,	A/RES/74/145 Freedom of religion or belief	Finland	Co-sponsor of the Resolution	Adopted by consensus
including alternative approaches to improve enjoyment of human rights and fundamental freedoms	A/RES/74/146 Implementing the Declaration on the Right and Responsibility of Individuals, Groups and Organs of Society to Promote and Protect Universally Recognised Human Rights and Fundamental Freedoms through providing a safe and enabling environment for human rights defenders and ensuring their protection	Norway	Co-sponsor of the Resolution	Adopted by consensus

	A/RES/74/147 Terrorism and human rights	Egypt and Mexico	Co-sponsor of the Resolution	Adopted by consensus
	A/RES/74/149 The right to food	Cuba	Co-sponsor of the Resolution	188 in favour, 2 against, no abstention
	A/RES/74/150 Promotion of a democratic and equitable international order	Cuba	Voted against	128 in favour, 53 against, 8 abstentions
	A/RES/74/152 The right to development	Cuba	Abstention	138 in favour, 23 against, 26 abstentions
	A/RES/74/154 Human rights and unilateral coercive measures	Cuba	Voted against	135 in favour, 55 against, no abstention
	A/RES/74/155 Promotion of equitable geographical distribution in the membership of the human rights treaty bodies	Cuba	Voted against	134 in favour, 52 against, 1 abstention
	A/RES/74/156 National human rights institutions	Germany	Co-sponsor of the Resolution	Adopted by consensus
	A/RES/74/157 The safety of journalists and the issue of impunity	Argentina, Austria, Costa Rica, France, Greece and Tunisia	Co-sponsor of the Resolution	Adopted by consensus

Subject	Resolution	Main sponsor of the Resolution	Information regarding Italy	Outcome of the Plenary Session
	A/RES/74/158 Strengthening the role of the United Nations in enhancing periodic and genuine elections and the promotion of democratisation	United States of America	Co-sponsor of the Resolution	Adopted by consensus
	A/RES/74/159 Human rights and cultural diversity	Cuba	Voted against	136 in favour, 55 against, no abstention
	A/RES/74/160 Protection of and assistance to internally displaced persons	Norway	Co-sponsor of the Resolution	Adopted by consensus
	A/RES/74/161 International Convention for the Protection of All Persons from Enforced Disappearance	Argentina, France and Morocco	Co-sponsor of the Resolution	Adopted by consensus
	A/RES/74/162 Subregional Centre for Human Rights and Democracy in Central Africa	Cameroon	Co-sponsor of the Resolution	Adopted by consensus
	A/RES/74/163 United Nations Human Rights Training and Documentation Centre for South-West Asia and the Arab Region	Qatar	Voted in favour	138 in favour, 1 against, 2 abstentions

	A/RES/74/165 Effective promotion of the Declaration on the Rights of Persons Belonging to National or Ethnic, Religious and Linguistic Minorities	Austria	Co-sponsor of the Resolution	Adopted by consensus
Human rights Situations and reports of Special Rapporteurs and Representatives	A/RES/74/166 Situation of human rights in the Democratic People's Republic of Korea	Finland	Co-sponsor of the Resolution	Adopted by consensus
	A/RES/74/167 Situation of human rights in the Islamic Republic of Iran	Canada	Co-sponsor of the Resolution Voted in favour	81 in favour, 30 against, 70 abstentions
	A/RES/74/168 Situation of human rights in the Autonomous Republic of Crimea and the city of Sevastopol, Ukraine	Ukraine	Co-sponsor of the Resolution Voted in favour	65 in favour, 23 against, 83 abstentions
	A/RES/74/246 Situation of human rights of Rohingya Muslims and other minorities in Myanmar	Finland and the United Arab Emirates	Co-sponsor of the Resolution Voted in favour	134 in favour, 9 against, 28 abstentions
	A/RES/74/169 Situation of human rights in the Syrian Arab Republic	Saudi Arabia and United States of America	Co-sponsor of the Resolution Voted in favour	106 in favour, 15 against, 57 abstentions

Subject	Resolution	Main sponsor of the Resolution	Information regarding Italy	Outcome of the Plenary Session
Crime prevention and Criminal Justice	A/RES/74/176 Improving the coordination of efforts against trafficking in persons	Belarus	Co-sponsor of the Resolution	Adopted by consensus
Countering the use of information and communications technologies for criminal purposes	A/RES/74/247 Countering the use of information and communications technologies for criminal purposes	Russian Federation	Voted against	79 in favour, 60 against, 33 abstentions
International Drug Control	A/RES/74/178 International cooperation to address and counter the world drug problem	Mexico	Co-sponsor of the Resolution	Adopted by consensus

Source: United Nations, General Assembly

II Human Rights Council

The Human Rights Council is the subsidiary body of the General Assembly responsible for addressing human rights violations, promoting worldwide respect of all human rights and fundamental freedoms for all, without distinction of any kind.

Established in 2006 under General Assembly resolution 60/251, the Council is an inter-governmental body made up of 47 United Nations Member States elected by the General Assembly for an initial period of three years, extendable for not more than two consecutive terms. It meets in Geneva, in three ordinary sessions per year, for an overall period of at least ten working weeks. Furthermore, although it is a body of Government representatives, the Council is open to the contributions of nongovernmental organisations which enjoy advisory status with the ECOSOC, which may participate in the meetings and submit written documents.

The Council has established several different "mechanisms" for monitoring human rights (resolution A/HRC/RES/5/1 of June 2007), including: the UPR, the Special Procedures (which include mandates by Country and thematic mandates), the Advisory Committee and a Complaints Procedure.

In 2019, the Council held:

- three ordinary sessions: 40th (25 February-22 March); 41st (24 June-12 July); 42nd (9–27 September);
- no special sessions;
- three UPR sessions: 32nd (21 January-1 February); 33rd (6–17 May), 34th (4–15 November).

In 2019, Italy was represented at the Human Rights Council by: Amb. Gian Lorenzo Cornado, Permanent Representative of Italy to the International Organisations in Geneva, First Counsellor Daniela d'Orlandi and First Secretary Massimo Baldassarre

A *Italy's Behaviour at the Human Rights Council in 2018*

In 2019, Italy participated in the ordinary sessions of the Human Rights Council as a Member State (hence, with the right to vote for the three-year period 2019–2021).

Over the course of 2019, the Human Rights Council adopted 92 resolutions (7 more than 2018): 29 resolutions during the 40th session; 26 during the 41st session; 37 during the 42nd session. Of these resolutions, 57 were approved with the consensus of all Member States, whereas a majority vote by Council members was necessary for 35 of them showing a slightly higher level of disagreement than in the previous year, when majority voting was required for 36 % of the resolutions adopted.

The following paragraph analyses Italy's behaviour at the Human Rights Council in 2019, with a particular focus on two issues: Italy's diplomatic efforts in the negotiation and presentation of resolutions and its voting behaviour.

On this first issue, 63 % of the resolutions adopted by the Council were negotiated with direct participation (sponsoring) or diplomatic support (co-sponsoring) from Italy. Of the 92 resolutions adopted, Italy sponsored 12 (compared to 11 in 2018) and co-sponsored 46 (same as 2018).

Half of the 12 resolutions sponsored by Italy are thematic and refer to children's rights (SDGs 2.2, 3.2, 4, 5, 8.7, 16.2), the right to freedom of religion and belief, human rights education and training (Goal 4: Ensure inclusive and equitable quality education and promote lifelong learning opportunities for all). The other six resolutions concern the situation of human rights in the Democratic Republic of Korea, Myanmar, Syria and Belarus.

Concerning Italy's voting behaviour, the country "won" in 21 of the 35 votes that took place; 11 resolutions were adopted by the majority vote of the Council despite Italy voting against them; Italy abstained in 3 votes. Italy supported resolutions that had been proposed by States from all the regional groups present in the Council: out of 21 favourable votes, 8 were resolutions presented by the Western Europe Group (United Kingdom, Finland, Sweden, The Netherlands, Iceland), 3 by the Eastern Europe Group (Romania, Georgia and Ukraine), 3 by the Asian group (Pakistan), 3 by the Latin America group (Argentina, Uruguay, Peru), and 4 votes were expressed in favour of resolutions presented by countries from two or more regional groups.

The votes against were on resolutions presented by Cuba (6 out of 11), Venezuela (3), Pakistan (1) and China (1). Finally, Italy's abstentions were distributed between the Asian group (2: Pakistan) and the African group (1: Angola).

The following table summarises the data on both dimensions considered above – in particular, it demonstrates that of resolutions sponsored and co-sponsored by Italy, 75 % were adopted by consensus by the Council, while the remaining 25 % were adopted by majority vote.

Synopsis of Italy's behaviour at the Human Rights Council in 2019

	Adopted by consensus by the Council	**Adopted by majority vote by the Council**			**Total**
		Italy: Vote in favour	*Italy: Voted against*	*Italy: Abstention*	
Resolutions sponsored by Italy	7	5	-	-	12
Resolutions co-sponsored by Italy	36	10	-	-	46
Resolutions not sponsored by Italy	14	6	11	3	34
Total	57	21	11	3	92

Adoption of HRC resolutions and Italy's behaviour (2019)

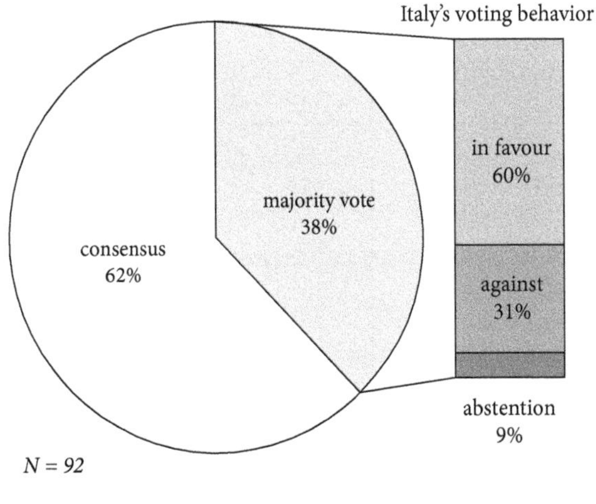

Resolutions sponsored and co-sponsored by Italy in 2019

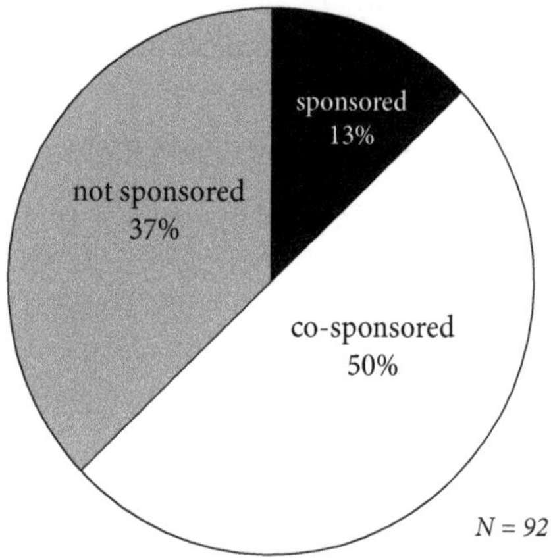

Human Rights Council: resolutions sponsored by Italy in 2019

Resolution	**Other sponsors of the resolution**	**Outcome of the voting process**
A/HRC/RES/40/10 Freedom of religion or belief	Romania et al.	Adopted by consensus
A/HRC/RES/40/14 Rights of the child: empowering children with disabilities for the enjoyment of their human rights, including through inclusive education	Uruguay and Romania	Adopted by consensus
A/HRC/RES/40/15 Thirtieth anniversary of the Convention on the Rights of the Child	Uruguay and Romania	Adopted by consensus
A/HRC/RES/40/17 The human rights situation in the Syrian Arab Republic	United Kingdom et al.	28 in favour, 5 against, 14 abstentions
A/HRC/RES/40/20 Situation of human rights in the Democratic People's Republic of Korea	Romania et al.	Adopted by consensus

Human Rights Council: resolutions sponsored by Italy in 2019

A/HRC/RES/40/29 Situation of human rights in Myanmar	Romania et al.	37 in favour, 3 against, 7 abstentions
A/HRC/RES/41/8 Consequences of child, early and forced marriage	The Netherlands et al.	Adopted by consensus
A/HRC/RES/41/13 Youth and human rights	El Salvador et al.	Adopted by consensus
A/HRC/RES/41/22 Situation of human rights in Belarus	Finland et al.	20 in favour, 6 against, 21 abstentions
A/HRC/RES/41/23 The human rights situation in the Syrian Arab Republic	United Kingdom et al.	26 in favour, 7 against, 14 abstentions
A/HRC/RES/42/7 World Programme for Human Rights Education: adoption of the plan of action for the fourth phase	Slovenia et al.	Adopted by consensus
A/HRC/RES/42/27 The human rights situation in the Syrian Arab Republic	United Kingdom, Qatar et al.	27 in favour, 6 against, 13 abstentions

Source: United Nations, Human Rights Council

Human Rights Council: resolutions co-sponsored by Italy in 2019

Resolution	**Sponsors of the resolution**	**Outcome of the voting process**
40th (25 February-22 March)		
A/HRC/RES/40/1 Promoting reconciliation, accountability and human rights in Sri Lanka	United Kingdom	Adopted by consensus
A/HRC/RES/40/2 Promotion and protection of human rights in Nicaragua	Argentina	23 in favour, 3 against, 21 abstentions

Human Rights Council: resolutions co-sponsored by Italy in 2019

A/HRC/RES/40/6 Promotion of the enjoyment of the cultural rights of everyone and respect for cultural diversity	Cuba	Adopted by consensus
A/HRC/RES/40/7 The right to food	Cuba	Adopted by consensus
A/HRC/RES/40/9 Human rights, democracy and the rule of law	Romania	Adopted by consensus
A/HRC/RES/40/11 Recognising the contribution of environmental human rights defenders to the enjoyment of human rights, environmental protection and sustainable development	Norway	Adopted by consensus
A/HRC/RES/40/16 Mandate of the Special Rapporteur on the promotion and protection of human rights and fundamental freedoms while countering terrorism	Mexico	Adopted by consensus
A/HRC/RES/40/18 Situation of human rights in the Islamic Republic of Iran	Sweden	22 in favour, 7 against, 18 abstentions
A/HRC/RES/40/19 Situation of human rights in the South Sudan	United Kingdom	Adopted by consensus
A/HRC/RES/40/26 Technical assistance and capacity-building for Mali in the field of human rights	Angola	Adopted by consensus
A/HRC/RES/40/27 Technical assistance and capacity-building to improve human rights in Libya	Angola	Adopted by consensus
A/HRC/RES/40/28 Cooperation with Georgia	Georgia	19 in favour, 3 against, 25 abstentions

Human Rights Council: resolutions co-sponsored by Italy in 2019

41st (24 June-12 July)		
A/HRC/RES/41/1 Situation of human rights in Eritrea	The Netherlands	21 in favour, 13 against, 13 abstentions
A/HRC/RES/41/2 Promotion and protection of human rights in the Philippines	Iceland	18 in favour, 14 against, 15 abstentions
A/HRC/RES/41/9 The negative impact of corruption on the enjoyment of human rights	Morocco	Adopted by consensus
A/HRC/RES/41/10 Access to medicines and vaccines in the context of the right of everyone to the enjoyment of the highest attainable standard of physical and mental health	Brazil	Adopted by consensus
A/HRC/RES/41/11 New and emerging digital technologies and human rights	Republic of Korea	Adopted by consensus
A/HRC/RES/41/12 The rights to freedom of peaceful assembly and of association	Czech Republic	Adopted by consensus
A/HRC/RES/41/14 Equal pay	South Africa and Iceland	Adopted by consensus
A/HRC/RES/41/15 Mandate of the Special Rapporteur on the human rights of internally displaced persons	Austria, Honduras and Uganda	Adopted by consensus
A/HRC/RES/41/16 The right to education: follow-up to Human Rights Council resolution 8/4	Portugal	Adopted by consensus
A/HRC/RES/41/17 Accelerating efforts to eliminate all forms of violence against women and girls: preventing and responding to violence against women and girls in the world of work	Canada	Adopted by consensus

Human Rights Council: resolutions co-sponsored by Italy in 2019

A/HRC/RES/41/18 Mandate of the Independent Expert on protection against violence and discrimination based on sexual orientation and gender identity	Argentina and Uruguay	27 in favour, 12 against, 7 abstentions
A/HRC/RES/41/25 Cooperation with and assistance to Ukraine in the field of human rights	Ukraine	20 in favour, 5 against, 22 abstentions
A/HRC/RES/41/26 Renewal of the mandate of the team of international experts on the situation in Kasai	Angola	Adopted by consensus
42nd (9–27 September)		
A/HRC/RES/42/2 Human rights situation in Yemen	The Netherlands	22 in favour, 12 against, 11 abstentions
A/HRC/RES/42/5 The human rights to safe drinking water and sanitation	Spain and Germany	Adopted by consensus
A/HRC/RES/42/6 The role of prevention in the promotion and protection of human rights	Ukraine and Uruguay	Adopted by consensus
A/HRC/RES/42/10 Special Rapporteur on contemporary forms of slavery, including its causes and consequences	United Kingdom and Australia	Adopted by consensus
A/HRC/RES/42/11 Human rights in the administration of justice, including juvenile justice	Austria	Adopted by consensus
A/HRC/RES/42/12 The human rights of older persons	Argentina	Adopted by consensus
A/HRC/RES/42/13 The right to social security	South Africa	Adopted by consensus
A/HRC/RES/42/14 Marking the 25th anniversary of the Beijing Declaration and Platform for Action	China and France	Adopted by consensus

Human Rights Council: resolutions co-sponsored by Italy in 2019

A/HRC/RES/42/15 The right to privacy in the digital age	Brazil and Germany	Adopted by consensus
A/HRC/RES/42/16 The right of everyone to the enjoyment of the highest attainable standard of physical and mental health	Brazil	Adopted by consensus
A/HRC/RES/42/17 Human rights and transitional justice	Switzerland	Adopted by consensus
A/HRC/RES/42/19 Human rights and indigenous peoples	Mexico and Guatemala	Adopted by consensus
A/HRC/RES/42/22 Arbitrary detention	France	Adopted by consensus
A/HRC/RES/42/24 The question of the death penalty	Benin and Republic of Moldova	26 in favour, 14 against, 6 abstentions
A/HRC/RES/42/28 Cooperation with the United Nations, its representatives and mechanisms in the field of human rights	Ghana e Ireland	36 in favour, 0 against, 11 abstentions
A/HRC/RES/42/30 Promoting international cooperation to support national mechanisms for implementation, reporting and follow-up	Paraguay and Brazil	Adopted by consensus
A/HRC/RES/42/32 Enhancement of technical cooperation and capacity-building in the field of human rights	Thailand et al.	Adopted by consensus
A/HRC/RES/42/33 Assistance to Somalia in the field of human rights	United Kingdom and Somalia	Adopted by consensus
A/HRC/RES/42/34 Technical assistance and capacity-building in the field of human rights in the Democratic Republic of the Congo	Angola	Adopted by consensus

Human Rights Council: resolutions co-sponsored by Italy in 2019

A/HRC/RES/42/35 Technical assistance and capacity-building to further improve human rights in the Sudan	Angola	Adopted by consensus
A/HRC/RES/42/36 Technical assistance and capacity-building in the field of human rights in the Central African Republic	Angola	Adopted by consensus

Source: United Nations, Human Rights Council

Human Rights Council: resolutions not sponsored by Italy in 2019

Resolution	**Sponsors of the resolution**	**Outcome of the voting process**	**Information related to Italy**
40th (25 February-22 March)			
A/HRC/RES/40/3 The negative impact of unilateral coercive measures on the enjoyment of human rights	Venezuela	27 in favour, 15 against, 7 abstentions	Voted against
A/HRC/RES/40/4 The negative impact of the non-repatriation of funds of illicit origin to the countries of origin on the enjoyment of human rights, and the importance of improving international cooperation	Angola	31 in favour, 2 against, 14 abstentions	Abstention
A/HRC/RES/40/5 Elimination of discrimination against women and girls in sport	South Africa	Adopted by consensus	-
A/HRC/RES/40/8 The effects of foreign debt and other related international financial obligations of States on the full enjoyment of all human rights, particularly economic, social and cultural rights	Cuba	27 in favour, 14 against, 6 abstentions	Voted against

Human Rights Council: resolutions not sponsored by Italy in 2019

A/HRC/RES/40/12 Question of the realisation in all countries of economic, social and cultural rights	Portugal	Adopted by consensus	-
A/HRC/RES/40/13 Ensuring accountability and justice for all violations of international law in the Occupied Palestinian Territory, including East Jerusalem	Pakistan	23 in favour, 8 against, 15 abstentions	Abstention
A/HRC/RES/40/21 Human rights in the occupied Syrian Golan	Pakistan	26 in favour, 16 against, 5 abstentions	Voted against
A/HRC/RES/40/22 Right of the Palestinian people to self-determination	Pakistan	41 in favour, 3 against, 2 abstentions	Voted in favour
A/HRC/RES/40/23 Human rights situation in the Occupied Palestinian Territory, including East Jerusalem	Pakistan	39 in favour, 3 against, 5 abstentions	Voted in favour
A/HRC/RES/40/24 Israeli settlements in the Occupied Palestinian Territory, including East Jerusalem, and in the occupied Syrian Golan	Pakistan	32 in favour, 5 against, 10 abstentions	Voted in favour
A/HRC/RES/40/25 Combating intolerance, negative stereotyping and stigmatisation of, and discrimination, incitement to violence and violence against, persons based on religion or belief	Pakistan	Adopted by consensus	-
41st (24 June-12 July)			
A/HRC/RES/41/3 Enhancement of international cooperation in the field of human rights	Venezuela	28 in favour, 14 against, 5 abstentions	Voted against

Human Rights Council: resolutions not sponsored by Italy in 2019

A/HRC/RES/41/4 Promotion of the right to peace	Cuba	32 in favour, 13 against, 2 abstentions	Voted against
A/HRC/RES/41/5 Human rights and international solidarity	Cuba	32 in favour, 14 against, 1 abstention	Voted against
A/HRC/RES/41/6 Elimination of all forms of discrimination against women and girls	Colombia and Mexico	Adopted by consensus	-
A/HRC/RES/41/7 The human rights of migrants	Mexico	Adopted by consensus	-
A/HRC/RES/41/19 The contribution of development to the enjoyment of all human rights	China	33 in favour, 13 against, no abstention	Voted against
A/HRC/RES/41/20 Impact of arms transfers on human rights	Ecuador and Peru	Adopted by consensus	-
A/HRC/RES/41/21 Human rights and climate change	Bangladesh, The Philippines and Vietnam	Adopted by consensus	-
A/HRC/RES/41/24 The Social Forum	Cuba	Adopted by consensus	-
42nd (9–27 September)			
A/HRC/RES/42/1 Composition of staff of the Office of the United Nations High Commissioner for Human Rights	Cuba	30 in favour, 13 against, 4 abstentions	Voted against
A/HRC/RES/42/3 Situation of human rights of Rohingya Muslims and other minorities in Myanmar	Pakistan and Finland	32 in favour, 2 against, 7 abstentions	Voted in favour

Human Rights Council: resolutions not sponsored by Italy in 2019

A/HRC/RES/42/4 Strengthening cooperation and technical assistance in the field of human rights in the Bolivarian Republic of Venezuela	Pakistan	18 in favour, 6 against, 23 abstentions	Abstention
A/HRC/RES/42/8 Promotion of a democratic and equitable international order	Cuba	25 in favour, 14 against, 8 abstentions	Voted against
A/HRC/RES/42/9 The use of mercenaries as a means of violating human rights and impeding the exercise of the right of peoples to self-determination	Cuba	29 in favour, 14 against, 4 abstentions	Voted against
A/HRC/RES/42/18 Terrorism and human rights	Egypt and Mexico	Adopted by consensus	-
A/HRC/RES/42/20 Human rights and indigenous peoples: mandate of the Special Rapporteur on the rights of indigenous peoples	Mexico and Guatemala	Adopted by consensus	-
A/HRC/RES/42/21 Protection of the rights of workers exposed to hazardous substances and wastes	Angola	Adopted by consensus	-
A/HRC/RES/42/23 The right to development	Venezuela	27 in favour, 13 against, 7 abstentions	Voted against
A/HRC/RES/42/25 Situation of human rights in the Bolivarian Republic of Venezuela	Peru	19 in favour, 7 against, 21 abstentions	Voted in favour
A/HRC/RES/42/26 Situation of human rights in Burundi	Finland	23 in favour, 11 against, 13 abstentions	Voted in favour

Human Rights Council: resolutions not sponsored by Italy in 2019

A/HRC/RES/42/29 From rhetoric to reality: a global call for concrete action against racism, racial discrimination, xenophobia and related intolerance	Angola	Adopted by consensus	-
A/HRC/RES/42/31 Technical assistance and capacity-building for Yemen in the field of human rights	Iraq	Adopted by consensus	-
A/HRC/RES/42/37 Advisory services and technical assistance for Cambodia	Japan	Adopted by consensus	-

Source: United Nations, Human Rights Council

B Universal Periodic Review

Italy was subjected to its first UPR in 2010 (7th session): on that occasion, 92 recommendations were addressed to Italy, of which it fully accepted (supported) 78, partially rejected (noted) 2 and fully rejected 12. Detailed information on the outcome of the first UPR for Italy is demonstrated in the 2011 edition of the *Italian Yearbook of Human Rights* (p. 169–173).

In 2014, Italy was subjected to its second UPR cycle (20th session), during which, 186 recommendations were addressed to Italy, of which it fully supported 176 and noted 12. Detailed information on the outcome of the second Universal Periodic Review for Italy is displayed in the 2015 edition of the *Italian Yearbook of Human Rights* (p. 169–173).

On 4 November 2019, Italy was subjected to its third UPR cycle (34th session, 4–15 November 2019) alongside other 13 countries: Angola, Egypt, Madagascar, Gambia, Fiji, Iran, Iraq, Kazakhstan, Bolivia, El Salvador, San Marino, Slovenia, and Bosnia-Herzegovina. During the review, supported by a troika made up of South Africa, Australia, and Slovakia, Italy was represented by a delegation of high-level officials (31 ministers, Members of Parliament and diplomats) and led by the Undersecretary of State for Foreign Affairs Manlio Di Stefano.

Documents relating to Italy's Third Cycle of the UPR

National Report of Italy	A/HRC/WG.6/34/ITA/1
Report of United Nations information on Italy	A/HRC/WG.6/34/ITA/2
Summary of stakeholders' submissions on Italy (NGO and Council of Europe)	A/HRC/WG.6/34/ITA/3
Final Report of Recommendations on Italy	A/HRC/43/4
Views on conclusions and/or recommendations	A/HRC/43/4/Add.1
Date of UPR at the Working Group of the Human Rights Council	4 November 2019, during the 34th session of the UPR (4–15 November 2019)

In his presentation, Undersecretary of State Di Stefano described actions that Italy has undertaken to promote human rights at the national and international level. In particular, the report notes that Italy had implemented 153 of the 176 recommendations it had accepted during the second UPR cycle, while the remaining recommendations are currently being implemented and concern the establishment of a National Human Rights Institution.

During the following interactive debate, the Italian delegation had to respond to questions, concerns and recommendations by representatives of 121 UN Member States.

The necessary information for this debate was provided both by the Italian Government's report and by two summary documents prepared by the UN Office of the High Commissioner of Human Rights: the summary of all recommendations of Treaty Bodies and of UN Special Rapporteurs; and the additional information provided by other stakeholders, in this case non-governmental organisations, the Council of Europe, FRA and the OSCE Office for Democratic Institutions and Human Rights. Furthermore, Italy had to consider the requests for clarifications sent to the Government before the session by the United Kingdom, Germany, Belgium, Portugal, Slovenia, Sweden, United States of America and Uruguay.

At the end of this first phase, Italy received 306 recommendations on possible measures (legal, political and institutional) to adopt to strengthen the national system of human rights promotion and protection (doc. A/HRC/43/4). Just over half of the recommendations concern four thematic areas, in order: racial discrimination (15.4 %), national human rights institutions (15 %), the rights of migrants, refugees and asylum seekers (14.1 %), and women's rights, gender equality and violence against women (10.5 %).

A diachronic analysis of the recommendations received by Italy in its three UPR cycles (2010, 2014 and 2019), disaggregated by thematic areas allows for the identification of trends and main critical issues (structural and/or contingent) of the national human rights protection system, as perceived by its "peers" within the international community.

The more evident statistic to emerge is that the most common recommendations (in terms of absolute numbers and percentage of the total) in all three UPR cycles for Italy concern racial discrimination and the rights of migrants. It is clear that for the international community, these issues represent the main structural critical issue for Italy; the State is called upon to take further and more decisive measures to combat the growing number of cases of hate speech in the public sector, discrimination at an administrative level, violations of the principle of non-refoulement, as well as improving conditions in migrant reception centres.

On top of these two issues, there were recommendations to create a national human rights institution, in line with the Paris Principles. The lack of this institution has caused more and more noise in the international community: the number of recommendations has steadily increased over the past few years, going from 16 in 2010 (10 % of the total number of recommendations) to 46 in 2019 (15 %).

Another two issues are gradually getting more attention, with a steady rise in the number of recommendations: they are respect for women's rights (particularly in reference to gender equality in the workplace and combatting all forms of violence), passing from 2 in 2010 (1.3 % of the total) to 32 in 2019 (10.5 %); and promoting economic and social rights (in the form of welfare state protection), passing from 2 in 2010 to 16 in 2019.

In addition to growing and constant concern, new issues have emerged over time, related to specific circumstances. For example, in 2019, some recommendations came up about the need for Italy to more effectively protect human rights defenders (following attempts at criminalising the work of NGOs carrying out search and rescue missions in the Mediterranean) and to combat modern slavery, above all in the agricultural sector.

Number of recommendations per thematic area received by Italy in cycles 1–3 of the UPR

	Thematic area	**III Cycle (November 2019)**		**II Cycle (October 2014)**		**I Cycle (February 2010)**	
		No.	*%*	*No.*	*%*	*No.*	*%*
1	Racial discrimination	47	*15.4*	33	*17.6*	25	*15.9*
2	National Human Rights Institution (NHRI)	46	*15.0*	25	*13.4*	16	*10.2*
3	Migrants and Asylum Seekers	43	*14.1*	20	*10.7*	24	*15.3*
4	Women's Rights, Gender Equality and Violence against Women	32	*10.5*	18	*9.6*	2	*1.3*
5	Economic and Social Rights	16	*5.2*	5	*2.7*	2	*1.3*
6	Trafficking	15	*4.9*	8	*4.3*	9	*5.7*
7	Torture and conditions of detention	15	*4.9*	6	*3.2*	5	*3.2*
8	Sexual Orientation and Gender Identity	14	*4.6*	5	*2.7*	4	*2.5*
9	Minorities	13	*4.2*	16	*8.6*	19	*12.1*
10	International Instruments	12	*3.9*	24	*12.8*	18	*11.5*
11	Children's Rights	11	*3.6*	9	*4.8*	10	*6.4*
12	Persons with disabilities	11	*3.6*	3	*1.6*	0	*0.0*
13	Right to Education and Human rights education	8	*2.6*	1	*0.5*	4	*2.5*
14	Justice and Civil Rights	6	*2.0*	3	*1.6*	4	*2.5*
15	Other	4	*1.3*	2	*1.1*	1	*0.6*
16	Human Rights Defenders	3	*1.0*	0	*0.0*	0	*0.0*
17	Development Cooperation	2	*0.7*	4	*2.1*	2	*1.3*
18	Freedom of expression and right to information	2	*0.7*	3	*1.6*	7	*4.5*

Number of recommendations per thematic area received by Italy in cycles 1–3 of the UPR

19	Contemporary Forms of Slavery	2	*0.7*	0	*0.0*	0	*0.0*
20	Arms Trade	2	*0.7*	0	*0.0*	0	*0.0*
21	Cooperation with UN (UPR, Treaty Bodies…)	1	*0.3*	2	*1.1*	2	*1.3*
22	Freedom of Religion	1	*0.3*	0	*0.0*	3	*1.9*
	TOTAL	306	*100*	187	*100.0*	157	*100.0*

Italy fully accepted 292 of the 306 recommendations made (around 95 % of the total: see A/HRC/43/4/Add.1).

Recommendations Nos. 2 and 6 ("Ratify the International Convention on the Protection of the Rights of All Migrant Workers and Members of Their Families, improve the protection of migrants, asylum seekers and refugees, and fully align immigration and asylum policies with international and European policies", Honduras and Djibouti) were partially accepted. The Government claims that, even whilst not ratifying the Convention, the current Italian legal system already guarantees the rights of both regular and irregular migrants.

However, Italy rejected 11 recommendations (compared to 9 in the second cycle and 12 in the first).

- Recommendations 1 and 276: *Ratify the International Convention on the Protection of the Rights of All Migrant Workers and Members of Their Families* (this recommendation had already been rejected in the first two UPR cycles). The Government reiterates that, in line with the traditional common position of the European Union, EU Member States will not ratify the Convention.
- Recommendation 7: Sign and ratify the Treaty on the Prohibition of Nuclear Weapons, and integrate a human rights impact assessment into its arms export control mechanisms (Ecuador). While Italy shares the goal of achieving a world free from nuclear weapons, the Government believes that Italy's approach is based on article VI of the Treaty on the Prohibition of Nuclear Weapons and on the idea that this objective can only be reached gradually, with the support of all relevant stakeholders and through a series of small, concrete steps; however, some of the provisions of the Treaty on the Prohibition of Nuclear Weapons make the Government doubt the treaty's

capacity to work as an irreversible, transparent and verifiable instrument for nuclear disarmament.

- Recommendation 135: *Consider revising the framework regulating the control of firearms, given the correlation between their use and feminicides* (Peru). The data on cases of feminicides in 2019 show that firearms were used only in 18 % of cases; moreover, under current legislation, the chief of police can take more appropriate measures on firearm withdrawal when cases of domestic violence and stalking are reported.
- Recommendation 271: *Investigate all allegations of ill-treatment and excessive use of force against asylum seekers and migrants, punish all the perpetrators and ensure that law enforcement officials receive appropriate professional training* (Pakistan). The Government clarifies that the use of force by law enforcement officers is regulated by the Criminal Code and there are no exceptions to the principle of obligatory criminal action; furthermore, the Department of Public Security already pays great attention to the strengthening of training courses for all law enforcement officials.
- Recommendations 279, 281 and 302: *Implement the principles of non-refoulement and relevant minimum standards, relating to the rights of migrants and asylum seekers* (Kenya); *provide humanitarian protection for all migrants, especially for those who are not eligible for refugee status but unable to return home* (Thailand); *review Law No. 132 of 2018 on the detention of asylum seekers to align it with international refugee law and human rights law* (South Africa). According to the Government, the principle of non-refoulement is already considered by Italian law and fully respected in practice. Furthermore, migrants and asylum seekers are fully protected under national, European and international law. Finally, the Territorial Commission for International Protection is able to issue a "special protection" permit if a foreign national or stateless person has not been recognised the status of refugee or subsidiary protection but are unable to be removed from the country due to the risk persecution or torture.
- Recommendations 289 and 298: *Guarantee the individual assessment of the situation of each migrant in order to put an end to the practice of collective expulsion* (Burkina Faso and Argentina). The Italian Government reiterates that it has never carried out any collective expulsions: every single expulsion order is drawn up after an assessment of the individual situation of the person involved.
- Recommendation 291: *Endorse the Global Compact for Safe, Orderly and Regular Migration* (Colombia). After abstaining on the adoption of the Global Compact, the Government declares that it cannot accept this recommendation as there is an ongoing discussion in the Italian Parliament on the State's future adhesion to the Compact.

C Special Procedures

In 2019, the Human Rights Council did not establish any special procedures. Consequently, there were 44 thematic and 10 country mandates.

It should be noted that in 2019, Maria Grazia Giammarinaro held the position of Special Rapporteur on trafficking in persons, especially women and children.

In 2019, Italy was subject to a thematic report (Special Rapporteur on contemporary forms of slavery, including its causes and consequences) and four communications.

Report of the Special Rapporteur on contemporary forms of slavery, including its causes and consequences, Urmila Bhoola (A/c).

Although the Italian legal framework provides protection of the human rights of migrant workers (particularly law No. 199/2016, the so-called anti-*Caporalato* Law) and this protection is extended by national and provincial collective agreements, the Special Rapporteur estimates there are over 400,000 agricultural workers at risk of being exploited and around 100,000 risk inhumane and degrading conditions. The Caporalato system creates the conditions for exploitation of workers, as it leads to dependency on a middleman, not only regarding access to the labour market, but also to access of other services, such as transport, food and water. This situation gives these middlemen (who are often members of criminal organisations or illegal trade unions) considerable power and control over the workers they recruit, as many workers have no choice but to continue working in slavery-like conditions. Other forms of coersion include: physical and sexual violence, threats of violence, withholding wages and documents, threats against family member in their countries of origin in cases of refusal to continue to work illegally.

Therefore, the Special Rapporteur recommends that Italy:

- Establish local public employment centres which are tasked with matching supply and demand of workers in the agricultural sector. In this way, the intervention of intermediaries will be avoided and the transparency of recruitment processes increased;
- Ensure public transportation systems in rural areas, particularly during harvesting seasons in order to avoid dependency on intermediaries;
- Create stronger incentives for reporting labour exploitation, inter alia by increasing the protection of victims and ensuring access to complaint mecha-

nisms, to justice and to an effective remedy regardless of the workers' migration status;

- Strengthen the Labour Inspectorates by allocating additional resources in order to ensure that inspections are effective, free from corruption and by also guaranteeing the safety and security of inspectors;
- Ensure access to basic services including adequate healthcare, housing and sanitation to everyone living in the Italian territory, regardless of their migration status, in accordance with international human rights standards;
- Ratify P029 (Protocol of 2014 to the Forced Labour Convention) and the International Convention on the Protection of the Rights of All Migrant Workers and Members of Their Families;
- Ensure greater transparency in agricultural supply chains and increase participation of employers and other key stakeholders such as trade unions in the Quality Agricultural Work Network in order to convert it into a multi-stakeholder platform to ensure ethical business that is committed to human rights implementation and due diligence.

Special Procedure Visits to Italy (2002–2019)

Date	Mandate of the Special Procedures	Report
3–12 October 2018	Modern forms of slavery, including its causes and consequences	A/HRC/42/44/ADD.1
10–16 May 2017	Extrajudicial, summary and arbitrary executions	A/72/335
1–5 June 2015	People of African descent	A/HRC/33/61/Add.1
2–5 December 2014	Human rights of migrants	A/HRC/29/36/Add.2
7–9 July 2014	Arbitrary detention	A/HRC/30/36/Add.3
11–18 November 2013	Freedom of opinion and expression	A/HRC/26/30/Add.3
12–20 September 2013	Trafficking in persons	A/HRC/26/37/Add.4
30 September-8 October 2012	Human rights of migrants	A/HRC/23/46/Add.3

Special Procedure Visits to Italy (2002–2019)

15–26 January 2012	Violence against women	A/HRC/20/16/ Add.2
3– 14 November 2008	Arbitrary detention	A/HRC/10/21/ Add.5
9–13 October 2006	Contemporary forms of racism	A/HRC/4/19/ Add.4
20–29 October 2004	Freedom of opinion and expression	E/CN.4/2005/ 64/Add.1
7–18 June 2004	Human rights of migrants	E/CN.4/2005/ 85/Add.3
11–14 March 2002	the independence of judges and lawyers	E/CN.4/2002/ 72/Add.3

Communications of Special Procedures regarding Italy.

In 2019, Italy received four communications from 14 thematic Special Procedures (around a third of the total number of Special Procedures operating within the Human Rights Council in 2019).

1) 3 May: joint communication from the *Special Rapporteur on adequate housing as a component of the right to an adequate standard of living*; *Special Rapporteur on the human rights of migrants; Special Rapporteur on minority issues*; and *Special Rapporteur on contemporary forms of racism, racial discrimination, xenophobia and related intolerance* on the violent and hate-fuelled protests which took place between 5 April 2019 against 75 people with Roma origins, who had been transferred into a temporary reception centre in Torre Maura, as well as a general increase in hate speech and forced eviction of Roma minorities.

In particular, the Special Rapporteurs expressed grave concern both on the violent and racist behaviour of far-right political organisations and their apparently complete impunity, on the escalation and normalisation of hate speech (based on racism), and on incitement of hatred and discrimination in the public and political sphere coming from some political leaders, high-level functionaries and State representatives, such as the Minister of the Interior Matteo Salvini. Using and spreading racist stereotypes, moreover, aggravates the incorrect perception and pre-existing cliches on minorities, who often find themselves in vulnerable situations. This contributes to an incitement of hatred and ultimately to the use of violence against them.

Therefore, the Special Rapporteurs invite the Government to provide information on the state of the ongoing investigations into the identification and prosecution of perpetrators of hate crimes against Roma communities, set up by the legal authorities; on measures taken to prosecute perpetrators of hate speech and incitement to hatred, on measures taken to provide adequate living solutions (long and short term) for Roma minorities, and on the way in which the National Strategy for the Inclusion of Roma, Sinti and Caminanti communities is implemented, particularly concerning the right to housing.

2) 15 May: joint communication from the *Special Rapporteur on the Situation of Human Rights Defenders*; *Independent expert on human rights and international solidarity*; *Special Rapporteur on the human rights of migrants*; *Special Rapporteur on contemporary forms of racism, racial discrimination, xenophobia and related intolerance*; *Special Rapporteur on torture and other cruel, inhuman or degrading treatment or punishment*; and *Special Rapporteur on trafficking in persons, especially in women and children*, on the "Directive for the unified coordination of surveillance measures on maritime borders and to combat illegal immigration pursuant to article 11 of lgs.d. 286/1998" (ministerial circular No. 14100/141), adopted on 18 March 2019 by Interior Minister Matteo Salvini.

According to the Special Rapporteurs, in asking the maritime authorities and Italian military to block private ships carrying out search and rescue operations in international waters (particularly to the north of Libya) from entering Italian territorial waters or ports, this directive could potentially compromise the human rights of migrants, asylum seekers and victims of arbitrary detention, torture, human trafficking and other grave violations of human rights.

Furthermore, the directive's provisions would constitute a violation of the principle of non-refoulement and would represent yet another attempt to criminalise the search and rescue operations in the Mediterranean conducted by civil society organisations and to intensify the climate of hostility and xenophobia against migrants.

In light of these considerations, the Special Rapporteurs urge the Italian Government to repeal the Directive and, alongside other EU Member States, to prepare a rapid, coherent, human rights-based response to the migration flows coming from Libya, ensuring adequate search and rescue missions in the Mediterranean in order to respect the primary obligation of saving living at sea and the principle of non-refoulement, pursuant to international humanitarian law and human rights law.

3) 27 May: joint communication from the *Special Rapporteur on the right to of everyone to the enjoyment of the highest attainable standard of physical and mental health*; *Special Rapporteur on adequate housing as a component of the right to an adequate standard of living, and on the right to non-discrimination in this context; Special Rapporteur on the human rights of migrants; Special Rapporteur on minority issues*; and *Special Rapporteur on the human rights to safe drinking water and sanitation* on the forced eviction of a Roma community of around 450 people residing in Ponte Riccio, in the municipality of Giugliano (Campania), on 10 May 2019.

The way that these evictions are carried out bring up numerous concerns for their compliance with international law and standards, as well as seemingly violating not only the right to adequate housing, but also the rights to water and sanitation, to health, to education and to human dignity. It is not an isolated case, as numerous reports by civil society organisations confirm.

The Special Rapporteurs urge the Italian Government to take all necessary measures to end the alleged violations, to prevent them from reoccurring and, if the investigations find any illegal conduct, to persecute the perpetrators of those alleged violations.

4) 12 July: in a joint communication, the *Special Rapporteur on the independence of judges and lawyers*, the *Special Rapporteur on the Situation of Human Rights Defenders*, the *Independent expert on human rights and international solidarity*, the *Special Rapporteur on the human rights of migrants* and the *Special Rapporteur on violence against women, its causes and consequences* express concern for the detention of and criminal proceedings against Carola Rackete, the German captain of the search and rescue ship Sea-Watch 3 in Italy. According to the Special Rapporteurs, this is yet another attempt to repress NGO search and rescue operations. This repression puts the lives of thousands of migrants at risk crossing the Mediterranean and could have a chilling effect on defenders of migrants' rights and civil society in general.

Furthermore, the Special Rapporteurs condoned the threats against the judge who ruled on the captain's release, denouncing them as illegal. The political charges and ideologies expressed by the executive authorities against the judge, who had simply complied with consolidate international public law (that there is an obligation to rescue persons in danger at sea), constitute a grave violation of the principles of an independent judiciary and separation of powers. The obligation to respect and adhere to judgments and decisions of the legal authorities is a necessary consequence of the separation of powers.

Therefore, the Special Rapporteurs urge the Italian Authorities to immediately stop the criminalisation of search and rescue operations: such legislative measures could potentially compromise the human rights of migrants, including the victims of arbitrary detention, torture and other grave human rights violations, and directly contravene Italy's obligations on human rights regarding search and rescue operations, including the binding obligation to respect and protect the right to life.

III High Commissioner for Human Rights (OHCHR)

The Office was established by the General Assembly in December 1993 with Resolution 48/141.

> The High Commissioner has a very broad mandate which includes the prevention of violations of human rights, ensuring the respect of all human rights, coordinating all United Nations activities involving human rights and strengthening national systems for protecting human rights and the rule of law. In this context, one of the crucial strategic activities for the High Commissioner's Office is supporting the establishment and development of independent human rights commissions at the national level. In order to fulfil its mandate, the Office of the High Commissioner has consolidated its presence "on the ground", establishing 13 regional offices and 13 national offices, sending experts on integrated United Nations peace missions or dispatching independent fact-finding operations, as well as mainstreaming the human rights component in United Nations teams' activities at Country or Programme level, and in those of specialised agencies of the United Nations (such as UNDP).

In 2019, Michelle Bachelet (Chile) covered the role of High Commissioner for Human Rights.

The Office of the High Commissioner is funded one-third by the regular budget of the United Nations, approved by the General Assembly every two years; the remaining two-thirds of the budget are voluntary contributions, mostly from States and additionally from international organisations, foundations, commercial enterprises, and private citizens.

In 2019, Italy contributed to the budget of the High Commissioner's Office with funds of around $1,234,000 (around 0.0.7 % of all voluntary contributions received by the Office in 2019, ranking 22nd among donors: see graph below).

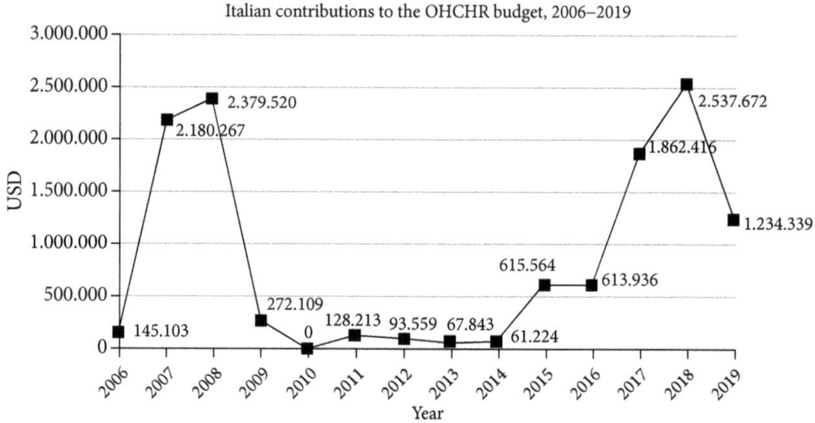

Source: OHCHR, Voluntary contributions to OHCHR in 2019

IV High Commissioner for Refugees (UNHCR)

This Office was established by the United Nations General Assembly on 14 December 1950, with resolution A/RES/428(V).

> The mandate of the Agency is to coordinate international action for the protection of refugees and the resolution of their problems all over the world. Its primary mission is to protect the rights and welfare of refugees and to ensure that all of them can exercise their right to request asylum and seek safe shelter in another State, with the option to return voluntarily to their home Country, integrate locally or to resettle into a third Country. The remit of the UNHCR also includes assistance to stateless persons.

On 1 January 2016, the General Assembly of the United Nations appointed Filippo Grandi (Italy) High Commissioner for Refugees, for a five-year mandate.

The UNHCR has had its own office in Rome since 1953. The Italian office participates in the procedures to determine refugee status in Italy and performs other duties regarding international protection, training, dissemination of information on refugees and asylum-seekers in Italy and in the various crisis areas all over the world, raising public awareness and fund-raising with Governments, companies and individual donors. Since 2006, the Italian UNHCR Office has performed as the Regional Representative for Albania, Cyprus, Greece, Malta, Portugal, San Marino, and the Holy See, besides Italy. In 2019, the UNHCR Spokesperson in Italy was Carlotta Sami.

According to the data provided by the UNHCR, in 2019, 11,500 migrants arrived in Italy by sea, almost half of the figure from 2018 (23,370): 23 % came from Tunisia, followed by Pakistan and Ivory Coast (10 % each), Algeria (9 %) and Iraq (8 %). The majority of people who arrived by sea were men (71 %), followed by minors (20 %) and women (9 %).

In a note from 6 August 2019, the UNHCR expressed its concern following the Italian Parliament's approval of the law conversion decree "*Security bis*" (law 8 August 2019, No. 77), imposing severe sanctions on vessels and individuals that conduct search and rescue operations in the Mediterranean. Under the amendments approved by Parliament, fines for private ships running the search and rescue operations and do not respect the entry ban for territorial waters have risen to up to one million euros; furthermore, these ships are immediately confiscated.

The UNHCR reiterated its concern about imposing financial penalties and other sanctions on captains of vessels that could hinder or block rescue operations by private ships, considering that European States have significantly reduced their own search and rescue operations in the Central Mediterranean. NGOs carry out an essential role in saving the lives of refugees and migrants who undertake the dangerous crossing to arrive in Europe: their work should not be criminalised or stigmatised.

Similarly, both commercial vessels and NGO ships must not be intimidated into allowing Libyan coast guards to transfer people who have been saved at sea nor allow them to disembark in Libya. In light of the extremely volatile security situation, the ongoing conflicts, the widespread human rights violations and use of arbitrary detention for people rescued or intercepted at sea or, Libya is not considered a safe port for disembarkation.

Furthermore, the UNHCR requested the States to continue discussion on creating a temporary and disembarkment mechanism for those rescued at sea, with shared responsibility among States for reception facilities and for the specific needs of migrants.

In 2019, Italy contributed to the UNHCR budget by allocating approximately $47 million (around 1.12 % of overall voluntary contributions for the office in 2019, ranking 15th among donors), showing a decrease of around $18 million compared to the previous year (see chart below).

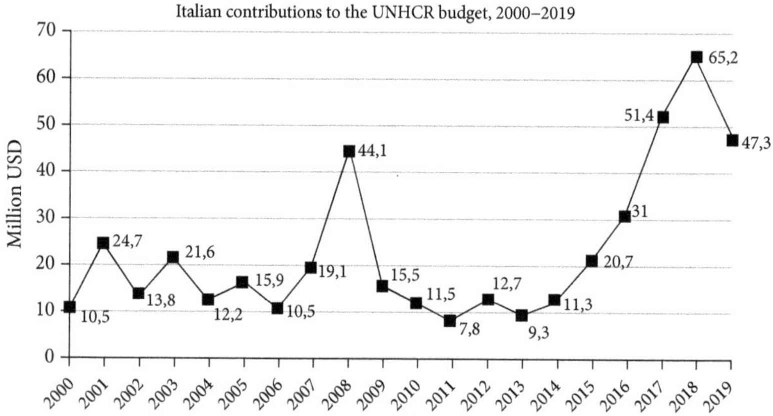

Source: UNHCR

V Human Rights Treaty Bodies

Over the years, the United Nations has established a comprehensive Human Rights Code (*International Bill of Human Rights*), whose backbone consist of the following nine conventions: International Convention for the Elimination of All Forms of Racial Discrimination (ICERD, 1965); International Covenant on Civil and Political Rights (ICCPR, 1966); International Covenant on Economic, Social and Cultural Rights (ICESCR, 1966); Convention against all Forms of Discrimination against Women (CEDAW, 1979); International Convention against Torture (CAT, 1984); Convention on the Rights of the Child (CRC, 1989); International Convention on the Protection of the Rights of All Migrant Workers and Members of Their Families (ICRMW, 1990); Convention on the Rights of Persons with Disabilities (CRPD, 2006);

and the International Convention for the Protection of All Persons from Enforced Disappearance (CPED, 2006).

Italy has ratified eight conventions and relevant optional protocols (as shown in the following table). However, it has not yet signed the ICRMW.

Convention	**Ratification law**	**Declarations/ reservations**	**Recognition of Specific Competences of the Committee**
ICERD	l. 13 October 1975, No. 654	Yes (article 4)	Individual Communications (article 14): Yes
ICESCR	l. 25 October 1977, No. 881	No	-
OP	l. 3 October 2014, No. 52	No	-
ICCPR	l. 25 October 1977, No. 881	Yes (article 15.1 and 19.3)	Individual Communications (article 41): Yes
OP-1	l. 25 October 1977, No. 881	Yes (article 5.2)	-
OP-2	l. 9 December 1994, No. 734	No	-
CEDAW	l. 14 March 1985, No. 132	Yes (general)	-
OP	ratification deposited on: 22 September 2000	No	Enquiry Procedure (articles 8 and 9): Yes
CAT	l. 3 November 1988, No. 498	No	Individual Communications (article 22): Yes Interstate Communications (article 21): Yes Enquiry Procedure (article 20): Yes

Convention	Ratification law	Declarations/ reservations	Recognition of Specific Competences of the Committee
OP	l. 9 November 2012, No. 195	No	Visits by the Subcommittee on Prevention of Torture (article 11) Yes
CRC	l. 27 May 1991, No. 176	No	-
OP-AC	l. 11 March 2002, No. 46	Declaration binding pursuant to article 3: 17 years	-
OP-SC	l. 11 March 2002, No. 46	No	-
OP-IC	l. 16 November 2015, No. 199	No	Individual Communications: Yes Enquiry Procedure (article 13): Yes
CRPD	l. 3 March 2009, No. 18	No	-
OP	l. 3 March 2009, No. 18	No	Enquiry Procedure (articles 6 and 7): Yes
CPED	l. 29 July 2015, No. 131	No	Enquiry Procedure (article 33): Yes

Legend:

OP = Optional Protocol

OP-AC = Optional Protocol to the Convention on the Rights of the Child on the Involvement of Children in Armed Conflict

OP-SC = Optional Protocol to the Convention on the Rights of the Child on the sale of children, child prostitution and child pornography

OP-IC = Optional Protocol to the Convention on the Rights of the Child on a Communications Procedure

In addition to recognising human rights in legally binding treaties, the UN has created monitoring mechanisms for each treaty. These committees or conventional bodies (Treaty Bodies) are composed of 10 to 23 independent experts selected on the basis of their probity and experience recognised in the field of human rights.

The main function of the Committees is to examine the periodic reports on the implementation of the internationally established standards in the Contracting Country. States are obliged to present these reports periodically (usually every 4 or 5 years). The Committees can carry out monitoring functions through three other mechanisms: field surveys; examination of inter-State communications; and examination of individual communications. The Committees provide their interpretation of the content of the provisions on human rights by publishing *General Comments* (for a more in-depth analysis of these functions, see *Yearbook 2011*, pp. 180–182).

Italy is monitored by eight Committees, as indicated in the following table. In 2019, Italy presented the XXI report on the International Convention on the Elimination of All Forms of Racial Discrimination; it received its concluding remarks from the Committee on the Rights of the Child and the Committee on Enforced Disappearances.

Italy's cooperation with UN Treaty Bodies

Committee	**Total reports presented**	**Last report presented**	**Latest concluding remarks**	**Reporting status**
CERD	21	February 2019	-	XXI report: presented and awaiting discussion
CESCR	5	August 2012	October 2015	VI report: due in 2020
CCPR	6	October 2015	March 2017	VII report: due in 2022
CEDAW	7	October 2015	July 2017	VIII report: due in 2021
CAT	6	October 2015	November 2017	VII report: due in 2021
CRC	6	July 2017	February 2019	VII report: due in 2023
CRPD	1	November 2012	September 2016	II, III and IV joint report: due in 2023
CED	1	April 2018	May 2019	II report: due in 2025

A Committee on Economic, Social and Cultural Rights

In 2019, the Committee held two sessions: 65th (18 February-8 March) and 66th (30 September-18 October). In the 65th session, the reports of Bulgaria, Cameroon, Estonia, Kazakhstan and Mauritius were analysed; in the 66th, those of Denmark, Ecuador, Israel, Senegal, Slovakia and Switzerland. During the year, no *General comments* were adopted.

The last periodic report of Italy was discussed by the Committee in September 2015, during its 56th session (see *Yearbook 2016*, pp. 160–162). Italy is required to present its sixth report in 2020.

On 7 March 2019, during the 65th session, the Committee released a view regarding Italy pursuant to the Optional Protocol on communication procedures (doc. E/C.12/65/D/22/2017). The authors of the communication (presented in March 2017) are a woman and a man of Italian nationality complaining of a violation of the right to sexual and reproductive health and informed consent (articles 3, 10, 12 and 15 of the Covenant), regarding Italian legislation on in vitro fertilisation.

In the light of the information provided and the particular circumstances of the case, the Committee considers that the prohibition on the withdrawal of the woman's consent to have an embryo transferred into her uterus and the restriction of both authors' access to reproductive rights constitute a violation of article 12 of the Covenant in respect of both authors, and of article 12 read in conjunction with article 3 of the Covenant. The Italian Government is under an obligation to provide the authors with an effective remedy, including by: (a) establishing the appropriate conditions to enable the authors' right to access in vitro fertilisation treatments with trust that their right to withdraw their consent to medical treatments will be respected; (b) ensuring that the woman is protected from any unwanted medical intervention and that her right to freely make decisions regarding her own body is respected; (c) awarding the woman adequate compensation for the physical, psychological and moral damages suffered; and (d) reimbursing the authors for the legal costs reasonably incurred in the processing of the present communication.

Furthermore, the Committee found that the Italian Government is obliged to prevent similar violations in the future, ensuring that its legislation and the enforcement thereof are consistent with the obligations established under the Covenant. Moreover, the State party has the obligation to:(a) Adopt appropriate legislative and/or administrative measures to guarantee the right of all women to take free decisions regarding medical interventions affecting their bodies, in particular ensuring their right to withdraw their consent to the transfer of embryos into their uterus; and (b) guarantee access to all reproductive treatments generally available and to allow all persons to withdraw their consent to the transfer of embryos for procreation, ensuring that all restrictions to access to these treatments comply with the criteria provided in article 4 of the Covenant.

B Human Rights Committee (Civil and Political Rights)

In 2019, the Committee held three sessions: 125th (4–29 March), 126th (1–26 July) and 127th (14 October-8 November). During the 125th session, the reports of Angola, Estonia, Niger and Vietnam were analysed; in the 126th, the reports of Mauritania, The Netherlands, Paraguay and Tajikistan; in the 127th, those of Belgium, Cape Verde, Czech Republic, Mexico and Senegal. During the year, no *General comments* were adopted.

> The last periodic report on Italy was discussed by the Committee in March 2017, during the 119th session (see *Yearbook 2018*, pp. 169–174). Italy is required to present its seventh report in 2022.

In 2019, the Committee adopted two decisions concerning Italy pursuant to the Optional Protocol on communication procedures:

- 26 July, 126th session (doc. CCPR/C/126/D/2570/2015). The Committee declared the communication presented by the Ukrainian citizen (subject to extradition to Ukraine in order to face criminal charges for a robbery allegedly committed in 2000) inadmissible. The complainant argued that this would violate his right to life, not to be subjected to torture and other cruel, inhuman and degrading treatment, and the right to non-refoulment (articles 7, 9 and 10 of the Covenant).

The Committee considers that the information at its disposal demonstrates that the State party took into account all the elements available, including the legal characterisation of the alleged crime and the human rights situation in the requesting country. The Committee therefore considers that, while the author disagrees with the factual conclusions of the State party's authorities and with their decision to uphold his extradition. He has not shown that the decisions of the Italian courts were arbitrary or manifestly erroneous, or amounted to a denial of justice. The author has equally not sufficiently substantiated his belief that he would suffer torture during pre-trial detention or why he would be held indefinitely in provisional detention and deprived of the right to have the lawfulness of his detention reviewed. Accordingly, the Committee considers that the communication is insufficiently substantiated for the purposes of admissibility.

- 6 November, 127th session (doc. CCPR/C/127/D/2656/2015), presented in July 2015, the authors of the communication are two Italian citizens (members of the Italian Radicals) who complained of an unreasonable restriction to the right to promote a national referendum initiative (article 25 and 2 of the Covenant). The authors submit that they encountered a number of arbitrary and unreasonable obstacles in the collection of signatures, caused by deficiencies in the system and by the actions and omissions of public authorities.

The Committee was of the view that the facts disclosed a violation by the State party of article 25 (a) read alone and in conjunction with article 2 (3) of the Covenant. The Italian State is under an obligation to provide the authors with an effective remedy. This requires it to make full reparation to individuals whose Covenant rights have been violated and is under an obligation to take all steps necessary to prevent similar violations from occurring in the future. In this connection, the Committee reiterates that the State party should review its legislation with a view to ensuring that the legislative requirements do not impose unreasonable restrictions on any of the modes of direct participation by citizens provided for in the Constitution. In particular, the State party should provide for avenues for promoters of referendum initiatives to have signatures authenticated, to collect signatures in spaces where citizens can be reached, and to ensure that the population is sufficiently informed about those processes and the possibility of taking part.

C Committee against Torture

In 2019, the Committee held three sessions: 66th (23 April-17 May), 67th (22 July-9 August) and 68th (11 November-6 December). During the 66th session, the reports of Benin, Democratic Republic of the Democratic Republic of Congo, Germany, Mexico, South Africa and the United Kingdom; in the 67th, the reports of Bangladesh, Greece, Poland and

Togo; in the 68th, those of Burkina Faso, Cyprus, Latvia, Niger, Portugal and Uzbekistan. During the year, no *General comments* were adopted.

The last periodic report on Italy was discussed by the Committee in November 2017, during the 62nd session (see. *Yearbook 2018*, pp. 175–178). Italy is required to present its seventh report in 2021.

D Committee on the Elimination of Racial Discrimination

In 2019, the Committee held three sessions: 98th (23 April-10 May), 99th (5–29 August) and 100th (25 November-13 December). During the 98th session, the reports of Andorra, Guatemala, Hungary, Lithuania and Zambia were analysed; in the 99th, the reports of the Czech Republic, El Salvador, Iceland, Mexico, Mongolia, Poland and Palestine; in the 100th, those of Cambodia, Colombia, Ireland, Israel and Uzbekistan. During the year, no *General comments* were adopted.

Italy presented its latest report in February 2019, but has not yet discussed it.

Latest report presented by Italy

Reporting round	XXI report
Date of the presentation of the Report	06/02/2019 (published 06/03/2019)
Report	CERD/C/ITA/21

The report presents the legal framework, policies and programmes adopted by Italy to implement laws contained in the Convention. In particular, this concerns the role of the UNAR and to the results of implementing *National Action Plan against Racism, Xenophobia and Intolerance* (concluded in 2017) and the *National Action Plan for interventions and measures to promote the integration of beneficiaries of international protection*, set out in 2017 by the National Coordinating Table at the Ministry of the Interior.

E Committee on the Elimination of Discrimination against Women

In 2019, the Committee held three sessions: 72nd (18 February-8 March), 73rd (1–19 July) and 74th (21 October-8 November). During the 72nd session, the reports of Angola, Antigua and Barbuda, Botswana, Colombia, Ethiopia, Myanmar, Serbia and the United Kingdom were analysed; in the 73rd the reports of Austria, Cape Verde, Ivory Coast, Democratic Republic of Congo, Guyana, Mozambique and Qatar; in the 74th, those of Andorra, Bosnia Herzegovina, Cambodia, Iraq, Kazakhstan, Lithuania and the Seychelles. During the year, no *General comments* were adopted.

The latest periodic report of Italy was discussed by the Committee in July 2017, during the 67th session (see *Yearbook 2018*, pp. 179–185). Italy is due to present its eighth report in 2021.

F Committee on the Rights of the Child

In 2019, the Committee held three sessions: 80th (14 January-1 February), 81st (13–31 May) and 82nd (9–27 September). During the 80th session, the reports of Bahrain, Belgium, Guinea, Italy, Japan and Syria were analysed; in the 81st, the reports of Botswana, Cape Verde, Ivory Coast, Malta, Singapore, Tonga; in the 82nd, those of Australia, Bosnia Herzegovina, Mozambique, Portugal and the Republic of Korea. In September 2019, *General comment* No. 24 on Children's rights in juvenile justice (doc. CRC/C/GC/24) was approved.

Latest report presented by Italy

Reporting round	V and VI joint report
Date scheduled for presentation of Report	04/04/2017
Date of the presentation of the Report	05/07/2017
Report	CRC/C/ITA/5–6
List of issues	CRC/C/ITA/Q/5–6
Concluding observations	CRC/C/ITA/CO/5–6
Date of the discussion of the Report	22–23 January 2019, during the 80th session of the Committee (14 January-1 February 2019)

During its 80th session (14 January-1 February 2019), the Committee examined the V and VI joint report of Italy, taking into account the numerous reports received from civil society organisations.

In its concluding observations, the Committee highlights the positive actions adopted by Italy, in particular: ratifying the Optional Protocol to the Convention on the Rights of the Child on a communications procedure in 2016; the International Convention for the Protection of All Persons from Enforced Disappearance in 2015; the Optional Protocol to the International Covenant on Economic, Social and Cultural Rights in 2015; the Optional Protocol to the Convention against Torture and Other Cruel, Inhuman or Degrading Treatment or Punishment in 2013; and the 2007 Council of Europe Convention on Protection of Children against Sexual Exploitation and Sexual Abuse (Lanzarote Convention), in 2013; adopting l. 71 of 29 May 2017 on protecting minors through prevention and the fight against cyberbullying, l. 47 of 7 April 2017 on protection measures on unaccompanied minors, lgs.d. 66 of 13 April 2017 on standards for promoting the inclusion of students with disabilities and the fourth National Action Plan on interventions for protecting the rights of adolescents, in 2016.

The main recommendations concerned the following issues:

- *Institutional Coordination:* The Committee urged Italy to define a clear mandate and sufficient authority within the Presidency of the Council of Ministers (Department for Family Policies) to coordinate all activities relating to the implementation of the Convention at the cross-sectoral, national, regional and local levels, and to strengthen the role of the National Observatory on Childhood and Adolescents under such an inter-ministerial coordinating body.
- *Economic Measures:* Italy was invited to conduct, with full participation of children, a comprehensive assessment of the impact of the austerity measures on the realisation of children's rights and, on the basis of the results of such an assessment, devise a strategy to more effectively address such impact and to ensure that the rights of children, in particular children from disadvantaged and marginalised communities, are not further adversely affected. Furthermore, the Committee recommended that Italy should allocate adequate human, financial and technical resources at all levels of government for the implementation of all policies, plans, programmes and legislative measures directed at children, in particular children in disadvantaged and marginalised situations. Finally, Italy should utilise a child-rights approach in the budgeting process by including specific indicators and a tracking system for the allocation and use

of resources for children throughout the budget and in relevant sectors and agencies, and use this tracking system for assessment of how investments in any sector may serve the best interests of the child, ensuring that the different impact of such investment on girls and boys is measured.

- *Independent National Human Rights Institutions:* The Committee urged Italy to provide full independence and autonomy to the Authority for Children and Adolescents and to establish, with no further delays, a national human rights institution in compliance with the Paris Principles.
- *Civil Society:* The Committee was deeply concerned by continuing smear campaigns against some civil society organisations engaged in search and rescue operations for migrants, including children, in the Mediterranean. The Committee urged the State party to guarantee the rights and freedom of action of civil society and to ensure that the rescue of migrants is not considered a crime.
- *Minimum age of marriage:* The Committee recommended that Italy amend its Civil Code to remove all exceptions that allow marriage under the age of 18 years.
- *Non-discrimination:* Taking note of targets 5.1 and 10.3 of the SDGs, the Committee recommended that the State party ensure full protection against all forms of discrimination, including advocacy of national, racial or religious hatred, by: (a) taking urgent measures to address disparities between the regions in access to health-care services, the minimum standard of living, adequate housing, including the prevention of forced evictions, sustainable development, and education of all children throughout the entire country; (b) Strengthening other preventive activities against discrimination and, if necessary, taking affirmative action for the benefit of children and in particular children in marginalised and disadvantaged situations, such as asylum-seeking, refugee and migrant children; stateless children; children belonging to minorities, including Roma, Sinti and Caminanti children; children born to unmarried parents; lesbian, bisexual, gay or transgender children and children living in lesbian, bisexual, gay or transgender families; intersex children; children with disabilities; and children in street situations.
- *Best interests of the child:* Italy was urged to develop procedures and criteria to provide guidance to all relevant professionals for determining the best interests of the child in every area and for giving the best interests of the child due weight as a primary consideration, in particular in relation to unaccompanied minors. Furthermore, the public authorities should disseminate to professionals working with and for children and the public at large, in particular children in a child-friendly manner, the Committee's General Committee No. 14 (2013) on the right of the child to have his or her best interests taken as a primary consideration.

- *Respect for the views of the child:* The Committee recommended that Italy Introduce a comprehensive legal provision establishing the right of the child to be heard without any discrimination due to age, disability or any other circumstance, both in the family environment and in any administrative, judicial or mediation procedure in which the child is affected, and ensure that the child's opinion is taken into account in accordance with the child's age and maturity, and adopt national uniform standard implementing regulations and guidelines accordingly, in particular in relation to all decisions concerning unaccompanied minors. Furthermore, Italy should develop toolkits for public consultation on national policy development to standardise such consultation at a high level of inclusiveness and participation, including consulting with children on issues that affect them.
- *Birth registration/Name and nationality:* In the light of target 16.9 of the SDGs, the Committee recommended that Italy: (a) take measures to prevent statelessness and ensure the effective implementation of the law regulating the acquisition of Italian citizenship at birth to otherwise stateless children; (b) resume the meeting of the working group on the legal status of Roma, Sinti and Caminanti, and take measures to improve the situation of undocumented or states children belonging to those communities; (c) consider ratifying the 1997 European Convention on Nationality.
- *Violence against children:* In the light of target 16.2 of the SDGs, the Committee recommended that Italy: (a) create a national system to monitor and collect data on violence against children, in particular on all cases of domestic violence against children and on violence against children in marginalised and disadvantaged situations, and undertake a comprehensive assessment of the extent, causes and nature of such violence; (b) further strengthen awareness-raising and education programmes – including campaigns – with the involvement of children in order to formulate a comprehensive strategy for preventing and combating violence against children, including child abuse and neglect; (c) introduce a comprehensive and precise definition of violence against children in legislation; (d) explicitly prohibit corporal punishment, however light, by law in all settings; (e) adopt, with the active involvement of children, a new national plan to prevent and combat the abuse and sexual exploitation of children, and ensure its uniform implementation throughout its entire territory and at all levels of government; (f) establish an independent and impartial commission of inquiry to examine all cases of sexual abuse of children by religious personnel of the Catholic church; (g) ensure that allegations of crimes relating to gender-based violence, including the trafficking of foreign children, in particular girls, are independently and thoroughly investigated and that perpetrators are brought to justice; (h) provide regular substantive training for judges, lawyers, prosecutors, the police and other relevant professional groups on standardised, gender- and child-sensitive procedures for dealing with victims and on how gender stereotyping by the judiciary negatively affects strict

law enforcement; (i)ensure the rehabilitation of child victims of gender-based violence.

- *Family environment and alternative care:* Italy was urged to: (a) continue to review its policies on alternative care for children deprived of a family environment to reduce reliability on civil society organisations, with a view to developing a more integrated, child rights-based and accountable system that integrates the traditional care provided by the extended family, with a particular focus on the best interests of the child; (b) ensure that the national guidelines are effectively and appropriately applied on an equal basis and to the same extent in different regions across the country; (c) ensure that the removal of children, including those with disabilities, from a family is permitted only after a careful assessment of best interests in each individual case, and is effectively monitored; (d) take measures to expand the system of foster care for children who cannot stay with their families with a view to go beyond the institutionalisation of children; (e) establish a national register of children deprived of a family environment, based on uniform and clear criteria across the entire territory of the State party; (f) ensure in practice that the child's views are heard in adoption processes in accordance with the child's evolving capacities.
- *Children with disabilities:* The Committee recommended that Italy set up a comprehensive strategy for the inclusion of children with disabilities; adopt national minimum standards on early childhood education quality services and on educational staff qualification and training that are suited to the special educational needs of children with disabilities; train additional specialised teachers and professionals in inclusive classed to provide individual support and all due attention to children with learning difficulties; undertake awareness-raising campaigns in order to combat stigmatisation of and discrimination against children with disabilities and to promote a positive image of such children.
- *Right to education:* The Committee expressed concern about high rates of school dropout, including from compulsory schooling, of Roma, Sinti and Caminanti children (also as a consequence of forced evictions); the dilapidated state of numerous school buildings that led to, for example, the collapse of ceilings on 112 occasions between 2014 and 2016; the phenomenon of bullying and cyberbullying, mainly in the school environment; the low rate of early childhood care and education in the south of the State party. Taking note of target 4.A of the SDGs, the Committee recommended that Italy: (a) accelerate the integration of the national student register and regional registers to identify all children of compulsory school age who do not attend school, are not in vocational training and not in an apprenticeship, and develop and promote quality vocational training to enhance the skills of children and young people, especially those who drop out of school; implement a human rights-based approach to the entire educational system that is more inclusive

towards children belonging to minority groups and migrant children and supports their aspirations; and effectively implement the national strategy for the inclusion of the Roma, Sinti and Caminanti for 2012–2020; (b) accelerate the creation of a register of school buildings, ensure that citizens have access to the register, and that school environments are welcoming and safe, and carry out systematic renovations of dilapidated buildings; (c) apply the guidelines on action contained in the *national plan for the prevention of bullying and cyberbullying at school for 2016/2017.*

- *Asylum-seeking and refugee children:* The Committee urged Italy to: (a) implement specific safeguards so that children are exempted from measures foreseen in law 132/2018 on urgent measures on international protection and public security; (b) facilitate access to the asylum system for children in need of international protection; (c) establish appropriate reception and protection mechanisms for unaccompanied and separated children, including those who may be in need of international protection, by ensuring adequate reception capacities for them throughout the State party on a needs-based approach; (d) implement a uniform protocol on age determination methods that is multidisciplinary, science-based, respectful of children's rights and used only in cases of serious doubt about the claimed age and in consideration of documentary or other forms of evidence available, and to ensure access to effective appeal mechanisms; (e) effectively implement the provision of voluntary guardians for unaccompanied and separated children by ensuring the timely appointment of a competent guardian who has the necessary expertise and availability and is free from any potential conflict of interest; (f) prioritise the immediate transfer of asylum-seeking children and their families out of regional processing centres, and to adopt permanent and sustainable resettlement options for refugees, particularly children and their families, to ensure that they are given lawful stay and reasonable access to employment and other opportunities; (g) to make relevant information and legal guidance on their rights and obligations available to migrant children, including information on human rights and fundamental freedoms, appropriate protection and assistance, options and pathways for regular migration and possibilities for return, in a language that they understand; (h) strengthen measures to reduce the statelessness of migrant children; (i) facilitate access to procedures for reunification of migrant children with their families; (l) take measures to provide inclusive and equitable quality education of migrant children, and to facilitate access to lifelong learning opportunities, on-the-job and vocational training, technical education, and language training, and by fostering partnerships with all stakeholders that can support this endeavour; (m) consider signing the *Global Compact for Safe, Orderly and Regular Migration* and ratifying the International Convention on the Protection of the Rights of All Migrant Workers and Members of Their Families.

Italy is due to present its seventh periodic report in October 2023.

G Committee on the Rights of Persons with Disabilities

In 2019, the Committee held two sessions: 21st (11 March-5 April) and 22nd (27 August-21 September). During the 21st session, the reports of Cuba, Niger, Norway, Rwanda, Saudi Arabia, Senegal, Spain, Turkey and Vanuatu were analysed; in the 22nd, the reports of Albania, Australia, Ecuador, El Salvador, Greece, India, Iraq, Kuwait and Myanmar. During the year, no *General comments* were adopted.

The latest periodic report of Italy was discussed by the Committee in August 2016, during the 16th session (see *Yearbook 2017*, pp. 178–182). Italy is due to present its joint second, third and fourth periodic report in May 2023.

H Committee on Enforced Disappearances

In 2019, the Committee held two sessions: 16th (8–18 April) and 17th (30 September-11 October). During these, two concluding observations were adopted relating to Chile, Italy and Peru (16th session) and Bolivia and Slovakia (17th session).

Italy presented its latest report in April 2018, but has not yet discussed it.

Latest report presented by Italy

Reporting round	I report
Date of the presentation of the Report	22 December 2017
Report	CED/C/ITA/1
List of issues	CED/C/ITA/Q/1
Concluding observations	CED/C/ITA/CO/1
Date of the discussion of the Report	8–9 April 2019, during the 16th session of the Committee (8–18 April 2019)

The Committee examined the I report of Italy during the 16th session (8–18 April 2019).

In its concluding observations, the Committee commended Italy for having established a national mechanism for reporting and follow up, the Inter-Ministerial Committee for Human Rights (at the Ministry of Foreign Affairs and International Cooperation), and the Office of the National Guarantor for the rights of persons detained or deprived of liberty, which is an effective monitoring body for the situation of those deprived of their liberty and serves as the NPM under the UN mandate.

At the same time, the Committee expressed concern about the recently implemented measures that converted into law the so-called Security Decree, in particular concerning the possibility of holding migrants due to be extradited in unspecified "suitable premises" provided by public security authorities. The Committee invited the Italian Government to immediately release information of immigration detention centres, ensuring all the necessary conditions for access by the National Guarantor and all supranational monitoring bodies with such competences.

The other main recommendations concerned the following issues:

- *Individual and inter-State communications:* Italy should recognise as soon as possible the Committee's competence to receive and consider individual and inter-State communications under articles 31 and 32 of the Convention.
- *National human rights institution:* The Committee recommends that Italy establish, with no further delays, a national human rights institution in full compliance with the Paris Principles.
- *Legislative measures:* The Committee urged Italy to take the necessary legislative measures to make enforced disappearance an autonomous offence and recognising enforced disappearance as a crime against humanity, in line with articles 2 and 5 of the Convention, and explicitly affirming that no exceptional circumstances whatsoever may to invoked as a justification for enforced disappearance, in accordance with article 1 of the Convention.
- *Duty to investigate and search for disappeared persons:* Italy should take measures necessary to prevent the disappearance of migrants, in particular children, and to find the whereabouts of those already missing and to provide the necessary judicial assistance to the authorities of other States parties in cases of enforced disappearance, to ensure that in practice no one may be extradited to another State where there is a risk of becoming a victim of enforced disappearance, in full respect of the principle of non-refoulement.

- *Unaccompanied minors:* The Committee recommends that Italy take the necessary measures to: (a) ensure that unaccompanied minors are promptly referred to child protection authorities as soon as possible after their arrival at an immigration detention centre; (b) ensure that effective application of the new harmonised multidisciplinary age-assessment procedures across all immigration detention centres, and ensure that anyone claiming to be a child is treated as such until a comprehensive and child-friendly age-assessment is undertaken; (c) prevent the disappearance of children from reception centres and find the whereabouts of those already missing.
- *Training:* The Committee encouraged Italy to further ensure that all law enforcement and security personnel (whether civil or military), medical personnel, public officials and other persons who may be involved in the custody or treatment of persons deprived of their liberty and migrants, including judges, prosecutors and other officials responsible for the administration of justice, receive specific and regular training on the provisions of the Convention.

Italy is required to present its second periodic report in April 2025.

I Committee on Migrant Workers

In 2019, the Committee held two sessions: 30th (1–12 April) and 31st (2–11 September). During these, concluding observations regarding Albania, Guatemala, Libya and Tajikistan (30th session) and Argentina, Bosnia Herzegovina and Colombia (31st session) were adopted. During the year, no *General comments* were adopted.

Italy has not ratified the International Convention on the Protection of the Rights of All Migrant Workers and Members of Their Families and therefore is not monitored by the Committee.

VI Specialised United Nations Agencies, Programmes and Funds

A International Labour Organization (ILO)

Established by the Treaty of Versailles in 1919, the ILO became the first specialised agency of the United Nations in 1946.

The ILO is devoted to promoting decent and productive work for men and women in conditions of freedom, equality, safety and dignity. Its chief objectives are: to promote rights at work, to encourage decent employment opportunities, to enhance social protection and to strengthen dialogue on work-related issues. The ILO is the only United Nations agency which has a tripartite structure: representatives of Governments, employers and workers jointly elaborate the policies and programmes of the Organisation. 185 States are members of the ILO.

Since its foundation, the ILO has adopted 189 conventions. Of these, the ILO has identified 8 which it defines as "fundamental" or "core" (No. 29 on Forced Labour, 1930; No. 87 on Freedom of Association and Protection of the Right to Organise, 1948; No. 98 on the Right to Organise and Collective Bargaining, 1949; No. 100 on Equal Remuneration for Men and Women Workers for Work of Equal Value, 1951; No. 105 on the Abolition of Forced Labour, 1957; No. 111 on the Elimination of All Forms of Discrimination in Employment, Occupation, Vocational Training and Terms and Conditions of Employment, 1958; No. 138 on the Minimum Age for Admission to Employment or Work, 1973; and No. 182 on the Elimination of the Worst Forms of Child Labour, 1999) and 4 defined as "priority" (or "governance": No. 81 on Labour Inspection, 1947; No. 122 on Employment Policy, 1964; No. 129 on Labour Inspection [Agriculture], 1969; and No. 144 on Tripartite Consultation [International Labour Standards], 1976).

Italy has been a member of the ILO since 1919 (amongst the founding members); it withdrew from the Organisation in 1937 but joined again permanently in 1945. The ILO is present in Italy with its offices in Rome, which have been operating since 1920, and the International Training Centre, established in Turin in 1965.

Italy has ratified 113 conventions adopted by the ILO (of which 82 are in force and 31 denounced), including the 8 fundamental ones, the 4 priority ones and 101 of the 177 technical conventions.

In order to monitor the application of conventions ratified by States, in 1926, the ILO established the *Committee of Experts on the Application of Conventions and Recommendations*, a body made up of twenty eminent jurists and social professionals, who are independent of Governments and appointed on individual merits. The monitoring mechanism requires each Member State to submit periodic reports on the steps they have taken, in law and in practice, to apply each of the conventions it has ratified. At the same time, Governments are required to submit copies of their reports to employers' and workers' organisations, which are entitled to make comments and supply further information. Government reports are initially examined by the Committee of Experts, which can make two different kinds of comments: *observations* and *direct requests*. The observations contain comments on fundamental questions raised by the application of a particular convention by a State, and are published in the Committee's annual report. On the other hand, direct requests relate to more technical requests or requests for further information; they are not published in the report but are communicated directly to the Governments concerned.

> Upon conclusion of its considerations, the Committee presents an annual report to the *International Labour Conference*, the most representative body of the ILO, comprising representatives from all the ILO Member States and including all its observations and recommendations, which are carefully examined by the *Conference Committee on the Application of Standards*, a tripartite standing committee made up of Government, employer and worker delegates. This Committee selects a number of observations from the report for more in-depth discussion. The Governments referred to in these comments are invited to respond before the Conference Committee to provide information on the situation in question. In many cases, the Conference Committee adopts conclusions recommending that Governments take specific steps to remedy a problem or to invite the ILO to come on a mission to their Country or to request technical assistance.

In 2019, Italy received:

- two observations regarding the following conventions: No. 81 on Labour Inspection (1947) and No. 129 on Labour Inspection (Agriculture) (1969);
- six direct requests regarding the following conventions: No. 81 on Labour Inspection (1947); No. 95 on Protection of Wages (1949); No. 102 on Social Security (1952); No. 118 on Equality of Treatment (1962); No. 129 on Labour Inspection (Agriculture) (1969); Maritime Labour Convention (2006).

In 2019, Italy contributed 3.75 % of the regular budget of the ILO, with a sum of around 17 million Swiss Francs. For the two-year period 2018–2019, Italy allocated a further voluntary contribution of $455,000, as one of eight donating countries, alongside Belgium, Denmark, Germany, Luxembourg, The Netherlands, Norway and Sweden.

B United Nations Educational, Scientific and Cultural Organisation (UNESCO)

The human rights which fall under the responsibility of UNESCO are the right to education, the right to benefit from scientific progress, the right to participate freely in cultural life and the right to information, including freedom of opinion and expression. In connection with these, the right to freedom of thought, conscience and religion, the right to seek, receive and impart information and ideas through any instrument and across borders, the right to protection of the moral and material interests resulting from any scientific, literary or artistic production are pertinent, as are the right to freedom of assembly and association, the right to education, the right to enjoy the benefits of scientific progress, the right freely to participate in the cultural life, and the right to information, including the freedom of opinion and expression.

Italy has been a member of UNESCO since 1948. In 2019, the post of Permanent Representative to UNESCO was filled by Amb. Massimo Riccardo. Since its establishment, UNESCO has adopted 31 conventions, 20 of which have been ratified by Italy.

In the field of education, it should be noted that in 1991, the 26th General Conference of UNESCO established the International Programme for University Cooperation (IUC – International University Cooperation). The Programme works to foster the creation of a network of centres of excellence (UNESCO Chairs) able to implement advanced teaching and research programmes in disciplines related to UNESCO policies, with particular reference to the issues of peace and human rights, democracy and intercultural dialogue. There are over 700 UNESCO Chairs created all over the world; in 2017 in Italy there are 25 Chairs (as in 2016), 3 of which deal specifically with human rights, reporting the wording in the denomination: Chair "Human Rights, Democracy and Peace", established in 1999 at the University of Padova; Chair "Human Rights and Ethics of International Cooperation", established in 2003 at the University of Bergamo; Chair "Bioethics and Human Rights", established in 2009 at the Pontifical Athenaeum "Regina Apostolorum", European University of Rome; Chair "Gender Equality and Women's Rights", established in 2019 at the University of Insubria.

In the field of bioethics, two committees operate at UNESCO: the International Bioethics Committee (IBC) and the Intergovernmental Bioethics Committee (IGBC).

The IBC was established in 1993, particularly thanks to the efforts of the then-Director-General of UNESCO Federico Mayor. It is a body made up of 36 independent experts coming from different geographical and disciplinary backgrounds. Its mission is to follow progress in life science and its applications in order to ensure respect for human dignity and human rights and to promote reflection on the ethical and legal issues raised by research in the life sciences and their applications. To this end, over the years the IBC has published a number of recommendations and other documents, the most significant of which is the Universal Declaration on Bioethics and Human Rights, adopted by the UNESCO General Conference in 2005. The Committee meets once a year when summoned by the Director-General of UNESCO.

The IGBC was created in 1998 pursuant to article 11 of the IBC Statute. It is composed of 36 Member States who are elected by the UNESCO General Conference and meets at least once every two years to examine the proposals and recommendations of the IBC and to forward these proposals, accompanied by its own opinions, to the other UNESCO Member States.

In 2019, Italy contributed about 4.3 % of the regular budget of UNESCO (which cover the regular expenses for the maintenance of the staff and for the main activities of the Organisation), which constitutes around $11.2 million. In 2019, Italy contributed a further voluntary extra-budget donation of around $7.6 million (with which the multi-annual cooperation programmes managed by UNESCO are financed), making it the 5th highest of donating countries.

UNESCO Machinery

In 2019, Italy was not involved with any of the organisation's monitoring mechanisms.

C Food and Agriculture Organisation of the United Nations (FAO)

The FAO was established in 1945 in Ville de Quebec, Canada, and has its headquarters in Rome. Since August 2019, Qu Dongyu (China) has been the Director-general of the Organisation. The Organisation budget for the biennium 2018–2019 amounted to $2.6 billion.

On 30 March 2020, Italy was the seventh highest contributor to the FAO with around $9 million in contributions. Italy collaborates with the FAO through the FAO/Italy Cooperation Programme, whose main components, financed by Italian voluntary contributions, are the Traditional Programme; the Italian Trust Fund for Food Security and the Decentralised Cooperation Programme.

D World Health Organization (WHO)

The World Health Organisation was established in 1948. Its primary objective is the attainment by all peoples of the highest possible level of health, understood not as the absence of disease but as a state of complete physical, mental and social well-being.

In Italy, there is a WHO office in Venice, with another 28 collaborating centres currently accredited (in terms of the number of this type of structure, Italy is the second in Europe and ninth in the world). These collaborating centres are specialised institutions to which the WHO does not grant any funding: they are identified by the WHO Director General and are part of a worldwide network of organisational support in the various medical-scientific fields. In Italy, their activity is coordinated by the Ministry of Health.

E United Nations Development Programme (UNDP)

The UNDP was established by the General Assembly in 1965 and has the role of central agency for the coordination and funding of development cooperation of the United Nations system.

NDP action pursues the general objective of "human development", understood as not only economic growth but also as social development, based on gender equality and respect for human rights. UNDP conducts research and analysis, preparing studies and reports. Of the most significant, worth noting are the Annual Report on Human Development and the report on the state of achievement of the Sustainable Development Goals.

In 2019, Italy contributed around $5.9 million to the regular budget of the UNDP, putting it in 17th place among the major contributing countries. This year, Italy allocated a further $74.6 million for specific projects and programmes coordinated by the UNDP.

F United Nations Environment Program (UN-Environment)

UN-Environment is the leading global environmental authority that defines the global environmental agenda, promotes the coherent implementation of the environmental dimension of sustainable development within the system of nations. Its mission is to coordinate and promote the creation of a global partnership for the development of projects and activities to protect the environment so that nations and peoples can improve their quality of life without compromising that of future generations.

Inger Andersen (Denmark) has been Direct General of the Program since February 2019. The representative at the UN-Environment and also the Head of Mission of the Italian Embassy in Nairobi is Amb. Alberto Pieri, succeeding Amb. Mauro Massoni in September 2018.

G United Nations Program for Human Settlements (UN-HABITAT)

United Nations Program for Human Settlements, UN-HABITAT is invested with the mission to foster sustainable urbanisation from the social and environmental point of view with the ultimate aim of guaranteeing everyone the right to decent housing.

The current General Director is Maimunah Mohd Sharif (Malaysia); the representative at the UN-HABITAT is Alberto Pieri, as of September 2018.

UN-HABITAT works in close collaboration with local authorities, including Municipalities, Provinces and Regions, thanks above all to the special relationship established with UNACLA, the UN Advisory Committee on Local Authorities. The latter is made up of mayors and representatives of umbrella organisations of local authorities chosen by the UN-HABITAT Director-General on the basis of their competence and commitment in implementing the UN agenda on human settlements.

H United Nations Children's Fund (UNICEF)

UNICEF is the permanent fund of the United Nations which is assigned the mandate to protect and promote the rights of children, girls and adolescents with the aim of improving their living conditions. Since 1 January 2018, the Executive Director is the American Henrietta H. Fore.

In Italy, the UNICEF Research Centre is located at the Istituto degli Innocenti in Florence. Since 1974, the Italian Committee for UNICEF has been working in Italy; it is a non-governmental organisation whose activities are overseen by a cooperation agreement signed with UNICEF International. Francesco Samengo has been President since 25 July 2018.

UNICEF has launched a vast programme in Italy for migrant and refugee minors, particularly minors who are not accompanied by a family member. The aim of this programme is to provide measures of assistance from first reception to their transferral to smaller, more stable structures, from monitoring human rights standards to school and cultural inclusion in the local community.

I International Organization for Migration (IOM)

Established in 1951, the IOM is the main inter-governmental organisation dealing with migrant issues. Its mission is to promote orderly migration based on respect for human dignity; to this end, it collaborates with Governments and civil society. From June 2018, the Director-General of the Organisation is António Manuel de Carvalho Ferreira Vitorino (Portugal).

The IOM Coordination Office for the Mediterranean countries is based in Rome and the main activities of the IOM offices in Italy concern: providing assistance to vulnerable groups and minors, migration and employment; migration and health; migration, climate and development, reuniting families; supporting voluntary return; and relocation and resettlement.

In 2019, the IOM did not publish any briefings concerning Italy.

Council of Europe*

The Council of Europe (CoE, 47 Member States) was established on 5 May 1949 and is the first and most advanced regional system for the promotion and protection of human rights.

The Permanent Representative of Italy to the Council of Europe from 1 February 2019 is Amb. Michele Giacomelli (up to January 2019 the role was covered by Amb. Marco Marsilli). The Italian official Gabriella Battaini-Dragoni holds the position of Deputy Secretary-General of the Organisation. Since 2011, Italy has been home to an external office of the CoE in Venice, directed by Luisella Pavan-Woolfe. The activities of this office focus on the integration of minorities, gender equality, participation of citizens in democratic processes, the role of women in the Euro-Mediterranean context, the integration of the Roma and the Day of Remembrance. The Office participates in many projects with local academic institutions, including the Venice International University, the European Inter-University Centre for Human Rights and Democratisation – EIUC/ Global Campus for human rights and Venice Ca' Foscari University. It hosts training courses on human rights and democracy with special reference to southern shore Mediterranean countries.

In 2019, Italia Italy made a contribution worth €35,873,440 to the activities of the CoE, of which €28,532,193 was allocated for the regular budget (in 2018, the overall contribution was €35,261,058 of which €27,515,762 for the regular budget). On 21 March 2019, Italy provided €80,161 in voluntary contributions to support the implementation of the Council of Europe Action Plan on Protecting Refugee and Migrant Children in Europe, bringing the total direct contributions to the action plan up to €238,161.

The following pages will illustrate the activities of the Parliamentary Assembly and the Committee of Ministers with reference to Italy; those of seven bodies established by a treaty: the European Court of Human Rights, the Committee

* Pietro de Perini

for the Prevention of Torture, the European Committee of Social Rights, the Advisory Committee on the Framework Convention for the Protection of National Minorities, the Group of Experts on Action against Trafficking in Human Beings Group of Experts on Action against Violence against Women and Domestic Violence and Lanzarote Committee on the Protection of Children against Sexual Exploitation and Sexual Abuse; and of four bodies established by the Committee of Ministers: Commissioner for Human Rights, the European Commission against Racism and Intolerance, the European Commission for Democracy through Law and the Group of States against Corruption.

As is coherent with the multi-year initiative calendar of various monitoring bodies of the Council of Europe, only some of these groups were able to analyse the human rights situation in Italy in 2019. The main issues tackled concerned corruption (Group of States against Corruption), violence against women and domestic violence (GREVIO and the Committee of the Parties), the conditions of detainees held in maximum security facilities or subjected to other isolation and segregation measures (Committee for the Prevention of Torture); the conditions of migrants with particular reference to the issue of *non refoulement* and the reception system in Italy (Commissioner for Human Rights, Committee of Ministers);social rights of children, families and migrants (European Committee of Social Rights); discrimination against Roma and Sinti communities with particular reference to the issue of evictions (European Committee of Social Rights). From an Agenda 2030 perspective which takes the SDGs into account, these issues mainly concern Goal 3 (ensure healthy lives and promote well-being for all at all ages), Goal 5 (achieve gender equality and empower all women and girls), particularly Target 5.2 (eliminate all forms of violence against all women and girls in the public and private spheres, including trafficking and sexual and other types of exploitation), Goal 10 (reduce inequality within and among nations), particularly Targets 10.2 (empower and promote the social, economic and political inclusion of all, irrespective of age, sex, disability, race, ethnicity, origin, religion or economic or other status) and 10.7 (facilitate orderly, safe, regular and responsible migration and mobility of people, including through the implementation of planned and well-managed migration policies) and Goal 16 (peace, justice and strong institutions), particularly Targets 16.3 (promote the rule of law at the national and international levels and ensure equal access to justice for all), 16.6 (develop effective, accountable and transparent institutions at all levels) and 16.5 (substantially reduce corruption and bribery in all their forms).

I Parliamentary Assembly

In the Parliamentary Assembly of the Council of Europe (PACE), made up of delegations from the national parliaments of the Member States of the CoE, 18 members of the Senate and the Chamber of Deputies sit for Italy; there are an equal number of alternate members.

PACE is a forum for discussing the main issues underlying the Organisation's mandate and it has advisory functions in relation to all international conventions drawn up in this context. It elects the judges of the European Court of Human Rights, the Commissioner for Human Rights, the Secretary General of the CoE and their deputy.

The following are the members and alternate members (a) of Italian PACE in: Deborah Bergamini, Marina Berlinghieri (a), Anna Maria Bernini, Francesco Berti (a), Simone Billi, Maria Elena Boschi, Maurizio Buccarella, Pino Cabras (a), Sabrina De Carlo, Fabio Di Micco, Piero Fassino (a), Claudio Fazzone (a), Gianluca Ferrara (a), Roberto Paolo Ferrari (a), Emilio Floris, Paolo Grimoldi, Barbara Guidolin (a), Francesco Laforgia (a), Francesco Lollobrigida (a), Alvise Maniero, Gianni Marilotti (a), Gaspare Antonio Marinello, Augusta Montaruli (a), Andrea Orlando, Gianluca Perilli, Daisy Pirovano, Alberto Ribolla (a), Maria Rizzotti (a), Tatjana Rojc (a), Gianfranco Rufa (a), Rosellina Sbrana (a), Filippo Scerra, Francesco Scoma (a), Simona Suriano (a), Manuel Vescovi.

Alvise Maniero, who carries out the role of President of the Italian Delegation, is also the Vice Chair of the Parliamentary Assembly. Concerning the role of Italian Members of Parliament within various committees, in 2019, Piero Fassino carried out the role of second Vice Chair of the Committee on Political Affairs and Democracy, Manuel Vescovi was the third Vice Chair of the Committee on Migration, Refugees and Displaced Persons and Roberto Rampi covered the role of the third Vice Chair of the Committee on Culture, Science, Education and Media.

Among the many documents adopted by PACE in 2019, five resolutions directly refer to the human rights situation in Italy. In some cases, recent developments on these issues were positively received, in others the documents highlighted shortcomings in the Italian situation and proposed recommendations to improve it.

Resolution 2261 on the progress of the Assembly's monitoring procedure (*June-December 2018 and the periodic review of the honouring of obligations by Iceland and Italy*; adopted 24 January 2019, *rapporteur:* Roger Gale), PACE encourages the Italian Authorities and those of other countries to implement the recommendations contained in the evaluation report of the Assembly. Specifically, PACE: expects Italy to remain committed to the promotion and protection of human rights, reduce regional disparities and welcomes the steps taken by the parliament to establish an independent national human rights institution; encourages Italy to ratify the European Charter for Regional and Minority Languages of 1992, Protocol No. 12 of 2000 and Protocols Nos. 15 and 16 of 2013 to the ECHR (see, on these latter, l.d.d. S. 2921), the European Convention on Nationality of 1997 and the Additional Protocol to the European Charter of Local Self-Government on the right to participate in the affairs of a local authority of 2009; concerning migration, PACE expresses its concerns about recent initiatives aimed at preventing rescue vessels from landing on Italian shores and urges the Italian Authorities to strengthen their action to combat trafficking in human beings in line with recommendations made by GRETA (see *Yearbook 2019*, pp. 250–256) and ensure that future legislation on migrants and refugees complies with Italy's European and international obligations; calls on the authorities to effectively combat all manifestations of racism, intolerance and xenophobia, particularly by preventing, investigating and prosecuting all racially motivated offences; recommends strengthening media freedom and address the issue of media ownership concentration and to decriminalise defamation to ensure the principle of proportionality of sanctions; regarding criminal justice reforms, calls on the Italian Authorities to further address the issues of, *inter alia*, excessive use of pre-trial detention, delayed justice and backlogs of court cases; on anti-corruption, while recognising the progress made, notes that corruption remains widespread and deeply rooted and that there is a persistent intertwinement of corruption, money laundering and mafia-type organised; concerning political party funding, PACE encourages the Italian Authorities to ensure transparency and the implementation of an efficient accountability control mechanism for the new system of party and election campaign funding based on private donations; urges Italy to implement all GRECO recommendations (see, in this Part, Council of Europe, XI; and *Yearbook 2017*, pp. 227–228), to consider lifting the reservation made to the Criminal Law Convention on Corruption and consider ratifying its Additional Protocol.

Resolution 2299 on *Pushback policies and practice in Council of Europe member States* (adopted 28 June 2019, *rapporteur*: Tineke Strik) recalls, among others, the judgment of the ECtHR on the *Hirsi Jama v. Italy* case to highlight the need for individual assessment of protection needs and of the safety of a return in order to prevent violation of article 3 ECHR and of the prohibition of collective expulsions, as enshrined in article 4 of Protocol No. 4 ECHR.

Resolution 2300 on *Improving the protection of whistle-blowers all over Europe* (adopted 1 October 2019, *rapporteur*: Sylvain Waserman), PACE notes with satisfaction Italy's adoption (as well as that of other European States) of law 30 November 2017, No. 179 (Provisions to protect those reporting crimes or irregularities that have come to light in the context of a public or private employment relationship).

Resolution 2305 on Saving lives in the Mediterranean: the need for an urgent response (adopted 3 October 2019, *rapporteur*: Domagoj Hajduković), PACE welcomes the agreement reached in Malta on 23 September 2019 on the redistribution of migrants by the Interior Ministers of Finland, France, Germany, Italy and Malta, strongly hoping that as many EU member States as possible will join it.

Finally, Resolution 2311 on *Human rights and business – what follow-up to Committee of Ministers Recommendation CM/Rec(2016)3?* (adopted 29 November 2019, *rapporteur*: Mikayel Melkumyan), PACE positively notes the Italian Government's adoption of the National Action Plan on business and human rights. one of the 18 NAPs to be adopted in CoE Member States of the Council of Europe, implementing the United Nations Guiding Principles on business and human rights.

II Committee of Ministers

On the subject of human rights, the Committee of Ministers (CM) relies on the work of the Steering Committee for Human Rights, an intergovernmental body composed of representatives of the 47 Member States which performs, among other things, standard-setting and follow-up.

The CM adopts recommendations regarding the Member States and on matters for which a common policy is agreed upon – in accordance with its role in the implementation of the European Social Charter (article 29) – with the aim of asking some States to adapt their laws and public policies with the provisions contained in the Charter. In addition, it is ultimately responsible for monitoring the Framework Convention on National Minorities (article 26). In this context, it adopts specific resolutions by country, based on the opinions of the Advisory Committee of the Framework Convention (see, in this Part III, Council of Europe, VIII).

With regard to its role in relation to the European Court of Human Rights, the CM has the function of supervising the execution of judgments of the Court, ensuring that Member States act in accordance with the rulings issued by the same. The Committee terminates each case by adopting a final resolution. Finally, the CM may apply to the Court for a ruling on issues related to difficulties of interpretation of the judgments of the Court itself which would impede their implementation and if it finds that a Member State fails to comply with a final judgment, it may refer the issue to the Court.

In 2019, the CM adopted 14 final resolutions on the execution of the EctHR judgments by Italy, regarding a total of 85 cases: CM/ResDH(2019)21 on the *Maggio and others* case and two other cases; CM/ResDH(2019)63 on the *Messana* case and four other cases; CM/ResDH(2019)121 on the *Piazzi* case and seven other cases; CM/ResDH(2019)120 on the *Mazzeo* case; CM/ResDH(2019)158 on the *Amati and others* case; CM/ResDH(2019)157 on the *Addazio* case and 36 other cases; CM/ResDH(2019)186 on the *Longobardi* case and one other case; CM/ResDH(2019)185 on the *Bozza* case; CM/ResDH(2019)221 on the *Orlandi and others* case; CM/ResDH(2019)238 on the *Francesco Quattrone* case and eight other cases; CM/ResDH(2019)255 on the *Casalino and Polichetti* case and one other case; CM/ResDH(2019)276 on the *Arras and others* case and seven other cases; CM/ResDH(2019)275 on the *Paudicio* case and one other case; CM/ResDH(2019)327 on the *Cirillo* case and five other cases.

Concerning the ongoing monitoring of the implementation of ECtHR judgments against Italy, the Committee of Ministers adopted six decisions in 2019.

On 14 March 2019, during its 1340th session, the CM adopted a decision (CM/Del/Dec(2019)1340/H46-9) on the *Khlaifia and others* case related to the condition of reception of immigrants in irregular situations in Italy and expulsion methods (see *Yearbook 2016*, pp. 255–256). In this decision, as regards the lawfulness and judicial review of migrant detention in hotspots, and whilst noting that l.d. 113/2018 allows the detention of asylum seekers in hotspots for identification purposes and also provides for a judicial review of such detention, the CM considered that more detailed information is necessary to fully assess the compatibility of this law decree with article 5 of the Convention (right to freedom and security) and the Court's case-law. The Committee therefore called therefore on the authorities to provide without delay comprehensive information on the current legislation governing detention of asylum seekers in hotspots, in particular on the grounds for detention and its possible extension, the decision-making process leading to it, and the information provided to the persons concerned about the grounds for their detention. It also called on the authorities to provide the Committee with details on the scope of judicial review of the decisions to detain asylum seekers in such centres and to prolong the detention, the time-frame set for this review, and the powers of the competent courts where they find the detention to be unlawful. The Committee invited the authorities to clarify whether migrants who have not applied for international protection may also be detained in hotspots and, if so, to provide information about the relevant legal basis and safeguards surrounding such detention. The CM invited the authorities to rapidly address the lack of an effective remedy enabling migrants to complain about the conditions of their detention in hotspots; it noted the information provided on the possibility (as communicated by the Government) to initiate urgent proceedings under article 700 of the Civil Procedures Code concerning conditions of detention in hotspots, and invited the authorities to provide additional detailed information on this remedy by 31 May 2019.

During the same session, the CM adopted a decision (CM/Del/Dec(2019)1340/H46-10) on the *Sharifi and others* case regarding the automatic return by Italy to Greece of irregular migrants intercepted as stowaways on ferries arriving in the Italian port of Ancona and the impossibility to have access to an individual assessment of their situation and of their need for international protection in Italy (see *Yearbook 2015*, p. 311). In this decision, as regards individual measures, the CM noted the information submitted by the authorities concerning the difficulties encountered in locating the three applicants who were not granted international protection in Italy and the assurances provided as to the safeguards they would grant them in case they manifest themselves again. Furthermore, the

Italian Authorities were called on to provide information on the concrete steps taken to locate these applicants and to clarify their situation, since no information has yet been provided. As regards general measures, the CM stressed the crucial importance of ensuring that migrants intercepted in the ports of the Adriatic Sea are protected from expedited unregistered returns to Greece, in view of the persistent deficiencies in the reception system for migrants and the asylum procedure, and have unhindered access in Italy to an individualised examination of their international protection needs in conformity with the requirements of the ECHR. The CM noted the information provided by the Italian Government on the current organisation and functioning of the reception of migrants, and also on the reduction since the events at issue in this case in the number of irregular migrants arriving at the Adriatic ports as well as in the number returned to Greece. However, it noted with concern that, notwithstanding the Committee's previous calls, the available information does not make it possible to ascertain the adequacy of the reception system established in the Adriatic ports to ensure that the individual situation of irregular migrants is thoroughly assessed; noted also the concerns expressed by the United Nations High Commissioner for Refugees in that respect. Finally, the CM noted with interest that the Italian authorities recently confirmed that since the European Court's judgment no transfer to Greece of asylum-seekers and of unaccompanied minors has been carried out and urged the authorities to provide the information requested by 31 May 2019 and to respond to the issues raised by the UNHCR in its communication.

On 6 June 2019, during its 1348th session, the CM adopted a decision (CM/Del/Dec(2019)1348/H46-13) on the *Di Sarno and others* case concerning waste refuge in Campania (see *Yearbook 2013*, p. 365). In the decision, the CM, noted with interest the efforts of the Italian authorities aimed at promoting systems of separate collection and the consolidation in recent years of the encouraging results previously achieved in terms of the sorting of waste, but was concerned that, at least until 15 February 2018, only a minimal part of the so-called historical waste accumulated prior to 2009 had been removed and called on the authorities to implement without further delay the plan for the removal of this type of waste. The CM invited the authorities to also provide information on the current daily functioning of the waste disposal system, including its capacity and long-term sustainability. It invited the authorities to submit information on the practical functioning and the level of coordination of the different monitoring mechanisms established including, as previously requested, on whether these mechanisms are entitled to make recommendations, and, if so, on the follow-up given to them and on their legal force. With regard to the current lack of concrete indications that the domestic legal system provides an effective remedy enabling persons to obtain redress for the damage suffered by poor management of waste collection, treatment and disposal, the CM called upon the authorities to rapidly address this shortcoming. Furthermore, it noted the information provided on the scope of proceedings before the administrative courts and invited the authorities to submit relevant and specific examples of case-law to assess the effectiveness of such proceedings in these particular circumstances. The authorities were called upon to provide this information no later than 16 December 2019.

During the same session, the CM adopted a decision (CM/Del/Dec(2019)1348/H46-12) on the *Agrati and others* group of cases regarding the retroactive application, in the absence of compelling public interest reasons, of law 266/2005 to pending judicial proceedings relating to the transfer of the approximately 310 applicants' length of service as local government civil servants (see *Yearbook 2012*, pp. 346–347). In this decision, As regards individual measures, the CM expressed their deep concern at the lack of any information in response to the outstanding questions previously identified by the Committee and urged the Italian authorities to indicate, by 30 September 2019 at the latest, the measures taken to ensure that the applicants in Peduzzi and Arrighi have retained the benefits flowing from the domestic court decisions delivered before the enactment of the legislation concerned. Furthermore, the CM urged the authorities to provide, by 30 September 2019 at the latest, information on the procedures available under national law to determine and remedy the consequences stemming from the retroactive application of Law No. 266/2005 for the applicants in Agrati and Others, De Rosa and Others and Bordoni and Others, for the period after 31 December 2011, and to indicate whether the other applicants have suffered pecuniary damage as a result of the violations found and, if so, whether it is possible to seek compensation in this respect at domestic level. As regards general measures the CM noted that the current application of the legislation concerned by domestic courts appears to ensure that no significant disadvantage as regards remuneration is suffered by staff who, like the applicants, are transferred to the national civil service within the Ministry of Education. The Committee welcomed the measures taken to ensure that laws with retroactive effect are adopted in strict conformity with the requirements of the Convention as underlined in the present cases, notably the procedures established inside Parliament to secure appropriate and effective verification of the compatibility of draft laws with the Convention and the Court's case-law, and encouraged the Italian authorities to pursue this good practice and decided to close their examination of the general measures in these cases.

On 25 September 2019, during its 1355th session, the CM adopted a decision (CM/Del/Dec(2019)1355/H46-12) on the *Olivieri and others* groups of cases regarding various shortcomings in the compensatory "Pinto" remedy available since 2001 to victims of excessively long proceedings (see *Yearbook 2017*, p. 312). In this decision, as regards individual measures, the CM noted that the question of individual measures has been resolved in nine repetitive cases of this group, and decided to close their supervision of the execution of these cases (see CM/ResDH(2019)238). It requested the Italian authorities to provide without further delay complete information on the payment of the just satisfaction in the cases of *GE.PA.F. S.R.L.*, *Selvaggio*, *Gaglione and others* and *Ambrosini*. As regards general measures, the CM noted with satisfaction that in its judgment of 21 March 2018 the Constitutional Court declared the provision which prevented applicants from applying for compensation for delay before the end of the main proceedings to be unconstitutional. It underlined the need for the authorities to respond without further delay to the other restrictions in the 2012 legislation, namely the exclusion of proceedings lasting six years or less and the cap on compensation, which encourage applicants to apply directly to the European Court, and requested the authorities to provide detailed information about the measures adopted or envisaged to this end. Concerning the ineffectiveness of the "Pinto" remedy in the context of administrative proceedings, the CM, recalling the *Olivieri and Others* judgment, invited the authorities to provide their assessment of the extent to which the new legislative provisions and the judgment of the Constitutional Court of 6 March 2019 have resolved this problem. Concerning the inapplicability of the "Pinto" Act to delays in preliminary investigations, recalling in the *Arnoldi* judgment, requested the authorities rapidly to inform the Committee how they envisage addressing the issue that that injured parties in criminal proceedings who have exercised at least some of their rights should be able to obtain compensation in respect of delays in preliminary investigations. The information should be provided by the end of January 2020 by the latest.

On 5 December 2019, during its 1362nd session, the CM adopted a decision (CM/Del/Dec(2019)1362/H46-14) on the *Cestaro* group of cases concerning the ill-treatment suffered by the applicants at the hands of State agents and the lack of effective investigations and court proceedings into these events (see *Yearbook 2015*, p. 20; *Yearbook 2016*, pp. 255–256). In this decision, as regards individual measures, the CM noted with deep regret that it is no longer possible to open a fresh investigation into the torture suffered by the applicants in *Bartesaghi Gallo and Others* due to the statute of limitation and therefore accepted that no individual measure is any longer possible in this case. It requested the authorities to clarify rapidly whether it is possible to carry out new criminal investigations into the applicants' allegations of ill-treatment in the remaining cases and, if so, to provide information on the steps taken or planned to rectify the shortcomings found by the European Court and their outcome; it invited also the authorities to provide information on any disciplinary investigations that have been initiated against the law enforcement agents who have been involved in acts of torture and other forms of ill-treatment, and their outcome. As regards general measures, the CM noted with satisfaction the reforms which in 2017 introduced the crime of torture into the Italian Criminal Code (see *Yearbook 2017*, pp. 21–22) and expressed their confidence that the law enforcement authorities, prosecutors and courts will be guided in their interpretation and application of these provisions by the requirements of the Convention and the European Court's case-law in this area. The CM regretted that the Italian authorities have not taken the opportunity to disapply the statute of limitation to torture; it therefore strongly invited the authorities to ensure that the remaining reforms in this area come into effect on 1 January 2020 and to keep the Committee informed of developments showing the effective application of these new provisions. The Committee recalled that the European Court found that the efforts of the prosecutors and courts adequately to investigate, try and punish those responsible for the ill-treatment suffered by the applicants were frustrated not only by gaps in the criminal law but also by the impossibility to identify all of the perpetrators and by the lack of cooperation from the police. It therefore invited the Italian authorities to ensure that adequate legal provisions are in place to ensure that agents taking part in law enforcement operations can be identified in all situations and that a message at high political level of zero tolerance of ill-treatment is formally delivered to law enforcement agencies. Furthermore, it invited the authorities to indicate how they have ensured, or intend to ensure, that law enforcement agents who have been charged with crimes involving ill-treatment are suspended from duty during the investigation or trial and dismissed if they are convicted, in conformity with the established case-law of the Court on this issue. Finally, the Committee noted with interest the information provided on the theoretical and practical training offered to law enforcement agents and encouraged the authorities to pursue their efforts to ensure that these officials undertake systematic and comprehensive training in the field of human rights throughout their career. The information should be provided by the end of 30 June 2020 by the latest.

On 11 September 2019, the CM adopted a Resolution CM/ResChS(2019)6 on the decision of the European Committee of Social Rights regarding collective complaints against Italy presented by the Italian General Confederation of Labour (CGIL) (140/2016, see *Yearbook 2017*, pp. 196–197). In the resolution, the CM acknowledges the decisions of the European Committee of Social Rights stating that Italian authorities violated articles 5 and 6 of the European Social Charter (revised) (see this Part, Council of Europe, V).

With Resolution CM/ResCPT(2019)3, adopted 9 October 2019, the CM appointed Gaia Pergolo as the new Italian member of the European Committee for the Prevention of Torture for the period 20 December 2019–19 December 2023 (see this Part, Council of Europe, IV).

Finally, on 5 November 2019, the CM adopted Resolution CM/ResCSS(2019)10 on the application of the European Code of Social Security (relating to the period 1 July 2017–30 June 2018), particularly the following parts of the Code: V (Old-age benefit), VI (Employment injury benefit), VII (Family benefit), VIII (Maternity benefit). On the basis of the Italian Government's report and the examination carried out by the ILO Committee of Experts on the Application of Conventions and Recommendations, the CM drew up a series of observations, on which it requested additional information from the Italian Authorities. With reference to part V of the Code, the CM invited the Italian Authorities to restore the right of all those protected pursuant to the issue of pension and social security reductions after 15 years of pension contributions. With regard to part VI, the CM requested that the Italian Authorities confirm that the work of INAIL includes the provision of dental care and dental supplies, at-home nursing assistance, and free glasses for victims of workplace accidents, as under article 34(2), lett. b), c) and e), of the Code. Regarding part XII of the Code, the CM requested further information on social security inspection services, in particular to explain the work of the National Labour Inspectorate (established with lgs.d. 149/2015) and the concrete benefits of the effectiveness and efficiency of the inspection services through a combination of social security and labour inspections.

III European Court of Human Rights

The European Court of Human Rights (ECtHR) guarantees the respect of the commitments laid down in the ECHR and its protocols by Member States of the CoE.

On 5 May 2019, Raffaele Sabato took on as the Italian judge on the ECtHR, taking over from Guido Raimondi who had also been the President of the ECtHR since September 2015.

The statistical data provided by the Court, and updated in December 2019, show that the total number of complaints pending against Italy amounted to 3,071, around 5.1 % of the total. In a worse situation are Romania with 7,879 complaints pending (13.2 % of the total), Ukraine (8,827, 14.8 %), Turkey (9,236, 15.5 %) and the Russian Federation (15,037, 25.2 %). 24.10 % of Italy's cases concern the right to a fair trial (article 6 ECHR), followed by 18.25 % of cases concerning the ban on torture and inhuman or degrading treatment (article 3 ECHR).

In 2019, the Court received 1,454 valid individual complaints about a violation of rights contained within the ECHR by Italy (1,692 in 2018 and 1,374 in 2017). In the same period, 2,403 complaints were declared inadmissible or removed; 14 were judgments as to substance, concerning 15 complaints, 13 of which found at least one violation of the Convention. Overall, the Court found the following violations: 1 with regard to inhuman and degrading treatment according to article 3 ECHR; 1 with regard to the lack of effectiveness of proceedings due to incomplete investigations according to article 3 ECHR; 1 with regard to the right to freedom and security according to article 5; 2 on the right to a fair trial according to article 6; 3 for excessive length of procedures according to article 6 ECHR; 1 with regard to the execution of a sentence according to article 6 ECHR; 3 on private and family life according to article 8 ECHR; 1 with regard to freedom of expression according to article 10; 2 for the absence of an effective remedy according to article 13 ECHR; 4 on the protection of property according to article 1, Protocol 1 ECHR.

136 complaints were communicated to the State in view of a hearing on their merits. The ECtHR also received 44 requests for urgent measures pursuant to article 39 of the Court's regulations, mostly regarding the suspension of deportation proceedings for as many applicants, only 6 of which were granted by the ECtHR.

An analysis on the Court's judgments concerning Italy in 2019 is presented in Part IV, Italy in the Case-law of the European Court of Human Rights.

IV Committee for the Prevention of Torture

The European Committee for the Prevention of Torture and Inhuman or Degrading Treatment or Punishment (CPT) was established by the 1987 Convention of the same name, conceived as complementary to the regulations under article 3 of ECHR which sets forth an absolute ban on torture. The CPT is a body composed of independent experts and has one member for each State Party to the Convention for the Prevention of Torture (all the CoE countries are party to it). The members of the Committee are elected by the Committee of Ministers. From 7 October 2015 to 19 December 2019, the Italian CPT member was Elisabetta Zamparutti. Gaia Pergolo was appointed by the CM with Resolution CM/ResCPT(2019)3 and will be in office until 19 December 2023.

> The Committee's main function is to verify, by means of inspections, the treatment of persons deprived of their liberty in order to strengthen, if necessary, their protection from torture and inhuman or degrading treatment or punishment (article 1). CPT is not an investigative body, but a preventive body. At the end of each visit, the Committee draws up a detailed report and sends it to the State involved, to which it requests an answer in relation to any critical issues raised in it. The action of the CPT is based on the principles of cooperation with national authorities and confidentiality. Therefore, its reports and the responses of the Governments are initially reserved and only subsequently, at the request of the country concerned, may they be made public together with the replies and observations provided by the national authorities.

In 2019, the CPT conducted 16 visits in the following countries: Armenia, Bosnia-Herzegovina, Denmark, France, Greece, Ireland, Iceland, Italy, North Macedonia, Poland, Portugal, Russian Federation, Turkey, the United Kingdom (2 visits) and Ukraine. During the year in question, the CPT published 12 reports related to the visits carried out in the following CoE Member States: Albania, Andorra, Bulgaria, Czech Republic, Estonia, Russian Federation, Georgia, Lithuania, Montenegro, Slovak Republic, Ukraine and United Kingdom.

Overall, the CPT conducted 14 visits in Italy (seven periodic visits and seven *ad hoc).* The most recent visit was from 12–22 June 2019 in order to evaluate the situation of detained persons in high or maximum security (the so-called regime 41-*bis*) and other isolation and segregation methods, such as the so-called daytime isolation. On the request of the Italian Government, the report of the Committee (CPT/Inf(2020)2) and the Authorities' response (CPT/Inf (2020)3) were published jointly on 20 January 2020.

During its visit, the CPT delegation visited prisons in Biella, Opera (Milan), Saluzzo and Viterbo. Cooperation on the part of the Italian Authorities was generally considered excellent, with the one exception of the Viterbo prison, where the management did not seem aware of the Committee's mandate. The delegation consulted with the Undersecretary of State for the Ministry of Justice, the head of the Department of Prison Administration (DAP) and other functionaries of the Ministry of Justice and the DAP and with various representatives from the Carabinieri, the Financial police and the State police force. Furthermore, CPT members met with Mauro Palma, president of the National Ombudsperson for the rights of persons detained or deprived of their liberty, who also carries out the national prevention mechanism (see Part II, National Bodies with Jurisdiction over Human Rights, VII, E) pursuant to OPCAT. The CPT members also met with representatives of civil society organisations working in this field.

In its report, the CPT notes positively the adoption of amendments to the Prison Administration Act in October 2018 (lgs.d. 121/2018; lgs.d. 123/2018; lgs.d. 124/2018). At the same time, it shows concern about the constant increase of the incarcerated population since its law periodic visit in 2016 (see *Yearbook 2017*, pp. 198–200) and that a large number of detainees are not guaranteed the minimum standards of $4m^2$ living space in multiple occupancy cells. Another further development is the recent judgment of the ECtHR on the *Marcello Viola (No. 2)* case, on 7 October 2019, on life sentences with parole (pursuant to article 4-*bis* of the Prison Administration Act). In the judgment, the ECtHR ruled that the current Italian prison system focuses on the lack of cooperation with the judicial authorities of inmates serving a full life sentence without taking their course of resocialisation into consideration.

In the prisons visited, the great majority of prisoners met by the delegation stated that they were treated correctly by staff. However, a few allegations of excessive use of force and physical ill-treatment were received at Biella, Milan Opera and Saluzzo Prisons. Further, at Viterbo Prison, a considerable number of allegations of physical ill-treatment were received and the CPT's delegation identified a pattern of deliberate infliction of ill-treatment by staff. The report describes several cases where the injuries observed and the medical evidence recorded were compatible with the allegations of ill-treatment made by the inmates. The report recommended that the Italian authorities should exert increased vigilance on staff, effectively investigate complaints made by prisoners and improve staff training, notably on the professional application of control and restraint and de-escalation techniques.

The conditions of detention for inmates under the medium-security regime varied at the prison establishments visited. In general, cells offered sufficient living space and adequate conditions of detention in terms of access to natural light, ventilation and state of repair. That said, material deficiencies were still visible, in particular in relation to the dilapidated and unhygienic common shower facilities, the austere design of the courtyards and in some cases the poor quality of food in terms of lack of variety and low protein content. The Italian authorities were recommended to remedy these deficiencies. In terms of regime, the CPT observed that both the out-of-cell and outdoor exercise entitlements offered to inmates were generous, but prison staff still did not engage in constructive relations with prisoners. Staff still misunderstood the concept of dynamic security. There was also the necessity to improve the programme of activities and vocational training opportunities at Biella and Saluzzo Prisons and to fill the vacant positions of educators.

The report described the situation of 28 internees subject to a court-imposed security measure who were accommodated in an ordinary section of Biella Prison in poor material conditions and provided with an impoverished regime. The CPT requested further information on the announced transfer of the internees to another establishment in order to provide them with adequate care and treatment in view of their specific legal status.

As regards inmates subject to the high-security regime, the CPT found certain material deficiencies such as absence of ventilation in the sanitary annexes and persistent problems with the provision of heating and hot water. The regime on offer was similar to the one in force for the medium-security population except that the range of work, vocational and educational activities and the visiting and telephone call entitlements were more limited. The CPT considered that more needs to be done to expand the range of activities on offer to high-security prisoners. The CPT also recommended that the Italian authorities review the classification and de-classification criteria for the placement of prisoners into the high-security regime, given the lack of a clearly defined procedure and legal certainty.

Turning to the various forms of isolation and segregation of prisoners, the CPT considered that the accessory punishment of court-imposed solitary confinement pursuant to article 72 of the Criminal Code ("*isolamento diurno*") is anachronistic and should be abolished. Such an additional punishment of prolonged solitary confinement can have harmful effects and is contrary to the principle of resocialisation of prisoners, particularly as it is usually imposed several years after the commencement of imprisonment. As regards the regime of special surveillance ("*sorveglianza particolare*") pursuant to article 14-*bis* of the Prison Law, the Committee found that prisoners subjected to this regime were de facto held in conditions of solitary confinement for prolonged periods. Given the potentially harmful effects of subjecting inmates to prolonged solitary confinement, the Committee called upon the authorities to provide such prisoners with an appropriate regime (i.e. at least two hours of meaningful human contact per day).

The report also described other separation measures of inmates for reasons of good order and criticises the lack of a regular review of such measures and the impossibility to appeal against them. Further, the report also included concrete recommendations in order to improve material conditions in the isolation and segregation units of the establishments visited.

The CPT again examined the extensive restrictions imposed on inmates subjected to article 41-*bis* of the Prison Administration Act (so-called hard prison regime) at the detention units of Milan Opera and Viterbo Prisons. The CPT called upon the Italian authorities to engage in a serious reflection on the current configuration of the "41-*bis*" regime by providing inmates throughout the prison system with a wider range of activities and increasing visiting and telephone entitlements, as well as remedying the observed deficiencies. It also considers that placement in the so-called restricted areas should be limited in time in light of their very restrictive conditions.

As to prison health-care, the CPT gained a generally positive impression of the quality of primary health-care provided to prisoners in the establishments visited. However, once again, regional disparities were found. The Committee recommended that vacant health-care posts at Biella and Saluzzo Prisons be filled, and that access to specialised and dental care in these prisons be improved. Further, the deficiencies concerning dental care and the conditions at the infirmary of Viterbo Prison should be remedied. It also recommended that measures be taken to ensure that confidentiality of medical examinations of inmates is respected.

The report also criticised the prolonged accommodation of mentally ill persons in a prison setting due to the absence of places in appropriate facilities (such as the so-called Residences for the Execution of Security Measures or REMS and the specialised psychiatric sections in prisons or ATSM). Measures should be taken to ensure that mentally ill prisoners are transferred to a health-care facility without delay. From the official statistics on suicide provided to the CPT and from the findings of its delegation, it appeared that persons who were placed in de facto solitary confinement were at much greater risk of committing suicide. Even persons who were assessed as being suicidal were often isolated from other prisoners, rather than being placed under direct staff supervision and offered both meaningful contact with other staff members and prisoners and access to activities, as appropriate.

The report also addressed the essential role of staff in prisons, and the necessity for staff to be better allocated throughout the prisons to ensure an effective presence on every section. The notion of dynamic security needs to be better promoted, and the training of staff enhanced, notably as concerns interpersonal skills. Finally, recommendations were made to increase telephone entitlements and family contacts for high-security prisoners, and to reinforce legal safeguards surrounding disciplinary proceedings for inmates.

V European Committee of Social Rights

The European Committee of Social Rights was established pursuant to article 25 of the European Social Charter of 1961 in order to determine whether the legislation and practice of States Parties comply with the provisions of the European Social Charter, its Protocols and the European Social Charter (revised) (ESC-R). Currently, the Committee is composed of 15 independent experts elected by the Committee of Ministers for a six-year mandate renewable only once. The Italian expert Giuseppe Palmisano was re-elected for the period 2016–2022, becoming the President of the Committee in 2017.

Italy ratified the European Social Charter in 1965 and the revised European Social Charter in 1999, accepting 97 of its 98 paragraphs. The only non-accepted provision is article 25 ESC-R, which protects the right of workers in the case of the insolvency of their employer. In 2002, the Committee of Ministers agreed that, every five years, countries must also inform the European Committee of Social Rights on the status of rights protected under provisions that they have not accepted. Italy's most recent communication was in 2019. On 6 June, the Italian authorities informed the Committee that on 13 December 2016, the Council of Europe representatives and Italy's competent authorities met to discuss obstacles that prevent Italy from accepting article 25 ESC-R. Following this meeting, the Directorate General of Labour and Industrial Relations of the Ministry of Labour and Social Policies took the necessary steps to clarify the situation regarding the operation of the Guarantee Fund. In conclusion, it was of the opinion that the problem of non-compliance of the national legislative framework – the reason given by Italy in 2014 for its non-acceptance of article 25 ESC-R (see *Yearbook 2016*, p. 183) – could be overcome. In fact, according to data from the INPS (National Social Welfare Scheme), the average period of payment of funds to workers is in line with the 60-day period prescribed by law No. 297 of 29 May 1982 and, consequently, with the deadline set by the case-law of the European Committee of Social Rights. The Ministry will therefore continue to analyse the matter, hoping to initiate the ratification procedure of article 25 of the Charter. In an opinion adopted on 3 September 2019, the Committee welcomed these developments and encouraged the Italian authorities to accept the article in question in the near future. If this does not happen, the next examination of the provision not accepted by Italy will take place in 2024.

In reference to the analysis of the provisions that were previously accepted, from 1967 to 2016, the Italian Government presented 20 annual reports on the application of the 1961 Charter and 17 or the revised Charter. On the basis of these reports, each year the Committee adopted conclusions on the state of protection of social rights in Italy. The most recent conclusions were published in March 2020 and refer to the seventeenth report, presented (late) on 10 May 2019; this year, they concern provisions for the thematic group "Children, Families, Migrants" (articles 7, 8, 16, 17, 19, 27, 31 ESC-R) during the period 1 January 2014–31 December 2017.

The Committee refers to the 36 paragraphs of these articles. It concluded that for 14 of these situations, Italy was in compliance, while for 15, the situation demonstrated in the country was in non-compliance. For seven of these paragraphs, the Committee postponed its conclusions and requested further information and details in the next report on the same issues.

Conclusions on Italy 2019 per paragraph

article ESC-R	**Conclusions: compliance**	**Conclusions: non-compliance**	**Postponed/request for information**
article 7 ESC-R (Right of children and young persons to protection)	para. 6 (time spent in vocational training during the normal working hours) para. 7 (paid annual holiday) para. 8 (prohibiting night work) para. 9 (regular medical control)	para. 1 (prohibiting employment under 15 years) para. 2 (prohibiting employment under 18 years for activities regarded as dangerous or unhealthy) para. 3 (prohibiting employment of children still subject to compulsory education) para. 4 (duration of working hours) para. 5 (fair wage)	para. 10 (special protection against physical and moral dangers)
article 8 ESC-R (Right of employed women to protection of maternity)	para. 1 (maternity leave), para. 4 (regulate night work) para. 5 (prohibiting dangerous, unhealthy or arduous work)	para. 2 (unlawful dismissal during maternity leave)	para. 3 (sufficient time off for mothers to nurse infants)
article 16 ESC-R (Right of the family to social, legal and economic protection)		Whole article	

Conclusions on Italy 2019 per paragraph

article 17 ESC-R (Right of children and young persons to social, legal and economic protection)		para. 2 (primary and secondary education with regular attendance at schools)	para. 1 (assistance, education and training)
article 19 ESC-R (Right of migrant workers and their families to protection and assistance)	para. 2 (departure, journey and reception) para. 5 (equality with regard to taxes and contributions) para. 7 (equality in respect of legal proceedings) para. 9 (transfer of earnings and savings) para. 11 (teaching of the national language)	para. 1 (assistance and information about migration) para. 4 (remuneration, membership of trade unions and accommodation) para. 10 (equal treatment for self-employed migrants)	para. 3 (cooperation between social services in emigration and immigration countries) para. 6 (family reunification) para 8 (guarantees against expulsion), para. 12 (teaching of the migrant worker's mother tongue)
article 27 ESC-R (Right of workers with family responsibilities to equal opportunities and equal treatment)	para. 1 (participation in employment) para. 2 (parental leave)	para. 3 (illegitimacy of dismissal due to family responsibilities)	
article 31 ESC-R (Right to housing)		para 1 (adequate housing) para. 2 (reduce homelessness), para. 3 (accessible housing prices)	

Regarding article 7 ESC-R (right of children and young persons to protection), the situation in Italy does not comply with the article's first five paragraphs. Concerning the regulations contained in para. 1 (prohibiting employment under 15 years) and 3 (prohibiting employment of children still subject to compulsory education), the Committee's analysis concludes that legislation regarding these paragraphs has not been concretely implemented. With reference to para. 2 (prohibiting employment under 18 years for activities regarded as dangerous or unhealthy), the situation is not considered in compliance as the Work Inspectorate does not conduct visits in training facilities where some dangerous or unhealthy roles could be carried out by minors. Concerning para. 4 (duration of working hours), according to the Committee, the Government's report does not show that working hours of 15- and 16-year-olds are reasonable. In relation to para. 5 (fair wage), the data presented by the authorities do not show that young workers' wages and the minimum allowance for apprentices are equal. Concerning para. 6 (time spent in vocational training during the normal working hours), the Committee requests further information on the extension of cover for all categories of young workers of all measures in force; in anticipation of this information, the Committee considers the situation to be in compliance with the Charter (revised). A similar approach has been adopted regarding para. 7 (paid annual holiday) and para. 8 (prohibiting night work). In both situations, the Committee adopts compliance decisions while requesting further information, particularly on the activities on work inspectors. The Committee concludes that the situation in Italy is in compliance in relation to para. 9 (regular medical control); other than requesting more detailed information on work inspectors, concerning to this paragraph, the Committee also asks for information on whether the medical tests undertaken in specific situations are adequate considering the risk to which some young workers are exposed. With reference to para. 10 (special protection against physical and moral dangers), the Committee postpones its conclusions in anticipation of more detailed information on various issues covered by the paragraph in question. The Committee asks particularly whether child victims of sexual exploitation can be held criminally responsible for their actions, and whether there are any training programmes for law enforcement agencies and social assistants to increase their knowledge on how to prevent and manage cases of sexual exploitation; it asks for information on the implementation of law 71/2017 (Provisions to protect minors and to prevent and tackle cyberbullying) and measures adopted to protect children from abuse via new technology; it also requests further information on measures adopted by the Italian Authorities to improve data collection on child victims of trafficking, and to protect and assist children living in vulnerable situations, especially in rural areas.

Regarding article 8 ESC-R (right of employed women to protection of maternity), the Committee concludes that the situation in Italy is in compliance with para. 1 (maternity leave), 4 (regulate night work) and 5 (prohibiting dangerous, unhealthy or arduous work), although concerning the first paragraph, this conclusion was made pending further information, particularly on the right to any type of allowance to female workers who do not qualify for maternity pay during their maternity leave. With reference to para. 2 (unlawful dismissal during maternity leave), the situation identified by the Committee is not in compliance, given that fair compensation may not be guaranteed in cases of wrongful dismissal during pregnancy or during maternity leave if the woman in question does not want to return to work. Regarding para. 3 (sufficient time off for mothers to nurse infants), the Committee decided to postpone its conclusion in anticipation of further information on existing guarantees to ensure that full-time domestic workers have the right to paid breaks to breastfeed, and on any laws in force on this right for part-time workers.

Regarding article 16 ESC-R (right of the family to social, legal and economic protection) – an article just one paragraph long –, the Committee concluded that the situation is not in compliance for the following reasons: the Government has not demonstrated that equal access for family benefits are guaranteed for citizens of other States party to the Charter; family allowances are not a sufficient additional income for a considerable number of families; Roma and Sinti families are not adequately protected concerning housing, especially in terms of eviction procedures and access to social housing (see also conclusions on article 31 ESC-R).

Regarding article 17 ESC-R (right of children and young persons to social, legal and economic protection), the Committee has postponed its conclusions on para. 1 (assistance, education and training); further information is needed in order to complete its evaluation. The Committee has requested information on the measures adopted to reduce the status of statelessness in children and the support the registration of children from the most vulnerable groups, such as Roma and Sinti communities and refugees. Furthermore, the Committee asked whether, in relation to child protection, the courts respected the legislation in practice, specifically referring to the use of corporal punishment as an educational method. Other information requested concerned the number of children in children's homes and foster homes, and progress made for the deinstitutionalisation of children and the ways and monitoring of fostering and all types of children's homes. The Committee asked for information on the maximum detention period that a child can be given, and in the case of minors in custodial sentences, it asked for confirmation that the detention period is regularly re-examined. It also asked whether minors can be subjected to solitary confinement, and if so, in what circumstances and for how long. Concerning the right to assistance, the additional information requested by the Committee concerns assistance for children in irregular situations to protect them from violence, negligence or exploitation, and whether children in these situations have access to healthcare. Regarding the situation of child poverty, the Committee asked the Italian Authorities to provide information in its next report on the levels of child poverty in the country, and the measures adopted to reduce the problem, especially through combatting discrimination and promoting equal opportunities for children from particularly vulnerable groups such as ethnic minorities, Roma communities, children with disabilities and in foster care. Concerning paragraph 2 of the article (primary and secondary education, regular attendance at schools), the Committee concluded that the situation in Italy is not in compliance given that the measures adopted to improve access to education for children from Roma communities have not shown to be sufficient.

Regarding article 19 ESC-R (right of migrant workers and their families to protection and assistance), the Committee concluded that the situation in Italy is in compliance with para. 2 (departure, journey and reception), 5 (equality with regard to taxes and contributions), 7 (equality in respect of legal proceedings), 9 (transfer of earnings and savings) and 11 (teaching of the national language). For all except the latter, the Committee still requested further information. However, the Committee found that the situation was not in compliance with para. 1 (assistance and information on migration) since the measures adopted to combat misleading propaganda on emigration have not been sufficient, particularly measures to prevent racism and xenophobia in politics and the propaganda against Roma and Sinti migrants. Moreover, the Committee reiterated that this reason was also at the basis of a violation ESC-R in the collective complaint (58/2009) presented against Italy by the *Centre on Housing Rights and Evictions* (see *Yearbook 2011*, pp. 218–219). Another non-compliance conclusion concerns para. 4 (remuneration, membership of trade unions, accommodation); the report presented by the Italian Government did not demonstrate the adoption of sufficient concrete measures to eliminate legal and de facto discrimination concerning access to accommodation. When the issues identified concerning these two situations are also applied to s self-employed migrant workers, the Committee concluded that the situation can be considered non-compliant with para. 10 (equal treatment for self-employed migrants). The Committee has postponed its conclusions with reference to the four remaining paragraphs, requesting further information from the Italian Authorities on these issues. Regarding para. 3 (cooperation between social services in emigration and immigration countries), the information requested was on the type and nature of contacts and information that maybe be exchanged with other countries' (origin or destination) social services; measures adopted to establish these contacts and promote cooperation between other countries' social services; agreements or international networks and any specific examples of cooperation (formal or informal) between State social services and other countries of origin or destination. Furthermore, the Committee has asked whether this cooperation only concerns social security (for example, on the family) and whether the Italian Authorities could give any examples of cooperation at the local level (and any cases in which this cooperation has been verified). Concerning para. 6 (family reunification) the Committee, reiterating a previously-made request from 2011 (see *Yearbook 2012*, p. 241), requested information on the existence of a complaint mechanism which, in cases of family reunification, allows for the examination of the merits of individual cases coherently with the principles of proportionality and reasonableness. Concerning para. 8 (guarantees against expulsion), the Committee requests further information on the reasons for which a magistrate can order an expulsion, as well as any circumstances in which a judge can order the same measure. It asked whether it is possible to review or appeal against such a decision or remediate the situation post factum, and whether these measures would have a suspensive effect; it also asked for further illumination on the concept of "social dangerousness", particularly related to committing minor offences. Regarding para. 12 (teaching of the migrant worker's mother tongue), the Committee presented a series of specific statistical data collection requests on the number of children receiving an education in their native language; the languages taught; the basis on which children of migrants have access to a multilingual education; and measures adopted by the Government to improve access to these schools for children of migrants. The Commission also asks whether the Government financially supports this access, what additional educational projects for teaching foreign languages and whether any non-governmental organisations provide educational teaching in migrants' languages and whether these receive support from the State.

Regarding article 27 ESC-R (Right of workers with family responsibilities to equal opportunities and equal treatment), the Committee concluded that the situation in Italy is in compliance with para. 1 (participation in employment) and 2 (parental leave). In relation to paragraph 1, the Committee asked the Italian Authorities to provide further information on how the period of parental leave is calculated given that family responsibility is taken into consideration when calculating pension rights. Regarding para. 3 (illegitimacy of dismissal due to family responsibilities), the Committee concluded that the situation in Italy is not in compliance on the basis that workers with family care responsibilities are not protected against wrongful dismissal for family responsibility if the worker does not want to be reintegrated into work.

Regarding article 31 ESC-R (right to housing), the Committee concluded that the situation in Italy is not in compliance with any of the three paragraphs within the article. Concerning para 1 (adequate housing), the Committee reached its conclusion based on the inadequate housing conditions of the Roma and Sinti communities in fixed camps and settlements. With reference to para. 2 (reduce homelessness), the measures adopted by the Government to reduce homelessness are considered insufficient. Furthermore, the evictions of Roma and Sinti communities continue without respecting the procedural guarantees that ensure respect for the human dignity for each individual person. Regarding para. 3 (accessible housing prices) the Committee concluded that the data presented by the Italian Authorities did not demonstrate that citizens of other States party to the European Social Charter legally working or residing in Italy have the same right to equal treatment in accessing social housing. Furthermore, there have not been sufficient resources invested to improve access for Roma and Sinti communities to social housing without discrimination. The Committee also observed that the citizens of other States party to the European Social Charter legally working or residing in Italy do not have the right to the same fair treatment regarding access to living benefits, as the criteria for the length of residency is excessive.

The next Italian report at the European Committee of Social Rights will be a simplified follow-up report on the decisions regarding collective complaints, in which the Committee found a violation. The deadline for the presentation of this report was 31 December 2019.

Collective complaints

In 2019, the Committee adopted two decisions on the collective complaints procedure established by the 1995 Protocol.

On 26 November 2019, the Committee adopted a decision on the complaint *Unione Generale Lavoratori – Federazione Nazionale Corpo forestale dello Stato (UGL – CFS) and Sindacato autonomo polizia ambientale forestale (SAPAF) v. Italy* (complaint 143/2016). The complaint, adopted on 3 July 2019, accuses the State of violating articles 1 ESC-R (right to work), 5 ESC-R (right to organise) and 6 ESC-R (right to bargain collectively), as well as articles E ESC-R (non-discrimination) and G ESC-R (restrictions). The complainant trade unions claimed that by applying lgs.d. 177/2016 (incorporating the State Forestry Authority into the Carabinieri Corps, thus acquiring military status), Italy was denying the State Forestry Authority of their trade union rights. In the decision regarding this complaint, after analysing the trade unions arguments and the response of the Italian Government, the Committee concluded that article 1(2) of the ESC-R is not applicable to the complaint in question. On the contrary, for the remaining complainant provisions, the Committee concluded by majority vote that there had been a violation of the Charter.

On 11 February 2020, the Committee made public its decision on collective complaint 158/2017 (adopted in September 2019, originally presented on 26 October 2017 by the *Confederazione Generale Italiana del Lavoro (CGIL)*). In this complaint, the trade union asked the Committee to confirm Italy's violation of article 24 ESC-R (right to protection in cases of termination of employment) concerning the provisions of lgs.d. 23/2015 on the protection of private sector workers against wrongful dismissal (articles 3, 4, 9 and 10). In particular, the complaint of the CGIL claimed that the compensation mechanism (established by the law in question) did not allow those who had been wrongfully dismissed to get sufficient compensation compared to the damage caused through internal judicial procedures, as well as not having a dissuasive effect on employers from continuing this practice.

In its analysis of the collective complaint (declared admissible on 20 March 2018), the Committee summarised the relevant national, European and international legislation on the matter, as well as the main legal developments that came out the adoption of lgs.d. 23/2015. Among others, the Committee mentioned l.d. 87/2018 (raising the minimum and maximum levels of compensation) and judgment No. 194 of 26 September 2018 of the Constitutional Court (overturning the method of calculating compensation for wrongful dismissal), declaring the illegitimacy of article 3(1) of lgs.d. 23/2015 in which it determines that the compensation be "the sum equal to two months wages of the last reference amount to calculate the final severance payment for each year of service".

On the basis of the Italian legal framework and after analysing the trade union's requests and the response of the Italian Government, and referring back to the Committee's own case-law on the issue (particularly the decision of 8 September 2016 on collective complaint 106/2014, *Finnish Society of Social Rights v. Finland*), the Committee concluded that the situation described in the complaint constitutes a violation of article 24 ESC-R.

Specifically, the Committee considered that neither the alternative legal remedies offered to victims of wrongful dismissal the possibility of compensation above the maximum threshold (imposed by law) nor the conciliation mechanism, as established by existing measures, allow all cases of wrongful dismissal to get adequate compensation, proportionate to the damage endured and able to discourage employers from continuing this practice of dismissal.

In 2019, three new collective complaints were presented against Italy.

The first (178/2019) was presented by Amnesty International and registered on 18 March 2019. In his, the NGO stated that the living situation of Roma and Sinti communities in Italy violated article 31 ESC-R (right to housing), read alone or jointly with article E (ESC-R) (non-discrimination), die to the continued practice of forced evictions, the provision of segregated and low-quality housing and the use of discriminatory criteria for assigning social housing. On 4 July 2019, the Committee unanimously declared the complaint admissible and decided, with 13 votes to one, to indicate immediate measures. Through these measures, the Committee asked the Italian Authorities to: 1) adopt all possible measures to eliminate the risk of grave and irreparable damage to evicted persons and others mentions in the complaint, in particular to ensure that those being evicted would not be left homeless and the evictions do not lead to unacceptable living conditions; and 2) ensure that all competent public authorities are updated about this decision and that they inform the Committee of all measures adopted to implement it without delay.

The second collective complaint was presented by *Sindacato Autonomo Europeo Scuola ed Ecologia* (SAESE) (No. 186/2019) and registered on 25 November 2019. It concerned article 30 ESC-R (right to protection against poverty and social exclusion). The complainant trade union claims that the pension reforms of 2011 (reducing the level of pensions) have caused thousands of precarious teachers to be at risk of poverty when they reach retirement age. Furthermore, the trade union complains that there is no comprehensive and coordinated approach to combatting poverty and social exclusion in Italy.

The third and final collective complaint *Sindacato autonomo Pensionati Or.S.A.* (187/2019) was registered on 3 December. The complaint concerned articles 4(1) ESC-R (right to equal remuneration), 12(1) ESC-R (right to social security), 16 ESC-R (right of the family to social, legal and economic protection), 20 ESC-R (right to equal opportunities and equal treatment in matters of employment and occupation without discrimination on the grounds of sex) and 23 ESC-R (right of elderly persons to social protection). The complainant trade union claims that the provisions introduced by article 1(41), of law 8 August 1995, No. 335 (Reforms to the compulsory and complementary pension system) and successive amendments (regulating the surviving spouse pension system) significantly reduce the amount of pension that is payable to a surviving spouse in the cases where the pension either goes to more than one recipient or one recipient has more than one source of income. This results in a discriminatory and unreasonable reduction of pension payments to which the deceased person would have had the right or had already received.

Finally, in 2019, the Committee adopted a series of decisions of the admissibility of complaints presented over the previous years. The complaints presented in *Unione sindacale di base (USB)* (complaint 170/2018, see *Yearbook 2019*, pp. 242–243) with a decision adopted on 3 July, and of *Associazione nazionale sindacato professionisti sanitari della funzione infermieristica – Nursing Up* (complaint 169/2018, see *Yearbook 2019*, pp. 242–243) with a decision adopted on 18 March were declared admissible. The complaints by the *Sindacato Autonomo Europeo Scuola ed Ecologia* (SAESE) (166/2018) and the *Associazione Medici Liberi* (177/2019) were declared admissible.

VI Commissioner for Human Rights

The Commissioner for Human Rights is an independent non-judicial institution established by the Committee of Ministers' Resolution (99)50 of 7 May 1999. On 1 April 2018, Dunja Mijatovic (Bosnia-Herzegovina) was elected Commissioner for Human Rights of the Council of Europe by the PACE. Mijatovic had served as the OSCE Representative on Freedom of the Media (see in this Part, Organisation for Security and Cooperation in Europe (OSCE), III), succeeding Nils Muižnieks (Latvia, 2012–2018), and will be in the role until April 2024.

> The Commissioner's duties are to promote effective respect for human rights, to support the 47 Member States in implementing the relevant CoE standards and to promote education and awareness of human rights. Its main activity is to conduct a permanent dialogue with Governments of the Member States, including visits to their respective territories. At the end of the mission, the Commissioner draws up a report that includes both an analysis on human rights and the improvement thereof; this report is published and spread widely. In addition, the Commissioner conducts follow-up visits to evaluate the progress made regarding the implementation of the previous recommendations and relevant reports are also rendered public.
>
> In 2019, the Commissioner conducted visits in Azerbaijan, Bosnia-Herzegovina, Bulgaria, France, Greece, Ireland, The Netherlands, Poland, Russian Federation, Turkey and Hungary. Furthermore, during the year in question, the Office of the Commissioner published the reports related to the visits conducted in 2018 in Armenia and Romania. The correspondence among the representatives of the CoE Member States' institutions was intense. Specifically, the Commissioner sent letters requesting information to Bosnia-Herzegovina, Czech Republic, Germany, Greece, Italy, Malta (2), Poland, Russian Federation, Scotland, Serbia and the Slovak Republic on their human rights situation.

Since its establishment, the Commissioner for Human Rights has conducted five visits in Italy. The last was held from 3–6 July 2012 and aimed to examine a series of critical issues, focussing on the excessive duration of judicial process and protection of the rights of Roma and Sinti communities, migrants and asylum seekers. The subsequent report was published on 18 September 2012 (CommDH (2012)26) (see *Yearbook 2013*, pp. 255–262). Although their last visit and report took place five years ago, the Commissioner has kept up a dialogue with the Italian authorities through various letters requesting clarifications, especially related to policies on Roma minorities and the management of migrants, refugees and asylum seekers (see, for example, *Yearbook 2017*, pp. 209–212 and *Yearbook 2018*, pp. 223–226).

On 7 February 2019, the Commissioner made public a letter (dated 31 January) addressed to the Prime Minister Giuseppe Conte (CommHR/DM/sf 004-2019). In this letter, the Commissioner expresses her concern about the negative consequences that the so-called security decree adopted in October 2018 (l.d. 113/2018, converted in law 132/2018) could have on the human rights situation of asylum seekers and those under international protection, including those under humanitarian protection. She asks for clarifications on the measures contained within the aforementioned legislation that will ensure continued access to reception and essential services. In particular, the Commissioner notes the apparent hastiness of transfers of residents of the Asylum Seekers Reception Centre (CARA) of Castelnuovo (Rome) in view of its closure, and expresses concern that these transfers could disrupt the commendable efforts put in place in the past years by local services for the integration and rehabilitation of the residents. Furthermore, recognising Italy's role over the past years in saving lives at sea and receiving asylum seekers and migrants arriving at its shores, the Commissioner states her deep concern about the recent measures hampering and criminalising the work of NGOs and relinquishing responsibility for search and rescue operations to authorities which appear unwilling or unable to protect rescued migrants from torture or inhuman or degrading treatment. The Commissioner urges the Italian Government to ensure that the human rights of persons rescued at sea are never put at risk because of current disagreements between Member States about disembarkation, and that humanitarian considerations always take priority.

The Italian Government sent a letter in response to the Commissioner on 12 March 2019. In this letter, the Permanent Representative of Italy to the Council of Europe, Michele Giacomelli, provides further updated information on the issues raised by the Commissioner. He focuses on describing the measures introduced by law 132/2018, particularly referring to the introduction of alternative measures for residence permits for humanitarian reasons, to the reformation of the reception system (establishing and the function of the SIPROIMI instead of the SPRAR system), and on the new criteria to acquire citizenship. The letter provides further information on the patrol action of the Italian Navy within the broad European framework, and gives statistical data on arrivals during the 2016–2019 period, describing initiatives undertaken following the closure of the CARA in Castelnuovo and the redistribution of residents into structures provided by the Lazio provinces, other Italian regions and the SIPROIMI system. According to the Italian Authorities, there were only three cases in which reception measures were revoked due to not meeting the new criteria.

On 21 November 2019, the Commissioner published her written observations presented at the ECtHR concerning the *S.S. and others v. Italy* case (21660/18). This case concerned the interception and rescue operation of a boat in distress in the Mediterranean Sea, carrying around 150 persons who had left Libya, and the alleged human rights violations resulting from this operation. In her submission, the Commissioner recalled that the effective protection and promotion of the human rights of refugees, asylum seekers and migrants, at sea and on land, requires the full implementation of member states' obligations under international maritime law, human rights law and refugee law, read consistently with each other. The Commissioner underscored that changes adopted in member states' migration practices in the Central Mediterranean, in particular certain types of assistance provided to the Libyan Coast Guard, have resulted in increased returns of migrants, asylum seekers and refugees to Libya, despite the fact that member states knew, or should have known, about the risk of serious human rights violations they would face in the country. In addition, the Commissioner highlighted that, at the receipt of distress calls originating from any search and rescue region, Member States' relevant authorities should not transfer responsibility for rescue operations to other state authorities, when they know or should know that such action would expose people in distress at sea to serious violations of their human rights. Lastly, she stressed that instructions issued in the course of such operations must be human rights compliant and that they should neither obstruct safety at sea and effective rescue, nor lead to the disembarkation of persons rescued at sea in a place that is not safe.

Among the Commissioner for Human Rights' work in 2019, the online publication of various Human Rights Comments (short posts in which the Commissioner analyses and summarises relevant human rights situations in Europe) is particularly noteworthy. Over the year, 7 comments were published (7 in 2018, 10 in 2017). Three of these refer specifically to the human rights situation in Italy.

European states must demonstrate resolve for lasting and concrete change for Roma people (4 April 2019). In this comment, the Commissioner uses the celebration of International Roma Day, 8 April, to highlight the urgent need to better protect the human rights of Roma Across Europe, the continuation of human rights abuses targeting Roma goes against all efforts otherwise made to improve their access to education, health care and employment and prevents them from fully participating in society. Among the various examples of episodes of human rights violations illustrated by the Commissioner, the issue of forcible evictions of Roma communities without due process and without provision of adequate alternative housing – a reoccurring practice that the Commissioner has already highlighted in Italy and other CoE Member States (Albania, Bulgaria, France, Serbia and Sweden). In the same comment, the Commissioner recalls that the failing of these countries to put an end to these practices was the reason that the European Committee of Social Rights of the Council of Europe found that these Member States had violated rights laid out in the European Social Charter (revised) (see, in this Part, Council of Europe, IV).

The independence of judges and the judiciary under threat (3 September 2019). In this comment, the Commissioner underlines the fundamental importance of the independence of the judiciary for the respect for the rule of law, the functioning of democracy and the observance of human rights. She then gives a series of examples of recent situations in which politicians and Governments of various CoE Member States have interfered with the judiciary and have even resorted to threats against judges rather than supporting and strengthening their independence, impartiality and efficiency. Among the examples, the Commissioner highlights the then-Interior Minister Matteo Salvini's public identification and attack on social media on 6 June 2019 on three magistrates who had challenged his immigration policies.

Time to deliver on commitments to protect people on the move from human trafficking and exploitation (12 September 2019). In this comment, the Commissioner underlines the importance that the fight against human trafficking and the eradication of what some call "modern slavery" is gaining prominence on the agendas of most Council of Europe Member States. One of the issues identified was the impact of migration policies on human trafficking victims. The Commissioner uses Italy as an example of this – in its second evaluation report on Italy (see this Part, Council of Europe, X),

GRETA found that, despite various areas of progress, new legislation excluding asylum seekers from access to reception centres focussed on social inclusion risked leaving possible victims of trafficking without assistance.

Finally, the Office of the Commissioner published various human rights reports in 2019; the most noteworthy are the *Unboxing artificial intelligence* report on the necessary steps for protecting human rights from the possible negative developments of artificial intelligence and the *Lives saved. Rights protected* report on the protection and rescue of refugees, asylum seekers and migrants at sea.

VII European Commission against Racism and Intolerance

The European Commission against Racism and Intolerance (ECRI), established in 1993, is a monitoring body of the Council of Europe specialised in combating any form of racism, xenophobia, anti-semitism and intolerance in a human rights perspective. The members of ECRI remain in office for five years. They are selected for their moral authority and their recognised experience in the field of combating racism, xenophobia, anti-semitism and intolerance; they act on an individual basis and independently. The Commission is composed by a member and, if a Government so wishes, a deputy member for each State of the Council of Europe. In 2018, the Italian expert was Vitaliano Esposito. Constance Hermanin was an alternate member. An Italian official, Stefano Valenti, was responsible for the External Relations of the Commission Secretariat, part of the Directorate-general Human Rights and the Rule of Law of the Council of Europe

The mandate of the ECRI covers all measures to combat violence, discrimination and prejudice against people (or groups of people) on the basis of racial, linguistic, religious, national, or ethnic preconditions. The Commission carries out an in-depth analysis of the situation regarding racism and intolerance in each of the Member States of the CoE and writes suggestions and proposals by drawing up reports. The report is on the basis of an analysis of documentary sources, site visits and a confidential dialogue with national authorities and civil society organisations. ECRI also directs general policy recommendations to all Member States and promotes cooperation with relevant actors, in particular NGOs, mass media and youth associations.

> In 2019, the Commission published reports of the fifth cycle of monitoring for Finland, Ireland, Latvia, The Netherlands, Romania, Russian Federation and Slovenia. Furthermore, the Commission presented the conclusions on the priority recommendations to the following countries in the context of the fifth cycle reports already published: Armenia, Azerbaijan, Cyprus, France, Georgia, Italia, Lithuania, North Macedonia, Principality of Monaco, Turkey and the United Kingdom. In 2019, the ECRI also conducted visits, within their respective cycles of monitoring, in: Albania, Austria, Belgium, Czech Republic, Germany, Slovak Republic and Switzerland. No new General Recommendations were adopted.

During the year in question, the ECRI published a report on the implementation of due priority recommendations for Italy within the fifth cycle of monitoring in September 2015 (report ECRI(2019)24, adopted on 3 April and published on 6 June 2019). The two recommendations concerned the following issues: 1) ensure the full independence and autonomy of the UNAR and extend its competences to all possible fields in which discrimination may occur; 2) provide all students and school pupils with the information, protection and support needed to live in harmony with their sexual orientation and gender identity (see *Yearbook 2017*, pp. 216–218).

In its initial analysis, the Commission recalled that in its last report on Italy, the ECRI had found that the UNAR still did not comply with the principle of independence and that its powers provided for by law were incomplete, pursuant to the General Policy Recommendations No. 2 on Equality Bodies and No. 7 on national legislation to combat racism and racial discrimination.

Regarding the powers of UNAR, the Italian authorities informed ECRI that in its day-to-day work UNAR continues to deal with grounds of discrimination other than those expressly provided for by law (ethnic origin and race), such as religion, skin colour, sexual orientation and gender identity. In addition, the authorities stated that the law provides that UNAR's remit also covers the fight against manifestations of "racism of a cultural and religious nature". In addition, since it was set up, UNAR has also been able to use article 43 of the pre-existing Consolidated Act on Immigration (legislative decree 286/1998), which prohibits direct and indirect discrimination on the grounds of race, colour, descent, national or ethnic origin, and religious beliefs and practices

These considerations could suggest that there is no particular need to extend UNAR's remit more explicitly in order to clearly cover discrimination based not only on ethnic origin and race but also on colour, language, religion, nationality and national origin. However, ECRI reiterates its opinion that, although in practice this remit has been considerably broadened (with the extension of protection against almost all forms of discrimination) – especially in the context of the 2015 National Action Plan against Racism, Xenophobia and Intolerance – the absence of a clear legislative framework has an impact on the effectiveness of UNAR's action. This view is also consistent with the general analysis regarding the main provisions in civil and administrative law to combat racial discrimination contained in ECRI's report on Italy within the fifth round of monitoring.

According to the information available to ECRI, UNAR was still not able to bring legal proceedings; moreover, its structure is still under the responsibility of the Department for Equal Opportunities of the Presidency of the Council of Ministers. Consequently, this body does not comply with the principle of the independence of national bodies specialised in the fight against racism and intolerance.

Referring to the second issue raised, the Italian authorities informed ECRI of a number of measures adopted since 2016 as part of the implementation of Act No. 107/15, "on good schooling", aimed at promoting mutual tolerance and respect at school. However, all the measures to provide pupils and students with the information, protection and support they need to be able to live in harmony with their sexual orientation and gender identity remain completely voluntary and, in most cases, are based on the initiative of non-governmental associations, although it is true that those associations may receive ministerial and local funding for the promotion of these activities. Furthermore, the ECRI noted that this type of extracurricular activities continues to meet with strong resistance from some parents, schools and regional authorities that are responsible for the provision of training. Initiatives to promote tolerance and respect among genders have often been openly criticised and consequently abandoned.

As already pointed out in the 2016 report on Italy, given this situation, extracurricular programmes involving teachers and children solely on a voluntary basis cannot suffice to rise to the challenge and may even be counterproductive. In conclusion, ECRI considered that its recommendation has been partially implemented.

VIII Advisory Committee on the Framework Convention for the Protection of National Minorities

The Committee is a monitoring body instituted pursuant to article 26 of the Council of Europe Framework Convention for the Protection of National Minorities. It is composed of 18 independent experts with recognised expertise in the field of the protection of national minorities. It is composed of 18 independent experts with recognised expertise in the field of protection of national minorities who sit on the Committee in their individual capacity for a period of four years. In 2019, there were no Italian experts on the Advisory Committee.

> The Advisory Committee serves to assist the CM in evaluating the implementation of the Framework-Convention in States Parties, through the examination of periodic State Reports. The results of this evaluation are expressed in a detailed opinion which serves as a basis for the preparation of the CM's conclusive resolutions on the Country in question. Follow-up meetings are generally organised by the Advisory Committee with a view to bringing together all actors – governmental and non-governmental – interested in the implementation of the Convention and to examine ways of implementing the results of the monitoring procedure. The CM concludes each cycle of monitoring of the Framework-Convention by adopting a resolution.
>
> In 2019, within their respective evaluation rounds, the Advisory Committee on the Framework Convention conducted visits in Finland, Portugal, and Serbia; it adopted (but not yet published by virtue of the confidentiality principle) opinions on Cyprus, Denmark, Finland, Georgia, The Netherlands, Poland and Portugal, while it published opinions on the national minorities situation in Albania, Azerbaijan, Finland, Ireland, Lithuania, Montenegro, Serbia and Russian Federation. Finally, it held follow-up meetings with representatives and stakeholders of Bosnia-Herzegovina.

On 8 April 2019, the Italian Government presented its new report on the situation of national minorities in the country (ACFC/SR/V(2019)009), launching the fifth cycle of monitoring for the implementation of the Framework-Convention. The report focuses on the main legislative and infrastructural developments over the past five years, as well as initiatives undertaken by individual regions and at the national level in line with implementing the Framework Convention and the Advisory Committee's guidelines.

In this report, the Italian Authorities reiterated that Italian legislation foresees various awareness-raising measures for preventing discrimination, intolerance, racism and xenophobia at all levels of society, and highlight that it is envisaged a specific form of protection through criminal law and aggravating circumstance for all crimes aimed to racial discrimination and hatred, which encompasses manifestations of thought aimed at disseminating ideas founded on superiority, racial or ethnic hatred along with incitement to commit discriminatory actions or acts of violence due to racial, ethnic or religious reasons.

Among the many new measures undertaken during this period, the report highlights those concerning the fight against gender-based and domestic violence against women, aiming to fully implement the constitutional principles of equality and ensuring, at the same time, the respect for diversity. In particular, the Government informed the Committee that, by ratifying the Istanbul Convention, the Italian Parliament has adopted in the course of the XVII legislature a number of measures to counter violence against women pursuing three strategic objectives: preventing crimes, punishing perpetrators and protection of victims. In line with this approach, the Criminal Code and the Criminal Procedure Code have been amended, increasing sanctions for some crimes usually committed against women and an Extraordinary Action Plan against gender-based violence and the related fund allocation to support victims. Moreover, in the current legislature, the Senate confirmed the establishment of an Inquiry Commission on Femicide, while the House Judiciary Committee is now in the process of examining some proposals for legislation aimed at strengthening the judicial protection for victims of violent crimes, with particular attention to sexual offenses and domestic violence.

The report underlines that Italy has enhanced the protection and the promotion of the rights of the linguistic minorities also through the regional legislation by addressing these safeguards –as recommended -also in a view to support the minorities' languages and culture.

The Department of Regional Affairs and Autonomous Regions of the Presidency of the Council of Ministers, accepting the Technical Advisory Committee's proposal on protecting historic linguistic minorities, allocated the necessary resources to institute new linguistic helpdesks or the continuation of their existing activities, which represent an effective contact point between citizens speaking a minority language and the Public Administration.

Despite the current economic contingency and the spending review, funds for projects involving minorities' languages continue to be allocated for supporting both activities pursuant to pursuant to laws 482/1999 (Regulations to protect historic linguistic minorities) and 38/2001 (Regulations to protect Slovenian linguistic minorities in the Friuli-Venezia Giulia region). The Permanent Institutional Panel on Issues concerning the Slovenian Speaking Minority in Italy, established at the Ministry of the Interior, continued its work in order to enhance cooperation activities for the protection of the Slovenian minority.

As well known, such regions as Aosta Valley, Friuli Venezia Giulia, Sardinia, Trentino Alto Adige/Sudtirol are regulated by specific legislation providing for additional funding for the support of linguistic minorities and the promotion of their languages and cultures. In this respect, the application of law No. 482/1999 and of law No. 38/2001 achieved a positive result, although the first one, 20 years after its application, would need to be updated. This positive impact of the law is confirmed by the increased demand in the use of minority languages and gives evidence of the greater awareness of their value.

As regards the protection of Roma and Sinti communities (which is one of the most problematic areas according to the last opinion of the Advisory Committee on Italia; see *Yearbook 2017*, pp. 218–221), the report stated that a concerted action of the Council of Europe Member States would be necessary. It added that the Italian government is implementing the National Strategy for the Inclusion of these communities within the framework of the four pillars: housing, work, health and education, by promoting or implementing projects aiming at an effective inclusion of the mentioned communities and focussing on crucial issues as housing conditions. The main objective aims at addressing such issues not in a mere emergency perspective – that is reductive from a political and institutional standpoint – but taking into account the development of integration-oriented actions planned in a medium and long-term perspective, in view of the definition of the 2020 European Agenda.

IX European Commission for Democracy through Law

The Commission, also known as the Venice Commission, is the Council of Europe's advisory body on constitutional issues; it was established in 1990 and receives financial support by a law of the Region of Veneto.

The Commission is composed of independent experts with extensive experience in the area of democratic institutions or excellence in the legal and political domains. Members are designated for four years by the participating countries which, as well as the 47 Member States of the CoE, include Algeria, Brazil, Chile, Israel, Kazakhstan, Kyrgyzstan, Mexico, Morocco, Peru, South Korea, Tunisia and the United States. Belarus is an associate member, while Argentina, Canada, the Holy See, Japan and Uruguay participate in the work of the Commission as observer countries. The European Commission, Palestinian National Authority, South Africa and the Association of Constitutional Courts using the French Language have a special co-operation status.

Since 2009, Gianni Buquicchio has been President of the Venice Commission. Two Italian experts participate in the Commission's activities as alternate members: Marta Cartabia and Cesare Pinelli.

Among its activities, the Commission puts forward studies and opinions on subjects covered by its competence, also at the request of other bodies such as the Parliamentary Assembly of the CoE, and promotes in-depth seminars. In 2019, the Venice Commission adopted 2 opinions with regard to the adoption of laws or bills of law on matters of constitutional importance in the following countries: Albania (2 opinions), Armenia (3), Bosnia-Herzegovina, Bulgaria, Georgia (2), Kosovo, North Macedonia (2), Peru, Republic of Moldova (5), Romania, Tunisia (2), Turkey, and Ukraine (3). No opinions or documents were adopted concerning Italy in 2019.

Even though it makes no specific reference to Italy, given the ongoing lack a national Ombudsperson, the adoption on 16 March 2019 of the Principles on the Protection and Promotion of the Ombudsman Institution (the so-called "Venice Principles", CDL-AD(2019)005, see Part II, Sub-national Human Rights Structures, II).

X Group of Experts on Action against Trafficking in Human Beings

The Group of Experts (GRETA) was established pursuant to article 36 of the Council of Europe Convention on Action against Trafficking in Human Beings and is charged, together with a Committee made up of the representatives in the CM of the States Parties to the Convention (Committee of the Parties), with monitoring the implementation of the obligations contained in the Convention.

The Group is made up of 15 independent experts known for their recognised competence in the fields of human rights, assistance and protection of victims of trafficking in human beings or having professional experience in the areas covered by the Convention. On 9 November 2018, the Italian national Francesco Curcio was elected as the latest member of GRETA, who will stay in the role until 31 December 2022.

> The monitoring procedure is divided into four-year rounds. The Group of Experts starts the dialogue with the Party under evaluation by sending out a questionnaire, which may be followed by requests for further information. If the Group of Experts deems it necessary, additional information may be requested from civil society organisations or gathered by organising a visit to the Country concerned. The draft report is sent to the relevant Government for comments. On receiving them, GRETA prepares its final report and conclusions and transmits it to the Country concerned and to the Committee of the Parties, which can adopt recommendations on the basis of the contents of the document. Each Party to the Convention appoints a contact person to cooperate with the Group of Experts.
>
> In 2019 the Expert Group published the evaluation reports on the implementation status of the Convention in: Andorra, Finland, Germany, Italy, Iceland, Liechtenstein, Lithuania, San Marino, Switzerland, Turkey and Hungary. . They conducted in-depth visits to the following countries: Albania, Austria, Bulgaria, Cyprus, Croatia, Denmark, Georgia, Principality of Monaco, Czech Republic, Republic of Moldova and the Slovak Republic.

On 7 December 2018, GRETA adopted its final report on the second evaluation round of the implementation of the Warsaw Convention in Italy (GRETA/2018/28, published on 25 January 2019). The report is based on the reply provided by the Italian authorities to the questionnaire sent by the Group of Experts in 2017 (GRETA/2017/23) and on the observations emerging from the evaluation visit conducted by a GRETA delegation between 29 January and 2 February 2018 in order to examine developments and improvements of the situation compared to the first round of monitoring (GRETA(2014)18, see *Yearbook 2015*, pp. 225–229) and the 2016 urgent procedure analysing the reimpatriation of possible human trafficking victims to Nigeria, within joint operations coordinated and organised by the European Agency FRONTEX (see *Yearbook 2017*, pp. 222–225).

The overview of the report of the second cycle was presented in the *Yearbook 2019* (pp. 251–257). On 5 April 2019, the Committee of the Parties adopted Recommendation CP/Rec(2019)02, closing the procedure. In the recommendation, the Committee of the Parties refers both to the most recent GRETA report and to the Government's response to this, and indicates what it considers the positive and negative actions that the country has undertaken against human trafficking. It requests updates from the authorities on highlighted areas and issues by 5 April 2020.

The positive actions highlighted by the Committee of the Parties included the further development of the legal framework for fighting trafficking in human beings. In particular, the Committee commended: the adoption of regulations strengthening the protection of unaccompanied minors, including child victims of trafficking; the adoption of the first National Action Plan against trafficking and exploitation on human beings in February 2016 (see *Yearbook 2019*, pp. 33–48); the development of an institutional framework for combatting trafficking in human beings, establishing an inter-institutional Control Room for planning, implementing and financing measures to combat trafficking in human beings; efforts to provide issue-specific training to a wide range of professionals in the field, following a multi-agency approach; the adoption of Guidelines for identifying victims of trafficking among seekers of international protection; the establishment of the "Single Programme for the rescue, assistance and social integration of victims of human trafficking and exploitation" and the substantial rise in fund allocation for anti-trafficking projects; the rising specialisation of law enforcement authorities and public ministries tackling cases of trafficking and their commitment to international cooperation in the fight against trafficking in human beings.

The Committee of the Parties goes on to recommend the Italian Authorities to commit to adopting immediate provisions to tackle a series of problematic situations identified in the GRETA report of Italy's second evaluation round. These immediate actions concern the following issues (for more details on recommendations, see *Yearbook 2019*, pp. 251–257):

- develop and maintain a comprehensive and coherent statistical system on trafficking in human beings by compiling reliable statistical data on measures to protect and promote the rights of victims as well as on the investigation, prosecution and adjudication of human trafficking cases. Statistics regarding victims should be collected from all main actors and allow disaggregation concerning sex, age, type of exploitation, country of origin and/or destination. This should be accompanied by all the necessary measures to respect the right of data subjects to personal data protection, including when NGOs working with victims of trafficking are asked to provide information for the national database;

- intensify their efforts to prevent trafficking of human beings for the purpose of labour exploitation;
- strengthen their efforts to prevent trafficking in children;
- adopt further measures to improve the proactive identification of victims of trafficking of human beings;
- ensure the availability of dedicated centres for asylum seekers who are presumed victims of trafficking;
- take measures to better identify and assist child victims of trafficking in human beings;
- review the legislation in order to ensure that the recovery and reflection period is specifically defined in law as provided for in article 13 of the Convention, and that all possible foreign victims of trafficking are offered a recovery and reflection period and all the measures of assistance envisaged in article 12, paragraphs 1 and 2, of the Convention during this period;
- adopt measures to assist and enable victims of trafficking to exercise their right to compensation;
- ensure that the return of victims of trafficking in human beings is conducted with due regard to their rights, safety and dignity, including the right to non-refoulement (article 40(4) of the Convention), and in the case of children, by fully respecting the principle of the best interests of the child;
- ensure compliance with article 26 of the Convention of Warsaw (non-punishment provision) through the adoption of a provision on the non-punishment of victims of trafficking for their involvement in unlawful activities, to the extent that they were compelled to do so, and/or by developing relevant guidance;
- take measures to ensure that offences of trafficking in human beings are investigated and prosecuted effectively, leading to proportionate and dissuasive sanctions;
- review the Code of Conduct for NGOs undertaking activities on migrants' rescue operations at sea with a view to enabling the identification of victims of trafficking amongst migrants and refugees at sea and in ports.

According to the provisional timetable of GRETA's third evaluation round on the implementation of the Warsaw Convention, Italy's evaluation will take place in May 2021. The Group of Experts will send its questionnaire to the national authorities, which this round will concentrate on the issue "access to justice and effective remedies for victims of trafficking".

XI Group of States against Corruption

The Group of States against Corruption (GRECO) was established in 1999 in order to monitor the compliance of CoE Member States with the anti-corruption standards and rules of the Organisation. These benchmarks are contained in the legal instruments adopted by the Council of Europe on actions against corruption – the Criminal Law Convention on Corruption with its Additional Protocol and the Civil Law Convention on Corruption – as well as the recommendations and resolutions adopted by the Committee of Ministers (in particular resolution (97)24 on the 20 Guiding Principles for the Fight against Corruption).

The Group comprises 49 States (47 Member States of the CoE plus Belarus and the United States). GRECO's main objective is to improve the capacity of its members to fight corruption by monitoring their compliance with Council of Europe anti-corruption standards through a dynamic process of mutual evaluation and peer pressure. It helps to identify shortcomings in national anti-corruption policies, prompting the necessary legislative, institutional and practical reforms. GRECO also provides a platform for sharing best practices. The GRECO monitoring system takes place in periodic cycles and includes: a "horizontal" evaluation procedure involving all the members and ending with the elaboration of recommendations on the necessary reforms in the legislative and institutional field; and a "compliance" procedure whose purpose is to assess the measures taken by Member States to implement these recommendations.

Italy has been a member of GRECO since 30 June 2007 and has undergone four evaluation rounds to date. The first two rounds were dealt with jointly and concluded in 2013 with the adoption by the Group of States of an addendum to the compliance report (see *Yearbook 2014*, p. 253). In 2014, on the basis of information previously provided by the Italian Government, GRECO adopted the compliance report (Greco RC-III(2014)9E) on the measures adopted by the Italian authorities to implement the 16 recommendations received in the course of the third monitoring round regarding two themes: I) incrimination for corruption and II) transparency of party funding (see *Yearbook 2015*, p. 220). In 2016, GRECO adopted the second compliance report, relative to the third monitoring cycle and the evaluation report on Italy after the fourth evaluation round (GrecoEval4Rep(2016)2) (see *Yearbook 2017*, pp. 226–228).

In December 2018, GRECO adopted its fourth evaluation round compliance report regarding Italy (GrecoRC4(2018)13) focusing on corruption prevention in respect to members of parliament, judges and prosecutors (see *Yearbook 2019*, pp. 257–260).

On 12 December 2019, GRECO published the second addendum to its second compliance report of the third evaluation round of Italy. It discusses the additional measures to implement the GRECO recommendations adopted by the Italian Authorities since its first addendum in 2018. The recommendations concerned: I) Incriminations and II) Transparency of Party Funding. In the first addendum of the second compliance report, GRECO concluded that Italy implemented satisfactorily eight of the 16 recommendations contained in the third round evaluation report, seven recommendations had been partly implemented and one had not been implemented. The evaluation presented in the second addendum is based on the information submitted by Italy in the situation report of 31 March 2019.

After analysing the progress made concerning eight recommendations received in the third round evaluation report which have not yet been fully implemented according to the first addendum analysis, GRECO concluded that four other recommendations have been fully implemented. The remaining four recommendations were evaluated as party implemented: recommendations i, ii, iii on theme I (Incriminations) and recommendation iv on theme II (Transparency of Party Funding). Therefore, in total, 12 of the 16 recommendations directed towards Italy in the second compliance report of the third round evaluation report were implemented satisfactorily or dealt with in a satisfactory manner. GRECO welcomed the measures progressively taken by Italy, in recent years, to step up its anti-corruption policy. In 2019, law No. 3/2019, so-called Bribe-Destroyer, entered into force. It introduced additional provisions to fight public sector corruption (theme I) and to increase transparency requirements in the private sector. More particularly, with regard to incriminations, GRECO congratulated Italy for its efforts to further align domestic legislation with the Criminal Law Convention on Corruption. Ratification of the Additional Protocol to the Criminal

Law Convention on Corruption remains a pending matter. Italy is one of only three countries (out of the 49 GRECO members) which have not ratified the Additional Protocol. The authorities are therefore invited to take action in this respect without further delay. With regard to political financing (theme II), Italy has introduced major reforms in this area. One of the most salient is the move from public to private funding – with the abolishment of public financing in 2017. There are several valuable features in the new system, such as a general ban on anonymous donations, lowered disclosure thresholds, increased sanctions, etc. In such an evolving context of change, and given the primacy role that private funding is now given in the system, it is obvious that a holistic and integrated approach regarding oversight and accountability mechanisms acquire prime significance. To this end, GRECO welcomed the upgraded transparency and publication requirements for campaign donations introduced in 2019.

According to the GRECO assessment, the new institutional agreements for supervising political financing need good coordination among the various authorities involved and must still show their feasibility and effectiveness. In this respect, it is essential that the monitoring goes beyond its formal nature and becomes substantial. To obtain this result, further improvements on the power, coordination and resources of various political financial monitoring bodies are necessary. Furthermore, the time and implementation will show if and how these existing laws will be perfected and refined to improve their effective supervision and application.

This second addendum concluded GRECO's third round of evaluation on Italy. The Group requested that the Italian Authorities continue to update them on future progress concerning the four partly implemented recommendations.

XII Group of Experts on Action against Violence against Women and Domestic Violence

The Group of Experts (GREVIO) is the body responsible for monitoring the implementation of the Council of Europe Convention on Preventing and Combating Violence against Women and Domestic Violence (Istanbul Convention) by the Parties which have ratified it.

> GREVIO's main purpose is to draw up and publish reports evaluating legislative and other measures taken by the Parties to give effect to the provisions of the Convention. If necessary, in the event of serious and persistent acts of violence covered by the Convention, GREVIO may initiate a special inquiry procedure. It can also adopt general recommendations on themes and concepts of the Convention.
>
> Other than electing the members of GREVIO, the Committee of the Parties completes the evaluation procedure of the Convention of Istanbul, acting on the GREVIO reports and conclusions and adopting recommendations regarding the countries concerned.
>
> GREVIO currently has 15 members with multidisciplinary expertise in the area of human rights, gender equality, violence against women and domestic violence or in the assistance to and protection of victims. Among them is the Italian expert Simona Lanzoni.
>
> In 2019, after receiving the respective national reports and civil society contributions on the state of implementation of the Istanbul Convention, GREVIO published the first evaluation reports on the implementation of the Istanbul Convention in the following countries: Finland, France, Portugal, and Sweden. It also conducted evaluation visits in Belgium, Italy, The Netherlands, Serbia and Spain.

On 15 November 2019, GREVIO adopted its baseline evaluation report on Italy (made public on 13 January 2020 together with the Government's comments). The document contains a complete analysis of the implementation of the provisions of the Istanbul Convention. It highlights all positive initiatives to prevent and combat all forms of violence against women and domestic violence at a national level and provides suggestions and proposals to improve the situation of women who are facing this type of violence.

GREVIO based its evaluation on the findings of its visit to Italy in March 2019; the visit saw the participation of national expert Professor Paola Degani of the University of Padova Human Rights Centre and numerous other contributors from civil society organisations, including AIDOS, D.i.Re (Women's network against violence), End FGM, Be Free, Italian Forum for Disability, Relive, UNIRE and others, in addition to other groups of experts and professionals working in the field of women's and children's rights.

Generally, in this report GREVIO recognised Italy's genuine political will to prevent and combat violence against women, shown through the range of measures taken to implement the Istanbul Convention. A succession of legislative reforms has created an extensive set of rules and mechanisms reinforcing the authorities' ability to match their intentions with concrete actions to stop the violence. Some of these legislative initiatives were particularly innovative, such as the legislation of 2009 on stalking, which contributed to creating a diffuse awareness as to the dangerousness of this criminal behaviour and the need to afford victims appropriate protection. GREVIO particularly welcomed the adoption of law 119/2013 which formalised the authorities' duty to support and to promote, including by attributing financial means, a vast network of support services for victims. This law acknowledged the experience and achievements of years of commitment on the part of women's organisations who were the first in the country to set up anti-violence centres and shelters for women and their children.

Another initiative the Group of Experts appreciated was the creation of the Senate committee of enquiry on femicide and all forms of gender-based violence in January 2017, which offered a commendable example of how a national parliament can put into effect the provision of article 70 of the Istanbul Convention regarding its role in monitoring the measures taken to implement the Convention. Positive references were also made in the report on the National Strategic Plan on Male Violence against Women (2017–2020), the third National Action Plan and the first and second GREVIO evaluation on its full embrace of the "4 Ps" approach of the Convention (the requirement for public interventions on violence against women to address concurrently prevention, protection, prosecution and integrated policies).

While acknowledging progress made to promote gender equality and further women's rights, the report finds that the cause of gender equality is facing resistance in Italy. GREVIO voiced its concern about the emerging signs of a tendency to reinterpret and refocus gender-equality policies in terms of family and motherhood policies. To overcome these difficulties, GREVIO considered that it is essential that the authorities continue to devise and effectively implement policies of equality between women and men and the empowerment of women which clearly acknowledge the structural nature of violence against women as a manifestation of historically unequal power relations between women and men.

According to the report, in Italy, specialist support services and shelters for victims are provided mainly by anti-violence centres run by NGOs. The report found that varying approaches in applying the relevant regulations lead to divergent conditions for accessing state funding and disparities in the quality of service provision. Moreover, different regional mechanisms for funding specialist services negatively impact the financial stability of women's NGOs and the continuity of service provision. Moreover, the report points to an issue of uneven spread of services throughout the country and of limited capacity of existing structures to respond to the needs of all victims of all forms of violence, including for example forced marriage. The report therefore called on the authorities to urgently expand the coverage and capacity of specialist services and to harmonise the provision of such services with the human rights-based approach and the standards of the Istanbul Convention.

According to the GREVIO report, further measures are urgently needed to fill the gap in the provision of specialist support services for victims of sexual violence in the form of rape crisis and/or sexual violence referral centres. Child witnesses' access to protection and support also poses a challenge, despite commendable progress made in Italian legislation and policies towards recognising the harmful effects on children of witnessing violence against women and reinforcing the support for children who become orphans as a consequence of violence against women. The report therefore suggested as a matter of urgency ensuring wider levels of awareness among the professionals concerned of the harmful effects of witnessing domestic violence on children and guaranteeing access for child witnesses to appropriate support services based on a gendered understanding of violence against women.

Several legislative reforms, including the recent law No. 69 of 19 July 2019 (known as the Red Code) have led to the development of a solid legislative framework in line with the requirements of the convention on the civil and criminal law remedies for victims of violence. Nevertheless, the report found a legislative gap caused by the absence of effective civil remedies against any state authority that has failed in its duty to take the necessary preventive or protective measures within the scope of its powers, in accordance with the requirements of article 29, paragraph 2, of the convention. Another area requiring urgent consideration by the authorities is that relating to the determination of custody and visitation rights. The report found that existing provisions in the law which would allow giving priority, in cases of violence against women, to the best interest of the child over and above the principle of shared parenting are rarely used.

In its report, GREVIO expressed its concern about the tendency of the system in place to expose to secondary victimisation mothers who seek to protect their children by reporting the violence. The report also found that legislative amendments are necessary to bring the Italian legislation in conformity with the requirement of ex officio prosecution set out in article 55, paragraph 1, of the Convention, as regards in particular the offences of physical and sexual violence.

The report further highlighted areas where the protection of women victims of violence is hampered by a partial implementation of the requirements of Chapter VI of the convention on criminal investigations, prosecutions and convictions of the various forms of violence covered by the convention. Despite the development of a number of guidelines on risk assessment – SARA (Spousal Assault Risk Assessment) – GREVIO finds that risk assessment and management procedures are not systematically applied by all relevant statutory agencies at all the relevant stages of proceedings and are not part of a multi-agency effort.

Despite the existence of an articulated system of emergency barring, restraining and protection orders in criminal, civil and administrative law, the report identified several critical shortcomings in its implementation. The report therefore required adopting urgent measures to lift the barriers preventing victims from accessing protective orders and to enhance their effective enforcement.

In the field of asylum, the report found that failures of vulnerability assessments to properly detect victims can lead to deportations or returns in violation of the obligation of non-refoulement. Recent policies of abandoning sea rescue and strengthening deterrence at sea, together with the closure of Italian ports to boats carrying rescued migrants, further increase the risk of refoulement. GREVIO therefore urged the authorities to uphold their obligation to respect the principle of non-refoulement and the human rights of victims rescued at sea.

Other than these fundamental points, GREVIO identified a number of priority issues requiring further action by the Italian Authorities to comply fully with the Istanbul Convention's provisions:

- ensure an application of the legal provisions on the offence of ill-treatment in the family which is sensitive to the gendered nature of domestic violence against women;

- ensure that the provisions of the Istanbul Convention are implemented without discrimination on any of the grounds listed in article 4, paragraph 3, which would include inter alia mainstreaming the prevention of gender-based violence in the activities of the national body(ies) mandated to combat discrimination and in programmes which are tailored to the specific needs of women who are or might be exposed to intersectional discrimination;
- ensure that policies and measures equally address prevention, protection, investigation and punishment, in accordance with the due diligence standard enshrined in article 5 of the Istanbul Convention;
- take further measures to ensure that policies address violence against women in a comprehensive and integrated fashion and are implemented and monitored by way of an effective co-ordination between national, regional and local authorities;
- ensure appropriate financial and human resources for measures and policies, while increasing the transparency and accountability in the use of public funds and developing appropriate long-term/multi-annual financing solutions for women's specialist services;
- reinforce the support and recognition of independent women's organisations and strengthen the national and local institutional framework for consulting and cooperating with women's organisations;
- provide a strong institutional basis for the bodies mandated to ensure the implementation and co-ordination of measures and policies to combat violence against women and pursue efforts to enable an effective monitoring and evaluation of policies;
- improve data collection in line with the requirements of article 11 of the convention;
- reinforce preventive actions in the fields of awareness-raising, education, training of professionals, perpetrator programmes and the employment sector, while pursuing proactive and sustained measures to promote changes in sexist social and cultural patterns of behaviour that are based on the idea of inferiority of women;
- step up victims' access to general support services which are adequately distributed throughout the territory, properly resourced and provided by trained staff members.

Other areas identified in the GREVIO report include: the need to consider amending the criminal offence of sexual violence so that it is based on the notion of freely given consent, in accordance with article 36, paragraph 1, of the convention, and introducing legislation to ensure that sexual harassment experienced in all areas of life is subject to a legal sanction; the call that the authorities should furthermore pursue their efforts aimed at enabling an expeditious handling of investigations and criminal proceedings into cases of violence against women, while ensuring that measures taken to this end are adequately funded; improvement in foreign victims' access to a residence entitlement and to gender-sensitive asylum procedures, reception and accommodation facilities and support services.

XIII Lanzarote Committee

The Committee of the Parties to the Convention on the Protection of Children from Sexual Exploitation and Abuse (or "Lanzarote Committee", named after the city in which this legal instrument was adopted), is the body established by the Council of Europe in order to monitor the implementation of this Convention.

The Committee is composed by the representatives of the current and potential States party to the Convention and has the function of assessing the situation for children's protection against sexual violence at national level on the basis of information provided by national authorities in response to two periodic questionnaires (a general questionnaire and a thematic questionnaire) and in other sources. The Italian member of the Committee is Tiziana Zannini of the Department for Equal Opportunities of the Presidency of the Council of Ministers.

The Committee also collects, analyses, and exchanges information, experiences and best practices to increase its capability to prevent and combat sexual abuse and violence against children. In this context, the Committee organises capacity-building activities aimed at exchanging information and organises hearings on the specific challenges raised by implementing the Convention. Since 2017, data and information has been gathered for the second evaluation round for the implementation of the Convention; this round focuses on protecting children against exploitation and sexual abuse online and via communication technology. A thematic report will be presented using the responses to a questionnaire sent out to the authorities of all countries which have ratified the Convention (among which Italy) and with the input of civil society organisations and children's organisations.

Within the monitoring activity of the Council of Europe, at the beginning of 2020, a new intergovernmental Directing Committee was set up. It will coordinate the Organisation's stand setting activities and monitor the progress of the Strategy 2016–2021 for children's rights. It will also supervise a newly founded body of independent experts: the Committee of Experts on the Rights and Best Interests of the Child in Situations of Parental Separation.

European Union*

I European Parliament

The EP, together with the Commission and the Council of the European Union, exercises a fundamental role in the promotion and protection of human rights within the overall framework of EU activities.

Following the elections of 23–26 May 2019, the Italian Member of Parliament David Sassuoli was elected President of the Assembly. Among the permanent EP Committees prominent in human rights issues, the following are highlighted: the Subcommittee on Human Rights within the Committee on Foreign Affairs (Italian members: Silvio Berlusconi, Anna Bonfrisco, Fabio Massimo Castaldo, Susanna Ceccardi, Giualiano Pisapia; substitute Italian members: Andrea Cozzolino, Raffaele Fitto, Pierfrancesca Majorino, Marco Zanni). For information on the Italian members of the various parliamentary committees and subcommittees previous to the elections of May 2019, see *Yearbook 2019,* p. 263).

Other Committees with significant involvement in human rights issues are the Committee on Civil Liberties, Justice and Home Affairs (Vice Chair: Pietro Bartalo; other Italian members: Caterina Chinnici, Laura Ferrara, Nicola Procaccini; substitute Italian members: Mara Bizzotto, Sabrina Pignedoli, Giuliano Pisapia, Franco Roberti); the Committee on Constitutional Affairs (Chair: Antonio Tajani; Vice Chair: Giuliano Pisapia; other Italian members: Fabio Massimo Castaldo, Antonio Maria Rinaldi; substitute Italian member: Brando Benifei); the Committee on Legal Affairs (Vice Chair: Raffaele Stancanelli; other Italian member: Franco Roberti; substitute Italian members: Brando Benifei, Andrea Caroppo, Caterina Chinnici, Sabrina Pignedoli, Luisa Regimenti); the Committee on Employment and Social Affairs (Italian members: Elena Lizzi, Daniela Rondinelli, Stefania Zambelli; substitute Italian members: Simona Baldassarre, Brando Benifei, Mara Bizzotto, Andrea Caroppo, Chiara Gemma, Pierfrancesco Majoirino, Antonio Maria Rinaldi); the Committee on the Environment, Public Health and Food Safety (Italian members: Simona Baldassarre, Sergio Berlato, Simona Bonafé, Marco Dreosto, Eleonora Evi, Pietro Fiocchi, Fulvio Martusciello, Alessandra

* Pietro de Perini

Moretti, Luisa Regimenti, Silvia Sardone; substitute Italian members: Carlo Calenda, Gianantonio Da Re, Danilo Oscar Lancini, Aldo Patriciello, Piernicola Pedicini, Daniela Rondinelli, Vincenzo Sofo, Annalisa Tardino, Lucia Vuolo); the Committee on Development (Italian members: Gianna Gancia, Pierfrancesco Majorino; substitute Italian members: Alessandra Basso, Ignazio Corrao, Valentino Grant, Patrizia Toia); the Committee on Women's Rights and Gender Equality (Italian members: Simona Baldassarri, Pina Picierno, Isabella Tovaglieri, March Zullo; substitute Italian members: Isabella Adinolfi and Alessandra Moretti) and the Committee on Petitions which will be discussed further on.

In 2019, the Sakharov Prize for Freedom of Thought was awarded to Ilham Tohti, renowned Uyghur human rights defender, economics professor and advocate of the rights of China's Uyghur minority who has for over two decades, worked tirelessly to foster dialogue and understanding between Uyghurs and Han Chinese.

Among the European Parliament's actions adopted in 2019 with themes regarding both human rights and specific initiatives carried out by Italy, the following activities are reported: resolution of 16 January on the situation of fundamental rights in the EU in 2017 (P8_TA(2019)0032); resolution of 13 February on the outcome of the Committee on Petitions' deliberations during 2018 (P8_TA(2019)0114); resolution of 4 April 2019 on waste management (P8_TA(2019)0338); resolution of 18 September 2019 on the mobilisation of the European Union Solidarity Fund to provide assistance to Romania, Italy and Austria (P9_TA(2019)0013).

Committee on petitions

The task of the Committee is to examine the petitions submitted by citizens (a right enshrined in the CFREU under article 44, as well as articles 24 and 227 TFEU), and to endeavour to resolve any breaches of their rights under EU law. The Italian members of the Committee are: Eleonora Evi, Mario Furore, Gianna Gancia, Massimiliano Smeriglio, Stefania Zambelli; the substitute members are Mara Bizzotto, Rosa D'Amato and Pina Picierno.

No significant actions concerning Italy took place in 2019.

II European Commission

The European Commission plays a central role in the development and implementation of European Union policies on human rights both within the Union and in regard to third countries.

Of the 27 members of the new Commission for the five-year period 2020–2024, particularly important are: Věra Jourová, Vice Chair, responsible for promoting values and transparency (related to upholding the rule of law, promoting democracy and monitoring the application of the Charter of Fundamental Rights), Dubravka Šuica, Vice Chair responsible for issues relating to democracy and demographics, Mariya Gabriel, Commissioner for Innovation, Research, Culture, Education and Youth, Nicolas Schmit, Commissioner for Jobs and Social Rights, Helena Dalli, Commissioner for Equality, Margaritis Schinas, Executive Vice Chair, responsible for promoting the European way of life (related to migration management, fighting hate speech and promoting interreligious dialogue); Frans Timmermans, Executive Vice Chair, responsible for implementing the new *Green Deal*.

The primary financial resources for the European Union activities on human rights is the European Instrument for Democracy and Human Rights (EIDHR), which supports the activity of the Global Campus of Human Rights.

On 6 June 2019, the Commission published the annual report of the implementation of the CFR of the EU, ten years on from the entry into force of the Lisbon Treaty, rendering the Charter legally binding. The aim of the report is to monitor the progress undertaken by competent sectors of the EU, showing how the Charter is taken into consideration in real situations, in particular when proposing new EU laws, and considering the role of the EU institutions and the Member State authorities in ensuring guaranteeing fundamental rights in the lives of citizens. The report was published alongside the results of a Eurobarometer survey on the awareness of European citizens of EU regional policy. In the report, it was highlighted that the decision makers of the Member States are increasingly more aware of the importance of ensuring that the various State initiatives respect the rights enshrined in the Charter and that, overall, the EU adopted measures aiming at protecting the fundamental rights of citizens, like the general regulation on data protection. National judicial bodies refer to the Charter in their decisions and ask for guidance from the EU Court of Justice. Furthermore, according to the monitoring carried out, the CFR is still not harnessed to its full potential and is still not well-known, above all when there are no national policies promoting the awareness of the Charter or its implementation. Furthermore, according to the Eurobarometer survey, even if there had been a slight improvement since 2012, only four out of ten citizens had heard of the CFR of the EU and only one in ten knew what it spoke about. The main critical areas concerning the implementation of fundamental rights in some parts of the EU regarded the protection of the rule of law and the shortcomings of asylum laws.

Further details on the Commission's action can be found in the section on EU Legislation in 2019 (see Part I, International Human Rights Law, III, B).

III Council of the European Union

Within the Council, there are the Human Rights Working Group (COHOM), the Working Party on Fundamental Rights, Citizens' Rights and Free Movement of Persons (FREMP), the Working Group "Asylum" and the Working Group "Public International Law"; within the latter, there is a training session dedicated to the International Criminal Court. With regard to promoting the guidelines for EU foreign policy on human rights, in 2019 the Council adopted two new guiding documents on, respectively, safe drinking water and sanitary services and non-discrimination in external action. It also updated the guidelines on torture and other cruel, inhuman or degrading treatment.

There were no decisions that contained specific references to Italy concerning human rights in 2019.

IV Court of Justice of the European Union

Following the entry into force of the Treaty of Lisbon, which made the Charter of Nice legally binding, the Court of Justice plays an ever more vital role for the promotion of human rights within the scope of EU law.

In 2019, Lucia Serena Rossi was a member of the court as a judge and Giovanni Pitruzzella as an advocate-general.

According to the data provided by the CJEU, in 2019, Italy ranked second in the number of preliminary rulings (article 267 TFEU) taken before the Court (70 out of 641), preceded only by Germany (114 rulings).

For a selection of the jurisprudence of the CJEU concerning Italy in 2019, see Part IV, Italy in the Case-law of the Court of Justice of the European Union.

V European External Action Service

The European External Action Service (EEAS) assists the High Representative of the Union for Foreign Affairs and Security Policy in upholding the CFSP/CSDP and ensuring the consistency of EU external actions in their functions both as President of the Foreign Affairs Council and as Vice-President of the Commission. The end of 2019 saw the handover by outgoing High Representative Federica Mogherini (Italy) to the incoming Josep Borrell (Spain).

There were no bills or specific EEAS initiatives regarding human rights and Italy in 2019.

VI Special Representative for Human Rights

Appointed by EU Council decision 2012/440/CFSP of 25 July 2012, the mandate of the European Union Special Representative for Human Rights involves enhancing dialogue with all relevant stakeholders concerning EU human rights policy, including international organisations, States and civil society organisations. From 1 March 2019, Eamon Gilmore (Ireland) took over the role of Special Representative (previously entrusted to Stavros Lambrinidis (Greece)).

No significant actions concerning Italy took place in 2019.

VII Fundamental Rights Agency (FRA)

An advisory body established in 2007, the FRA is the main technical instrument available to the EU with the task of supporting European and national institutions in the promotion and protection of human rights. Since 16 December 2015, Michael O'Flaherty (Ireland) has been Director of the Agency. Since July 2015, Filippo di Robilant has sat on the FRA Management Board for Italy (Vice President as of 29 September 2017, as well as a member of the Agency's Executive Board). The substitute Italian member is Laura Guercio. Italian professor Francesco Palermo (former member of the Advisory Committee on the Framework Convention for the Protection of National Minorities) is part of the Scientific Committee.

The research element of FRA's work consists mainly of the gathering and comparative analysis of data concerning the fundamental rights situation in the various EU Member States, including Italy. The Agency can also adopt opinions on issues related to the protection of fundamental rights in the EU.

Among the many FRA activities of 2019, one of the most relevant for Italy is the publication of the update (as of February 2019) of the November 2016 opinion on the situation of fundamental rights in the Italian and Greek "hotspots". The document was adopted on 4 March. The FRA underlines how many of the 21 recommendations of 2016 on how to tackle violations of fundamental rights identified in the implementation of the hotspot approach in two countries are still relevant despite sincere efforts to improve the situation. Only three of the issues raised by the FRA were tackled effectively. In eight of the identified cases, there had been developments that had, however, not concretely or significantly improved the situation. There has been no significant progress regarding the other 10 recommendations.

The FRA has identified some principle challenges that Italy has to tackle – particularly concerning *child protection*. Despite important legal developments and shorter stay periods for unaccompanied minors in hotspots, there are still serious issues. Shelters for unaccompanied minors are insufficient and the conditions in their dedicated areas in hotspots are inadequate. Other issues included *identifying vulnerable people* (since there is no structured approach to subsequent structure referral that can respond to specific needs of vulnerable people) *security issues*, in light of violent incidents which occur in hotspots in both countries, and *returns* and *readmissions*. Even though Frontex staff are better trained in their operations and national human rights monitoring mechanisms regularly visit the hotspots to check on repatriation and readmission processes, in both countries, the deprivation of liberty with no assessment of the need or proportionality on a case-to-case basis.

The FRA document shows fewer arrivals in Italy since July 2017, which has resulted in an improvement in hotspot sites. However, since it is currently being underused, it is difficult to assess if the system is currently equipped to adequately manage future emergencies on fundamental rights, if there is an increase in arrivals once again. In Italy, the main challenges related to fundamental rights now concern the cooperation agreements with Libya, refusal to open the ports to search and rescue ships and the criminalisation of search and rescue vessels in the Central Mediterranean.

VIII European Ombudsman

The European Ombudsman, an institution established in 1992 by the Treaty of Maastricht and provided for in articles 24 and 228 TFEU, examines the complaints lodged by European citizens about maladministration in the institutions and bodies of the European Union. The Ombudsperson is elected by the EP, and their duties are performed with complete independence. Emily O'Reilly, previously the National Ombudsperson of the Republic of Ireland, currently holds this position.

According to the report on the activities of the European Ombudsman concerning 2019, over the period considered, the Office processed 2,171 complaints, of which 94 were from Italy. It launched 456 investigations (of which 29 for complaints from Italy), and overall concluded 560. In the same year, two investigations were initiated by the Ombudsperson on their own initiative.

In its annual report, the Ombudsman referred to its own intervention (decision of 13 December 2019) concerning a complaint by the NGO Amnesty International, in relation to the way in which the Commission managed a previous complaint on Italy's possible violation of the directive on racial equality and living conditions of Roma communities. Amnesty International presented the issue to the Commission in 2012 which then launched a pilot procedure to investigate the situation. After almost six years, the Commission still had not made a decision on implementing formal infraction procedures against Italy; the delay pushed the NGO to take the issue to the Ombudsman, which found that the delay was not unjustified, but urged the Commission to take a position on the matter as soon as possible.

IX European Data Protection Supervisor

Established by Regulation 45/2001, the European Data Protection Supervisor is responsible for ensuring the right to the protection of individual privacy in the handling of personal data by EU institutions and bodies, as specified in articles 7–8 of the Nice Charter. It is an independent body elected by the Parliament and the Council of the EU and the current Supervisor (as of 5 December 2019) is Wojciech Wiewiórowski (Poland). Until his death in August 2019, the role was covered by the Italian magistrate Giovanni Buttarelli.

No significant actions concerning Italy took place in 2019.

Organization for Security and Cooperation in Europe (OSCE)*

Through a multi-dimensional approach to security, the OSCE (57 participating States) deals with conflict prevention, crisis management and post-conflict rehabilitation. Among its specific mechanisms and bodies are the Office for Democratic Institutions and Human Rights (ODIHR), the High Commissioner on National Minorities, the Representative on Freedom of the Media and the Special Representative and Coordinator for Combating Trafficking in Human Beings. Thomas Greminger (Switzerland) was Secretary General of the OSCE until July 2017.

The Permanent Representative of Italy to the OSCE is Amb. Alessandro Azzoni. members of the Chamber of Deputies and the Senate sit in the OSCE Parliamentary Assembly, with its headquarters in Warsaw. Following the general election of 4 March 2018, the Head of the Parliamentary Delegation is Paolo Grimoldi. The other 12 Italian Members of Parliament are: Luigi Augussori, Alex Bazzaro, Mauro Del Barba Gianluca Ferrara, Niccolò Invidia, Massimo Mallegni, Francesco Mollame, Emanuele Scagliusi, Paola Taverna, Achille Totaro, Valentino Valentini, Vito Vattuone. From 1 January 2016, the Italian Roberto Montella assumed the duties of Secretary General of the OSCE Parliamentary Assembly.

Italy is one of the major contributors to this organisation. In 2019, the Italian contribution to the budget was around €14.3 million (about 10.3 % of the total budget), lower to those of the United States of America (12.9 %), of Germany (10.9 %) and of France (10.4 %). Italy also contributed 2.6 % of the extra budgetary expenses with a commitment of €1.3 million (this figure was €5.5 million, equally 13 % of the total in 2018 in which Italy held the Annual Presidency of the OSCE), ranking 6th. In 2019, Italy was in second place for the number of officials involved in the Secretariat, in OSCE institutions and in field missions (89).

---

* Pietro de Perini

In 2019, the OSCE institutions organised a relatively limited number of initiatives and activities on the human rights situation in Italy which were developed around the work of the Representative on Freedom of the Media. From an Agenda 2030 for Sustainable Development perspective, the recommendations that were addressed to the Italian authorities aimed at improving access to information, diversity and independence of the media and protecting journalists from threats and violence. These contribute to the implementation of Goal 16 (peace, justice and strong institutions), particularly to targets 16.3 (promote the rule of law at the national and international levels and ensure equal access to justice for all) and 16.10 (ensure public access to information and protect fundamental freedoms, in accordance with national legislation and international agreements).

I Office for Democratic Institutions and Human Rights (ODIHR)

The ODIHR is the main institution of the OSCE which has been assisting Member States in the implementation of their commitments on the human dimension since 1991. Ingibjörg Sólrún Gísladóttir (Iceland) has been in the role of Director of the Office since 19 July 2017.

In 2019, the two-year project "Building a Comprehensive Criminal Justice Response to Hate Crime" (launched by the ODIHR in February 2017) came to a conclusion. The project aimed at improving the competences and collaboration between legal professionals in four OSCE Member States – Bulgaria, Greece, Italy and Poland – and at improving their cooperation with civil society, in order to build a criminal law response to hate crimes in each of these countries. In Italy, the focus was on training police forces, public ministers, judges, lawyers and civil society groups working with hate crime victims at a regional level in Lombardy, as well as analysing data on hate crime collected by the Milan District Court. The results were presented in a workshop in Milan on 15 January 2019.

Among the other work promoted by ODIHR in 2019 regarding Italy, the report related to monitoring the freedom of peaceful assembly in a group of participating OSCE States was published. The States included Italy, alongside Belgium, Canada, Germany, Lithuania and Norway, studying these assemblies in the period 24 May 2017–9 June 2018 in order to form conclusions and general recommendation for the States involved. 4

of the 29 assemblies observed by the ODIHR took place in Italy – more specifically the protests against the G7 Summit in the Giardini Naxos in May 2017.

II High Commissioner on National Minorities

The office of the High Commissioner on National Minorities is the institution responsible for identifying, and as far as possible addressing, situations of inter-ethnic tension in the OSCE area. As well as serving as a conflict-preventing mechanism, the High Commissioner can also support quick solutions which can defuse processes of escalating violence. On 19 July 2017, the Italian diplomat Lamberto Zannier, former Secretary-General of the OSCE from 2011 to 2017, became the High Commissioner on national minorities.

The High Commissioner carried out no significant actions concerning Italy took place in 2019.

III Representative on Freedom of the Media

Established in 1997 with a view to ensuring a high level of compliance with the rules and standards on freedom of expression and freedom of the media accepted by the States Parties to OSCE, the Representative on Freedom of the Media acts as an early warning instrument in cases of violation of the right to freedom of expression, with particular attention to any obstacles or impediments to the activities of journalists. On 18 July 2017, Harlem Désir (France) was appointed as the new OSCE Representative on Freedom of the Media.

In 2019, the OSCE Representative had to comment on the situation of freedom of the press in Italy, via declarations and comments through his official social media channels. On 8 January, the Representative wrote to the Italian Authorities to express his concern about the budgetary decision of the Government in 2019 which brought about the end of direct funding for certain types of media publications in Italy, which a plan to abolish them completely by 2022, and to request information on the possibility that the country carry out an assessment on the impact of the measure, including on potential consequences to the pluralism and diversity of the media. Once again in January, the Representative formally condemned the physical attack on two journalists from the magazine *L'Espresso* in Rome on 7 January, carried out by neo fascists who had taken the video camera and deleted the recording of the attack before the police were able to intervene; the Representative asked that the perpetrators be quickly arrested and prosecuted. In another declaration, the OSCE Representative publicly expressed his concern for the appeal of the four-month prison sentence of the journalist Davide Falcioni (of Fanpage.it) for conducting an investigation into a protest in Turin in 2012. Furthermore, the Representative was horrified by the physical assault which took place in February 2019 on the journalist Daniele Piervincenzi and his team from the public television channel Rai 2 in Pescara, declaring that the perpetrators must be brought to justice. In reference to violence against journalists in Italy, the Representative was shocked to hear about the brutal attack on journalist Valentino Gonzato of the daily newspaper *Il Giornale di Vicenza* in April 2019 while reporting on a crime in a park. In this case, in a declaration, the OSCE Representative welcomed the quick reaction of local police, and asked that the perpetrators be identified and punished.

On 6 March 2019, the OSCE Representative wrote to the Italian Authorities to express his concern on the threat of closure of *Radio Radicale* after a significant drop in public funding, requesting further information since there had been no plan to establish another public radio service to broadcast parliamentary sessions or important court proceedings. A few months after, on 13 June, the Representative expressed his satisfaction that the budgetary commission for the Italian Parliament had voted in an amendment to allocate €3 million for *Radio Radicale* for the year, thus saving the station from closure.

On 18 November 2019, the representative of the OSCE strongly condemned the ambush of journalist Mario De Michele (director of the website *Campania Notizie*), which took place in Gricignano d'Aversa on 14 November. In a declaration, the Representative stated that it was unacceptable that a journalist had to suffer these threats on his life to carry out his work, and welcomed the Italian Authorities' investigations to find the perpetrators and bring them to justice. He also referred to the decision by the OSCE Council of Ministers on the security of journalists, which urges Member States to publicly and unequivocally condemn the attacks and the violence against journalist, including murders, torture, enforced disappearances, arbitrary arrests, detention and expulsions, intimidation, harassment and threats of any kind (physical, legal, political, online, economic) that are used to repress their work and force them to close their offices, even in conflict situations.

IV Special Representative and Coordinator for Combating Trafficking in Human Beings

The Office of the Special Representative and Coordinator for Combating Trafficking in Human Beings is responsible for assisting OSCE States to progressively meet their commitments in this area under the 2003 Action Plan. It also serves as the body co-coordinating all OSCE activities combating trafficking. In 2019, Valiant Richey (United States of America) was the OSCE Special Representative and Coordinator.

The activities of this office in 2019 regarding Italy include the first simulation training exercise for professionals from all parts of the Mediterranean region. More than 74 professionals from 38 countries attended the five-day training. Participants came from law enforcement agencies, the judiciary, social service providers, civil society organisations and asylum agencies. For the first time, the training also included participants from six Partners for Cooperation as well as ten participants from six African countries whose participation was sponsored by the UN.

The first simulation-based training sought to enhance the capacity of participants to effectively identify, investigate, and prosecute human trafficking cases amongst migrants and refugees in mixed migration flows. Particular emphasis was given to the importance of a coherent and multidisciplinary response to human trafficking, involving close coordination between relevant governmental and non-governmental organisations, to meet the multiple protection needs of victims and support law enforcement efforts.

This project, entitled *"Combatting human trafficking along Mediterranean migration routes"*, was undertaken by the Office of the Special Representative in partnership with the *Carabinieri* and the CoESPU and with support from the UNODC, UNHCR, Office of the UN Special Representative of the Secretary-General on Sexual Violence in Conflict, and also the Financial Police ("*Guardia di Finanza*"), Italian State Police, the University of Padova, Municipalities of Venice and Vicenza and independent experts. Two further simulation training courses are planned for 2020 and 2021.

Humanitarian and Criminal Law*

I Adaptation to International Humanitarian and Criminal Law

Italy is party to all the main international conventions concerning the law of armed conflicts and international criminal law. With the l. 4 December 2017, No. 200, Italy ratified and implemented an amendment to the Rome Statute establishing the International Criminal Court, adopted in 2015, concerning the elimination of article 124 of the same Statute. The latter provision, better known as "opting out clause", provisionally provided that each State may declare that it does not accept, for a period of seven years from the entry into force of the Statute against it, the jurisdiction of the Court with respect to war crimes committed by their own citizens or on their territory. 2018 celebrated the 20th Anniversary of the Rome Statute, signed in 1998. 2018 was also the year that The Philippines deposited a notification of withdrawal from the International Criminal Court. The decision was communicated on 17 March 2019. The Philippines is the second State to withdraw from the Rome Statute (article 127) after Burundi in 2017.

Italy has not yet ratified the amendments to the Rome Statute adopted in 2010 during the Review Conference of Kampala (Uganda) and related to the statutory provisions on war crimes and crime of aggression.

On 6 December 2017, the Assembly of States Parties elected Rosario Salvatore Aitala as the Italian Judge of the International Criminal Court, whereas on 10 March 2018, Cuno Tarfusser (Italy) completed his mandate, which had started in March 2009.

In connection with the arms sector, the obligation to present periodic reports on the state of implementation of the provisions of the various conventions is particularly important. In this regard, in 2018, Italy presented its annual report required by article 7 of the Oslo Convention on

---

* Ino Kehrer

the banning and limitation of deployment of conventional arms; the annual report required by article 7 of the Convention against anti-personnel mines; the report requested by the Protocol on Mines, Booby-Traps and Other Devices and concerning the Protocol on Explosive Remnants of War, required by the Convention on Prohibitions or Restrictions on the Use of Certain Conventional Weapons; the annual report required by the Convention of Oslo on Cluster Munitions (April 2018).

On 7 July 2017, the Treaty on the Prohibition of Nuclear Weapons. It was opened for signature on 20 September 2017, as of April 2018, 70 States had signed and 23 had ratified it. The United Nations General Assembly convened a working group to develop the treaty: Italy voted against the resolution, and therefore did not participate in the drafting process and is not one of the States that has signed the Treaty.

II Italian Contribution to the "Peacekeeping" Missions and Other International Missions

With the entry into force of the l. 21 July 2016, No. 145 regarding the participation of Italy in international missions, the procedures for authorisation and financing of the missions follow two distinct procedures: the procedure for the launch of new missions pursuant to article 2 (resolution of the Council of Ministers, transmission to the Chambers, parliamentary authorisation by means of guidelines) and the procedure for the extension of the same for the following year, included in the so-called parliamentary session on the progress of the authorised missions (articles 3 and 4). article 3 of the law also provides that, by 31 December of each year, the Government present to the Chambers, an analytical report on the missions in progress for discussion and subsequent parliamentary deliberations.

On 23 April 2019, the Council of Ministers discussed the analytic report concerning the international missions carried out between 1 October-30 December 2018 (Doc. XXVI, No. 2). This deliberation also aimed to authorise the continuation of these missions in 2019, pursuant to 3 of law 21 July 2016, and Italy's participation in a new international mission, pursuant to article 2, para. 1, of the same law (DOC. XXV, No. 2). It deals with the bilateral cooperation mission in Tunisia, which, at the same time, sees the conclusion of Italy's participation in the NATO support mission to the country, foreseen by part No. 3 of the Council of Ministers deliberation on 28 November 2018 (Doc. XXVI No. 1). Both Council of Ministers deliberations were approved on 13 May 2019 of the Chamber of Deputies Commissions III (Foreign and EU affairs) and IV (Defence).

The resolutions of the Chamber of Deputies (No. 6-00080) and of the Senate of the Republic (Doc. XXIV, No. 9), were approved, respectively, on 4 July 2019 and 9 July 2019. They authorised the continuation of on-going international missions and development cooperation initiatives to support the peace and stability process in 2019, and to launch a bilateral cooperation mission in Tunisia.

The following list shows the military and police missions to which Italy participated with its own personnel in 2019. The total annual average number of armed forces' contingents used in the theatres operating in 2019 was 6,290 units. €1,426,481,331 were allocated to extend ongoing missions and €2,072,880 to launch a new bilateral mission of the armed forces. It is estimated that the total financial needs for 2019 was equal to €1,428,554,211.

Country/geographical area of mission	Mission
Asia	Global Coalition Against Daesh
Afghanistan	NATO Resolute Support Mission (RSM)
Africa	United Nations Mission for the Referendum in Western Sahara-MINURSO
	European Union Training Mission Central African Republic-EUTM RCA
	NATO Support Mission in Tunisia to develop their interforce defence capacities
Albania	Bilateral Cooperation Mission of Italian Police Forces in Albania and Balkan countries
Bosnia-Herzegovina	European Union Mission ALTHEA
Cyprus	United Nations Peacekeeping Force in Cyprus (UNFICYP)
Egypt	Multinational Force and Observers in Egypt (MFO)

United Arab Emirates/Bahrain/ Qatar/Tampa, USA	Military personnel in the United Arab Emirates, Bahrain, Qatar and Tampa for needs connected to missions in the Middle East and Asia
Kosovo/Balkans	European Union Rule of Law Mission in Kosovo (EULEX Kosovo)
	United Nations Mission in Kosovo (UNMIK)
	Joint Enterprise Operation (NATO)
	United Nations Military Observer Group in India and Pakistan (UNMOGIP)
Libya	United Nations Support Mission in Libya (UNSMIL)
	Support and Assistance Bilateral Mission for the Libyan military Coast Guard
	European Union Border Assistance Mission in Libya (EUBAM Libya)
	Bilateral Assistance and Support Mission in Libya
Lebanon	Bilateral Training Mission for Libyan Armed Forces
	United Nations Interim Force in Lebanon (UNIFIL)
Mali	United Nations Multidimensional Integrated Stabilization Mission in Mali (MINUSMA)
	EUCAP Sahel Mali
	European Union Training Mission Mali (EUTM Mali)
Mediterranean	EUNAVFOR MED Operation SOPHIA
	NATO Sea Guardian in the Mediterranean Sea (formerly Active Endeavour)
Niger	Bilateral support mission in the Republic of Niger
	EUCAP Sahel Niger
	Temporary International Presence in Hebron (TIPH2)
Palestine	Bilateral Training Mission for Palestinian Security Forces
	European Union Police Mission for the Palestinian Territories (EUPOL COPPS)
	European Union Border Assistance Mission in Rafah (EUBAM Rafah)
Palestine/Egypt	EUNAVFOR Operation Atalanta

Somalia/Horn of Africa	European Union Training Mission Somalia (EUTM Somalia)
	EUCAP Somalia (ex EUCAP Nestor)
	Bilateral training mission of the Somalian and Djibouti police forces
	Personnel based in the national military base in the Republic of Djibouti for needs connected with international missions in the Horn of Africa and surrounding areas
Strengthening national and NATO provisions	NATO: provisions for the defence of the South-East borders of the Alliance, (NATO Support to Turkey)
	"Mare Sicuro": National naval air provisions in the Mediterranean Sea, which includes the bilateral mission supporting the Libyan Coast Guard
	NATO: provisions for surveillance of the South-west Alliance Air space
	NATO: provisions for presence in Latvia (Enhanced Forward Presence)
	NATO Support in Tunisia
	NATO Air Policing for surveillance of the Alliance Air space

Part IV

National and International Case-Law

Human Rights in Italian Case-law*

Continuing the work started in the previous editions of the Yearbook, Section IV presents an overview of the case-law of the Italian courts in 2018 and highlights the theme of internationally recognised human rights. The focus is on the jurisprudence of the Constitutional Court and the Court of Cassation and on the aspects of case-law of the international courts that are closest to Italian judicial practice and have specific competence on human rights: the European Court of Human Rights (ECtHR) and the Court of Justice of the European Union (CJEU). The section also contains a brief presentation of rulings passed by these two courts referring to Italy and human or fundamental rights.

As always, the intent is not to provide an exhaustive examination, but rather to cite and note the guidance and the new paths that were recorded in 2019 within Italian and European judicial practice regarding human rights standards, following an approach that aims at consolidating information given in previous editions.

While the parts concerning the ECtHR and CJEU judgments (which have been divided into subjects, given the modest number of cases) follow strict criteria relating to the sequential articles of each respective instrument, the presentation of Italian case-law instead is divided into 13 thematic areas, one more than last year. The area of women's rights has, this year, been divided into two separate points. This choice came about in light of reflections carried out last year on the relationship between the various arguments within this section of the Yearbook and the SDGs, promoted worldwide by the United Nations, among which the task of combatting discrimination, especially against women and based on gender (Goal 5: Achieve gender equality and empower all women and girls) has a huge relevance.

---

* Paolo De Stefani

I Aspects of the Relationship between the Italian Justice System and European Case-Law

A Foreign State Immunity and International Crimes

The Florence Court of Appeal returns to the issue of the responsibility of Germany for international crimes committed against Italian citizens deported to Germany and held in Nazi forced labour camps during the Second World War. The Florence District Court (judg., 12 November 2019, No. 2694) had rejected the application for compensation for damages against the Federal Republic of Germany by a person who, at the age of 14, had been deported to the Mauthausen Concentration Camp. Recalling the judgment of Constitutional Court 238/2014, which was in conflict with the conclusions of the International Court of Justice in the 2012 judgment *Germany v. Italy* (see *Yearbook 2015*, pp. 240–241, *Yearbook 2016*, pp. 218–219, *Yearbook 2017*, pp. 255–256), the Court of Appeal repealed the decision of the lower Court, stating that "International norm on State Immunity from civil jurisdiction for to damages caused by war crimes and crimes against humanity is in complete opposition with article 24 of the Constitution, as it blocks judicial protection of a fundamental right, that of human dignity, enshrined in article 2 of the Constitution".

Two judgments of the Court of Cassation (Civil Cassation, sec. III, judgments 2 September 2019 Nos. 21995 and 21996) deal with the reopening of forced execution in Italy of the judgments of the Supreme Court of the Hellenic Republic (decided by the Rome District Court in 2017), recognising the civil responsibility of the German State for the massacre of around 300 people in Distomo (Greece) on 10 June 1944, and sentenced the German State to pay just under €50 million for the costs of the proceedings. The judgments on damage of the Greek judiciary were enforced in Italy by the Florence Court of Appeal. The Greek Regional Government of the district where Distomo is located had requested that an Italian court seize some properties of the German Railway Company located in Italy. The first executive proceedings were concluded in 2012, declaring the seizure inadmissible, on the basis of the aforementioned decision of the International Court of Justice which upheld the foreign State's immunity rule. Judgment 238/2014 of the Italian Constitutional Court reopened the possibility to implement judgments in Italy that ascertain and enforce the civil responsibility of foreign States for international crimes, thus excluding that Italy can be bound to the 2012 decision of the International Court of Justice. The Court of Cassation notes that the 2012 ICJ judgment does not directly bind the Italian judges, as it intervened in terms of international law. The 2013 Italian law which enforced the ruling of the ICJ was declared unconstitutional in 2014. The 2013 law did not take into account enforcement proceedings that had already started in Italy. In its current state, the Italian judges (both those involved in civil proceeding for damages and those involved in the enforcement of previous decisions – albeit based on a non-final judgment) must retain their own jurisdiction in regards to foreign States for international crimes attributable to them. This applies to procedures for damages, procedures that uphold a foreign judgment affirming such liability, or procedures aiming at enforcing foreign judgments on State liability. Such judgments can be challenged before another court, but the outcome of this examination does not hinder the implementation of the judgment within the Italian system. The complaint of the German Railway Company was therefore rejected and the enforcement procedure can continue.

B Sanctions of the CONSOB: the Constitutional Court Applies the Rule of the So-Called Dual Preliminarity

The judgment of Constitutional Court No. 269/2017 (see *Yearbook 2019*, pp. 293) identified the principle by which in cases where Italian law is contrary to the EU law framework under the CFR and therefore also to the ECHR, the Italian judge had to raise a question of constitutionality, even when the norms of the CFR of the EU are directly effective; the preliminary referral to the ECJ can only work at a later stage, and not before the national Constitutional Court has ruled on the matter. This decision will need to be harmonised with EU law and with the ECHR. The principle was followed in judgment Constitutional Court 112/2019 of 10 May 2019. The question concerns article 187-*sexies* of lgs.d. 58/1998, Consolidated Act on provisions on financial intermediation. This law, introduced in 2005 and left substantially unchanged despite a reform enacted in 2018, establishes that the National Commission for Companies and the Stock Exchange (CONSOB) can sanction perpetrators of insider trading with financial sanctions and with confiscation of illegal products. In the case at hand, the person exploited private information obtained through his job as a company administrator, buying stocks to the value of about €125,000 and making a profit of around €25,000. The person was issued with a fine of €200,000 and had his property (worth around €150,000, that is, the entire product of the financial transaction) confiscated. The Constitutional Court considered the incompatibility between laws imposing this type of confiscations and the CFR of the EU and the ECHR (article 47 and article 1, Protocol 1 respectively, the latter through article 117 of the Constitution), as well as its inconsistency *vis-à-vis* articles 24 and 111 of the Constitution, concluding that it represented a violation of this framework. The total fine that the law is able to place on the perpetrator is disproportionate. The obligation to confiscate the entire product of the operation gained by use of insider information (instead of solely the profit made), alongside the large administrative sanction issued by the CONSOB (200,000 euros), results in excessive punishment. The principle of proportionality of fines, while being specifically applicable to criminal sanctions, must also be applicable to administrative sanctions.

II Dignity of the Person, Right to Identity

A *Prostitution and Its Solicitation*

In the context of proceedings involving, among others, ex-Prime Minister Silvio Berlusconi, the Bari District Court brought up the question of constitutional legitimacy of the measures of law 20 February 1958, No. 75, the so-called Merlin Law against the exploitation of others' prostitution, which sets out solicitation of prostitution as a crime. This law, according to the remitting judge, assumes that prostitution is always coercive and exploitative, whereas in the judge's opinion and that of the parties to the proceedings declaring it unconstitutional, this is not the case of escorts who freely choose to offer sexual services in exchange for payment (though widespread and unknown at the time of the Merlin Law). Their work comes under the manifestation of the freedom to sexual self-determination, guaranteed by article 2 of the Constitution by way of individual dignity, and furthermore linked to the principle of freedom of economic initiative (article 41 of the Constitution). It follows that punishing with criminal law those who provide intermediation services between escorts and their potential clients, in the context of legal and non-exploitative or coercive prostitution, contradicts the constitutional principle (set out in articles 13, 25 and 27 of the Constitution) which excludes punishing conduct which does not compromise a protected asset. Article 25(2) of the Constitution on the necessary determination and legality of criminal law would be infringed since the law would put different behaviour on the same legal footing: facilitating forced prostitution and facilitating freely chosen prostitution carried out by escorts.

The judgment of Constitutional Court developed ample treatment of these models which, at an international level, were processed in various legal frameworks to tackle the issue of prostitution: regulatory and neo-regulatory models, prohibition and neo-prohibition models and abolition models. This latter forms the basis of the Italian legislation of 1958. All of these models (except the traditional regulatory model) have passed the scrutiny of the various European Constitutional Courts; the neo-prohibition model is particularly popular in the legal framework of the EU (as shown, for example, by Directive 2011/36/EU, on combatting human trafficking for sexual exploitation). The argument that Italian law aiming to combat all prostitution activities was contrary to article 2 of the Constitution was directly rejected. "Offering sexual services for remuneration and/or for hire is not – according to the Court – a protective or developmental instrument for the person, but constitutes, much more simply, a particular form of economic enterprise". It is therefore justified that when discussing the crime of solicitation of prostitution, the Court recalls article 41 of the Constitution. However, the same article 41, while confirming the freedom of economic enterprise, specifies that this "may not be carried out against the common good or in such a manner that could damage safety, liberty and human dignity". In this case, dignity is objective, irrespective of what everyone can subjectively develop their own sense of dignity. Human dignity is effectively – in light of recent case-law – the judicial good protected by laws on solicitation of prostitution. The solicitation of prostitution makes the practice of commercialising sexual activities (prohibited under Italian law) possible. Nor can it be assumed that the idea of solicitation as applied in the case of prostitution is unspecified and inaccurate, since the same judicial parameters are widely applied in other cases which are just as complicated. Ultimately, it follows that the crime of solicitation of prostitution, just as more generally the abolition-based legal framework introduced by the 1958 law is in no way contrary to the Constitution, although it is not the only with that is compatible with constitutional parameters.

Regarding the present crime of solicitation of prostitution, the Court of Cassation clarified that this crime consists of any action that renders the work of prostitution easier, with no reference to the aim or reason for this conduct. In this specific case, the action consisted in driving the women to the place of prostitution, with a small fee in cash (Criminal Cassation, sec. III, judg. 12 December 2019, No. 5910).

B Right to Know One's Origins

The Genoa Juvenile Court (judg. 23 May 2019) extended the reflection developed by Court of Cassation (see *Yearbook 2019*, pp. 296–297) on the right to know one's own family origins, even if there is an explicit declaration from the mother to remain anonymous, unless the woman does not show persistent willingness to break that confidentiality. Balancing the interests of these circumstances means recognising the right, on one hand, of a person to know their own origins and, on the other, the anonymity of the mother and also, in some cases, the existence of other children. The present case concerned the request on an individual, adopted at birth, to know their biological mother's personal data after her death. The request was rejected as the woman had had other children, and it was not possible to get their consent to divulge the information on their biological brother without revealing the anonymous birth to them (which they may have been kept in the dark about). It was therefore impossible to give the requested information on the birth without interfering with the privacy of others, nor by obtaining their consent on sharing this kind of information.

C Advance Provisions on Treatment of Personal Data and the Role of Support Services

The Constitutional Court (judgment 144/2019 of 13 June 2019) rejected the question of constitutionality, as raised in relation to article 3, paragraphs 4 and 5, of law 22 December 2017, No. 2019 (Regulation on informed consent and advance provisions on treatment of personal data), as unfounded. The matter concerned attributing power of attorney of an ill person to a support administrator. The person had been in a vegetative state for some time. The concern raised by the remitting judge was that from the cited article, in can be inferred that a support administrator who has been given power of attorney over a person can single-handedly (that is with no authorisation of a tutelary judge) deny necessary treatments to keep the person alive (naturally if there have been no advanced provisions on treatment stating otherwise). In this way, a support administrator would have the power of life and death over the person, taking into account that the decision to stop any treatment can be challenged in front of a tutelary judge only if it goes against the opinion of the doctor. This violates articles 2, 13 and 32 of the Constitution as its takes away a life and death decision from the person who is directly involved, by entrusting this exclusively to a support administrator. If the person is incapable of making a decision on their own health, refusal of treatment that would ensure their survival should instead be the result of an extensive consultation process, with the involvement of a judge.

The Constitutional Court rejects this interpretation. Law 219/2017 implements the principle of informed consent. The contested article 3 regulates cases in which informed consent to treatment or to procedures necessary for survival cannot be provided by the interested party and there is no declarations on advance provisions. The contested law however does not attribute the task of deciding on sustaining the life of an individual necessarily and automatically to a support administrator. The figure of a support administrator (according to the Civil Code) is very flexible. If the tutelary judge attributes the power of attorney of an individual to a support administrator, this does not automatically mean that the person is given the task to decide whether to deny medical treatment to the individual. This responsibility will be attributed on a case-by-case basis in light of specific circumstances, even after granting power of attorney.

> This issue is affronted also by the decision of the Rome District Court, judg. 23 September 2019. The tutelary judge dismissed the question presented by a support administrator of a woman in a vegetative state, aimed at authorising the suspension of lifesaving treatment. In fact, the tutelary judge stated that this suspension can only be carried out with informed consent provided by the same support administrator (representing the ill woman), relying on declarations made by the woman herself on multiple occasions and by other friends and family members. With no exceptions by doctors, and in light of absolute power of attorney over healthcare conceded to the support administrator upon their nomination in the case at hand, any authorisation procedure ordered by the judge would be superfluous.

One particular case occurred of the nomination of a support administrator by a person coming from the Jehovah's Witnesses community. In this particular case, the support administrator was the individual's wife (also a Jehovah's Witness). The private designation act was drawn up in 2014 under article 408 of the Civil Code, on the basis that "the support administrator can be appointed by the individual anticipating any future eventual incapacities". The law foresaw that, in the case that the serious illness worsened, the support administrator should assess if it is the case to continue the absolute refusal of any treatment involving blood transfusions, due to the religious principles of Jehovah's Witnesses. In 2015, the private document was taken to the Genoa tutelary judge to appoint the support administrator named within. The judge opposed this appointment, noting that the document was written by an individual who was still fully mentally capable, and therefore seems to set out the treatment choices in case of the loss of mental capacity to understand or choose their own treatment as a preventative measure. This is not compatible with the appointment of a support administrator. This rejection by the tutelary judge was brought to the attention of the Supreme Court, which had to take into account that, in the meantime, law 219/2017 on biological testament (or living will) entered into force, regulating advance provisions on medical treatment. Moreover, the law only has applied from 2018 onwards and does not cover the document formed in 2014.

The Court of Cassation (sec. I, judg. 15 May 2019) firstly established that naming a support administrator does not assume the lack of mental capacity of the individual, but can also apply to an illness that, even temporarily, impedes a person from directly managing their own interests. Either way, the alternative to appeal the nomination of a support administrator can be the interdiction or incapacitation of a nominee, not the banning of the measure entirely, as this would deprive the vulnerable individual of any form of protection. Above all, the Court held that advance provisions for medical treatment, including refusals of blood transfusion for religious reasons, can be legitimately kept alongside the nomination of a support administrator. Italian law recognises the self-determination of treatments and the principle of informed consent (article 32 of the Constitution). Doctors must respect the wishes of the patient, even if that leads to the death of the patient themselves. However, there is no reference to positive actions to end the life of a patient (consented murder or assisted suicide), but allows the patient to choose their own treatments and also to stop or refuse them. The fact that these choices reflect a religious belief of the individual (article 19 of the Constitution) should further justify the observance of this principle. The Court of Cassation recalls the principle of human dignity as established by the CFR of the EU (articles 2, 3 and 35) and by the UN Convention on the Rights of Persons with Disabilities. ECtHR case-law was also cited, in particular judgment *Lambert v. France* (*Lambert and Others v. France* [GC], No. 46043/14, 5 June 2015).

D Personal Injury and Consent of the Victim; Commercialisation of Gametes

This case and the subsequent case-law across the years has brought to the forefront the situations of extreme existential precarity lived in Italy. This includes the shocking realities of people who, through scams set up by criminal organisations posing as insurance companies, accepted to undergo injury and mutilations for a modest fee. However, the sums of money received simulating road accidents or workplace accidents mostly ended up in the hands of the organisations running the scams, leaving the injured person with very little. The Court of Cassation established that in these types of cases, the victim's consent to the injury cannot be viewed as free and informed. Unlike provisions concerning one's own body that are regulated by laws (organ donation, sex change, sterilisations), consent in the circumstances in question is given for an illegal act – that is, inflicting injury and mutilations. Article 5 of the Civil Code bans an individual from using their body in any way that permanently compromises its physical integrity or when it is against the law, public order or public morality. These notions are constantly evolving, especially in light of medical and scientific progress. The right to use one's own body (linked to the right to health) does not cover forms of self-inflicted injuries (in the case in question, the victim obtained injuries to the fibula and ankle) which aimed to commercialise the body or to committee fraud (which is punishable by law). Since the perpetrators of the injury are fully aware of the illegal nature of the injuries obtained, the consent of the victim cannot excuse this behaviour according to article 50 del Criminal Code (Criminal Cassation, sec. I, judg. 2 October 2019, No. 46895).

A case brought in front of the Supreme Court (Criminal Cassation, sec. III, judg. 6 June 2019, No. 36221) is similar in nature. The question came from an appeal by the Procurator of Milan of a judgment acquitting individuals who had, alongside foreign clinics, put in place a system that purchased eggs directly from women or from foreign clinics, or paid foreign women to undergo hormonal treatments to produce gametes for the organisation; the biological material was therefore used to allow access to assisted procreation for couples and the cost to obtain the gametes was taken off the price of clinical treatment (the Court ruled that a crime had not taken place). The organisation also offered an extra pay-for service which facilitates contact between couples and donors. This conduct can be criminally sanctioned by article 12, law 40/2004 on medically assisted procreation, which bans carrying out, organising or publicising the selling of gametes or maternal surrogacy. According to the judge who ruled on the case, since the Constitutional Court (judg. 162/2014 – see *Yearbook 2015*, pp. 252–254) had ruled that the ban on heterologous fertilisation (originally foreseen by l. 40/2004), contradicted the Constitution in cases in which couples suffered from pathologic and irreversible sterility and infertility. The law which punishes the production of gametes and making them available to the public should also be overturned. In reality, the judgment of the Constitutional Court does not mean that the law punishing the commercialisation of gametes has been repealed. In line with Directive 2004/23/EC on treatment of human cells, to be legally used in assisted heterologous fertilisation, gametes must be donated voluntarily by the woman. Although the directive does not completely exclude the possibility of compensating the donor, the law transposing the directive into Italian law bans any retribution for the donor. That implies that the selling of gametes for assisted heterologous fertilisation is still a crime, even in cases where heterologous fertilisation is permitted.

E Diagnostic Tests that Affect the Sexual Freedom and Consent of the Patient

The Court of Cassation (Criminal Cassation, sec. III, judg. 22 February 2019, No. 18864) repealed an appeal judgment which had acquitted a case in which a gynaecologist, during normal patient visits, had sexually stimulated them without their consent for the practice. Even though the stimulation carried out by the doctor could be used for diagnostic purposes, in three cases reported to the authorities, the actions of the health professional caught the patients by surprise, and was carried out without their consent, and accompanied by generic requests to "collaborate". Beyond the circumstances in which there is strict necessity, a medical procedure cannot disregard the informed consent of a patient; this would represent a violation of the dignity of the person, the right to integrity of the person and the right to health (articles 2, 13, 32 of the Constitution). The idea of "implicitly" given consent is also unacceptable, even more so if those actions intrude in any way on the sexual sphere. Sexual violence is, by nature, the lack of consent by the victim concerning actions that could be considered sexual. Therefore, even if a health professional carries out these actions to treat the person, if those actions are sexual in nature, without consent the doctor takes responsibility for that violence. The aim of an individual to get sexual pleasure is not an element of the crime of sexual violence. Nor can it be said – as the territorial judge suggested – that there is any doubt on the fact that the doctor acted with malice: given that the lack of verified consent is, in itself, evidence that the procedure was carried out against the patients' will, and with no other way to justify the conduct with other reasons or to suggest that getting their consent would have been impossible.

F Conscientious Objection and Abortion

According to the Council of State (sec. V, judg. 9 April 2019, No. 2327), the case of the Municipality of Genoa's ban is legitimate – the Municipality had refused the request to put up a poster manifesto by the Union of Rationalist Atheists and Agnostics (UAAR) which implicitly criticised the practice of conscientious objection of health workers to abortion (in particular). The poster featured a doctor and a priest, topped with the slogan "Head or Cross?" ("*Testa o Croce?*"), and "Don't leave it up to faith. Ask immediately if your doctor is a conscientious objector". According to the judges, the campaign aimed at striking the free expression of the conscientious objection of medical staff, for religious or ethical reasons, by inferring that these are in contrast with reason ("head"), therefore introducing a discriminating factor between medical staff based on belief or religion. Critical expressions or campaigns that seem legal when linked to social or political rhetoric are instead discriminatory and harmful to the rights of the people they are in reference to, when presented as an initiative rather than pure information.

G Adoption of Partner's Child within Civil Unions and the Right to a Name

The norms on "adoption in specific cases" (l. 184/1983, article 44 – see also *ultra*, paragraph XI, D) are generally used to allow the reciprocal adoption of the respective children of components of a civil union (law 176/2017), on the assumption that the legitimising adoption is possible even if the child of the partner was conceived through medically assisted fertilisation procedures. In the case in question, two women in a civil union had both given birth to a child via medically assisted fertilisation procedures. By overcoming the literal reading of the law, the Juvenile Court established that both children would have the same surname, formed by putting together the two surnames of the mother in the same order. According to the letter of the law, each child would have had to add the surname of the adoptive "second mother" to their biological mother's surname, and consequently the two siblings would have different surnames. The constitutionally guided interpretation of the law allows the correction of this conclusion without the need to bring up the question of constitutional legitimacy of the law (Genoa Juvenile Court, judg. 13 June 2019).

On the subject of the right to a name, a judgment with which the Parma District Court (judg. 27 February 2019, No. 2) is worthy of mention: it was a case of the adoption of an adult, interpreting (in line with the Constitution) article 299 of the Civil Code (surname of the adopted person). The Court accepted the application to change the adopted person's name by adding the surname of the adopting parent to the individual's original surname (instead of replacing it completely, pursuant to the Civil Code). This allowed the individual to maintain ties with their biological father, while also recognising the deep relationship with the adopting parent. According to the Court, the current social role of adult adoption – not to protect the descendancy or heritage of the individual, but to recognise a profound emotional tie between the two – justifies the departure from the rules of the law, which otherwise would be contrary to article 2 of the Constitution.

H Transcription of Foreign Documents and Alleged Contrast with Public Order: Adoption by Homosexual Couples, Surrogate Maternity

The Joint Sections of the Civil Cassation (Civil Cassation, joint sections, judg. 8 May 2019, No. 12193) pronounced on a case in Italy (in the Municipality of Trent) of the denied transcription by the Municipality registrar of the parental relationship of one of two partners of a civil union (the two men married in Canada) and two children, born in Canada with the aid of a surrogate mother with egg donation. The minors were the biological children of one member of the couple, but not of the second. On the basis of local law, the Ontario Supreme Court had already confirmed the parental status of the second partner for the children. This relationship was the subject of the transcription in Italy, pursuant to l. 218/1995 on international private law. The Trent registrar had argued it was at the limit of public order, but the exception was rejected by Trent Court of Appeal. The joint sections ruled therefore on the complaint put forward by the Mayor of Trent and the Ministry of the Interior on the decision, as well as by the Public Ministry of the Trent Court of Appeal (although the legitimacy of this latter challenge this decision was subsequently excluded by the Court of Cassation and its complaint was declared inadmissible). The judgment developed an ample treatment on the notion of international public order, not intended as a defensive limit opposed to all new entries of laws and judicial acts, but rather as a tool to open up domestic legislation to shared international values (see also *Yearbook 2018*, pp. 267–8). Based on these assumptions, the Supreme Court ruled to fix the criteria of the scope of international public law in order to be effective in Italy in the following terms: this can be implemented in Italy if it is compatible with the fundamental principles laid out in the Constitution and in sources of international and supranational law, just as they are embodied in the frameworks of Italian law and constitutional and ordinary case-law. Legislation and case-law constitute "living rights" necessary to define the notion of public order, which together determine the founding values of the legal framework of any given historic moment. In light of this notion, according to the Joint Sections, the ban on recognising surrogate mothers should be encompassed within the principles of public order – it is not explicitly found in constitutional and international sources, but is undoubtedly expressed in Italian law, particularly law 40/2014 on medically assisted fertilisation. Unlike other cases, in which the transcription of foreign acts that recognise parental status were found admissible, this case deals with a total maternal surrogation, and therefore between one of the parents and children born through assisted maternity, there is no genetic or biological relationship ("parent with intention"). The situation reflects a case dealt with by judgment of Civil Court of Cassation 24001/2014 (see *Yearbook 2015*, pp. 254–255). "Pure" maternal surrogation is not valued by Italian law and therefore the transcription of foreign acts that fully recognises it to all its effects cannot be permitted (like the one emitted by the Canadian Court. According to the Court of Cassation, it is not valid to oppose this conclusion with the [RB1] the principle of the best interests of the child, confirmed by the CRC, by the CFR of the EU, by the European Convention of 1996 on the exercise of rights of minors and by the Hague Convention on Jurisdiction, Applicable Law, Recognition, Enforcement and Co-operation in respect of Parental Responsibility and Measures for the Protection of Children of 1996. The rights of the child can be balanced with other important principles and values (in this case, the woman's dignity), and, in a situation like the one in question, parental status was finally recognised to one of the partners. In conclusion, the non-transcribable nature of foreign acts, which confirm a parent-child relationship when the child was born abroad to a surrogate mother and the parent (an Italian citizen) has no biological link with the child, is affirmed.

Intervening on the complaint of the Mayor of Samarate (Varese), a section of the Court of Cassation decided to request the judgment of the Joint Sections to clarify the subject of transcribability in Italy of child adoption acts by a same-sex couple made up of one person with double citizenship (Italian and American) and one American citizen, married in the United States of America. The adoption act was emitted in compliance with local laws from a New York Court. The Milan Court of Appeal ordered the Municipality in Lombardy to transcribe the child adoption act and the concurrent recognition of the child's adopted status within the couple. The Municipality challenged this, however, stating that the current law, despite the adoption of law 76/2016 on "civil unions", continues to oppose adoption by homosexual couples, which is banned by article 29 of the Constitution and represents an international public order law. The Court of Cassation identified a clear disrespect of Italian law regarding legal adoptions by unmarried couples (therefore also homosexual couples or civil union couples). The Joint Sections will have to establish whether this constitutes a limit of international public order (to which the legislation refers this decision). (Civil Cassation, sec. I, ord. 23 September 2019, No. 29071).

I Sex Changes of Married Partners

The Grosseto District Court ruled on an issue which in part coincides with the judgment Constitutional Court 170/2014 (see *Yearbook 2015*, p. 279). The Constitutional Court (as well as the Court of Cassation in many circumstances) stated that, in the case of a sex change of one part of the couple, the couple was not "obliged" to legally end their marital relationship, but would have to continue the relationship as a civil union, pursuant to law 76/2016 on civil unions. The case in question instead concerned the simultaneous sex change of both spouses. The Court established that a constitutionally orientated reading of the current law discipline leads to maintaining the relationship in its pre-existing form of a marriage even after the correction of the attribution of sex of both members of the couple (Grosseto District Court, judg. 3 October 2019, No. 740).

III Freedom of Religion, Rights to Freedom of Speech, Association, and Political Rights; Right to Inform; Hate Crimes; Crime of "Injury"

A Authorisation to Gather to Celebrate an Islamic Festival

On 1 August 2029 (decree No. 1003), the Lombardy Regional Administrative Court suspended the bill with which a Municipality in

Lombardy denied a Muslim association the authorisation for around 200 people to celebrate the Festival of Sacrifice (Eid al-Adha – one of the main Islamic holidays) in a public area on 14 August 2019. The request had been made following all written rules and the reasons given for its rejection made no reference to a "proven reason of security or public safety"; the only reason for which restrictions can be placed on a peaceful reunion according to article 17 of the Constitution. The reasons given by the Municipality may be valid for the opening of a fixed place of worship, but are not adequate for the temporary use (one day) of a public space, even if it is for religious activities. The suspension measure (which anticipate the effects of a judgment) was issued by the presiding judge via an urgent decree; there was not enough time for the bench to meet before the start of the holiday period, and it would have been impossible to celebrate the Festival in another period, given that the Islamic religious calendar fixed the festival between 11 and 15 August. For the Municipality, it is ordered to identify the area within five days.

B Limits of the Right to Inform

According to a judgment of the Court of Cassation (Criminal Cassation, sec. V, judg. 21 June 2019, No. 43569), the right to inform cannot supersede the punishment of a crime (impersonation) committed by a journalist to get potentially useful information in a journalistic bit for a popular TV show (*"Le iene"*). In a similar case, Criminal Cassation (sec. II, judg. 7 June 2019, No. 38277) adopted a different stance. The case concerned the purchase made by the owner of a leading chain of supermarkets on behalf of the then-director of *"Panorama"* and a well-known journalist of *"Libero"*. The item was a CD of telephone recordings taken from the sales team of an investigation agency, in which it was stated that another chain of supermarkets was carrying out wiretapping operations on its own employees. The Court of Cassation defers the conviction, requesting that the judge consider the contribution that the journalist's investigation (using the stolen CD) has made to the public debate on privacy. According to the judges, it is the duty of journalists to report on issues of public interest (the businessman's role was rendered irrelevant by the death of the interested party) and this, in some cases, can justify the use of illegal practices, as the ECtHR seemed to confirm.

C Propaganda of Racist Ideas and other Manifestations of Hatred

The Supreme Court (Criminal Cassation, sec. V, judg. 7 May 2019, No. 32862) reformed the appeal judgment which, in 2018, convicted the politician Mario Borghezio. At the time (2013), he was a Member of the EP, who during a well-known radio show was speaking about Roma and Sinti communities, said about them (among other things) that they had "a certain high-tech tradition for breaking into the homes of honest people". The conviction was for racially-aggravated libel. Ruling on the application, the Court of Cassation firstly excluded that the statements made by the ex-Member of Parliament could have been protected by the "right to satire", as well as failing to exercise self-restraint when satirising certain subjects and issues. The conviction was revised on the type of crime committed: it could not be defined defamation – since the offensive statement did not concern one particular individual but in general the Roma and Sinti ethnic communities -, but the crime (introduced by law 654/1975 ratifying the Convention against racial discrimination, now article 604 Criminal Code), of propaganda of idea based on racial or ethnic hatred or superiority, punishable with a fine of up to €6000 euro and a prison sentence of up to 18 months. It was excluded that this crime was in any way contrary to the principles of freedom of expression of the ECHR (article 10); any reason that would constitute non-criminality given the link between his statements on the radio and the contents of speeches made by Parliament was also ruled out, since, while hinting at the situation of Roma and Sinti communities in Europe, these speeches did not contain any of the discriminatory content heard on the radio programme. The Court took the opportunity to clarify some specific aspects on the crime of propaganda of racist ideas, currently sanctioned by Italian law. This propaganda consists of spreading messages "aimed at influencing the behaviour or psychological reaction of a vast public audience in order to attract followers"; racial or ethnic hatred (which is different to a superficial dislike or intolerance) is a "feeling that create the concrete danger of discriminatory behaviour", based on the ethnical or racial identity of an individual, regardless of their personal behaviour.

During a meeting of the Municipal council of Milan dedicated to the issue of evicting some Roma community settlements, one citizen (a well-known member of a right-wing political group) raised his arm to imitate a fascist salute. The person was charged in 2018 for the crime under article 2 of law-decree 122/1993 (Mancino Law), which punishes "anyone who during a public meeting, outwardly demonstrates or flaunts emblems or symbols (specific or general) of organisations, associations, movements or groups" which aim to instigate discrimination or violence based on race, ethnicity, nationality or religion. The circumstances in which the gesture was carried out rendered it unmistakable as a reference to the fascist ideology – no exception could be made for its tenuous nature. The sentence (40 days in prison and a €1000 fine) was therefore confirmed (Criminal Cassation, sec. I, judg. 27 March 2019, No. 21409).

The Criminal Court of Cassation held that the crime of hate propaganda (currently foreseen by article 604-*bis* of the Criminal Code) does not cover putting up a poster on a mobile advertising van, in which a shop's advertisement was placed next to a complaint about a particularly violent news article of the previous days, with the caption "Illegal immigrant kills three Italians with a pickaxe. Death penalty immediately" (*"Clandestino uccide tre italiani a picconate. Pena di morte subito"*), alongside a picture of a guillotine decapitating a black man. According to the Court of Cassation, the message did not concern migrants or African in general, but referred particularly to a news article, stigmatising the behaviour of an individual and not the way of life of a collective (Criminal Cassation, sec. I, judg. 13 December 2019, No. 1602). Similarly, the Supreme Court confirmed the appeal judgment which acquitted the defendant. It concerned a Provincial Councillor in Monza and Brianza who, on her own Facebook page, had posted paradoxical comments (following other equally surreal comments insulting Southern Italians) on a satellite photo of Italy which seemed to be missing the central and southern regions of the country. The paradoxical and nonsensical nature of the politician's comments led the Court to exclude the idea that, even in theory, the pictures would have created a risk of discriminatory behaviour (Criminal Cassation, sec. I, judg. 26 November 2019, No. 6933).

With regards to the aggravating factor of racial, ethnic or religious hatred (established by the so-called Mancino law – l.d. 122/1993, now article 604-*ter* of the Criminal Code), the Court of Cassation reiterated that this refers both to when these comments made when committing a crime are intentionally aimed at eliciting racial hatred (in this case, it concerned personal injury to an African man), but also when, by using discriminatory stereotypes about a certain ethnicity, the comments could invoke hostile sentiments (Criminal Cassation, sec. VI, judg. 7 June 219, No. 40014).

D Abolition of the Crime of "Insult"

The Constitutional Court (judg. 37/2019 of 6 March 2019) dismissed the issue of constitutionality as manifestly unfounded, with reference to the laws adopted in 2014 and 2016 repealing the crime of "insult" (article 594 of the Criminal Code). The Constitutional Court agrees that the honour of a person should be fundamental right, protected by articles 2 and 3 of the Constitution, and by international law (article 17 IICPR, 8 ECHR, 7 CFR of the EU). This recognition does not necessarily impose the use of this instrument of Criminal law for the statement. The choice to maintain the crime of defamation (article 595 of the Criminal Code) and decriminalise "insult" falls within the area of discretional choices which only Parliament (while exercising its legislative function) can take; since it is not a groundless, illogical or discriminatory choice, it does not come under the consideration of the Constitutional Court.

IV Asylum and International Protection

A Repatriations to Libya Violate Asylum Seekers' Human Rights

The Rome District Court (judgment 28 November 2019, No. 22917) pronounced on one of the various cases (more than ten years after the facts of the case) of refoulement towards Libya by the Italian military navy in the summer of 2009, the most noteworthy of which was the subject of the *Hirsi Jamaa and Others v. Italy* judgment of the ECtHR (see *Yearbook 2013*, pp. 257–259; see also *Yearbook 2019*, p. 256). On 30 June 2009, the ship "Orione" of the military navy took 87 (or 82) migrants back to Libya (the majority of whom Eritrean) who had been intercepted attempting to cross the Mediterranean, drifting 26 miles off the coast of Lampedusa. After their re-entry into Libya and their stay at the migrant detention centres, most migrants slipped under the radar. Some, however, managed to reach Israel, where they were also held in deplorable conditions, although here they were able to contact legal aid in Italy who, over the past few years, brought the civil case before the Rome District Court. The judgment of the Court went over the dramatic events of 2009 and, confirming the same reading provided by the ECtHR judgment, ruled that the Italian State must be held responsible for violating the ban on collective expulsions to a country in which they were at high risk of persecution, death, torture, and other inhuman treatment. The defence of the Italian State (that it had not received any requests for international protection from any of the rescued migrants) was rebuked. Even if no request had been made, this would not have justified the complete ignorance of the inhuman conditions and treatment of irregular migrants in Libya (at the time and in subsequent years) as was described. The judges concluded that Italy is required to pay compensation for non-material damages (article 2043 of the Civil Code) suffered by the migrants due to the legal activity of the Italian State, more precisely by the Prime Minister and the Ministry of Defence, whose repatriation policy violated the fundamental rights of the applicants. The compensation was set at €15,000 euro each, the same sum which (on an equitable basis) was defined by the ECtHR with the *Hirsi Jamaa* judgment. Additionally, the judgement confirmed the applicants' right to re-enter Italy (re-entry method to be stipulated by the Government) in order to present an international protection application, which had been illegally blocked ten year previously.

B Constitutional Legitimacy of Some Measures of the Law-Decree "Security and Immigration". Civil Registration of International Protection Seekers

The regions of Umbria, Emilia-Romagna, Marche, Tuscany, Calabria, Basilicata and Sardinia have contested law-decree 113/2018 ("security and immigration decree": see *Yearbook 2019, passim*), considered in all aspects and in reference to some of its articles before the Constitutional Court (the latter two successively renounced their cases). The complaint was considered inadmissible with judgment 194/2019 of 24 July 2019. Although it complies with the decree as a whole, it was challenged by the Regions under article 77 of the Constitution (the law which regulates exceptional legislative power of the Government) as it was adopted with no urgent or necessary foundation. The Constitutional Court held that the Regions had not adequately motivated the connection between the alleged violation of article 77 of the Constitution and any reduction of their competencies, as granted to them by the Constitution itself. The decree impacts on issues and policies strictly pertaining to the State, in particular concerning the management of immigration and public security, although it may have consequences for other sectors (health, social assistance, professional training, etc.) which is of regional competency. It is therefore legitimate to challenge individual provisions which fall under regional competency, but not the decree in its entirety. The individual issues raised by the Regions, therefore, first and foremost concerned article 1 of the decree, which removes the residence permit for humanitarian protection and (partially) replaces it with various other type of permit. Humanitarian protection was introduced in Italy in 1993, in connection with the Schengen Agreement for the protection of foreign citizens, although not defined as refugees or holders of subsidiary protection (introduced in 2004 by EU Law), they still have "serious motives" which are humanitarian in nature, or other serious motivation resulting from constitutional or international obligations, to avoid repatriation and to obtain a temporary permit to remain in Italy. Other laws (which are humanitarian in nature) protected the victims of forced prostitution ("social protection"), victims of serious labour exploitation and victims of domestic violence. Decree 113/2018 upheld these "special" permits, alongside others (for medical treatment, disaster, acts of particular civil value and risk of persecution or torture). All these measures impact on the principle enshrined in article 10, para. 3 of the Constitution which sets out the Republic's duty to give asylum to foreign nationals "of whom, in their own country, the effective exercise of the democratic freedoms, guaranteed by the Italian Constitution, have been restricted". Moreover, the regulations laid down in article 1 of l.d.113/2018 can be investigated for a violation of article 10(3) of the Constitution, as well as article 117(1) of the Constitution, as regards to international obligations in humanitarian law. However, the Italian regions cannot take on this unconstitutional aspect, as it deals with issues outside their competence, and can only hypothetically influence the regions on matters that do fall within their scope. At the same time, the Court discussed the issues raised about articles 12 and 13 of the l.d. 113/2008, which radically reformed the first and second reception system for asylum seekers, and established that the residency document issued to asylum seekers did not allow them to register within their host municipality. These measures come under the issue of "immigration", over which the State and regions share competences. However, according to the Constitutional Court, this specific issue relates to the right to asylum and the legal status of foreign nationals at the registry office, which entirely fall under State jurisdiction.

The explicit ban on allowing the registration of a person with a temporary residence permit issued with a request for international protection formed the basis of a number of judgments. These rulings also brought up the question of its constitutionality – the judgment on this is due in 2020. The complaint regarding this ban was presented by a number of asylum seekers in various courts. The applicants complained that, without registering their presence on the territory with the Municipality, they were unable (or found great difficulty) to access essential health, banking, and labour services among others, for which it is necessary to show a residence document. The Courts of Florence (ord. 18 March 2019), Bologna (ord. 2 May 2019), Genoa (sec. XI, ord. 22 May 2019), Prato (ord. 28 May 2019) and Lecce (ord. 6 December 2019) established that, without challenging the validity of this provision, in reality, no "status" is necessary to register in a municipality, as a statement of the individual and the local authorities' assessment to ascertain the effective residence of the person requesting international protection in the territory should be sufficient. This interpretation has undoubtedly limited the negative effects that the law provision could have had on the many people seeking international protection. Over the year, however, the validity of this law has led to a huge difference in its application across the country, with many Municipalities applying these restrictions in their most literal form, while others chose the opposite approach. In some cases, municipalities gave the responsibility of this registration act to their mayors (making them a registrar), hence relieving officials of any responsibility.

C Complaints against the Ban on Recognising International Protection

The Court of Cassation ruled out that the 2017 law eliminating the double degree of judgment for procedures to recognise the right to international protection could violate the Constitution. Double degree judgments were not carried out under constitutional law and may not be foreseen when the need for promptness is prevalent. Moreover, the facts of the case, assessed by judicial bodies, were already established by administrative proceedings in front of the Territorial Commissions, with which any further judgment could be considered superfluous. The question of constitutionality of law 46/2017 on this point (in reference to articles 24 and 11 of the Constitution) is therefore manifestly ill-founded (Civil Cassation, sec. I, ord. 9 January 2019, No. 295).

The procedures to recognise the status of a holder of international protection requires the active participation of the Territorial Commission and a judge to assess whether the applicant is in a situation of persecution or danger that may justify protection. Moreover, according to Supreme Court, if statements made by the applicant are found to be unreliable or contradictory, the judge does not need to investigate the information further to find out if there is indiscriminate violence and persecution in the country of origin (in this case, Senegal) (Civil Cassation, sec. I, judg. 30 September 2019, No. 24410).

In various judgments, the territorial courts have reiterated the burden of proving the existence of conditions that would justify international protection regarding the foreign national applicant; territorial commissions and judges must unofficially integrate the information provided by the individual (see, for example, Cagliari Court of Appeal, judgments 13 February 2019, No. 136; 17 July 2019, No. 635; Milan Court of Appeal, sec. IV, judg. 30 July 2019, No. 3370; Turin Court of Appeal, sec. IV, judg. 2 October 2019, No. 1593; Ancona District Court, judg. 10 October 2019). The Court of Cassation clarifies that the credibility of the evidence provided by the applicant is a point of fact that the Territorial Commission or the judge must investigate. This can only subsequently be taken up by the Court of Cassation in cases of missing or incomprehensible information (Civil Cassation, sec. VI, judg. 31 July 2019, No. 20582).

In a case concerning an international protection seeker from Mauritania, the Bari District Court (judg. 19 September 2019) recognised that in the country in question, there are no tools to effectively guarantee human rights of persons who have been reduced to a state of slavery. The situation of the applicant as a victim of persecution must be recognised, and consequently must be given refugee status.

The hearing in front of the territorial commission for international protection can be legal even when only one member of the commission is present, even when the individual has been not priorly informed (as expressly foreseen by law), as long as the circumstance did not cause a specific violation of the individual's fundamental rights – in the case at hand, the exception must be presented within the court appeal (Civil Cassation, sec. VI, judg. 25 July 2019, No. 20250; see *Yearbook 2019*, p. 306).

The Venice District Court noted that the critical political and economic situation of the country of origin of the individual requesting protection – in this specific case, Nigeria – is not in itself enough to justify recognising refugee status or conceding subsidiary protection with no proven link between this situation and the individual situation of the applicant. However, in the case of a woman from Nigeria who had been trafficked to then exploited in Libya, there are other conditions present that allow for the recognition of humanitarian protection (which is possible, since her application was processed prior to the entry into force of law-decree 113/2018 abolishing humanitarian protection) (Venice District Court, judg. 24 May 2019). The Florence District Court's previously cited judgment of 23 May 2019 came to similar conclusions concerning a Bangladeshi citizen.

Catanzaro Court of Appeal (sec. I, judg. 21 May 2019), reforming a previous ruling, held that the proven homosexuality of an applicant for international protection on the basis of a psychological relationship and his membership to an Arcigay (LGBT) association in Italy. It follows that any eventual repatriation to his country of origin (the Gambia) would have led to his arrest for alleged sexual violence on a young person (and presumable sentence which could be up to a life sentence) given that all homosexual activities are illegal in that country. The Court also acknowledged that, on the basis of reports by international bodies (among which Amnesty International), in the Gambia, being homosexual exposes the person to graves forms of persecution. This therefore justifies the recognition of refugee status for the individual.

D Humanitarian Protection

Humanitarian protection (which is different to those defined as refugee status or subsidiary protection status) was abolished in Italian law by l.d. 113/2018. The Court of Cassation clarified that this repeal does not have retroactive effect. Civil Cassation sec. I, judg. 19 February 2019, No. 4890, confirmed that the new categories that have replaced humanitarian protection can only be applied for proceedings opened after the date of entry into force of the aforementioned law-decree, while the previous legal must be applied in any situation that was already open or was ongoing at that date. See, also, the Florence District Court, judg. 23 May 2019, where the Court recalled the observations of the President of the Republic on the adoption of law-decree 113/2018, aimed at reiterating the need to guarantee the right to asylum for foreigners who "have had the effective exercise of their democratic freedoms impeded in their own country", even if the presence of a law abolishing humanitarian protection.

This form of protection is not a category in itself in precise terms, since it is necessary to protect the subjective situation of vulnerability in which a person (even if the individual does not have the prerequisites for protection as a refugee or subsidiary protection, who cannot be expelled from Italy may find themselves; Civil Cassation, sec. VI, judg. 4 October 2019, No. 24864; see also Palermo Court of Appeal, sec. I, judg. 12 June 2019, No. 1210).

Unlike those with refugee or subsidiary protection status, holders of humanitarian protection who do not have a passport from their country of origin do not have the right to be issued with a travel document (which would replace a passport) by the Italian Authorities. They are therefore not allowed to leave the State. This does not constitute discrimination, as, given their less vulnerable status, the conditions of those with humanitarian permits are (in many aspects) less guaranteed than those with refugee or subsidiary protection status. The judge added that this was also confirmed by the recent removal of humanitarian protection, which has been replaced by forms of temporary residence permits for particular cases (Regional Administrative Court Molise, Campobasso, sec. I, judg. 21 February 2019, No. 65).

E Migrants' Reaction to Repatriation to Libya and Resisting Public Arrest of a Ship's Captain: Justified Legitimate Defence and Line of Duty

On 8 July 2018, the Italian salvage-ship Vos Thalassa went ahead to rescue a boat carrying 67 migrants drifting in high. After the rescue, the ship's crew were threatened by some of the survivors when it became clear that the boat was turning south toward Libya in order to hand over the migrants to the authorities (on the order of the Italian Authorities) (the rescue operation was carried out in Libyan search and rescue waters). The Trapani District Court, after reconstructing all details of the case, wondered whether the threats to the crew and the acts of resistance and insulting a public officer of some of the rescued migrants could be justified as self-defence. The Court noted that migrants hold a series of rights to life and personal safety, which the State whose authorities were managing search and rescue operations (in this case Italy) had to duty to guarantee. According to international law, in particular the 1979 Convention of Hamburg on Search and Rescue mission, when one of the Contracting Parties finds out about a person in danger at sea, the State must immediately take the necessary steps to assist them and allow the person to disembark in a safe place. Given the circumstances, including the witness testimonies of the rescued migrants, there is no doubt that, in summer 2018, no disembarkation in Libya could be considered a return to a safe place (the conditions of arbitrary killings, torture, sexual violence and exploitation faced by irregular migrants in Libya were well-known). This does not take into account that it was impossible to apply for recognition of refugee status, which presumably many of the rescued migrants had the right to do. Returning migrants to Libya did not only constitute a form of refoulement (in contravention of the Geneva Convention relating to the

Status of Refugees), but a violation of the right to life and to not undergo torture and inhuman treatment. According to the Trapani District Court, the Italy-Libya Protocol (concluded in 2017) to regulate the collaboration between the two countries to combat human trafficking and illegal immigration could not be considered legally binding, as the deal was concluded in its simplified form without the sanction of the Italian Parliament, and also in light of the clear non-compliance of the obligations undertaken by Libya, in particular those related to the treatment of migrants and those applying for international protection. The resistance shown by the migrants to the prospect of refoulement to Libya was therefore not a reaction to an arbitrary act by the ship's authorities (who was acting under orders from the State search and rescue coordinator), but rather was legitimate form of self-defence in front of behaviour that unfairly exposed them to a violation of their fundamental rights. Nor can it said that the migrants had voluntarily placed themselves in that situation, since their escape from Sub-Saharan Africa afflicted by armed conflicts and disasters could be considered anything but voluntary. Therefore, there was a serious and grave danger of unfair treatment endangering the lives and dignity of the migrants if they were taken back to Libya and realistically the only way to avert this was the violent reaction of some migrants. It follows that the alleged offences against those migrants must be justified by self-defence (Trapani District Court, judg. 3 June 2019, No. 112).

Along the same lines as this previous story, the decision of the Agrigento District Court must be recalled, which intervened on the highly-covered case of the Sea Watch 3 ship from 29 June 2019. The ship docked at Lampedusa port to allow 50 shipwrecked migrants to disembark, contravening the orders of the port authorities and lightly striking a patrol boat that was attempting to block the manoeuvre. The alleged crime for the Sea Watch 3 captain, Carola Rakete, was resisting arrest (article 337 of the Criminal Code). The Agrigento District Court (judg. 2 July 2019) reconstructed the entire case which resulted in a clash between the humanitarian NGO ship and an armed forces vessel in Lampedusa port. Sea Watch 3 had rescued 53 migrants from international waters. Despite the orders to stop from the Italian Authorities, and declaring that she had no other alternative to transfer the migrants to a safe port, the ship's captain decided to disembark the rescued migrants in the Italian port of Lampedusa. The Libyan and Tunisian ports were not able to ensure adequate treatment of the migrants, and Maltese ports were too far. The ship (with the migrants on board) stayed outside the port of Lampedusa for 14 days, awaiting authorisation which continued to be delayed, in part due to the political tug-of-war that occurred on the issue, both in Italy and in Europe. With the health and security situation deteriorating aboard the ship, the captain decided to proceed with the approach without an order from the authorities. It was at this point that the two vessels collided. The Court acknowledge that the captain of the ship find herself with a duty to respect international maritime law on rescuing shipwrecked persons, which the Italian coastguard authorities were opposing in that moment. On the basis of article 51 of the Criminal Code ("the fulfilment of a duty imposed by a legal norm [...] excludes punishment"), her behaviour, which could abstractly be equated with the crime of resisting arrest, is therefore not punishable by law.

V Discrimination – General Issues

A Discrimination Based on Nationality or Ethnic Origin

Some decisions applied the regulations set out in lgs.d. 215/2003 (implementing directive 2000/43/EC) against discrimination on the basis of race or ethnic origins. (For other cases regarding "hate crimes" concerning the right to freedom of expression and opinion, see in this Part, Human Rights in Italian Case-law, III B)

Brescia Court of Appeal (sec. I, judg. 18 January 2019, No. 96), rejecting the appeal in the first instance, held that the posting and sharing of a comment on Facebook reading *"This is the list of all cooperatives and foundations and other operatives that with the smug face of those doing charity are actually PROFITING from trafficking illegal immigrants... These institutions get MORE THAN 1000 EUROS A MONTH PER IMMIGRANT! It's our money, but if the government has to use our money to maintain someone, it should at least be its own citizens, not Africans!"* constitutes discriminatory behaviour. The judge consequently ordered the cessation and non-repetition of this conduct, compensation for damages, and the adoption of measures to prevent similar casing from arising in the future, as well as the publication of this decision in the media). Publishing a similar text would constitute a form of collective discrimination which vilifies asylum seekers and the associations which assist them. It can therefore be seen as a form of harassment based on racial and ethnic origins of migrants. The Court therefore confirmed the legal stance of some associations, registered with the ministerial list of bodies and agencies that assist migrants.

The Rome District Court (sec. II, judg. 28 January 2019, No. 798) ascertains the discriminative nature of a public call for tender for cultural mediators to work within the judicial administration which was open only to Italian citizens and excluded both EU citizens and non-EU citizens holding a long-term or permanent residence permit, refugees and holders of subsidiary protection (see also *Yearbook 2019*, pp. 310–311).

B Discrimination towards Homosexual Couples on Assisted Reproduction

The Constitutional Court (judg. 221/2019 of 23 October 2019) discussed the issue of the discriminatory nature of law 40/2004 on medically assisted reproduction, allowing access of these practices solely to heterosexual couples and makes the use of these techniques by homosexual couples sanctionable. According to the Court, the law addresses pathological sterility and infertility, and is not meant as an instrument to fulfil the desire of an individual or couple who don't have these conditions to become parents. However, it is clear that the law is directed at a procreation with a mother and a father of different sexes. This legislative choice takes into account a multitude of traditionally identified social and culture elements and fulfils the aim of protecting human dignity. The applicant complains that the violation of articles 2, 3, 31 and 32 of the Constitution and articles 8 and 14 ECHR was accurately weighed up both in a parliamentary discussion and in the framework of many Constitutional Court decisions on the issue, as well as international standards, in particular articles 2, 17 and 23 ICCPR and 5, 6, 22, 23 and 25 of the Convention on the Rights of Persons with Disabilities. The idea that a couple formed of two fertile, living parents of different sexes is by and large the best place to welcome and bring up a new-born child does not seem irrational or arbitrary. In the case of homosexual couples (in this case, the procedure regarded a couple made up of two women), the infertility is not pathological, but physiological and "structural". The two situations are deeply and existentially different. Therefore, it is not possible to cite discriminatory treatment in this case; that is, different treatment for structurally similar situations. The access ban for medically assisted reproduction for homosexual couples therefore does not constitute a discrimination contrary to the Constitution.

VI Rights of Persons with Disabilities

A Leave to Assist Persons with Disabilities: Assistance Benefit

Law 104/1992 allows employees to benefit from special leave to assist family members with disabilities. Any abuse of this system would constitute an offense causing damage to the employer and the social security institution reimbursing the employee's salary. However, this does not mean that the worker using this extra leave to steadily care for family members must constantly be with the disabled person. In this case, the Court of Appeal received a challenge on the judgment at first instance and annulled the dismissal of a cashier who, in the days taken on leave to assist her disabled mother at her family home, as well as looking after her during the night and in other moments during the day, she took care of other personal matters, while the mother managed her own life and relationships in her daughter's absence (calling on others for assistance when necessary). The daughter was always contactable and available to assist her mother during these times). This was enough to rule out any abuse (Campobasso Court of Appeal, judg. 26 October 2019, No. 257).

According to the Rome District Court, this support benefit (foreseen by law 18/1980) is also directed for people who assist a person with learning difficulties who, even if they are able to look after their own physical needs (eating, taking medication, getting dressed, and so on), would not be able to carry out these activities without a helper in the way or in the amount of time necessary to respect their personal dignity or health, or in a way that created danger or distress for others (Rome District Court, sec. Labour, judg. 28 May 2019, No. 5159).

B Inclusion in Education

The joint sections of the Civil Cassation ruled on the Individual Education Plan (IEP), that is the document produced jointly by the school and local social-health services, which are defined year by year according to the needs of students with disabilities to be integrated into the school system from infant school onwards. In particular, the document sets out the need for hours of teaching support for the student. Disputes relating to the initiation and definition of the IEP, including those relating to hours of work involved in covering the support role, are the responsibility of administrative authorities. Once approved, the IEP establishes a fundamental right for the student and a duty for the school which if not carried out (often "justified" by financial or staffing problems) constitutes a violation of the school administration's duty towards the child and the family, and represents indirect discrimination based on disability. All related issues therefore fall under the competence of an ordinary judge (Civil Cassation, joint sections, judg. 8 May 2019, No. 25101; see also Sicily Regional Administrative Court, Palermo, sec. III, judg. 7 February 2019, No. 343).

Various Regional Administrative Court judgments reiterated that the school administration has the duty to define (via an IEP) the basic number of hours needed by students with disabilities. This must happen on a yearly basis, depending on the practical needs of the child, which could vary greatly according to the student's progress or regressions; if an IEP is not adopted, or it is incomplete, it is impossible to calculate the correct number of hours to assign to support teachers. This could lead to the condemnation of the administration for its failure to produce and apply the IEP (see Aosta Valley Regional Administrative Court, Aosta, sec. I, judg. 14 January 2019, No. 2; Campania Regional Administrative Court, Naples, sec. IV, judg. 2 January 2019, No. 15; sec. VIII, judgments 11 February 2019, No. 737; 5 March 2019, No. 1233; 1 April 2019, No. 1825; sec. IV, judg. 22 October 2019, No. 5005; Molise Regional Administrative Court, Campobasso, sec. I, judg. 5 December 2019, No. 435). The lack of financial resources cannot be a valid reason to not assign support teachers to students with disabilities as determined by their IEP (Campania Regional Administrative Court, Naples, sec. VIII, judg. 5 March 2019, No. 1214; 10 June 2019, No. 3140; Lazio Regional Administrative Court, Rome, sec. III, judg. 4 April 2019, No. 4471). Legal confirmation of the right to a support teacher can only go ahead for the year specified by the related IEP, since this must be rewritten every year (by 30 July) for the following school year. It is therefore not possible to request the confirmation of the right to support in advance – it is only possible to confirm that of the year for which the IEP has been written (Campania Regional Administrative Court, Naples, sec. IV, judgments 21 January 2019, No. 314; 4 November 2019, No. 5211). Compensation for the non-material damage of the failure to assign a support teacher to a student with disabilities is calculated taking into consideration the related damage that may be caused by the lack of assistance that the teacher would have been able to given, and the reduced integration of the child in the classroom environment. Moral suffering must also be added to this as a consequence of the discrimination suffered (Campania Regional Administrative Court, Naples, sec. IV, judg. 2 December 2019, No. 5668).

VII Social Rights

A Right to Health and Access to Medicine

The Council of State (sec. II, judg. 15 July 2019, No. 4967) rejects the complaint presented by the pharmaceutical company Novartis against a series of measures that allowed the use of Avastin as a treatment for some forms of maculopathy that is associated with age despite the fact that the drug had been released into the market as a treatment for tumours. The off-label use of Avastin should be monitored by the health authorities, guaranteeing single dose portions of the drug bottled by hospital pharmacies. This off-label use was also treated as reimbursable by the national health system as an alternative medicine; Lucentis, which is also produced and sold by Novartis and by a subsidiary of Roche, was much more expensive (ten times more expensive). The two pharmaceutical companies were also at the centre of an investigation brought up by AGCOM. Novartis and Roche were fined in 2014 for €180 million given that, while well-aware that both medications could be effective in ophthalmological treatments, they had agreed to not request the release of Avastin on the European and Italian market for use in the treatment of maculopathy, but to only authorise the use of a much more expensive drug (Lucentis) for the same treatment. They also overstated the potential side-effects of using Avastin to maintain the use of the more costly Lucentis, the production and sale of which would benefit both companies. According to Novartis, prescribing– and then charging the national health system – Avastin for off-label use in treatment (but which studies had widely demonstrated to be effective for maculopathy) violated EU law. However, the ECJ contradicted this interpretation with a 2018 judgment. For the Italian judge, it is scientifically proven that the two drugs – Avastin and Lucentis – are interchangeable in the treatment of maculopathy, and the former, if administered in the forms recommended by the Italian Pharmaceutical Authority, has no side-effects for the patient. The Council of State further recognised the legal status of the choice of the Italian authority to charge the national health system with the cost of the off-label use of Avastin to treat age-related maculopathy, as due to the cost of Lucentis, it was no longer a valid alternative to Avastin. To be considered "valid", the judges noted, the alternative drug would not only have to be equivalent from a medical and scientific perspective, but also from an economic perspective. The cost of Lucentis would have led to the failure to treat all patients in need, which would have violated their right to health.

B Workplace Security. Individual Protection Provisions

The Supreme Court (Criminal Cassation, sec. IV, judg. 21 March 2019, No. 27971) ruled on proceedings on the death of an employee at work sent to do essential maintenance work on a railway line. The work was carried out on a double track railway and the worker was run over by a train coming the other way on the second track. The Court decided that the verdict of murder for the manager of the maintenance company was justified. The maintenance team of the subcontracted company had been sent to the point without being told that the railway traffic had not been suspended on both tracks. The hypothetical imprudence of the workers therefore cannot be considered to exclude the criminal liability of the owner of the company.

In cases of workplace accidents, the culpable conduct of the worker removes the employer's responsibility only when the behaviour can be considered grossly negligent and "abnormal". In a case of the Civil Court of Cassation, a person who was dissembling a warehouse of a company employed by a Municipality was killed when the structure collapsed. The person who the employer had placed in charge had suggested suspending the operation, but had not made it clear that this was due to serious safety issues. The judge held that the victim had behaved recklessly, applying article 1227 of the Civil Code (contribution of the creditor's negligent act to damage); however, the Court of Cassation held that the civil responsibility of the death of the worker (pursuant to article 2087 of the Civil Code) is attributable to the employer, who had not adequately informed and trained the person appointed to do the job (Civil Cassation, sec. Labour, judg. 25 November 2019, No. 30679).

A cleaner working in a factory was hit by a mechanical arm that fell of a production chain to package oven products. The employee had begun working while the machines were still in motion. Although working while the machines are still working was prohibited for cleaning staff, her behaviour cannot be considered seriously reckless or unpredictable; the contractor was supposed to turn off the machines and supervise the safety of the worker. Therefore, the responsibility of the employer still stands up to examination pursuant to article 2087 of the Civil Code (Civil Cassation, sec. Labour, judg. 25 February 2019, No. 5419; Trent Court of Appeal, judg. 18 May 2019, No. 58; Rome Court of Appeal, sec. III, judg. 4 September 2019, No. 5349).

The Court of Cassation held that personal protective equipment (PPE) does not just constitute products used specifically to protect a person from specific risks, but also any tool that could be an effective barrier to risks to the individual's health. An employer must therefore provide their employees with both PPE and manage its upkeep and treatment. In the case at hand, the employees of a waste disposal company had requested a reimbursement of the money they had paid (out of their own pocket) over the years to clean their work clothes, that had been provided by the company. According to the Court of Cassation, article 2087 of the Civil Code, closure laws for systems to prevent workplace accidents and illnesses requires the employer to wash the clothes supplied, which is essential for their functionality to protect the health of workers (Civil Cassation, sec. Labour, judg. 16 December 2019, No. 33133; see also sec. VI, judg. 9 October 2019, No. 25401).

Article 2087 of the Civil Code is at the centre of the decision concerning the dismissal of a State Railway driver (Civil Cassation, sec. Labour, judg. 29 March 2019, No. 8911) who had repeatedly refused to operate the vehicle without a second driver present. The Court noted that the duty of the employer (under article 2087) concerns the preparation of all necessary provisions to protect the safety of the worker, both those foreseen by law and those imposed by the best technical and experimental knowledge available. This responsibility is not objective, and the worker has the burden of demonstrating that the measures they are challenging are effectively inferior to established standards. According to the Milan Court of Appeal, article 2087 of the Civil Code, although primarily concerning employees, this applies to all professionals working in a company; the local health organisation is therefore responsible for an incident that occurred concerning a dentist working (with a private contract) in a company's medical clinic. The dentist had fractured her thumb due to a chair malfunctioning – the one which she was using while examining a patient (Milan Court of Appeal, sec. Labour, judg. 3 October 2019, No. 1219). The Court of Cassation also held that it is necessary to assess the responsibility of a regional body managing university accommodation for the killing of a security guard who had been robbed during his work shift. Since the institution should have known that it was customary to keep large sums of money relating to the students' accommodation for a certain time in the security guards' office, the accommodation managers should have installed adequate anti-theft devices (Civil Cassation, sec. Labour, judg. 18 November 2019, No. 29879).

C Consumers' Rights. Misleading Advertising

The Council of State (judg. Sec. IV, 15 July 2019, No. 4976) discussed reports from the AGCOM concerning misleading messages on the Tripadvisor website. According to the AGCOM, some of the reviews of tour services offered on the platform, even though they were false, written by people who had never used the services, they had still been highlighted on the site, for their efficient nature (both positive and negative). More generally, TripAdvisor's control system to avoid false reviews has shown itself to be inept at completely blocking them from getting posted. This created the conditions to distort the competition and mislead consumers, which goes against the company's assurance that its consumer guidance system is trustworthy and transparent. The €500,000 fine imposed by AGCPM in 2014 was contested by the two companies that manage the online portal – TripAdvisor and TripAdvisor Italy – at the Rome Regional Administrative Court which received the complaint and annulled the fine. However, the Council of State confirmed the misleading nature of a series of statements within the online portal concerning the trustworthiness and objectivity of the information (phrases such as "TripAdvisor offers trustworthy travel advice, published by real travellers") and therefore found contrary to articles 20, 21 and 22, of the Consumer Code (lgs.d. 206/2005). The Council of State reduced the fine to €100,000, considering that in the portal there are more than just the above-mentioned statement – there are also disclaimers that warn consumers that the monitoring system that checks individual reviews has limitations.

The Lazio Regional Administrative Court examined the case of a publicity campaign for the sports club Calcio Napoli and of the Deutsche Bank, which was launched to advertise season tickets for the football season 2011–2012. The season ticket came with advertising for a series of financial products, including the possible financing to purchase the subscription itself. In 2012, AGCOM deemed the advertisement deceptive, fining the football club €100,000 and the bank €200,000. The financing for the season ticket, in various ways, was publicised as *"zero-interest rate"* ("*2° tasso zero*"); while in reality there were no essential information gaps (in particular the Annual Effective Global Rate – APR) – except in the form of the difficult-to-read fine print – from which the consumer could have inferred the existence of undeclared costs. The Regional Administrative Court held that, although more detailed information was available in the documents accompanying the contract for the financial support, under the laws on deceptive advertising, the most important part is the "hook" which the consumer first hears. This is all the more important in the field of consumer finance, where the knowledge gap between the service provider and the average consumer is notoriously large. Since the laws on deceptive advertising apply regardless of the economic damage caused to the consumer, it is not necessary to decide if the economic damage for season ticket holders was insignificant. Therefore, the sentence was confirmed, as was the fine to be paid (Lazio Regional Administrative Court, Rome, judg. 1 August 2019, No. 10193).

D Right to Strike

The Constitutional Court ruled out that the circumstance dictated by the current legislation (in particular law 146/1990 on regulating the right to strike) which prohibits the practice of lawyers' associations to call multiple abstentions from hearings constitutes a violation of constitutional principles (articles 3, 24, 11 of the Constitution, also referring to article 6 ECHR). The lawyers had all united in their reason to protest without, however, prior notification of the overall duration of the abstention. The Constitutional Court ascertained that to avoid disproportionate damage to citizens and violation of their right to access justice, laws and self-regulation norms already existed to limit the effects of actions to "block hearings" which would potentially harm the rights of citizens (judg. 14/2019 of 31 January 2019).

Even if they are not expressly mentioned in the list (which is not exhaustive) of the activities for which law 146/1990 foresees restrictions on the right to strike, airport security services are among those essential public services as they carry out a direct role in protecting the right to life and personal safety of an individual. Therefore, the right to strike of workers in these services can be exercised under limitations defined by the laws on essential public services (Civil Cassation, sec. Labour, judg. 2 October 2019, No. 24633). Regarding "picketing" actions (protest measures adopted by striking workers to block their colleagues (not adhering to the strike) from entering a workplace), the Council of State excluded that this activity in itself be considered banned or dangerous; it is part of the right to strike and can happen legally, as long as there is no violent or threatening behaviour that may impinge upon the freedom of the workers or jeopardise public security (Council of State, sec. III, judg. 6 November 2019, No. 7575).

E Social Security Withholdings and Wages

The economic and financial crisis of 2008 left many companies facing cash shortages, with little possibility of getting loans from banks. Some business owners had to face a double obligation which was difficult to manage – that of paying taxes and pension contributions for workers, and also of ensuring their employees' regular wages. One business owner from Brescia decided to prioritise her obligations to her workers, omitting the pension contributions (paid to the INPS and therefore indirectly to the worker) in order to keep up the monthly wages. The Supreme Court (Criminal Cassation, sec. III, judg. 15 May 2019, No. 36421) refutes the assumption of the business that the obligation to pay employees' wages justified (under article 51 of the Criminal Code: the fulfilment of a duty imposed by a legal excludes punishment) the omission of pension payments for those same workers. According to the Court, the two obligations cannot be compared, since they both deal with the rights of employees; in addition, only the obligation to pay pension contributions is supported in criminal law, which sanctions the crime with a prison sentence of up to three years if the missing contribution goes over €10,000 a year (article 2, l.d. 463/1983).

VIII Immigration, Citizenship

A Memorandum between Italy and Libya of 2017: Its Nature as an International Treaty

In 2018, the Constitutional Court declared the question of constitutionality inadmissible due to conflicting attributions brought up by some Members of Parliament related to the Italy-Libya Memorandum of Understanding 2017. The Memorandum was adopted through a simple bill of the Prime Minister and not with a parliamentary bill. The motivations given for the rejection were based on the fact that only Parliament (and not individual MPs) can bring up this type of issue (see *Yearbook 2019*, p. 219). In 2019, the Council of State (Judg. Sec. III, 2 September 2019, No. 6028) rejected the issue of civil access, pursuant to Chapter V of law 241/1990 on administrative procedures and the right to access, and bills concerning the implementation of the Italy-Libya Memorandum, put forward by a private citizen and by the Italian Coalition for Civil Liberties and Rights (CILD). According to the Council of State (which confirms a similar decision of the Rome Regional Administrative Court), the law on civil access (lgs.d. 33/2013) ruled out that this could be admitted on the grounds of military defence and issues, as well as international relations (article 5-*bis*), all of which are clearly referenced within the Memorandum. Access to the documents concerning meetings of the mixed Italian-Libyan committee and concerning data on combatting illegal immigration, human trafficking and so on, including the financial aspects of this activity was legally denied, firstly as it consists of purely technical acts, and secondly as there is justified confidentiality measures, due to its connection to combatting criminal organisations. Moreover, it would not be possible for the administrative judge to enter into the scope of executive bodies in order to verify the existence of other unspecified documents illegally kept secret. Council of State noted that the internal structures of the administration and Italian Anticorruption Authority (ANAC) supervise these aspects, with the possibility of more incisive action than that regulated by civil access.

B Iure Sanguinis *Access to Italian Citizenship of Descendants of Subjects of the Austro-Hungarian Empire*

A Brazilian citizen, descended from emigrants from Trentino, immigrated to Italy in 2005. He requested Italian citizenship on the basis of law 14 December 2000, No. 379 (Provisions for recognising Italian citizenship for persons born or already residing in territories that constituted the Austro-Hungarian empire and their descendants). Between 2005 and 2008, he was also able to work, given that he had a residence permit awaiting citizenship. However, in 2008, the Autonomous Province of Trent sent out a notice, based in turn on an act emitted by the Ministry of the Interior, declaring that a residence permit awaiting citizenship did not allow the holder to work on Italian territory. Having obtained Italian citizenship in 2012, the individual requested without success for the authorities to annul the measure that had blocked him from working from 2008 to 2012, as well as compensation for the damages suffered. The administrative judge on this issue brought up the question of constitutionality of law 2000 (and the correlated article 6 of the Consolidated Act on Immigration) in the part where it did not foresee that a Residence permit pending the acquisition of nationality issued to descendants of the Austro-Hungarian Empire who emigrated before 16 July 1920 allowed the person to work. This regime brought about a difference in treatment for immigrants awaiting citizenship (in Italy with different statuses), and, due to this different status, they were able to carry out work-related activities. The Constitutional Court (judg. 149/2019 of 19 June 2019) starts by considering the peculiar nature of law 379/2000, which attributed citizenship purely on the basis of *ius sanguinis*, with no minimum residency period in Italy, to anyone who had the correct documentation and carried out a declaration by 2005 either in Italy or via an Italian consulate abroad. The commission was established to examine all questions which should have been resolved by 2010, but were still open in 2019. Therefore, there are numerous similar situations to the one which brought about the case in question. Residence permits issued awaiting citizenship were issued to individuals whose status was still being assessed with the aim of granting citizenship, on the basis of law 379/2000, on the assumption that the process would have been completed promptly; and since citizenship could be conceded without the individual necessarily being in Italy, the possibility to work in Italy for the holder of this permit was not even regulated. In conclusion, the question of constitutionality was ruled inadmissible given that it is the duty of the judge to provide a constitutionally orientated interpretation of the law on immigration to put a person in the necessary conditions to get a residence permit, allowing them to exercise their constitutional rights to work to overcome the critical recurring problem of delays in the assessment of criteria for granting citizenship.

C Access to Citizenship

Granting Italian citizenship is one of the measures which the Italian Authorities enjoy the widest discretion. This means that the final decision can only be challenged when it is based on insufficient investigation, on non-existent facts, or on an illogical, inconsistent or nonsensical reasonable. The objective requirements assessed by the authorities include whether the person earns an income that is higher than the social minimum (set at around €8,600 a year for a single person and €11,000 a year for a couple, plus €500 for every dependent child). This economic criterion prevails even when the foreign national has completely integrated in Italian society, and therefore the requirement must also refer to the family unit as a whole. Therefore, the Regional Administrative Court annulled the decree due to its illegitimacy – the decree which withheld the granting of Italian citizenship to an individual who, while not earning the minimum personal wage themselves, the requirement was met when considering both the person and their spouse's social allowance as a single unit (Lazio Regional Administrative Court, Rome, sec. I, judg. 6 September 2019, No. 10791).

The information and conclusions used to justify denying the granting of citizenship are confidential. Under the law, the individual has no right to know the information in detail, as it is sufficient that the decree refers to "reasons relating to the security of the Republic" (Lazio Regional Administrative Court, Rome, sec. I, judgments 3 April 2019, No. 4391; 4 September 2019, No. 10728).

One of the conditions for granting citizenship is residency in the State for at least ten years. Demonstrating residency can only occur through providing municipal registration data. Any other evidence is inadmissible and no administrative delays or other obstacles can be used to justify anomalies in this regard (Friuli-Venezia Giulia Regional Administrative Court, Trieste, sec. I, judg. 30 April 2019, No. 186). Refusing to undergo a standard road check to verify the physical and mental conditions of the driver could lead to the rejection of an application for citizenship, even if the individual has been legally residing in Italy for over ten years and is well integrated in society (see, for example, Lazio Regional Administrative Court, Rome, sec. I, judg. 4 January 2019, No. 110).

D Statelessness

The Court of Cassation heard the complaints of an individual from the former-Yugoslavia, who had arrived in Italy before its break up. In 2016, he was the recipient of two expulsion orders, due to his lack of a valid Italian residence permit. The applicant's situation can be considered as stateless. However, it does not reveal that the applicant has never initiated the procedure to recognise his state of statelessness. According to the 1954 New York Convention on the Status of Stateless Persons which Italy ratified in 1962, the term "stateless person" means a person who is not considered as a national by any State under the operation of its law. The formal recognition of this status does not have constitutive value but simply recognises the stateless status of the person, which can exist as a "de facto" situation. In fact, none of the States of the former Yugoslavia recognises the applicant as a citizen – in particular not Bosnia-Herzegovina, the territory where the person lived before moving to Italy. The New York Convention sets out a general prohibition on the expulsion of stateless persons by the State in which the person has been admitted (apart from cases of a threat to national security). This law must be extended to also cover *de facto* stateless persons (Civil Cassation, sec. I, judg. 19 June 2019, No. 16489).

E Social Rights of Immigrated Citizens

The Constitutional Court, with judgment 50/2019, ruled on some cases brought up in passing during proceedings proposed by non-EU citizens, who had residence permits for family reasons and who had been refused social allowance benefits by INPS due to their lack of a "residence permit" (now "EU Long Term Residence Permit"). Social benefits are available to any person residing legally in Italy for 10 years or more, who are over 65 years in age and have an income under a certain threshold: the limitation in access to this benefit that the person must hold a long stay residence permit was introduced in the Budget Law of 2001. According to the remitting judges, this law constitutes a discrimination founded on nationality, as it introduces a distinction in access to social benefits based exclusively on nationality, contrary to articles 3, 38 (right to social assistance) and 10.2 of the Constitution (the latter jointly with article 14 ECHR: banning discrimination based on nationality). The Constitutional Court recognises that, in respect of the social benefits which satisfy a primary need of an individual, article 2 of the Constitution on the guarantee of inviolable rights – more so than article 38 of the Constitution – excludes all forms of discrimination based on the recipient's nationality or length of residency in Italy. The social benefits for over-65-year-olds, however, is not an essential social benefit, since it exceeds the satisfaction of a person's primary needs and is subject to changes by the Government in terms of the individual's long-term proven link with the territory (as seen in the case of non-EU citizens, who hold a long-term residence permit). The criteria identified by the law does not seem nor unreasonable nor arbitrary. The criteria are linked to the nature of solidarity of social allowances, paid for by an individual's prolonged stay in the State as a worker (or for another legal reason). The judgment reiterates the decisions previously taken by the Constitutional Court in judgment 222/2013 (see *Yearbook 2014*, p. 270). The question of constitutionality is therefore rejected.

In 2019, some judgments found discriminatory behaviour in INPS procedures to deny foreign citizens the birth allowance, which is a means tested benefit for low income family households on the birth of a child (law 190/2014) (see *Yearbook 2019*, p. 313). The Turin District Court (ord. 28 May 2019) held that the ban on recognising the "baby bonus", under article 74 of lgs.d. 26 March 2001, No. 151 (opposed by the Municipality of Turin and by INPS) was discriminatory in nature. This ruling went in favour of two Egyptian women, holders of a single residence and work permit, who had had children in 2018. The reason for the ban was that the law required that the individual held a long-stay residence permit (which the women did not have). The Court held that the principle of equal treatment of all workers, as set out in Directive 2011/98 on the single residence permit for non-EU citizens, should apply. Equating national and EU workers with non-EU citizens therefore does not consent different treatment of holders of a residence and work permit and a long-stay residence permit. (The principle was also implicitly reiterated in Constitutional Court, ord. 52/2019). The conduct of INPS was deemed discriminatory by Brescia Court of Appeal with judgments 26 February 2019, Nos. 89 and 90.

According to the Milan District Court (sec. Labour, judg. 27 March 2019), the decision of the Municipality di Vigevano (obliging non-EU resident citizens to request a series of certifications and documents from their country of origin in order to access certain social benefits) was discriminatory and illegitimate. Although general laws on self-certification already give wide scope to limit foreign nationals to self-certify in many situations, provisions on ISEE (Equivalent Economic Situation Indicator) are more specific to even out the situation for Italian residents than they are for non-EU resident citizens. Therefore, these are the rules that the Municipality should have followed.

IX Freedom of the Press – Right to Report and Criticise. Right to Private and Family Life

A Freedom of the Press and the Crime of Defamation

The Court of Cassation decided to annul without delay a judgment of defamation. The judgment refers to the circumstances of a case brought up in the context of a 2011 "gossip" TV show that spoke about people from a reality show, one of whom (a so-called *"tronista"*) had been accused of demanding a fee to participate in charity events. The Supreme Court decided that the right to a reputation of the person in question must yield to the right to freedom of the press, as exercised by the presenters of the TV show. The right to criticise should be distinct from the right to freedom of the press, as it is not linked to specific facts, with no need to prove the truthfulness of the allegations. They are characterised more as a personal evaluation of facts or characteristics of a person. Furthermore, the Court admitted that the personal behaviour of the individual is of public interest, on which one can exercise the right to freedom of the press – it recognises that "gossip" TV shows enjoy a lot of popularity based on the characters and people they talk about, attracting a wide range of people. As for the "self-restraint" of the expressions used to criticise the individual, this too must be assessed in reference to the characteristics of the programme itself, in which colourful and scathing expressions are standard language and these are acceptable as long as there are in theme and pertinent. In this case, the "tronista" was well-aware of the type of discussion that would have arisen, and had chosen to take part in the programme voluntarily and consciously (Criminal Cassation, sec. V, judg. 20 March 2019, No. 32829).

On the distinction between right to criticise and the right to freedom of the press, see also Criminal Cassation, sec. V, judg. 24 January 2019, No. 7340, in which (referring to ECtHR case-law) the Court defines right to freedom of the press as relating strictly to the facts of a matter, while critical opinion consists of conjecture and speculation.

The right to freedom of the press does not extend to considering a statement in an online journalistic publication as libellous if the author has listed their sources (and adequately verified them). The news or comment must also be considered of public interest and using standardised language. It is not, however, sufficient to verify the information used in an article on Wikipedia. The journalist had erroneously accused someone in an article of taking part in the 1980 Bologna massacre on the basis of some general references found on Wikipedia. The Court found that article constituted libel (Criminal Cassation, sec. V, judg. 15 April 2019, No. 38896). In another case the Supreme Court, ruled on a complaint in which the two daughters of a partisan accused a historian of defamation who, in an essay, had (tentatively) conferred their parent with an active role in planning the Rovetta Massacre (Brescia). The Rovetta massacre is the name given to the summary execution of 43 Italian soldiers (from the Republic of Salò) captured by a group of partisans in the days after 25 April 1945. According to the judges, if the historical data were collected correctly with no intention of offending the memory of the individuals involved, and even if thc bibliographical references and conclusions about these individuals are incomplete or unambiguous, this constitutes an exercise of the right to historical criticism, and in no way can this be translated into defamation. Countering or refuting the conclusions of the scholar must be conducted with academic tools, and not with those of criminal law (Criminal Cassation, sec. V, judg. 9 September 2019, No. 42755).

An activist published a phrase on a blog which had falsely attributed to the leader of the political party Northern League (*Lega Nord*) Matteo Salvini, in which he accused Southern Italians of not participating in the Resistance against Nazi-fascism due to their cowardice. According to the judges and the Court of Cassation, inserting the fake citation among other real statements made by the politician constitutes libel. It cannot be considered satirical, since the article was not written in ironic tones and the mix of real statements and fake citations overall rendered the article misleading (Criminal Cassation, sec. V, judg. 10 May 2019, No. 34129).

A decision of the Rovigo District Court (judg. 12 June 2019, No. 331) confoirms that, if investigations cannot identify the IP number from which defamatory posts were sent on the Facebook profile of an accused person, this individual cannot be charged with the crime of defamation. This is due to the fact that, no matter the contents of a comment published, it is impossible to rule out that a different person did not use the profile of the accused persons to publish the offensive text on their behalf.

B Defamation and Discrimination

The Milan District Court ruled on a complaint of discrimination, pursuant to article 43 of the lgs.d. 286/1998 (Consolidated Act on Immigration). The complaint was made against the daily newspaper "*Libero*" by a cooperative which (among other things) work within the migrant reception sector. In 2017, the newspaper published an anonymous article entitled "Sinister speculation. The list of leeches getting rich off trafficking black people. In 2016, millionaire turnover for Coop and Catholic associations" ("*Turpe speculazione. Elenco dei papponi che si arricchiscono con la tratta dei neri. In 2016, fatturati milionari per Coop ed associazioni cattoliche*"). The cooperative in question was named on the list in the article's title. Articles 43 and 44 of the Consolidated Act on Immigration (integrated by lgs.d. 215/2003 and by l.d. 59/2008 transposing European Directive 2000/43) foresee that individuals and bodies are able to propose civil cases against discrimination based on race, ethnicity, nationality or religious belief. The aim is to stop and sanction acts that directly or indirectly contribute to discrimination, including discriminatory harassment. According to the cooperative, the article denigrated, with discriminatory effect, its foreign national users and its work in general. The piece should have therefore been censured, according to laws against racial or ethnical discrimination. The Court noted that the antidiscrimination law censures the behaviour of individuals whose actions may directly or indirectly harm the applicant considering the power relationship between the two: employer, service manager or administrative authorities. In this case, however, the harassment comes a journalistic exercise. Therefore, it is more appropriate to report the dispute within the context of liability for defamation (as indeed requested by the applicant in the alternative application to investigate the discriminatory act). The Court noted that the way in which the information on public funds of the cooperatives working with immigrants and asylum seekers was reported by the paper exceeded the limits of the right to report and constituted defamation. The Court therefore condemned the editor of "Libero" to pay €25,000 in compensation for reputational damage (at the time, Vittorio Feltri was the editorial director of the newspaper, and was originally indicated to be the author of the discriminatory piece. Since then, he has been removed as editorial director since his position was not comparable to that of a "responsible director". It has not been proven that he was the author of the article in question). (Milan District Court, sec. I, ord. 13 June 2019, No. 60124).

On discriminatory conduct, see, in this Part, Human Rights in Italian Case-law, V.

C Right to be Forgotten

The Court of Cassation, overturning the judgment of the Court of Appeal, postponed the judgment of a case brought by two victims of a crime, who had given testimony in a trial filmed for a show by RAI, since in the transmission the witnesses' faces were only partially distorted, and their voices were completely recognisable. This constitutes a violation of their right to privacy, given the nature of the personal information which was broadcast, which disproportionately placed their privacy second to the right to report. Instead of taking for granted that the witnesses could have been recognised, and justifying the balance between privacy and right to report made by the company by the limited number of people who would have recognised them, the court should have concentrated on the suitability of the technical measures taken by RAI to avoid the possibility of a person recognising the witnesses, both in this case and future cases (Civil Cassation, sec. III, judg. 4 April 2019, No. 9340).

25 years after the events of the case, a daily newspaper from Sardinia reprinted the details of the murder of the applicant's wife, who, at the time, had been sentenced to a 12 years prison sentence, fully served. The publication of the article brought back the applicant's feelings of anguish and fear, compromising his health and his public image. The appeal for damages brought against the newspaper was rejected in the first and second instance. The Court of Cassation examined the case with an interlocutory order and a Joint Sections judgment. These deeply analysed the law and case-law at a national and European level on the conflict between the right to report and the right to private life, particularly from the prospective of the right to be forgotten, recalling legislation on privacy. Regarding this specific case, however, the joint sections observed that the right to report should also refer to the right to report historical events, since the criticised article was not reporting on current events, but recalled news from over a quarter-century before. Linked to this alternative perspective is that the need to report every detail of the painful event (including the name and surname of the perpetrator) does not seem as convincing. On the right to report events of the part, therefore, the Court of Cassation stated that the

right to privacy for the people of that event prevails, unless it is of renewed public interest to know those historical events, that is if those mentioned in the event have done something or cover a role that makes them noteworthy. In the case at hand, there was no specific reason to justify particular public interest in the details of the event and the persons involved did not have a public profile to justify repressing their right to privacy. The complaint was therefore accepted and the judgment was annulled (Civil Cassation, joint sections, judg. 22 July 2019, No. 19681).

D Illegal Use of Personal Data

The new law on privacy (lgs.d. 101/2018) did not substantially amend the law on illegal use of personal data (article 167). Consequently, the mass sending of emails (advertisements) continues to be irrelevant from a criminal law perspective. It is only a crime when a person sends those emails with the intention of causing harm to the receiver. It is difficult for an individual recipient of an e-mail advertising campaign to demonstrate that deleting one or more unwanted e-mails causes significant harm – regardless of the fact that sometimes the person receiving spam emails has not requested to have their email address deleted from the sender's mailing list, as is their right (Criminal Cassation, sec. III, judg. 20 June 2019, No. 41604).

The crime of illegal use of personal data occurred instead in the case of a man who, for a "prank", briefly postet photo-montages of 17 Facebook profile pictures of women he knew on a porn website (without their consent). The women withdrew the libel suit after the perpetrator had voluntarily offered them the payment of compensation. However, the relevant article of the Privacy Code can be applied autonomously (Criminal Cassation, sec. III, judg. 19 June 2019, No. 43534).

X Women's Rights

A Femicide

Other than the issue of femicide (according to the Eures databanks on murder in Italy, of the 130 women killed in the country in 2018, 108 were killed by a family member, partner or ex-partner), the Supreme Court also dealt with a number of cases on the issue of abuse within the family (article 572 of the Criminal Code). In a case of a brutal murder of a woman committed by her boyfriend who, for years, had been reported for abusive behaviour, the Court of Cassation clarified that the accusation of murder should not be confused with that of abuse within the family, aggravated by the victim's death. The case showed how the extreme violence with which the woman had been assaulted was a clear expression of the desire to kill her and therefore justified the sentence for wilful murder, and not for aggravated mistreatment (Criminal Cassation, sec. I, judg. 11 July 2019, No. 12292). The Supreme Court rejected a case in which a man found guilty of femicide pleaded that the aggravating factor of premeditation should be ruled out given that, while he had undoubtedly prepared himself by illegally purchasing a gun and other behaviour to this end, the killing of his ex-girlfriend had happened during the day and without hiding from various surveillance cameras in the phases before the death. His determination to act must have therefore been formed hastily, and the murder should be defined as an impulse killing. Instead, the Court found that the interpretation of the charges as premeditated murder is not contradictory, as it is indisputably true that perpetrator had already been reported to the authorities (although not yet prosecuted, subject to a precautionary restraining order, which had obviously not been respected) for the crime of stalking against the same woman (Criminal Cassation, sec. I, judg. 27 May 2019, No. 1396). Finally, the Court of Cassation confirmed the order of the territorial judge establishing pre-trial detention in prison for perpetrators of violence against an ex-girlfriend. The way this violence took place (hits to the head with a hammer) supports the theory of attempted murder rather than (as offered by the accused party) of personal injury; nor is it adequate to grant house arrest with an ankle (electronic) tag because the woman fortunately recovered from the violence. Considering the high risk of reoffending, in light of the perpetrator's profile, suggests that the decision of the judge who ordered the man's detention to be correct (Criminal Cassation, sec. I, judg. 13 March 2019, No. 38865).

B Abuse within the Family; Sexual Violence

Regarding abuse within the family, one case concerned the systemic harassment of a widowed women who had been married to a Mafia associate. The woman had been segregated at home by members of her husband's family through threats of severing ties with her daughters, among other things. The Court decided that this type of behaviour cannot be excused through references to a deeply patriarchal culture within the family in question. The law does not foresee any kind of "cultural" justification as an exception for this behaviour (Criminal Cassation, sec. V, judg. 25 March 2019, No. 21133). The Supreme Court also integrated the crime of maltreatment towards the wife with the behaviour of husband who imposes the presence of a lover or girlfriend into the family home or a connected apartment, even in the absence of explicit violent and threatening behaviour (Criminal Cassation, sec. VI, judg. 50 May 2019, No. 35677).

The Turin judge for the preliminary investigations ruled against the accusation of abuse within the family of the daughter of a couple who had witnessed violence against her mother by her father (who was suffering from a mental illness) during a difficult and conflictual separation, as the Court ruled out that the man conscientiously and wilfully wanted to inflect any suffering on the child. Alongside law 69/19 (so-called code red for crimes against women and children), article 572 of the Criminal Code on abuse within the family establishes that the minor is always to be considered harmed when abuse takes place in their presence, and therefore this is regardless of any will or awareness of the perpetrator. The facts of the case at hand, however, occurred before this law had come into force, and therefore it cannot be applied. Excluding that the father intentionally inflicted suffering on the child may be inferred by the child herself, who always spontaneously supported her father and had never "perceived" the behaviour effecting her mother as directed at her (Turin District Court, judg. 28 October 2019, No. 1715).

> Regarding sexual violence (article 609-*bis* of the Criminal Code), the Court of Cassation reiterated that the procedures have been set up to deal with cases where the victims are adults, but the perpetrator of the crime is their parent or guardian. This clarification confirmed the consolidated case-law, but was still necessary in light of the unclear nature of article 609-*septies*, para. 4, No. 2. The Court noted that, since the basis of admissibility is the condition that the victim may be at risk from the perpetrator if the individual decides to report the violence, there is no reason to reserve this protection exclusively for minors, as this situation may exist into adulthood (Criminal Cassation, sec. III, judg. 7 February 2019, No. 14021).
>
> The Supreme Court nullified an appeal judgement which had reformed the sentence given at first instance to two individuals who had been found guilty of sexual violence against a twenty-two-year-old. The Court of Appeal had reconstructed the information ascertained by the first instance Court, twisting the information to an alternative perspective, claiming that the young woman had asked the two to join for a night out, then invented the violence to justify

the situation to her mother. Among the elements supporting this "alternative" reconstruction of the facts was, among other things, the girl's not particularly attractive appearance. The Court firstly recalls that on the basis of the principle that a sentence is given in criminal proceedings when the accused is found guilty beyond any reasonable doubt, and therefore that it is admitted that the appeals judge can reform the first instance sentence on the basis of criticising the arguments underlying the sentence. The Supreme Court then reiterated the growing importance even within trials of ongoing legislation on the role of the victim of a crime, and confirms that, to overturn statements made by a victim a more solid argument framework than one that calls into question the physical appearance of the victim, especially regarding this type of crime. The acquittal was therefore reversed and the case has been sent back to another appeal judge (Criminal Cassation, sec. III, judg. 5 March 2019, No. 15683).

According to the Court of Cassation, the crime of sexual violence (and not the lesser crime of harassment) has been integrated with the act of inducing the victim – an under-14-year-old girl – via incessant and continuous online – to take place in virtual sexual relations. It was shown that this behaviour is not only highly distressing for the victim, but greatly restricts their sexual freedom, consistent with the crime of sexual violence (Criminal Cassation, sec. III, judg. 5 July 2019, No. 41951).

XI Children's Rights

A Community Service in Juvenile Justice

The Court of Cassation doubted the constitutional legitimacy of the community service regime within juvenile justice proceedings. In the event of the failure of the regime of community service and therefore the renewed obligation for the Juvenile Court to proceed with a sentence for the minor, the law does not foresee that the time served in community service can be detracted from the overall time given in the sentence. This situation is only applied to minors and not to adult perpetrators of crime. This results in the imposition of inevitably disproportionate penalties, since the time spent doing community service is added to the requirement of the sentence, in violation of articles 3, 27 and 31 of the Constitution. According to the Constitutional Court (judg. 68/2019 of 29 March 2019), unlike volunteer working in social or community services for adult inmates, the institution of community service in cases regarding minors (articles 28 and 29 of the Decree of the President of the Republic 448/1988 (Provisions on criminal trials regarding juvenile offenders)) does not aim to punish, but to re-educate the minor. It therefore cannot be considered equal to a criminal punishment. On the contrary, it could lessen the re-education of the minor, as the individual may consider the assignment of community service as a training or education tool as a lighter way of serving their punishment.

B Special House Arrest – Community Service in Juvenile Justice

The Constitutional Court acknowledged the constitutional illegitimacy of the legal mechanism (focussed on article 58-*quater*, para. 1, 2 and 3 of law 354/1975 on Prison Administration Code) which allows special house arrest as an alternative to prison, allowing mothers (or in some cases, fathers) with children under ten years old to serve part of their sentence with their children within their home. In the event that the detainee has undergone the revocation of another alternative measure, the authorities must wait another three years before granting this measure. In fact, the law suggests that the prisoner be burdens with the consequences of their previous failure to comply with the requirements of a benefit. Special house arrest, should be viewed as a way to prioritise the protection of the rights of the child, implementing article 31 of the Constitution (child protection) and of the CRC (see also *Yearbook 2015*, pp. 215–216). The law imposing this rigidity is therefore declared unconstitutional (Constitutional Court, judg. 18 July 2019, No. 187).

C Crime of Child Pornography

The crime of distributing child pornographic material (article 600-*ter*, para. 3 of the Criminal Code) includes the sending of child pornographic content via WhatsApp to a solitary person, even if the original photo was taken by the victim themselves (selfie). The Court of Cassation deals with the case of a university student who, using a female friend's phone to take a group photo, came upon some intimate selfies of the girl in the phone's memory and saved them for himself. By successively sending the photos to a third party, the distribution of the images became uncontrollable. Article 600-*ter* does not explicitly mention the possibility of material being produced by the victim themselves, but it undoubtedly constitutes a method of committing the crime that is fully compatible with the letter of the provision and consistent with the purposes of the law. The Court of

Cassation therefore confirmed the sentence and excluded that there can be retroactive application of the incriminating interpretation of the law when it was not foreseeable in the moment of the event (Criminal Cassation, sec. III, judg. 21 November 2019, No. 5522).

The crime referred to in article 600-*ter*, para. 1, No. 1 (use of minors for the creation of pornographic shows or for the production of pornographic material) also includes inducing the minors to produce this material themselves by giving them the idea. The law aims at punishing anyone who uses the minor in order to obtain child pornographic material, even if the material was created by the minor themselves (Criminal Cassation, sec. III, judg. 18 April 2019, No. 26862).

D State of Abandonment and Adoption

In various decisions of both the Court of Cassation and the territorial district courts, the courts reiterated the principle the state of abandonment and removal of children from their parents must only be put into practice in extreme situations and after all measures to keep the family united have been exhausted. These principles are founded on the CRC and on the ECtHR case-law as well as article 1 of law 184/1983.

The Court must issue a prospective judgment on the possibility of recovering parenting skills and competences, which should also take any possible support for parents into account, that may come from family and with the assistance of local social services (Civil Cassation, sec. I, judg. 11 December 2019, No. 32412; the positive influence of an extended family is also highlighted in Civil Cassation, sec. I, judg. 4 November 2019, No. 28257). Expressing the wish to take care of the child is not enough to prevent the court from opening a state of abandonment, if the actual situation of the family would lead to the prevention of the harmonious development of the child (Civil Cassation, sec. I, judgments 11 December 2019, No. 32410, 17 July 2019, No. 19154). The presence of fourth-degree relative (grandparents) who are willing to take care of the minor could justify blocking the declaration of a state of abandonment; the suitability of these relatives must be assessed case by case (Civil Cassation, sec. I, judg. 4 December 2019, No. 31672). Even if the relative have adequate material conditions, the lack of the parents' moral assistance that is necessary for a child's development (deprived of the so-called "right to love") may justify declaring a state of abandonment and therefore opening adoption procedures (Caltanissetta Juvenile Court, judg. 15 November 2019). Similarly, the progress made by alcoholic parents does not necessarily lead to the disappearance of the situation that had originally led to the child being put up for adoption, unless they are able to permanently recover from their alcohol dependency (Civil Cassation, sec. I, judg. 6 November 2019, No. 28522). Only long-term situations, and not short-term dysfunctions deriving from *force majeure*, can justify putting a child up for adoption. These long-term situations are linked with the parents' persistent inability to provide the child with the minimum physical and emotional care necessary for their development. These situations may occur in the presence of mental illness (Civil Cassation, sec. I, judg. 31 October 2019, No. 28207), or the parents' conditions of disability when State services are unable to adequately provide assistance (Civil Cassation, sec. I, judg. 11 June 2019, No. 15730). In all cases, the inability to perform parental functions must be ascertained, not the mental state, illness or disability of the parent (Milan Court of Appeal, judg. 14 January 2019, No. 5). The recovery of the father's suitability to play the role of parent of a minor given in pre-adoptive foster care to another family justifies revoking the state of abandonment and re-establishing the relationship between the child and the natural parent. The Court of Cassation confirmed the 2018 Court of Appeal judgment, recognising the declaration of a state of abandonment of 2014 of the Juvenile Court without assessing (due to late transmission) a social services report from October 2013, which showed that the father had recovered parental capabilities. Therefore, the state of abandonment had to be annulled. Even if four years had passed in which the child had successfully integrated into their foster family, the Court of Cassation reiterated that the law prioritises the right of a minor to live with their original family over the right to emotional continuity that comes from foster parents (Civil Cassation, sec. I, judg. 3 October 2019, No. 24790).

Children's participation in court proceedings for adoption is guaranteed under Italian law. The minor must be able to be heard in all phases of the proceedings, including during the appeals process (Civil Cassation, sec. I, judg. 23 January 2019, No. 1887). The Court of Cassation revoked an investigation on the status of a child to be put up for adoption during which the child was not given the chance to participate via their representative; the latter may require the nomination of a specialised advocate (lawyer) (Civil Cassation, sec. I, judg. 7 May 2019, No. 12020).

The participation of children in judicial proceedings which concern their own wellbeing is reiterated as necessary in procedures on international child abduction. The repatriation decree, therefore, is unlawful if the child was not given the opportunity to speak, given that the child could oppose repatriation when ordered more than one year from the date of the abduction (Civil Cassation, sec. I, judg. 4 June 2019, No. 15254).

For some time (it is generally reported as preceding a judgment of Bari Juvenile Court of 2008), case-law has held that it can set out a form of so-called "mild adoption", which can be used in cases where the family of origin is not completely unsuitable to support the child, and other individuals (guardians) are able to carry out all parental functions. The legal basis of "mild adoption" is established in article 44 of l. 184/1983 on the rights of minors to a family, concerning "adoption in particular cases". Unlike normal adoption, "mild adoption" does not severe ties with the child's biological family and can be arranged in whatever way is in the best interests of the child. The Civil Court of Cassation (sec. I, judg. 23 October 2019, No. 27206) reiterated its legitimacy, while acknowledging that, in the present case, the territorial court had correctly excluded it, given that it had already recognised the unsuitability of the biological parents to be of any benefit to their children.

The Court of Cassation, with a judgment clarifying the function of a "residual rule" set out in letter d of article 44 of law 184/1983, established that non-legitimising adoption "in particular cases" can be arranged for a child in couples (married or unmarried) or with individuals, and without the sexual orientation of the adopters having any direct or indirect significance. Adoption "in particular cases" is possible when all other forms of pre-adoptive custody would be unfeasible. The only legal requirement is that the adopting person and the adoptee must have an age difference of at least 18 years. The only assessed criterium is that the individual is working in the adopted person's best interest, in particular to ensure emotional and educational continuity. Any eventual opposition of the biological parents – deprived of parental authority – cannot constitute an obstacle to this adoption (Civil Cassation, sec. I, judg. 26 June 2019, No. 17100; see also Genoa Juvenile Court, judg. 3 July 2019).

E Recognition of Children; Shared Custody

The right for a father to recognise an under-14-year-old child born out of wedlock is fundamental, but it also coincides with the best interest of the child and their right to parenthood. The fact that the father's motivations also include avoiding repatriation (as a foreign citizen) does not invalidate this right, unless the mere fact of ascertaining paternity does not involve specific damage to the child's development. The Court of Cassation (Civil Cassation, sec. I, judg. 14 February 2019, No. 4526) confirmed that the father's criminal record for non-violent crimes does not hinder the recognition of paternity. The Grosseto District Court (judg. 15 January 2019, No. 21) instead decided not to proceed with the recognition of the biological children of a foreign national with a criminal record for violent crime, including crimes against the mother of the children, and who had generally shown minimal interest in the children.

The norms on shared custody of children in the event of parental separation, must also be applied when one of the parents lives abroad, according to the Court of Cassation. An exception to this principle may be admitted only if applying this shared parenthood is shown to be detrimental to the mental and physical well-being of the child (Civil Cassation, sec. I, judg. 6 March 2019, No. 6535).

F Right of Parents to Be Informed of Their Child's Progress at School

The Apulia Regional Administrative Court established that not promoting a school student at the end of the year is not unlawful if the parents have not been informed during the previous months on the student's academic progress. The high school in question had uploaded an electronic register available for families online, where all the student's results and attendance figures were displayed. This however did not exempt the school from checking whether the parents could effectively use this communication tool or from creating further means of communication with the family. Without this, the school is guilty of a serious procedural failure which made the judgment to not promote the student to the successive year unlawful. (Apulia Regional Administrative Court, Bari, sec. I, judg. 5 September 2019, No. 1184).

G Listening to Minors and Self-determination in Relationships

Caltanissetta Juvenile Court rejected with its own decree the request of the father of a 16-year-old staying in an institution for minors to not authorise the permanent stay of the girl at her boyfriend's house, despite the positive approval of his family. The judge assessed the maturity of the girl and recalled that as minors, the legal system recognises significant levels of self-determination (ability to carry out work activities, to recognise one's own child, to enter into marriage with a judge's consent, and so on). There is therefore a space of autonomy in the relationship and emotional sphere that the parent and institutions themselves must respect. The father's opposition does not rule out that the girl could spend weekends (without staying overnight) at her boyfriend's family home, recommending the family to ensure a suitable environment and the social services and housing community to monitor this authorisation (Caltanissetta Juvenile Court, decree 13 August 2019).

H Doubts on the Extension of the Crime of Failure to Provide Means of Assistance to Children Born Out of Wedlock

The Constitutional Court (judgment 189/2019 of 18 July 2019) had to intervene on a referral from seven separate Courts to clarify the scope of a legislative simplification operation carried out in 2018, with which a series of criminal provisions were inserted into various laws contained in the Criminal Code. Among these, there were also some criminal safeguards for the obligation to provide child assistance, established by article 570 of the Criminal Code, even in cases of separation or divorce. However, the new article 570-*bis* begins with the words: "The penalties set out in article 570 [concerning the event in which a person does not provide their children with support] is applied to the spouse who attempts to avoid their obligation to pay any maintenance checks…". The reference in the text to "spouse" suggested that the law did not extend to children born out of wedlock, in clear violation of the principles of equality and child protection (articles 3 and 30 of the Constitution). Though a complex interpretation endeavour, anticipated by some judgments of the Court of Cassation, the Constitutional Court found the question of unconstitutionality unfounded, despite the reference to "spouse" in the article in question, instead of parent. However, the Court invited the legislator to clarify this point through rewriting the text of article 570-*bis*, and condemns the fact that a measure intended to simplify legislation by reporting rules in the Criminal Code which are available in other laws has actually created uncertainty with respect to legal situations which, before the "clarifying intervention, had not produced doubts of constitutionality".

I Violence against Children

In various judgments, the Court of Cassation clarified some aspects of the criminal law protecting minors from sexual violence. According to Criminal Cassation, sec. III, judg. 15 January 2019, No. 11509, the aggravating factor of the young age of the victim could be combined with the handicapped defence) article 61.1 of the Criminal Code). In the specific case at hand, a young girl had become the victim of sexual violence in a moment where she was no longer being supervised by her mother, and could not ask for help from any other adult. In the case of sexual violence, although the crime includes abuse of authority as one of the prerequisites, the aggravating factor (established by article 61, No. 9 of the Criminal Code) of committing the crime abusing power as a religious minister can also be applied (Criminal Cassation, sec. III, judg. 24 January 2019, No. 23463).

XII Due Process: The Pinto Act on Unreasonable Length of Proceedings

A Questions of Constitutionality

Law 83/2012 introduced a provision in law 89/2001 (Pinto law, on just compensation in cases of excessive length of judicial proceedings). The new provision establishes that the defendant must file an acceleration request within thirty days of going over the time limit for excessive length of proceedings in order to be entitled to complain of excessive length of criminal proceedings. Likewise, in administrative proceedings, within the administrative proceedings reform and with a law that entered into force in 2011, the party had already been exposed to the burden of filing a withdrawal request to speed up proceedings after the reasonable limit has ended. The measures were introduced to "prevent" a person deliberately chasing an excessive length of legal proceedings (instead of only sanctioning the Government to pay fair compensation after the incident), by placing an obligation on the parties to supervise compliance in terms of reasonableness. The Constitutional Court investigated the question of constitutionality regarding a series of cases in which the request for fair compensation had been rejected due to the failure to present a "preventive" application. The Court held that laws introduced in 2011 and 2012 were contrary to the right to trial within a reasonable time and to effective access to justice to guarantee one's rights enshrined within ECHR (articles 6.1 and 13), and therefore are unconstitutional due to their non-compliance with article 117.1 of the Constitution. The withdrawal application and acceleration application do not speed up the proceedings and serve only to test the how invested the defendant is in the case (Constitutional Court, judgments 34/2019 of 6 March 2019 and 169/2019 of 10 July 2019).

B Application Problems

2019, like every year, saw numerous sentences of the Court of Cassation (and of trial courts) on the application of the "Pinto" Act. Some of the most significant of these cases are detailed in the following paragraphs.

The joint sections of the Civil Cassation (judgments No. 19883 of 23 July 2019 and No. 20404 26 July 2019) ruled on a widespread issue coming from so-called Pinto on Pinto cases, that is the unreasonable length of administrative procedures (which should be concluded within six months and five days) aiming to implement a judgment of fair compensation adopted for the unreasonable length of proceedings prerequisite. In particular, in the event of an enforcement procedure or a compliance order for the failure to implement a judgment confirming the excessive length prerequisite and to award fair compensation, the proceedings go over the reasonable limit once again, it is unclear whether it is possible to apply for a new "Pinto" complaint, whether the second delay is linked to the first, or whether it is possible to complain to the ECtHR only once, invoking article 6.1 ECHR. With two "twinned" judgments, (modelled on the letter of the Supreme Court and ECtHR case-law), the Joint Sections continue along the same lines as the 2014 judgments (see *Yearbook 2015*, p. 288), in which it was established that delays in enforcement or compliance judgments could only be asserted for the purposes of compensation for excessive length before the ECtHR. This issue was also discussed in 2016 (see *Yearbook 2017*, pp. 288–289); on that occasion, the Joint Sections highlighted the compliance with the six-month deadline within which State administration must have implemented the "Pinto" judgment: if compliance with the deadline has been duly requested by the applicant but rejected by the administration, the proceedings can be considered joint; otherwise they must be separated. The enforcement of this is the competence of the European judge. The Court also recalls the ECtHR judgment in *Bozza v. Italia* (see *Yearbook 2018*, pp. 312–313), in which the Court reiterated that excessive length of proceedings must take into account both the length of proceedings themselves and the length of the Pinto proceedings, including all necessary arrangements for the latter. Moreover, the access to possible compensation must not depend on a request being made by the individual for a specific procedure. According to the ECtHR, an individual who had already obtained a judgment against the State should not have to request a separate proceeding to forcefully receive the compensation they are owed. The Italian Government recognised its own non-compliance regarding some cases brought in front of the ECtHR, in which it seemed that no compensation had ever been paid, despite the passing deadline to implement the judgment which recognised the right to fair compensation. Welcoming the insight of the ECtHR, and reviewing its own 2016 decision, the Joint Sections confirmed that the "final decision" (that can be challenged within six months to obtain fair compensation under the "Pinto" Act) can be not only the one which closes a "Pinto" procedure, but also the one which ends the implementation of the duty to pay fair compensation. This cannot affect the availability of measures that an individual applicant must take within a certain period to claim fair compensation. The Court definitely established that: "Pinto on Pinto" complaints can be presented within six months not of the judgment recognising the excessive length of proceeding prerequisite, but also within six months of the final conclusion of the implementation phase (enforcement procedure or a compliance order); the length of the implementation phase (from the foreclosure of goods by the State until the effective payment of compensation) can be used to calculate the excessive length of a procedure; the delay does not include the time between a "Pinto" decision which recognises the unreasonable length of procedures and the start of the enforcement procedure by the individual; an excessive delay by the State outside the scope of the Pinto Act can only be asserted under the ECtHR.

Civil Cassation, sec. VI, ord. 21 January 2019, No. 1527 established that even in administrative cases, suspending the implementation of disputed measures was arranged for the benefit of citizens, and even if the outcome of the case is expected to be unfavourable to the citizen themselves, this suspension does not prevent further extension of the procedure from constituting a violation of the right to a trial within a reasonable time. The excessive length causes a non-pecuniary damage, although presumably this is less than would result from implementing the disputed measures.

The Court of Cassation clarified a point which is not considered by the Pinto Act: in case in which none of the parties appears in the council chamber in front of the Court of Appeal to determine the unreasonable duration of a process. The judges in this case must declare the "no-place" to proceed on the question of compensation; this does not permanently stop the judgment, but it means that the applicant must request its reopening in a second moment (Civil Cassation, sec. III, judg. 29 August 2019, No. 21776).

A worker had tried to accede the procedure (established by the Pinto Act) to receive a settlement regarding an employment dispute, which began in 2002 and had still not concluded by 2011. In 2012, the Court of Appeal held that the delay was greater than the five-year limit and awarded him fair compensation of around €4,000–€800 non-pecuniary damages per year of the delay. In 2017, the worker applied for more compensation, as the dispute was still ongoing. The employment dispute finally concluded with the rejection of the citizen's application. The Court of Appeal once again investigated the issue of excessive length of the procedure, and held that it had exceeded the reasonable limit by ten months, awarding the worker €266 in compensation. With the entry into force of the Budget law for 2016 (l. 208/2015), in 2016, the minimum and maximum amounts that can be awarded per year of delay for excessive length of judicial proceedings were lowered to €400 and €800 euro (in 2012 these were set at €500 and €1500; see law 89/2001, article 2-*bis*). Furthermore, in 2016, the judge was able to reduce that amount under €400 when proceedings involve a high number of people or when the proceedings conclude with a rejection of the applicant's complaint. This different treatment for the two cases (even when referring to the same case) was found to be illegitimate by the applicant. The Court of Cassation, however, rejected this doubt, highlighting that the second complaint began in 2017 and without laws regulating the intermediary period, the new laws had to be applied in their entirety (Civil Cassation, sec. II, judg. 14 October 2019, No. 25837). The new laws set out that no compensation should be awarded to an applicant who applied to or persisted in the proceedings while knowing their own position (l. 89/2001, article 2.2-*quinquies*): while taking a consolidated case-law perspective, the law has only been applicable from 2016 and has no influence on the decision on the amount of compensation awarded, but on the applicant's right to request it (Civil Cassation, sec. II, judgments 14 January 2019, No. 595; 14 October 2019, No. 25826). On applying such criteria and deciding the amount of compensation due, the district judge (Court of Appeal) has a wide margin of appreciation over which (except in cases of evident unreasonableness) the Court of Cassation has no power (Civil Cassation, sec. II, judg. 28 May 2019, No. 14521).

According to the Trentino-Alto Adige Regional Administrative Court (sec. I, judg. 30 September 2019, No. 113), the right to just compensation for non-pecuniary damages caused by an excessively long administrative procedure is a personal right of the individual concerned in the proceedings; the lawyer involved therefore cannot act on his own account at the Ministry of Justice as a substitute for his client.

XIII Criminal Matters

A Self-defence

Law 26 April 2019, No. 36 amended article 52 and others of the Criminal Code on the issue of legitimate defence. The fundamental definition of this cause to rule out the illegality of an individual's behaviour who reacts to assault has not changed ("those who resort to self-defence, when such a response is needed in the face of a clear threat of wrongful injury to their own or others' right, cannot be punished. However, the defence must be proportional to the offense."), but the new law has introduced a series of measures extending its scope. In particular, on reacting with a weapon or other means to a home intrusion, it was established that there must always be an element of proportionality, when defending with one's own or others' safety or property from a persistent aggressor. Furthermore, the perpetrator of an act of legitimate defence of their personal safety which was deemed disproportionate, the further exemption of having acted in a state of serious disturbance caused by the situation must apply.

Some judgments of the Court of Cassation have helped clarify some finer points of the new law. The judgment Criminal Cassation, sec. V, judg. 13 June 2019, No. 40414, discussed the case of a person who had hit an individual with a baseball bat who he had found in this home (the person was famous, but the agent involved had not recognised him). The person had entered into his home with no violence nor threatening behaviour. The Court upheld the conviction for personal injury, without applying legitimate defence of the home, which can only be applied when the home intrusion is violent. Criminal Cassation, sec. III, judg. 10 October 2019, No. 49883, confirmed the conviction for murder by a person who surprised a burglar who was entering into the individual's home at night, having given up and taking refuge in the courtyard, the individual shot him a number of times with a shotgun. According to the Court of Cassation, even in its new form, article 52 of the Criminal Code underlines the principle that the killing of an aggressor can only be justified through legitimate self-defence if the lethal use of force is necessary (with ex-ante assessment) to protect the injury or property of the individual. In other words, even if the new reform states that there must always be an element of proportionality between the aggressor and the defender, in cases of home intrusion, it is still necessary to prove the existence of aggression or a risk of aggression that could cause personal injury or harm the property that the individual is defending. In the case of assault or risk of assault judged by mistake, as in the case in question, there is liability for culpable excess of self-defence. Even the further non-punishment factor brought on by the serious mental disturbance caused by the situation can only come into operation when an individual acts in the face of a risk of aggression, not when this is averted.

B Torture: Article 613-bis of the Criminal Code

The Criminal Court of Cassation took advantage of one of the first judgments that applies the crime of torture under article 613-*bis* of the Criminal Code, introduced in 2017, to provide clarifications on the interpretation of a law which has raised a number of issues. The case dealt with a number of young people from a city in Apulia who systematically and for a long time inflicted physical and moral harassment and violence against an adult described as unable to defend themselves due to psychological limits. Following yet another assault by the "gang", the man died. He had already been suffering from numerous mental health problems. Various members of the group were convicted of a number of crimes, including torture. The question of torture was brought up by the complaints presented in from of the Supreme Court. The Court, placing article 613-*bis* in a systemic framework (among crimes against personal freedom and particularly moral freedom) and in connection with international instruments (in particular article 3 ECHR), defended the choice of the legislator to write that the law does not just sanction State-mandated torture (mainly referring to the Convention against Torture of 1984), but also sanctions any act that causes intense physical or mental suffering to a defenceless person, independent of the perpetrator's status as a public official or private citizen (even if the law provides for an aggravated liability for public officials). According to the Court of Cassation, criminologically speaking, this choice hits the mark. The crime is malicious, it must consist in serious violence or threats or in cruelty, and it must produce acute physical suffering or verifiable mental trauma for the individual who undergoes it. The victim must be a person deprived of their liberty, or in the custody, care, assistance of the perpetrator or find themselves in a vulnerable situation. Furthermore, the conduct must occur habitually or multiple times; although a single act of violence could constitute torture as long as it is inhuman or degrading to the dignity of the person. Torture is, therefore, a habitual crime (multiple acts of violence or serious threats), but can also occur with a single act when this consists of inhuman and degrading treatment (for example *waterboarding*). Concerning the "seriousness" requirement, this refers to both the violence and threats (and not just the latter); it is the reoccurring nature, whether close together or distant in time, or even at the same time, but the work of more than one person. "Cruelty" does not necessarily require the repetition of the act, as this defines itself in the perpetrator's gratification for the violent acts being carried out. Cruelty is not necessarily linked to physically harmful behaviour (such as mutilations, burns and so on) but can also consist of forcing the individual to do humiliating acts that have an effect on the personality of the victim. The victim may have a particular relationship with the torturer. One of these situations is demonstrated by the condition of impaired defence of the individual – which could be in light of age, sex, mental state and so on. Finally, the "verifiable mental trauma" as an alternative to "acute physical suffering". The trauma in question must be identifiably distinct from the individual's general mental state (hence the expression "verifiable", which refers to a demonstrative finding, since a medical confirmation is not necessary), and can consist in a situation that is resolved quickly, and does not have to lead to a structured psychological trauma causing deep, long-lasting effects on the victim. Applying all these parameters, the Court of Cassation confirmed the judgment in merit and the convictions (Criminal Cassation, sec. V, judg. 8 July 2019, No. 47079).

C Inhuman Treatment and Article 35-*ter* Prison Administration Act

The Court of Cassation ruled on some issues concerning the application of article 35-*ter* of the Prison Administration Act (l. 354/1975), establishing a compensation procedure in favour of prisoners who are victims of inhuman treatment.

The Supreme Court (Civil Cassation, sec. III, ord. 20 January 2019, No. 2350) established that compensation can be made between the amount owed by an inmate to the State (due to monetary fines) and the amount the individual is entitled to receive in compensation for damages for detention in inhuman or degrading conditions. Action set out in article 35-*ter* can also be presented by an inmate serving a full life sentence even if the main benefit for going through with this request (that is, parole) is not a prospect at that moment, given that the impediment to any benefit of the sentence can change depending on the offender's choices (Criminal Cassation, sec. I, judg. 3 May 2019, No. 41649).

The liveable space of a cell (which can be no smaller than three square-metres per person) includes tables, stools and other non-fixed furniture that have many functions and do not limit the liveable space within the room. The liveable space is impeded by hygiene services and non-removeable furniture, such as bunk-beds and other similar furniture (Criminal Cassation, sec. I, judgments 10 January 2019, No. 1562; 22 January 2019, No. 15104; 21 March 2019, No. 23596; sec. VI, No. 1562; 22 January 2019, sec. III, No. 1564; 25 June 2019, No. 38933;). The area taken up by a single bed, which, since it can have various functions and can generally be moved is calculated within in liveable space (see, in particular, Criminal Cassation, sec. I, judgments 22 January 2019, No. 151047; 7 March 2019, No. 29476). There is a mobile separating wall between the cell (over seven metres squared) and the bathroom area, without automatic ventilation systems, it does not constitute an inhumane condition (Criminal Cassation, sec. V, judg. 4 March 2019, No. 30469).

The Court of Cassation annuls the decree with which the supervisory court rejected the question of compensation for an inmate who, for a certain period, had to share a cell of less than three metres squared, although he had access to external spaces for around eight hours a day. The Court of Cassation does not consider the decision sufficiently motivated. The fact that there are elements – such as the access to outside spaces – which compensate the discomfort of a cell which the law cannot assess in the abstract. In a case which dealt with an inmate who could not walk without assistance, any compensation had to be assessed more specifically and in the light of the applicant's personal characteristics (Criminal Cassation, sec. I, judg. 21 March 2019, No. 23496). The decision of the Supreme Court mirrors this; a complaint of inhuman treatment presented by an inmate. The complaint was rejected by the supervisory court exclusively on the basis that the cell was ascertained to be above the limit of three metres available per person (in a cell occupied by three inmates). According to the Court of Cassation, the fact that the cell was larger than the limit of three metres (in this case, it was 3.2 metres squared per person in a three-person cell) eliminates the presumption of inhuman treatment, but does not exclude that this may emerge from considering other elements of the inmates' overall treatment (Criminal Cassation, sec. I, judg. 20 September 2019, No. 43440).

The complaint relying on article 35-*ter* can be presented by a person under house arrest, with regard to the amount of time that a person must be detained in a cell (Criminal Cassation, sec. I, judg. 14 November 2019, No. 51302).

The amount of money granted in compensation for every single day of detention in inhuman conditions (up to ten years) is €8 a day; for those released from prison before the date of entry into force of article 35-*ter* (28 June 2014), the limitation period does not apply before this date (Civil Cassation, sec. VI, judg. 22 October 2019, No. 26974).

According to the Court of Cassation (Criminal Cassation, sec. VI, judg. 24 October 2019, No. 1024), prison detention for an inmate who has on multiple occasions attempted suicide (generally corresponding with unfavourable judgments) by obtaining and ingesting psychiatric drugs does not constitute inhuman and degrading treatment. The prisoner asked to be transferred in a health structure outside the prison. According to the Supreme Court, unless a prisoner cannot be kept in prison for health reasons, repeated self-harm behaviour could imply the transfer of the person to another prison facility or providing more effective measures to protect the prisoner's safety, but not necessarily their release. The applicant's detention does not in itself constitute torture or inhuman treatment and the lack of surveillance which allowed the prisoner to attempt suicide are attributable to organisational difficulties within the prison, but that are not the direct responsibility of prison administration.

The case of a prisoner who complained about the fact that he received a different brand razor blades than the ones he had requested does not refer to article 35-*ter*, but to 35-*bis* of the Prison Administration Act (judicial complaint for the violation of rights). The Court of Cassation (Criminal Cassation, sec. I, judg. 25 June 2019, No. 38937) noted that having the preferred brand of razor blades is not a subjective right of a detained person and cannot, therefore, be the subject of a complaint in front of the supervisory judge. The applicant was ordered to pay a €2000 fine on top of court costs.

D Life Sentences and Article 4-bis of Prison Administration Act

The regime of whole-life sentences is regulated by article 4-*bis* of the Prison Administration Act and established for anyone committing crimes under article 416-*bis* Criminal Code (mafia crimes, among others) who will not cooperate with the judicial authorities. These continue to be the subject of complaints brought up in front of the Constitutional Court (see, for example, *Yearbook 2019*, pp. 347–248).

The most controversial of these is the whole-life sentence without parole, also based on article 4-*bis* which prevents prisoners with whole-life sentences to accede parole or conditional release if they fail to cooperate with the judicial authorities, even in cases where 26 years have been passed in prison, and therefore making it impossible to return to civil life. In 2019, whole-life sentences were the subject of an important judgment of the ECtHR – see, in this Part, Italy in the Case-law of the European Court of Human Rights (*Viola v. Italy*).

With judgment 253/2019 (4 December 2019) the Constitutional Court ruled on different issue: the compatibility of provisions that exclude the admission of prisoners under a special regime to the use of bonus permits with constitutional principles (in particular article 27 Cost.). The law is applied not only to those affiliated with the mafia or similar organisations but also perpetrators of crimes committed in "mafia contexts". Automatically extending the disputed measure to the latter as well would lead to an unreasonable extension of the rationale of the provision, according to the referring court. The absolute preclusion of considering any specific reason for not cooperating with the judicial authorities constitutes an unjustified flattening of the rule on a particular type of offenders, or particularly members of mafia organisations whose sentence cannot be reduced. It does not allow to take into account in an individualised way of the different positions. In favour of this declaration of unconstitutionality was, among others, the National Ombudspersons on the rights of persons deprived of personal liberty, even if his request to intervene in the proceeding was not accepted, nor was his request to present his own brief under the title of *amicus curiae* (a figure which is currently not foreseen for procedures before the Constitutional Court).

The judgment carried out an extensive historical reconstruction of legislative interventions and case-law on the differentiated treatment of perpetrators of mafia-related crime. At the centre of this issue is the question of whether it is possible to maintain the legislative presumption that committing certain crimes demonstrates the perpetrators' affiliation with organised gangs and indicates a danger to society that is incompatible with admittance into any prison benefit programmes that take place outside the prison complex, or whether it should consider the possibility that other reasons, not related to maintaining links with the mafia, may determine the unwillingness to cooperate with the justice system. The conclusion of the Court was that, even in the absence of cooperation with the justice system, if the supervisory judge has elements that rule out all links to organised crime, but also any danger that those links might be restored, taking into account the concrete personal and environmental circumstances, the authorities must be able to provide the prisoner with access to benefits (i.e. the use of the bonus permits) as a re-educational measure for the sentence. Article 41-*bis* of the Prison Administration Act, which does not allow for this assessment, must be declared unconstitutional.

> There are certain provisions of article 4-*bis* which do not refer to life sentences, including the judgment of the Constitutional Court 229/2019 (8 November 2019). The decision follows those made in 2018 (see *Yearbook 2019*, pp. 248–249), concerning the possibility of granting benefits such as bonus permits to prisoners serving sentences for kidnap, aggravated by the death of their victim. For this crime, article 4-*bis* sets out the same rigid exclusions as those for perpetrators of mafia-related crimes: cooperation with judicial authorities and serving a fixed portion of the sentence. In judgments 149/2018 and 174/2018, the Constitutional Court had already considered this rule contrary to the Constitution as it was applicable to "obstructive" perpetrators who were sentenced to full life sentences and women who were convicted of these crimes but who are also mothers of children under the age of 10. With this judgment, the declaration of unconstitutionality for incompatibility with the principle of the re-educative objective of punishment (article 27 of the Constitution) and the principle of equality and proportionality (article 3) was also extended to "obstructive" perpetrators (such as prisoners serving sentences for kidnap, aggravated by the death of their victim) who are not serving life sentences but a prison detention. The rigid parameters established by article 4-*bis* (serving at least two-thirds of the sentence) should not bind the supervisory judge when granting benefits that are present in other conditions of law. The judgment also recalled that this conclusion had been anticipated by a number of 2018 decisions, with which Parliament had been invited to amend the law in question, something which has not happened yet.

E Prisoners' Conditions, Particularly of Prisoners under the Special Prison Regime (Article 41-bis of the Prison Administration Act)

The Supreme Court (Criminal Cassation, sec. I, judg. 9 January 2019, No. 11597) carried out an articulated reading of the laws in force on national and local ombudsperson for the rights of detained persons, addressing the opportunity for persons subjected to the special prison regime defined by article 41-*bis* of the Prison Administration Act reserved interviews, which are foreseen for members of mafia organisations, among others. The case concerned the judgment of the Sassari tutelary judge, who had allowed the Municipal Ombudsperson on the Rights of Prisoners to have a confidential interview, with no surveillance video-filming, with a prisoner held under special prison regime of article 41-*bis*. The Ministry of Justice challenged this decision, complaining that the Municipal Ombudsperson should not be allowed to carry out confidential interviews with prisoners without prior authorisation and without the presence of prison staff. The Court carried out an extensive analysis of the Italian and international legislation on the subject of Ombudspersons on the rights of prisoner. The current article 67 of the Prison Administration Act allows some institutional roles to carry out visits in prisons, including the Ombudspersons – both the National Ombudsperson (which is also the NPM against torture on the standards of the Optional Protocol of 2002 to the Convention against Torture – OPCAT), and the regional and local ombudspersons. The right to make visits with no prior authorisation is granted only to the National Ombudsperson, as well as granting "the opportunity to have private interviews with the persons deprived of their liberty without witnesses, either personally or with a translator if deemed necessary, as well as with any other person who the national preventive mechanism believes may supply relevant information" (article 20 OPCAT; see also article 7, l.d. 146/2013, established by the National Ombudsperson for the Rights of Persons in Prison or Deprived of Liberty). For the other Ombudspersons, the general limitations set out for interviews with relatives remain, in particular the presence (without listening) of prison officers in the interview room. Concerning the special regime for prisoners affiliated with mafia organisations, interviews with all Ombudspersons can always take place, even if they are more strictly regulated by article 41-*bis*, that is with prior authorisation and video-filming, without these reducing the number of visits allowed from close family members (one a month); only the National Ombudsperson (not regional or local) can carry out visits and confidential interviews with all prisoners (including those held under article 41-*bis*) with no witnesses or video-filming, by virtue of its function as a National Torture Prevention Mechanism. In conclusion, the authorisation of the Sassari tutelary judge to the local Ombudsperson was not legitimate, since only the National Ombudsperson is allowed a private interview with no video-filming with a prisoner held under a special regime.

The current Prison Administration Act (l. 354/1975) established that the refusal by a supervisory judge to concede grant a prisoner a "prize permit" could be presented as the subject of a complaint in front of a Supervisory Court, but sets an extremely short time limit for this process: 24 hours; a time limit which is further restricted by the fact that to deposit the complaint in the correct offices during work hours, prisoners first have to obtain authorisation to leave their cell. The Court of Cassation (Criminal Cassation, sec. 1, judg. 30 October 2019, No. 45976) considered that this time limit is excessively short, especially considering that recent legislative reforms imposed that the complaint must include detailed motivations, or it will be declared inadmissible. In 1996, the Constitutional Court had raised concern about the short time limits place of complaints, and invited the legislator to intervene. Over twenty years later, there has still been no reform on the subject. The Court of Cassation held that the question of constitutionality of the norm that fixes the 24-hour time limit for filing complaints is not ill-founded and forwarded the issue to the Constitutional Court.

The Court of Cassation (sec. I, judg. 3 July 2019, No. 32337) reiterated the legitimacy of the standard of the constitutional principles of "hard prison regime" established by article 41-*bis* of the Prison Administration Act for criminal organisation members, especially Mafia-type organisations. An important member of the Palermo mafia detained in Rome under the 41-*bis* regime, complained that this regime contravened the rights sanctioned by the ECHR, especially considering the fact that it had been applied to him for many years and that, according to the person concerned, the influence of his "family" in Palermo had greatly diminished over the years. The judges reiterated that the differentiated regime was not only imposed to break existing ties with the prisoner and their mafia gang, but also to prevent any restoration of those ties. The aim of the differentiated regime is not to punish or re-educate the prisoner, but to "neutralise" them via ending all connection with the mafia system. This also explains the administrative nature of the procedures (albeit subject to judicial control by the supervisory judge) to regularly monitor those ties.

The Court of Cassation (Criminal Cassation, sec. I, judg. 19 November 2019, No. 5450) ruled on a complaint presented by an inmate subjected to the special prison regime contained within article 41-*bis* of the Prison Administration Act, who complained about the administration's refusal of his request for a CD-ROM containing educational material. The applicant attended school courses and had accessed a video file containing educational material. The prison administration refused to allow him to receive a (rewritable) CD-ROM. The complaint filed regarding this refusal was not considered to be subject to assessment by the supervisory judge, as it concerns an ordinary situation that did not affect the rights of the inmate. The reason for the refusal was evident, given the particular surveillance regime under article 41-*bis*. The Court of Cassation approved this approach, noting that not only the administration's behaviour had not resulted in a significant prejudice to the prisoner's rights, but that the administration could not reasonably take on the task of managing excessively complex authorisation procedures.

According to the Supreme Court (Criminal Cassation, sec. I, judg. 15 November 2019, No. 5446), where the norm foresees that the prisoner can have one visit a month with family members, article 41-*bis* does not allow these interviews to take place on two consecutive days (the last day of the month and the first day of the following). The law in fact establishes a balance between the inmate's needs to maintain contact with family members and the goal of managing the flow of information that can be transmitted outside the prison for security reasons; maintaining this balance requires that the visits be organised at a safe distance and therefore excludes their rapid succession in consecutive days.

The Court of Cassation held that it was legitimate that newspapers delivered to the prisoners under the article 41-*bis* regime were censored, as the prison authorities removed the articles which referred to organised crime in the home city or area of the prisoner in question (Criminal Cassation, sec. I, judg. 11 October 2019, No. 48522). On the other hand, prohibiting a person under the special regime pursuant to article 41-*bis* to access local news cannot be automatically arranged on the basis that it could help maintain relations with a criminal organisation, but requires specific justification (Criminal Cassation, sec. I, judg. 13 June 2019, No. 35766).

Prisoners, including those under the 41-*bis* regime, are not allowed to speak with their family members via videoconference (Criminal Cassation, sec. I, judg. 22 March 2019, No. 16557). In the absence of a specific legal provision, the supervisory judge cannot allow meetings via Skype. On the other hand, the Court of Cassation acknowledges that an inmate held under the special regime still has the right to use both the time to go outside (for health reasons) and to be able to spend some time with other inmates in order to facilitate the prisoner's re-education. The inmate cannot be excluded from shared activities on the assumption that during the time spent outside, the individual may meet other prisoners. However, socialisation measures must not allow the prisoner to meet or have contact with any members of their previous criminal organisation. Except in exceptional cases, the inmates must spend at least two hours outside (Criminal Cassation, sec. I, judgments 19 February 2019, No. 15572; 28 February 2019, Nos. 17579 and 17580; 21 March 2019, No. 18898).

F Political Rights of Prisoners

The Court of Cassation (Civil Cassation, sec. 1, judg. 29 January 2019, No. 2479) excluded that the law laying out the temporary or permanent suspension from the electoral register of prisoners who have committed serious crimes (that is, those whose punishment is more than three years imprisonment or a life sentence) constitutes a violation of article 3 of Protocol 1 to the ECHR. The measure is not applied indiscriminately to all prisoners, rather adopting the criteria of the seriousness of the crime committed and the subsequent length of sentence (the judgment refers back to ECtHR case-law on the *Scoppola 3* case, see *Yearbook 2013*, pp. 347–348).

G Sanctions Imposed by Independent Authorities

According to the Civil Court of Cassation (Sec. 2, judgments 3 January 2019, Nos. 4 and 5), the sanctions imposed by the *Banca d'Italia* and the CONSOB (the independent authority which regulates the Stock Exchange) as regard the respective monitoring competencies on financial actors, are not criminal in nature. Moreover, it is not possible to apply the standards established by articles 6 and 7 of the ECHR. The recipients of these fines are fully entitled to challenge them in a judicial court, where the standards of a fair trial are determined by the Constitution and by the ECHR.

H Lawyers' Use of a Computer with Clients in Prison

The Court of Cassation ruled on a case of a lawyer who was stopped from bringing his laptop into an interview with a client in pre-trial detention in prison. The legal representative had not justified the choice to use the computer instead of printing the relevant documents that he was going to share with his client. The legal representative opposed the ban however, stating that this would create a disparity between the prosecution and the defence since there is no similar restriction for the prosecution magistrates. The Court of Cassation (Criminal Cassation, sec. III, judg. 18 April 2019, No. 38609) recognises that there is no ban on using laptops during interviews with defendants within the Criminal Procedure Code or Prison Administration Act; however, in order to bring a computer into a prison, it is necessary to adequately justify not directly printing the documents needed or why it is not possible to use the computers already available in the prison.

I Extradition, European Arrest Warrant

Carrying out a European arrest warrant issued by the judicial authorities of an EU Member State, which involves the removal of a person to a foreign State, cannot go ahead if there are grounded reasons to believe that the detention conditions in foreign prisons are inhuman or degrading. There are many standards that must be considered, and information concerning the lack of space made available to the prisoner (under three metres square per person) are not the only factors to keep in mind, as the judgment must be made in reference to general detention conditions. The decision to allow the removal of the applicant to Romania to serve his sentence is therefore confirmed (Criminal Cassation, sec. II, judg. 4 June 2019, No. 25066). At the same time, the Court of Cassation places the condition on the implementation of a European arrest warrant issued by Belgium of receiving updated information on the steps taken to tackle the situation of overcrowding reported by the European Committee for the Prevention of Torture in 2017 and in 2018 (Criminal Cassation, sec. VI, judg. 20 October 2019, No. 44397). The laws regarding the European Arrest Warrant system, prohibiting the extradition of a person requested by a foreign authority to serve their sentence when that person is a mother to a child of under three years, are only applied among EU Member States. An Albanian woman who was requested by her country of origin to serve her sentence there has no recourse. The decision of the Italian Court, therefore, was issued after verifying that the prison conditions of the only Albanian penitentiary structure able to accept her were in compliance with international standards. The extradition was therefore confirmed (Criminal Cassation, sec. VI, judg. 11 December 2019, No. 1677). Article 698 of the Criminal Procedure Code explicitly rules out the possibility of extraditing a person to a State which punishes the crime in question with the death penalty. This blocks any extradition to China, despite the fact that the bilateral treaty on extradition only briefly mentions the well-founded fear of punishment or cruel, inhuman or degrading treatment. The possible use of the death penalty evidently goes beyond this provision (Criminal Cassation, sec. VI, judg. 11 June 2019, No. 39443). According to the Supreme Court, the outstanding matter of a procedure to recognise international protection does not rule out a possible extradition request for the same person, in order to serve their sentence in their country of origin. Naturally, the potential rejection of the extradition request on the basis of an established risk of a death sentence or of detention in inhuman conditions could affect the application for international protection. However, the two proceedings are completely separate (Criminal Cassation, sec. VI, judg. 12 June 2019, No. 29910). The Spanish judicial authorities requested the implementation of a sentence of 630 days imprisonment (as regulated by the laws on the European arrest warrant) for a

Spanish citizen sentenced in Spain for fraud against the EU. The Italian judge recognised the conviction issued by Spain but declared it condoned by virtue of the pardon issued by the Italian State, applicable to this type of criminal sanction. The Court of Cassation annulled this decision. It is the sovereign prerogative of a State to right to apply the sentences issued by its national judges without other States undermining the decision; therefore, this principle is also laid out in the framework for collaboration among EU Member States. The pardon issued by Italy cannot therefore make the Spanish Court's conviction disappear into thin air. The same EU law foresees that in this type of case, there are consultations allowing the implementation of the judgment (Criminal Cassation, sec. VI, judg. 19 November 2019, No. 47445).

Italy in the Case-law of the European Court of Human Rights*

I Right to Life, Ban on Torture and Inhuman and Degrading Treatment

In the *Knox* case (No. 76577/13 judgment of 24 January 2019), the applicant complains of a violation of articles 3 and 6 paragraphs 1, 3 and 8 of the ECHR. The case concerned the criminal proceedings leading to the conviction of the applicant to three years imprisonment for malicious accusation against D.L., having accused him of killing her flatmate M.K. during a police interview held at 1.45 and 5.45 on the morning of 6 November 2007. The applicant complains that those accusations were made having been subjected to ill-treatment in violation of article 3 ECHR. In particular she complained of being slapped on her head twice by the police force. Furthermore, the same police officers were accused of subjecting her to extreme psychological pressure, including shouting and threats of imprisonment, at a moment in the shock and extreme confusion of the situation had made her incapable of showing discernment or willpower. The applicant claims that this was in violation of the right to respect of private life pursuant to article 8 of the ECHR. Her state of confusion, difficulty in recalling the facts of the case and, therefore, the unreliability of her statements and the impairing of her capacity for self-determination were all reported by the applicant two days after on 8 November 2007. Moreover, the emotional shock during her interrogation caused by the aggressive and offensive treatment was described repeatedly by the applicant, including constantly complaining about those conditions in her ordinary appeal and her appeals on points of law. Given these circumstances, the ECtHR found that the facts complained of by the applicant had attained the minimum threshold of severity to engage article 3 ECHR (*Poltoratski v. Ukraine*, No. 38812/97, 29 April 2003) and that therefore the National Authorities were required to carry out an official investigation. The treat-

* Ino Kehrer

ment complained of had not left to any investigation, in violation of article 3 ECHR in its procedural aspect, as the applicant had not been given the benefit of an investigation capable of shedding light on the facts and the possible responsibilities. However, in its substantive aspect, the ECtHR found that there was insufficient evidence for it to conclude that the applicant had actually sustained inhuman or degrading treatment. Regarding the complaint of a violation of article 6 ECHR, the ECtHR held that there had been a violation of that article of the ECHR (specifically, paragraphs 1 and 3 letter c), considering that her statements were made without legal assistance, even though the Italian Government declared that, according to settled case-law of the Court of Cassation (judgments Nos. 10089 of 2005, 26460 of 2010 and 33583 of 2015), statements made by persons under investigation in absence of a lawyer could only be used when these themselves constitute a crime. The applicant had been particularly vulnerable, being a foreign young woman, 20 at the time, not having been in Italy for very long and not being fluent in Italian Given these circumstances, in the Court's opinion, it is not possible to exclude that the restriction of the applicant's access to a lawyer had not irreparably undermined the fairness of the proceedings as a whole, considering that the impugned statements had constituted the offence with which she was charged. Similarly, the ECtHR found that there had been a violation of article 6, paragraphs 1 and 3 letter e, of the ECHR, concerning the right to the assistance of an interpreter. In this case, as raised repeatedly by the applicant, the police interpreter, by her own admission, had played a role that went beyond interpreting and had played the role of mediator. The authorities failed to assess this conduct or its impact on the outcome of the criminal proceedings. The Court therefore concluded that this failure had compromised the fairness of the proceedings as a whole. Therefore, the ECtHR ordered the Italian Government to pay €10,400 compensation for non-pecuniary damage and €8,000 for costs and expenses.

In the *Marcello Viola* case (No. 77633/16), on 13 June 2019, the ECtHR gave their decision on the incompatibility of an irreducible life prison sentence with article 3 ECHR. Life imprisonment, under article 4-*bis* of the Prison Administration Act, foresees no possibility for an inmate to benefit from parole or other prison benefits when the detainee has not previously cooperated with the judicial authorities. Under domestic law, in order to incentivise cooperative behaviour from the prisoner, the Court had previously held that a legal presumption of dangerousness could be justified given the ongoing links with the Mafia-type group and the lack of cooperation with the judicial authorities. The applicant complains that, given his life sentence pursuant to article 416-*bis*, there was no possibility of his sentence being reviewed nor could he benefit from parole. The applicant had not cooperated with the judicial authorities in order not to put himself and his family at risk of retaliation from mafia groups. Furthermore, it was highly improbable that any cooperation would be considered 'impossible' or 'enforceable pursuant to article 58-*ter* of the Prison Administration Act and to the Court of Cassation case-law, owing to the existence of the aggravating circumstances linking to his role as head of the Mafia-type group. The applicant argued that, no matter what his behaviour in prison had then been, there was no possibility of social reintegration nor was there any prospect of release. Considering that the lack of any *de jure* and *de facto* prospect of release is a violation of article 3 ECHR, the Court examined the only option available to the applicant to reduce his sentence. The Court recognised that by requiring prisoners to cooperate with the judicial authorities and a severance of ties with criminal organisations in order to demonstrate the positive outcome of resocialisation courses, article 4-*bis* was designed to for general prevention and public protection against mafia crime, aiming at "cutting off" an inmate from their mafia contacts and restoring law and order (judgments Nos. 306/1993 and 273/2001 of the Constitutional Court). Despite this, the Court recalls that the aims of resocialisation and reinsertion into society of inmates as possible release prospects are fundamental elements that must be considered when deciding on an imprisonment sentence. To this regard, the Court had doubts as to the free and deliberate nature of the choice to cooperate with judicial authorities, considering, for example, the fear of retaliation expressed by the applicant by his former Mafia circles. According to the third-party intervener "*L'altro diritto* NGO", this fear is the main reason why prisoners refused to cooperate for Mafia-related crimes. The Court inferred from this that the lack of cooperation did not necessarily reflect continuing adherence to criminal values or ongoing links with the Mafia-type organisation. The "severing of ties" with Mafia circles might be expressed in ways other than cooperation with the judicial authorities. In particular, the applicant had made progress in his resocialisation as demonstrated by the L'Aquila Surveillance Judge order revoking the measures of article 41-*bis* of the Prison Administration Act (so-called hard prison regime). However, by equating an irrebuttable presumption of dangerousness with a lack of cooperation fails to reflect the individual's actual progress towards rehabilitation and therefore makes it impossible for the applicant to demonstrate that his detention was no longer justified on legitimate penological grounds (*Murray v. The Netherlands* ([GC] No. 10511/10, 26 April 2016)) and deprived the applicant of any realistic prospect of release. This presumption effectively prevented the competent court from examining the sentence, limiting them to finding that the conditions of cooperation had not been met.

According to the Court, therefore, article 4-*bis* restricted the applicant's prospects for release and the possibility of review of his sentence to an excessive degree. Accordingly, his sentence could not be regarded as reducible for the purposes of article 3 ECHR. To remedy this violation of article 3 ECHR, the Court suggests a review of life sentences entailing a review of the sentence in light of re-educational and resocialisation progress, in order to overcome the automatic assumption that cooperating with the judicial authorities reflects the only possible way of severing ties with Mafia-type groups. In the Court's opinion, this legislative measure must ensure that "A whole life prisoner is entitled to know, at the outset of his sentence, what he must do to be considered for release and under what conditions" (*Hutchinson v. United Kingdom*; [GC], No. 57592/08, 17 January 2017). The Court decided six votes to one that the violation of article 3 ECHR was sufficient in respect of non-pecuniary damage. In the separate opinion, Judge Wojtyczek expressed his objection to the violation of article 3 ECHR by Italy, since it is essential that every State Authority can adopt necessary measures to "dismantle criminal organisations that constitute a threat to the lives of people" keeping in mind the specific situation of each country. The judge underlined that sentences are multi-dimensional and multi-functional tools. Their goal is not only to resocialise the prisoner, but serve as retribution, as a deterrent and can contribute to the fight against crime. According to Judge Wojtyczek's separate opinion, the reasons given in the judgment seem to suggest that the only legitimate objective of sentencing is the resocialisation of the offender, even though other ECtHR judgments have highlighted the deterrent effect of a sentence (*Sidiropoulos and Papakostas v. Greece*, No. 33349/10, 25 January 2018, *Zeynep Özcan v. Turkey*, No. 45906/99, 20 February 2007). Judge Wojtyczek also noted that the judgment had reversed other principles like, for example, the existence of presidential clemency as a measure ensuring that the sentence is compatible with the need for it to be reducible (*Iorgov v. Bulgaria* (No. 2) No. 36295/02, 2 September 2010, *Harakchiev and Tolumov v. Bulgaria*,

Nos. 15018/11 and 61199/12, 8 July 2014). For these reasons, the judge believes that this judgment makes legislation on life sentences less comprehensible and even more unpredictable.

On 26 November 2019, the ECtHR declared the *Verri* case (No. 41130/18) inadmissible. The complaint was presented by the son and daughter of Mr Valerio Verri (now deceased). On 8 April 2017, while carrying out supervisory tasks to combat poaching as a volunteer environmental guard, Mr Verri was shot and killed by N.F. The applicants complained of a violation of the right to life of their father under the material and procedural aspects of article 2 ECHR. They claimed that their father's death could have been prevented if law enforcement agencies had acted with due diligence. According to the applicant, by promptly analysing the biological material recovered, it would have been possible to deduce that the killer was the same person wanted by the Ferrara Police Force for the murder of a bar owner and could have informed the environmental guard service of the danger or alternatively suspended the service altogether in the days before the killing. The ECtHR rejected the complaint, holding that the accusations were manifestly ill-founded in light of article 35 para. 1 and 2 of the ECHR. Regarding the material respects of the case, although article 2 of the ECHR includes the positive obligation for States to take necessary preventative measures to safeguard individuals whose life is at risk due to the criminal activities of others (*Bljakaj and others v. Croatia*, No. 74448/12, 18 September 2014), this obligation must not impose an impossible or disproportionate burden on the authorities. In the case at hand, the suspension of the service would have been unreasonable and disproportionate, as the law enforcement agencies had not known, nor should they have known, of the existence of a real and immediate risk to the life of an identified individual or individuals given the vast expanse of territory and the fact that the criminal did not seem to have a specific target. Regarding the procedural aspects, following the complaint, Italian authorities swiftly began a criminal investigation to investigate any wrongdoings by the law enforcement agencies.

II Right to Freedom, Security and Free Movement

In the *Rizzotto* case (No. 20983/12), the ECtHR gave a judgment on the complaint of a violation of article 5 para. 4 ECHR on 5 September 2019.

This article guarantees anyone arrested the right of any person arrested to appeal in front of a court to determine the legitimacy of their detention. This specific case concerned the applicant's lack of opportunity to get an objective judicial review on the legitimacy of the pre-trial detention undergone. Since the applicant had been declared untraceable, the Palermo District Court ordered the pre-trial detention and appointed a lawyer to represent him, presenting an appeal against the order. As the lawyer had been officially appointed, the applicant had therefore never had any previous contact with him. The lawyer requested the appeal, however, in the meantime the applicant had been extradited from Malta and was being held in Regina Coeli prison in Rome. The appeal against the pre-trial detention order was rejected as inadmissible on the basis of the "single appeal" principle. The applicant, therefore, had never had the opportunity in person to support the application for release: firstly, because he was untraceable; secondly, because of the rejection of his appeal. Considering that no element of the case suggests that the applicant attempted to evade justice or had unequivocally waived his right to a defence, the Court held that article 309 of the Criminal Procedure Code had not afforded the appropriate pursuant to article 5 para. 4 ECHR, especially the right to an effective hearing by a judge examining in appeal against detention. This right, according to the Court, was not even ensured by the remedy established in article 299 of the Criminal Procedure Code, offering the possibility of applying to set aside a detention order with a view to securing a review of the lawfulness of ongoing detention. In any event, since this was the first time the applicant had sought to secure a review of the lawfulness of his detention and no new facts had thus been submitted to the court's scrutiny, a request for a hearing would in any event have been declared inadmissible under the relevant legislation. The Court unanimously concluded that there had been a violation of article 5 para. 4 ECHR, since the applicant had not had the opportunity of effectively being heard by a competent judge to ensure the legitimacy of his detention. The Government was ordered to pay a total of €11,000 in respect of non-pecuniary damage and of costs and expenses.

The *Torresi* judgment (No. 68957/16) of 17 December 2019 concerns the complaint of a violation of freedom to leave a country pursuant to article 2 of protocol 4 to the ECHR through the refusal to issue a passport to the applicant by the Italian Authorities. This refusal is established in article 3 letter b), of law No. 1185 of 21 November 1967, amended by article 24, para. 1, of law No. 3 of 16 January 2003 in order to restrict the freedom of parents (who shared parental custody) to leave the country and not fulfil their obligations to their children. In the case at hand, the mother of the applicant's two children refused to give her consent for him to apply for a passport, fearing that if the applicant moved away from the country, he would have contributed less financially and emotionally to his daughters' well-being. This refusal was examined by the Italian Authorities, who held that it was justified and in compliance with the best interests of the children, as it aimed to protect the bond between the father and his daughters, and to guarantee the children's right to receive maintenance payments. This conclusion was shared by the Court, finding that the interference in the right for a person to leave a country for another (pursuant to article 3 letter b), of law No. 1185 of 21 November 1967) was legitimate when aimed at protecting the interests of the applicant's daughters. Furthermore, the Court noted that the internal judicial authorities had regularly re-examined the temporary restriction on the applicant's freedom of movement, assessing whether there had been developments in the situation that made the measure unjustified or disproportionate. The Court therefore unanimously decided that the complaint manifestly ill-founded pursuant to article 35, para. 3 and 4 ECHR.

III Right to a Fair Trial

With the *Ajmone Marsan and others* judgment (No. 21925/15) of 10 January 2019, the ECtHR ruled on the alleged violation of the right to a trial within a reasonable length of time pursuant to article 6 para. 1 ECHR. On 20 November 1986, the applicants presented a complaint to the Lazio Regional Administrative Court, which, on 1 February 2011, rejected the application. In 2011, the applicants presented complaints on the excessive length of proceedings in front of the Perugia Court of Appeal, pursuant to the so-called Pinto Act (l. No. 89/2011). These complaints were declared inadmissible by the Court of Appeal, since during the administrative proceedings, the applicants had not presented a withdrawal request which, pursuant to article 54 of law-decree No. 112 of 25 June 2008, was one of the conditions of admissibility for Pinto procedures. The ECtHR recalled that the procedure to complain about the excessive length of an administrative court case does not constitute an effective remedy pursuant to article 13 of the ECHR (*Olivieri and others v. Italy*, Nos. 17708/12 and 3 others, 25 February 2016, see *Yearbook* 2017, p. 312). Since it was evidently in the interest of both parties to deal with the appeals in a reasonable time (given that they presented a request to set the date of the hearing in front of the Regional Administrative Court twice), the Court held that 25 years of proceedings exceeded the reasonable length of proceedings as established by article 6 para. 1 ECHR. The Court therefore found a violation of article 6 para. 1 ECHR, but did not order any compensation payment since the applicants had not applied for just satisfaction.

On 22 January 2019, the ECtHR decided to strike the *Ugliano* (No. 53247/10) and *Capua and others* cases (No. 53787/11 and 66122/11) which had been presented for excessive length of civil proceedings in light of article 6 ECHR – though pursuant to article 39, the dispute had already been resolved. In all cases, the Italian State offered a friendly settlement, offering compensation payments for damages and expenses. In the *Di Blasi and others* (No. 42256/12), *Barone* (No. 64105/13) and *Della Rocca* (No. 16627/16) cases on the same subject, the Court held that, under article 37 para. 1 letter c, and given the copious amount of case-law on excessive length of civil proceedings in Italy (*Bozza v. Italia*, No. 17739/09, 14 September 2017, see *Yearbook 2018*, pp. 312–313), the unilateral proposal made by the Italian State to resolve the case through quarterly payments no longer justified the existence and continuation of the examination of the appeal.

On 31 January 2019, the ECtHR decided to strike the *Abagnale and Sicignano* case (Nos. 69795/14 and 69800/14) from the list. The case was presented pursuant to article 6 ECHR for excessive length of administrative judicial procedure and inefficiency of the "pinto" compensation remedy due to its new condition of admissibility of the complaint (i.e. the urgent request to arrange a date for the hearing (withdrawal request) in the main procedure). The controversy was resolved by friendly settlement pursuant to article 39 ECHR.

On 14 February 2019, the ECtHR decided to strike by friendly settlement (pursuant to article 39 ECHR) the *Masetti and others* case (No. 4281/04 and 161 others); on 7 March 2019, the *Ricci and others* case (No. 43420/06 and 13 other cases); on 21 March 2019, the *Fraccola and others* case (No. 36358/07; 25183/09; 35659/16); on 16 May 2019, the *Muratore and others* case (No. 5740/19); on 14 November 2019, the *Sconamiglio* case (No. 32082/15), which presented an application pursuant to article 6 ECHR and article 1 of the protocol No. 1 to the ECHR for the missing or late implementation of internal court decisions. On the same subject, on 14 February 2019, the ECtHR decided to strike the *Biagini and others* case (No. 43089/04 and 116 other cases) and on 7 March 2019, the *Capozzi and others* case (No. 11543/

04 and 839 other cases) holding that the unilateral proposal made by the Italian State to resolve the case through quarterly payments no longer justified the existence and continuation of the examination of the appeal pursuant to article 37 para. 1 letter c.

In the *Arnaboldi* case (No. 43422/07), with a judgment of 14 March 2019, the ECtHR ruled on the ongoing case of an indirect expropriation through with the applicant had been deprived of his land which had been bought by the Government and transformed irreversibly. The public administration, through ANAS asked a private real estate company to carry out the work on their behalf and, therefore, to enforce the expropriation procedure. The applicant had already filed a claim with the Florence Court of Appeal and through their judgment obtained the right to compensation from the private company. The applicant had, however, never received this compensation due to the company going into "extraordinary administration". The Court recognised that, in this case, the responsibility of the State cannot be excluded just because it had decided to exercise its power to delegate the work to a private company. State responsibility to exercise power that subsequently have an effect on rights and freedoms protected by the ECHR exists regardless of how these powers are exercised even if these are delegated to a private companies or individuals (*Sychev v. Ukraine*, No. 4773/02, 11 October 2005, and *Kotov v. Russia* [GC], No. 54522/00, 3 April 2012). According to the Court, in the case at hand, the State is responsible for not taking necessary measures for the applicant to receive the due compensation. The Court stated that the Government, as the delegating administration, is responsible and cannot refuse to enforce a final judgment against a company in a state of insolvency. Therefore, the Court held that there had been a violation of the right of the applicant to a fair hearing pursuant to article 6 para. 1 ECHR which protects the right to see a binding and definite judgment enforced, as it is considered an integrant part of a trial pursuant to the article (*Bourdov v. Russia*, No. 59498/00, 7 May 2002) and the violation of the right to property established by article 1 of the protocol 1 according to which a credit, especially if definitive and collectable, can be considered an asset. The Government was ordered to pay €880,000 in compensation for pecuniary damage and non-pecuniary damage for the failure to pay the compensation awarded to the applicant by the Florence Court of Appeal

On 16 May 2019, the ECtHR decided to strike the *Adami and others* (No. 26056/07) and *Aiello* cases (No. 20035/07) which had been presented pursuant to article 6 ECHR for legislative interference in pending legal proceedings. The Italian State recognised these interferences, and presented a unilateral proposal to resolve the cases through monetary payments. Given the clear and ample ECtHR case-law on legislative interference in pending legal proceedings in Italy, the Court held that admission of the Government and the proposed amount of money, the continuation of the examination of the appeal was no longer justifiable pursuant to article 37 para. 1 letter c.

On 18 June 2019, the ECtHR declared the *Valia* case (No. 16320/14 and 7 others) inadmissible. The case was presented pursuant to article 6 ECHR for excessive length of proceedings for administrative decisions which had been taken on access to the civil service and, pursuant to article 13 ECHR, for the ineffective "Pinto" remedy alongside provisions on a withdrawal request. However, the Court found the complaint to be inadmissible as it had been presented after the 6-month limit, from the date of the final internal decision pursuant to article 35 para. 1 ECHR.

The *La Posta* case (No. 5425/10) was declared inadmissible by the ECtHR on 8 October 2019. The complaint was presented pursuant to article 6 ECHR for excessive length of real estate enforcement proceedings. The applicant was the part owner of some real estate properties subjected to foreclosure, of which he had been nominated the legal guardian. The excessive length of proceedings was due to many different factors: the difficulty in selling the foreclosed properties, the intervention of many creditors, the procedure coinciding with another enforcement proceeding, and the co-ownership of all the foreclosed properties. To make a decision on the case, the Court verified its admissibility pursuant to article 35 ECHR, in particular para. 3 letter b, which foresees the inadmissibility of a complaint in which the applicant has not suffered serious harm, unless the case has been duly examined by an internal court. Therefore, the ECtHR assessed whether the specific circumstances of the case (*Korolev v. Russia*, No. 25551/05, 1 July 2010) meet the minimum threshold requirements for the seriousness of the situation, considering the "right allegedly violated, the seriousness of the incidence of the violation inferred in the exercise of a right and/or any consequences of the violation on the personal situation of the applicant" (*Giusti v. Italia*, No. 13175/03, 18 October 2011, see *Yearbook 2012*, p. 356). In light of these elements, in the case at hand, the Court did not find that the applicant had suffered any serious harm, above all because he had the opportunity to reduce the procedure times. Pursuant to article 495 of the Civil Procedures Code, the applicant could have not only converted the foreclosures into a payment of the equivalent sum of money as credit, but also, as the legal guardian, he could have profited from the gains of the foreclosed properties (especially rents) to pay their debtors. Pursuant to article 35 para. 3 ECHR, the ECtHR therefore decided to not continue examining the complaint as: the applicant had not suffered any substantial harm; respect for human rights (as guaranteed by the Convention or its Protocols) did not require any examination on the merits; and the complaint had already been thoroughly examined by an internal court, given that the appeals judge and the judges of the Court of Cassation (pursuant to the "Pinto" Act) had examined the request for compensation put forward by the applicant.

On 14 November 2019, the ECtHR decided to strike the following cases by friendly settlement: pursuant to article 39 ECHR, the *Violi* case (No. 34279/09), the *Scottoni* case (50294/10 and 39 others), *Cerfoglia* (No. 50295/10 and 44 other cases), *Poletti* (No. 50328/10 and 13 others) and *Canale and others* (Nos. 41107/18 41111/18 42563/18); and pursuant to article 37 para. 1 letter c ECHR, the *Caratti and others* case (No. 29827/10) *Stefanelli* (No. 43180/11), *Provenzano* (No. 3602/15), *Passaseo* (No. 46798/11), *Pisino* (No. 46804/11), *Vesuvio* (No. 4488/14), *Pisino* (No. 30814/14), *Letizia* (No. 32026/14) and *Maghini* (No. 50297/10 and 44 others). The applicants complained of a violation of article 6 ECHR and of article 1 protocol 1 to the ECHR, introduced with the Budget Law for 2007 (l. 296/2006), of an interpretive law with retroactive effect on pension calculations which harmed Italian citizens who had already earned the right to a certain level of pension after working in Switzerland. The applicants argued that this was contrary to the principles of a fair trial and the division of power. The Italian Government recognised that there had been a violation of article 6 ECHR in these cases, in light of ECtHR case-law (*Maggio and others No.* 46286/09 52851/08, 53727/08, 54486/08 and 56001/08 of 31 May 2011; see *Yearbook 2012*, p. 347–8 and *Stefanetti and others* No. 21838/10 and 7 others of 15 April 2014; see *Yearbook 2015*, p. 320), and therefore decided to award each applicant with compensation in respect of non-pecuniary damage and of costs and expenses.

On 14 November 2019, the Court decided to On 14 November 2019, the Court decided to strike the *Galiotta and Rosafio* cases (Nos. 30344/18 and 31236/18) (on the alleged legislative interference in legal proceedings pursuant to article 6 para. 1 ECHR and article 1 protocol 1 to the ECHR) and also the *Schievano* case (No. 4277/11) (on the alleged failure to hold a public hearing during a procedure to apply preventative measures pursuant to article 6 ECHR). The cases were struck as the applicants had not presented their cases within the deadline set out by Court requests, the circumstance of which was interpreted as the non-intention of the applicants to continue with their complaint, pursuant to article 37 para. 1 ECHR.

With the *Scervino and Scaglioni* judgment (No. 35516/13) of 5 December 2019, the ECtHR ruled on a violation of the "reasonable length" of an administrative judicial procedure pursuant to article 6 para. 1 ECHR. The applicants presented their complaint in front of the Tuscany Regional Administrative Court in 1998 and 2011, and had begun a "Pinto" procedure which concluded in the recognition of the excessive length of the case by the Genoa Court of Appeal. However, this decision was annulled by the Court of Cassation in 2013, as, during proceedings in front of the Regional Administrative Court, the applicants had not presented a withdrawal request, which is a new condition for admission of "Pinto" complaints, introduced by law-decree No. 112 of 25 June 2008. The applicants also complained of lack of effective remedy pursuant to article 13 ECHR of the Pinto complaint following the introduction of these new admission conditions. The Court recognised a violation of article 13 ECHR, since, in line with the *Olivieri and others v. Italy* judgment (Nos. 17708/12 and 3 others, 25 February 2016, see *Yearbook 2017*, p. 312) as shown by the joint reading of article 54, para. 2, of law-decree No. 112 of 2008 (amended by legislative decree No. 102 of 2010) and of the "Pinto Act", a Pinto complaint cannot be considered an effective remedy pursuant to article 13 ECHR. Furthermore, the Court recognised a violation of article 6 para. 1 ECHR for exceeding reasonable length of proceedings, given that the first instance of justice had lasted 13 years, without adopting any information or arguments to justify such a duration, and the two requests to fix the date of a hearing had not had any effect. The Government was sentenced to paying €12,200 in compensation in respect of non-pecuniary damage and of costs and expenses.

IV Private and Family Life

In the *Cordella and others* case (No. 54414/13 and No. 54264/15 judgment of 24 January 2019), the ECtHR decided to jointly examine complaints by various applicants living in Taranto and the surrounding areas, from a right to private life perspective pursuant to article 8 ECHR. The applicants' complained that the damage caused by pollution from toxic emissions from the steel plant in Taranto and the lack of legal and administrative measures taken to ensure the de-pollution of the area to protect the health of its workers and the environment. The Court, stating the inadmissibility of an *actio pupularis* (*Perez v. France* [GC], No. 47287/99, 12 February 2004, and *Di Sarno and others v. Italia*, No. 30765/08, 10 January 2012, see *Yearbook 2013*, pp. 321–322) and the lack of general environmental protection pursuant to the ECHR (*Kyrtatos v. Greece*, No. 41666/98, 22 May 2003), highlighted that it could only assess whether the environmental damage had a detrimental effect on the family and private lives of the individuals, compromising their well-being or depriving them of the enjoyment of their homes (*López Ostra v. Spain*, No. 16798/90, 9 December 1994, *Guerra and others v. Italia*, No. 14967/89, 19 February 1998). Article 8 ECHR imposes positive obligations on the State, other than abstaining from arbitrary interferences: adopting necessary measures to regulate authorising, commissioning, exploiting, securing and checking dangerous activities. Furthermore, in this specific case, the Court assessed whether the national authorities had acted with due diligence in its evaluation of all interested parties involved in trying to effectively reduce pollution. To this end, scientific studies going back to 1970 were taken into consideration showing the health and environmental effects of the toxic emissions from the steelwork plant and the lack of measures taken from 2012 onwards by the Integrated Environmental Authorisation (AIA) to reduce pollution. This also led to an infraction procedure in front of the European Court of Justice (C-50/10 judgment of 31 March 2011). In light of these circumstances, the ECtHR ruled that the national authorities had not taken necessary measures to effectively protect the right to private life of the persons involved. In particular, the adoption of urgent measures by the Government (the Save-Ilva decrees) to ensure the continued running of the steelworks despite the fact that the judicial authorities identified a serious risk to the health and life of the workers were found in violation of article 8 ECHR by the Court. It was found that it did not respect the balance between "the interest of the applicants to not suffer grave damage to the environment that would compromise their private life and, on the other hand, the interests of the company as a whole". Therefore, the ECtHR ordered the full reimbursement of the applicants' legal fees, finding that the violation was sufficient to receive just satisfaction.

In the *Minervino and Trausi* case (No. 63289/17), with the judgment of 12 February 2019, the ECtHR ruled on the controversy on the compatibility between the right to respect for family life (pursuant to article 8 ECHR) and housing the five children of the applicant firstly in a foster home and subsequently in foster families. From 2008 onwards, the applicant family had been looked into by social services due to the poor hygiene conditions and the parents' emotional, educational and learning incapacity, (one of whom was alcohol dependent) and their inability to take care of and provide for the children's needs. Social services had therefore requested that the children be removed from the parents and be placed in a fostering institution, which took place in 2009 under the authority of the Juvenile Court – the three eldest children were placed in institutional care and were able to visit the parents at weekends. These visits were suspended in 2014, when the Court ordered that parental authority over the children should be suspended, and that all children (including the youngest born in 2012) should be housed in an institution. This was due to: the youngest child contracting scabies from the deterioration of the hygiene conditions in the home; the further deterioration of the social and environmental situation despite the social, economic and parental support actions implemented by social services since 2008; and the continued refusal of the applicant to undergo therapy to overcome alcohol addiction. Furthermore, given the lack of interest shown by the parents towards their children (demonstrated by the very few visits they made to the institution), the desire expressed by the children to not return to their family home and the persistent incapacity of the parents to take care of the children (having not collaborated with the authorities or changed their lifestyles), and despite continued support from social services, in 2015, the Juvenile Court declared that the children could be put up for adoption. The parents presented a complaint against this decision, in particular, the mother requested an evaluation of her parental capacity. The Court of Appeal rejected the complaint and did not order an expert opinion, considering that the various social services reports and the Juvenile Court investigation were sufficient to assess the applicants' parental capabilities. For the same reasons, the Court of Cassation rejected the complaint in 2017. The Court noted that interference in family life, as protected by article 8 ECHR, is admissible only where it is "in accordance with the law", is pursuing one or more legitimate objective, and is "necessary in a democratic society" to achieve them (*Gnahoré v. France*, No. 40031/98, 19 September 2000). The notion of "necessity" implies an interference based on an essential social need and, above all, an interference which is proportionate to the legal aim it is pursuing (*Couillard Maugery v. France*, No. 64796/01, 1 July 2004). The Court also evaluated whether (according to para. 2 of article 8 ECHR) the adoption measure is necessary in a democratic society, as it constitutes a grave interference in family life: during this evaluation, the ECtHR considered the best interest of the child. Furthermore, recalling that, wherever a family connection exists, pursuant to article 8 ECHR, the State has an obligation to favour the adoption of appropriate measures in order to unite the parent and child (*Kutzner v. Germany*, No. 46544/99, 26 February 2002) – the removal of a child from a family environment can only take place as a last possible course of action (*Neulinger and Shuruk v. Switzerland*, [GC], No. 41615/07, 6 July 2010). Therefore, the Court examined whether, before allowing a permanent adoption process to begin, the judges should have assessed and adopted all possible measures to facilitate the parent/child bond.

To this end, the ECtHR considered that the adoption had been arranged six years after the undertaking of the family by the authorities, also recognising that maintaining contact between the children and their parents had always been a priority of the authorities during these 6 years. In light of the fact that, despite the support and assistance offered throughout the period by the social services, there had been a further deterioration of the family and social environment and no improvement of the applicants' parental capacity or the bond between them and their children had emerged (as happens in many social services cases), the ECtHR decided that it was necessary to place the children in a more protected environment. The Court also noted that the specific measures adopted were the result of a careful examination of the situation of the applicants and the children, and also the result of the children's requests. The ECtHR unanimously declared the complaint inadmissible as manifestly ill-founded pursuant to article 35 para. 3 and 4 ECHR.

With the judgment of 14 February 2019 in the *Narjis* case (No. 57433/15), the ECtHR ruled on the complaint of a violation of the right to respect for private and family life pursuant to article 8 ECHR by the Italian authorities who refused to renew the residence permit of the applicant, residing in Italy, and consequently expelled him from Italy to Morocco, forcing him to leave his family who also reside in Italy. The authorities had decided to not renew his residence permit to protect public order, in light of his numerous convictions for criminal offences (including for aggravated theft, handling stolen goods, possession and carrying of illegal weapons, and evasion) and a trend of reoffending. The Court considered that, given the very long period (20 years) that Mr Narjis had been resident in Italy, the refusal to renew his residence permit and the decision to remove him from the national territory had amounted to an interference with his right to respect for private life (*Hasanbasic v. Switzerland*, No. 52166/09, 11 June 2013 and *K.M. v. Switzerland*, No. 6009/10, 2 June 2015), but not family life, given his status as an unmarried man with no children (*Slivenko v. Latvia* [GC], No. 48321/99, 9 October 2003). The Court noted that any interference must be necessary in a democratic society in light of the criteria set out in *Üner v. The Netherlands* ECtHR judgment (No. 46410/99, 18 October 2006). According to the Court, these criteria were weighed up both by the Council of State and by the Lombardy Regional Administrative Court, which had examined the complaint presented by the applicant against his expulsion decree. In view of his criminal record, regular use of drugs and his apparent inability to integrate into professional life and that if he were to return to Italy, he would have had to serve a prison sentence of four years and six months for receiving stolen goods, the Court did not find a violation of article 8 of the ECHR in the domestic judges' decision.

In the *R.V.* case (No. 37748/13), the ECtHR with the judgment of 18 July 2019 ruled on the complaint of a violation of the right to respect for private and family life pursuant to article 8 ECHR caused by the decision to take the children of the first applicant into the care of the local authorities. In particular, not only were the parents of the children complaining that the fostering placement (while temporary) had gone on for over ten years, they also noted that its extension was not supported by sufficient reasons. Furthermore, the applicants claimed that the fostering process did not prioritise reunifying the children with their biological parents, as shown by the limitations of the family visits (which from weekly became monthly, and in some periods were suspend altogether). Therefore, the parents complained that custody without any judicial measure had turned into an adoption which constitutes a measure of last resort that must be justified by ascertaining the lack of parental suitability. The Court therefore assessed whether the interference into the applicant's family life was necessary in a democratic society. These interferences were established by the law pursuant to articles 333 and 336 of the Civil Code and aim to safeguard the "health and morale" and the "rights and freedoms" of children. In this case, the Court noted that the temporary fostering should aim at reunifying the family by taking all necessary measures (*Covezzi and Morselli v. Italia*, No. 52763/99, 9 May 2003, *R.M.S. v. Spain*, No. 28775/12, 18 June 2013). The Court noted that in the case at hand, custody was arranged on the basis of a temporary measure that is foreseen in case of urgent need that does not allow for long-term custody outside the family. According to the Court, these provisions were adopted within judicial decision-making processes which presented (from the first judgment in 2005 onwards) critical issues on the lack of diligence and promptness of technical appraisals delivered to the Courts. Furthermore, over ten years, the Juvenile Court assigned with monitoring the situation only ruled once on the need to extend the custody provisions. Therefore, the Court stated a series on doubts with respect to the care requirements and exceptional diligence of the Italian Authorities which should be carried out in the best interests of the children. In light of the various delays and unlimited extensions to these temporary measures foreseen specifically for emergency situations, with no provision of the duration of the measures or its judicial review, which led to the uninterrupted removal of children from their parents for over 10 years, the Court unanimously found a violation of article 8 ECHR, ordering the payment of €50,000 in compensation in respect of non-pecuniary damage and of costs and expenses.

On 17 September 2019, the ECtHR declared the *Raimondo* case (No. 42401/13) inadmissible. The case dealt with the intolerable acoustic and light emissions suffered daily by the applicant on his property due to the construction of a prison about forty metres from his home and the failure of the authorities to take steps to ensure effective respect of private and family life pursuant to article 8 ECHR. The ECtHR held that, pursuant to article 35 para. 1, the applicant had not exhausted all domestic remedies. The Court noted the applicant had not filed the complaint pursuant to article 844 of the Italian Civil Code to halt the emissions and an eventual compliance judgment if the administration failed to observe the judgment. Due to the subsidiary nature of the ECtHR, the applicant did not give the national authorities the opportunity to prevent or remedy the violation of the Conventions. Furthermore, the Court sustained that there was no evidence that these elements would have brought adequate compensation to the applicant, and that the mere presence of doubts about the potential success of a given remedy does not constitute a valid reason to justify the non-use of a domestic remedy (*Sejdovic v. Italia* [GC],

No. 56581/00, 1 March 2006, *Alberto Eugénio da Conceicao v. Portugal*, No. 74044/11, 29 May 2012).

In the *Luzi* judgment (No. 48322/17) of December 2019 the complaint deals with the violation of the right to respect of family life pursuant to article 8 ECHR. According to the applicant, exercising his full right to visit his daughter for eight years running was rendered difficult. For this reason, the applicant complained that, despite the numerous court decisions recognising his right to visit the child, the Italian Authorities did not take the measures necessary for him to effectively exercise that right, particularly considering the mother's lack of respect for the courts' decisions and the instructions given by social services. According to the applicant, this situation caused a state of parental alienation and a progressive estrangement from the daughter. The ECtHR stated that article 8 ECHR does not aim at blocking arbitrary interferences in family life, but also imposes positive duties that, in this context, include facilitating contact between parents and children to maintain emotional attachment (*Bondavalli v. Italia*, No. 35532/12, 17 November 2015, see *Yearbook 2016*, pp. 265–266), taking all necessary preparatory measures to reach this objective (*Nuutinen v. Finland*, No. 32842/96, 2000, *Ignaccolo-Zenide v. Romania*, No. 31679/96, 25 January 2000, *Sylvester v. Austria*, Nos. 36812/97 and 40104/98, 24 April 2003). The Court notes that since 2010 (when the child was one year old) the applicant had repeatedly asked to recognise his right to visit his daughter. Although this right had been recognised by various court decisions, the applicant had only been able to exercise this right in very limited situations, due to the opposition of the mother. The damaging behaviour of the mother was reported to the judicial authorities multiple times, both by the applicant and the social services. In 2015, the Court of Appeal, following expert intervention, conceded the care of the child to the social services. Despite further complaints to the Court of Appeal after 2015 by the social services and the applicant regarding the manipulative attitude of the mother and the continued incapability of the father to exercise his right to visit the child, the authorities did not take any further measures. Concerning the persistent opposition of the child's mother to allow the father's visits, the Court noted that the national authorities had not adopted all necessary measures, which should be reasonably be put in place in order to respect the right of the applicant to maintain contact with his daughter and establish a relationship with her (*Strumia v. Italia*, No. 53377/13, 23 June 2016, see

Yearbook 2017, p. 248). Given the failure to adopt measures to respect the visiting rights of the applicant, the Court therefore unanimously held that there had been a violation of the right to respect of family life of the applicant pursuant to article 8 ECHR. The Italian Government was ordered to pay €23,000 in compensation in respect of non-pecuniary damage and of costs and expenses.

V Freedom of Expression

In the *Sallusti* case (No. 22350/13) with the judgment of 7 March 2019, the ECtHR ruled on the complaint of a violation of freedom of expression pursuant to article 10 ECHR of the applicant. The applicant was charged with libel and sentenced to imprisonment pursuant to article 13 of law 8 February 1948 No. 47 pursuant to article 57 of the Criminal Code. As the director of a newspaper, the applicant had failed to proofread an article which had been submitted by an anonymous author. The article in question contained false information on a case concerning a minor, despite the clarifications disseminated the day prior to their publication, and tarnished the reputation of the persons involved. Therefore, the Court assessed whether the interference in the right to the freedom of expression had been necessary in a democratic society, determining: a) whether it corresponded to a "pressing social need"; and b) whether it was justified by the Italian Authorities for "relevant and sufficient" reasons; c) and whether the sanction imposed was "proportionate to the legitimate aim pursued" (*Belpietro v. Italia*, No. 43612/10, 24 September 2013, see *Yearbook 2014*, p. 249). The ECtHR found that the interference corresponded to a "pressing social need", given the false information of the news reported on a minor, its defamatory nature towards all those involved and the obligation of a newspaper director to check such articles. On the proportionality of the sanctions issued, the Court noted that the provision of a prison sentence for libel is in compliance with the freedom of expression of journalists (guaranteed by article 10 ECHR) only in exceptional circumstances. The Court therefore found that there was no justification for the imposed prison sentence, even if suspended and commuted to a fine through an *ad hoc* provision of the President of the Republic, given the absence of exceptional circumstances, such as the infringement of other fundamental rights that may occur for example in cases of hate speech and instigating violence. The Court also noted that (as also observed by opinion No. 715/2013 of the Venice Commission of 9 November 2013) prison sentences for the crime of defamation as established by article 13 of law 8 February 1948 No. 47 are the subject of parliamentary debate and a reform bill (bill 925 presented by Hon. Costa). The bill is currently under revision for a second reading before the Senate Standing Committee on Justice, proposing the removal of imprisonment as a sanction. In the case at hand, the Court found that there had been a violation of article 10 ECHR as the prison sentence was disproportionate to the legitimate aim invoked and unnecessary in a democratic society. The Italian Government was therefore ordered to pay €12,000 in compensation in respect of non-pecuniary damage and €5,000 in respect of costs and expenses.

VI Right to Private Property and to Peaceful Enjoyment of Possessions

The *Colazzo and others* case (No. 36944/06) was found manifestly ill-founded and therefore rejected pursuant to article 35 para. 3 and 4. The applicants complained of not receiving "sufficient and appropriate" compensation due to the taxes imposed on them in light of law No. 413 of 1991 and the and the fact that no award had been made in respect of non-pecuniary damage they had suffered as a consequence of being unlawfully deprived of their property, violating their right to peaceful enjoyment of their possessions based on article 1 of protocol 1 to the ECHR. The ECtHR recognised that the Lecce Court of Appeal acknowledged that the deprivation of property had been unlawful and had been entitled to compensation in conformity with the criteria established by the case-law (*Armando Iannelli v. Italy* No. 24818/03, 12 February 2013, see *Yearbook 2014*, p. 325). It found that the taxes implemented had also been justified considering the wide margin of appreciation that each State enjoys in the area of taxation.

In the *Condominio Porta Rufina* (No. 14346/05) and *Mideo* (No. 19169/02) judgments of 6 June 2019, the ECtHR ruled on the violation of the respect for private good pursuant to article 1 of protocol 1 to the ECHR. The applicants had been deprived of their property through indirect expropriation as a result of the irreversible transformation of their assets. In light of the principles established in ECtHR case-law on indirect expropriation (*Belvedere Alberghiera S.r.l. v. Italy*, No. 31524/96, 30 May 2000, *Scordino v. Italy* (No. 3), No. 43662/98, 17 May 2005, and *Velocci v. Italy*,

No. 1717/03, 18 March 2008), in this case at hand, the Court decided that there had been an illegal occupation of the terrain, of which the administration was able to take advantage. Without a formal expropriation act, the principle of indirect expropriation can be considered effectively applied and the land acquisition by public authorities can be legitimised only with a final legal provision rending the deprivation of the right of ownership predictable in light of the principle of legal certainty. In both cases, given that several years had passed between the loss of the property and the final legal decision, the Court found it incompatible with the legality principle of interferences and therefore, in both cases, a violation of the right to peaceful enjoyment of possessions pursuant to article 1 protocol 1 to the ECHR. Furthermore, in the *Mideo* case, having passed 10 years on one level of judicial proceeding, the Court found that, considering the sums acknowledged in similar cases concerning a failure to take the "reasonable length of time" clause into account, Rome Court of Appeal (conceding only €600 in compensation in respect of non-pecuniary damage to the applicant) had not afforded a sufficient and adequate remedy for the violation. Therefore, the Court held that there was a violation of article 6 para. 1 ECHR.

On 6 June 2019, the ECtHR decided to strike the *AZ S.R.L.* case (No. 9284/10), which had been presented in reference to article 1 of protocol 1 to the ECHR for the failure to receive compensation following the lack of opportunity to profit from land in public domain on which the individual had been given a thirty-year (renewable) leasehold and public funds to create a tourist project. The Italian Government recognised the violation and unilaterally proposed to settle the case with a payment of €30,000 in compensation in respect of non-pecuniary damage and of costs and expenses. The applicant considered the sum unsatisfactory since it was not sufficient to cover neither the emerging damage nor the loss of profits. Given the Government's declaration and the circumstances of the situation, the ECtHR considered the proposed compensation to be appropriate and that pursuant to article 37 para. 1 letter c, further examination of the case is not justified.

In the *Zappa S.A.S* judgment (No. 43842/11) of 4 July 2019, the ECtHR ruled on a complaint of a violation of the right to respect for property pursuant to article 1 protocol 1, as the applicant (a company managing fishing valleys) had been intimidated by the Padova Revenue Office to vacate the bodies of water she had been occupying on the grounds that they were State property, and to pay the State compensation for damages caused by her *sine titulo* occupation. The complaint is very similar to that in *Valle Pierimpiè Società Agricola S.p.A. v. Italy* (No. 46154/11) judgment of 23 September 2014 (see *Yearbook 2015*, p. 324). In this decision, the Court recognised that, before being intimidated to vacate the fishing valley that she occupied, the applicant had a legitimate expectation connected to her financial interest which was sufficiently important to constitute a substantial interest as protected by the Convention (*Di Marco v. Italia*, No. 32521/05, 26 April 2011, see *Yearbook* 2012, p. 358) and a 'property' with regard the applicability of article 1 of protocol No. 1. On this occasion, the Court found an interference to the right to respect of the applicant's property pursuant to article 1 of protocol No. 1 to the ECHR, as her property had been bought by the State, and the applicant had lost any possibility to assert her claim. This interference was carried out without compensation for the deprivation of the property of the individual. Furthermore, the Court considered that imposing additional burdens on the applicant, like paying a fee for unlawful occupation in the Pierimpiè Valley was disproportionate for the legitimate aims pursued, that is to protect the environment and ecosystem of the laguna and to ensure effective public use of the area. The Court therefore found a violation of article 1 protocol 1 to the ECHR in the case at hand, given the similarity of the two cases.

Italy in the Case-law of the Court of Justice of the European Union*

I Rights of Justices of the Peace to Paid Leave

Some decisions of the ECJ declared the request for a preliminary ruling made by some of the Italian Justices of the Peace is manifestly inadmissible. The case questioned the compatibility of Italian law with EU law that set out that Justices of the Peace (as honorary magistrates) were paid on the basis of their fixed-term work contract with a salary calculated on each hearing or trial assigned to them, while not being considered public employees and without benefitting from paid holidays (which ordinary judges are able to take) – despite the amount of work that they do – even though the amount of work carried out is the same as other judges. According to the referral court, these provisions are not in compliance with article 31(2) CFR of the EU ("Every worker has the right to limitation of maximum working hours, to daily and weekly rest periods and to an annual period of paid leave"). Moreover, in referral orders, it has already been recognised that the Justices of the Peace should not deal with these disputes, which should be under the scope of labour or administrative judges. However, since a judgment of the Joint Sections of the Court of Cassation 2017 explicitly banned the Labour Court and the Regional Administrative Court from ruling on causes relating to holidays raised by the Justices of the Peace, the latter are the only judicial body willing to address the issue raised by their colleagues. In their opinion, this circumstance constitutes a possible contradiction with EU law, in particular with article 47 CFR of the EU, which recognises the right to a fair and public hearing within a reasonable time by an independent and impartial tribunal previously established by law. The conflict of interest that may occur when a Justice of the Peace is called to rule on the right

* Paolo De Stefani

to paid leave for honorary judges is therefore clear. The ECJ declared that these preliminary requests were manifestly inadmissible as there is a lack of jurisdiction of the referring court to adjudicate on the dispute in the main proceedings (as admitted by the applicants themselves). The ECJ was requested to provide an opinion on the alleged anomaly of Italian law on this issue, which would be able to produce some concrete judicial effect and therefore incompatible with the aims of article 267 TFEU. (see cases C-600/17; C-626/17; C-618/18).

II Unconditional Right of Pre-emption Granted to Employees of the Pharmacy Being Sold

Italian law foresees that if a municipal pharmacy is sold to private ownership, the pharmacy employees enjoy a right of pre-emption to that service. Other pharmacists complained that this contravened the principles of free competition and equal treatment, all of whom had participated in a public tender, submitting their most economically advantageous bid for the business. On the contrary, given their confidence in their right of pre-emption, that pharmacy employees had not even participated in the public tender. The Council of State requested that the ECJ clarify whether Italian law contradicts the principles of freedom to choose an occupation and right to engage in work (article 15 CFR of the EU) and with the freedom to conduct a business (article 16 CFR of the EU), considering that the law favouring the former employees also contributed to preventing pharmacists from other EU countries from working in Italy, contravening article 49 TFEU on the right to establishment ("restrictions on the freedom of establishment of nationals of a Member State in the territory of another Member State shall be prohibited"). The ECJ states that an unconditional right of pre-emption to pharmacists employed by a municipal pharmacy (that allows them to become the owner of a pharmacy without participating in the call for tenders) could be justified in the interest of the best management of the pharmacy, and therefore in the interest of the protection of the health of citizens. There is no reason to think that a former employee is necessarily preferable to a pharmacist with the same qualifications and experience, but who has previously worked elsewhere. The Italian law must therefore be disregarded (ECJ, case C-465/18).

III Protection of the PDO Brand

Over the years, the EU has set out a vast array of laws to protect "typical" agricultural food and production. Designation of origin comes within the rights of industrial and commercial property that are protected in EU law through regulations and frameworks, as well as the laws of Member States themselves. Therefore, according to the ECJ, the rules introduced by the Italian laws and ministerial regulations (which state that *Mozzarella di Bufala Campana* PDO (Protected designation of origin) must take place) must be produced in spaces that are completely separate from those used to store or process other types of milk that cannot be used in Mozzarella di Bufala Campana PDO production), is perfectly in compliance with EU law. Some dairies complained that the specific clause stipulating the separate processing spaces for PDO and non-PDO production imposed excessive costs, leading to discrimination among companies. The ECJ instead held that the protection of the reputational value of PDO production justified, the rigorous provisions of Italian law, which make monitoring of each production phase very efficient and prevents any contamination (whether intentional or accident) of packaging of PDO mozzarella with milk that comes from areas outside the protected buffalo farming zone (ECJ, case C-569/18).

IV Customer Protection and Unfair Practices of Gas and Electricity Companies

Some of the main companies providing electricity and gas were fined by the Italian Competition Authority (AGCM) for contravening regulations with aggressive commercial practices using contracts not requested by the consumer and concluded via telephone or by representatives at home. These practices were found to be contrary to EU law provisions on unfair commercial practices between companies and consumers – transposed into Italian law through the Consumer Code (lgs.d. 206/2005). The competence of the AGCM to impose these fines was challenged by the companies in question, since a different public agency (The Authority for Electrical, Gas and Hydrosystems Energy (AGEECSI), which in 2017 became the ARERA: Regulation Authority for Energy, Networks and the Environment) monitors the electrical and natural gas providers, according to specific EU directives and corresponding Italian law. The Council of State put this issue to the ECJ: whether Italian law on the AGCM's monitoring of unfair practices of companies providing electricity and natural gas is in compliance with EU law within this sector. The ECJ ruled that the application of Consumer Protection laws (attributing the AGCM with the competence to fine electricity and gas companies) should take priority over energy distribution market regulations, moreover given that market regulations have substantially left the issue of consumer protection up to the AGCM monitoring processes (ECJ, joint cause C-406/17, C-407/2017, C-408/17; C-417/17).

V EU Law and Italian Criminal Proceedings

EU directive 2012/29 invited States to introduce measures for victims of crime, including the right to receive compensation as part of criminal proceedings (if domestic legislation foresees the establishment of a civil action) and the right to not sustain other forms of victimisation and secondary victimisation. The law, established by the Italian Criminal Procedure Code, on renewing evidence (including the testimony of a victim of a crime), challenges these principles, in the event that there has been a change in the composition of the judging panel, it is not sufficient to read the minutes of previous declared to the new panel. In a case presented in front of the Bari District Court, the judge decided to forward the issue to the ECJ for a preliminary ruling. One of the three judges (who was in the process of commenting on accusations of fraud and money-laundering) was assigned to another location and therefore, due to a request by one of the defendants, it was necessary to renew the witness of one of the victims of fraud. The circumstance, however, risked exposing the victim (who became a civil party) to further pressure, as well as an inevitable lengthening of the timing of any compensation, contrary to the aims of Directive 2012/29. The ECJ (judgment in C-38/18) was called on to balance protecting the right to defend oneself in court and protecting the victims of crime (article 52 CFR of the EU). The Court concluded that Italian law setting out the renewal of witnesses under discussion before the same panel of judges which then rule on the criminal judgment does not necessarily disproportionately compromise the right of a victim of crime to receive compensation and to enjoy necessary protection; it is the duty of the judge to assess on a case-by-case basis whether this procedure does not disproportionately compromise the rights of the victims, with reference to their specific vulnerability, notwithstanding the right to a fair trial and ensuring the rights to defence (articles 47 and 48 CFR of the EU).

Another directive (2012/13) sets out shared minimum EU laws on right to information in criminal proceedings, in line with the principles of a fair trial, presumption of innocence and right to defence by the CFR of the EU (articles 47 and 48). Its aim is to harmonise criminal procedure regulations between Member States and to enhancing mutual trust on criminal matters among Member States. In a trial for handling the proceeds of crime, which was then reclassified as theft, the Bari District Court noted that the current Italian law allows the accused to apply for a negotiated penalty (*patteggiamento*) only in cases in which a mere legal reclassification of the act occurs, as opposed to a change in facts. The doubt is as to whether this limited provision to apply for a negotiated penalty complies with Directive 2012/13, which lays down the standards that the accused has the right to information about the accusation filed against them, and the instruments to prepare their defence, under article 48 CFR of the EU on the right to a defence. The ECJ firstly confirmed that it had competence to rule on the question, despite the fact that the case has no transnational aspects (a crime committed in Italy by an Italian against other Italian citizens). If it is true that the CFR of the EU does not apply unless the issues falls under the scope of the application of EU law (article 51(1) CFR of the EU) and among these, there is no definition of the crimes of theft or handling the proceeds of crime, then it is also true that it falls under the competences of the EU to legislate in order to facilitate the mutual recognition of judgments and judicial decisions (article 82 TFEU). The Directive in question falls within this framework, as therefore does the question of a possible violation of article 48 CFR of the EU. On the issue, the ECJ concluded that there was no incompatibility between Italian law and EU law. EU law makes no mention of negotiated penalty procedures and can therefore not be called to rule on an alleged limitation of the possibility of an accused person to benefit from such a possibility (ECJ, case C-646/17).

VI Public Contracts and Super-accelerated Procedures

In 2017, a super-accelerated procedure on public contracts foresees, among other things, the possibility for a company to challenge the admission of another participant to the assignment for a public contract within 30 days of the decision on the admission or exclusion, that is, when the assignment of the role has not yet been decided. In this way, however, challenging the decision (other than being based on unknown elements) could present unnecessary costs to a company: an applicant admitted to the tender may not ultimately receive the contract, and contesting her admission would prove completely inconclusive. To not do so, however, would render the next challenge inadmissible, due to the ongoing use of a sunset clause. According to the referring court, this constitutes a violation of the principle of a fair trial (article 47 CFR of the EU). According the ECJ, Italian law on this issue was in compliance with EU law, which is not opposed to rapid procedures and with stringent deadlines; however, the act must admit applicants to a tender in the knowledge they will be notified of any decision with motivated reasons, in order to make any appeal on the grounds of a violation of EU law possible. As for the actual interest in challenging an admission provision before knowing the outcome of the procedure, the ECJ held that challenging an illegal measure is significant in itself, regardless of the outcome of the administrative procedure.

VII Age-Based Discrimination

An airline pilot (an employee of a private company working in the national security sector) was sent automatically in retirement on his sixtieth birthday, despite an EU regulation establishing an age limit for commercial pilots of 65 years and directive 2000/78 which establishes a blanket-ban on every type of discrimination in employment and work conditions based on age, as well as religion, personal beliefs, disabilities, or sexual orientation. A difference of treatment may be justified where a characteristic constitutes a genuine and determining occupational requirement as well as when, in a democratic society and laid down by national law, it is to protect public security, to maintain public order and prevent criminal offences, to protect health and protect the rights and freedoms of others and when the objective is legitimate and the requirement is proportionate. The issue of aviation safety could justify the establishment of a lower retirement age limit for pilots, especially given that the case dealt with non-commercial flights (that is, operating aircraft used for activities associated with protecting national security). However, while an age limit of 60 years may be essential and instrumental to carry out this type of work, the fact that it occurs automatically could be disproportionate. In conclusion, the ECJ ruled that Italian law laying out the automatic dismissal of company-employed pilots operating in activities associated with protecting national security once they reach the age of 60 does not respect the principle of non-discrimination based on age. It must therefore be decided by a judge on a case-by-case basis on whether the circumstances justify a ban of persons to fly for public security or for medical or psychological reasons (ECJ, C-396/18).

Research and Editorial Committee

Andrea Cofelice, MA in Institutions and Policies of Human Rights and Peace, University of Padova. PhD in Political Science – Comparative and European Politics, University of Siena.

Pietro de Perini, Lecturer of Human Rights in International Politics in the Master's Degree Programme in Human Rights and Multi-Level Governance at the University of Padova. MA in Institutions and Policies of Human Rights and Peace, University of Padova. PhD in International Politics, City, University of London.

Paolo De Stefani, Aggregate Professor of International Law of Human Rights in the Master's Degree Programme in Human Rights and Multi-level Governance at the University of Padova. He is National Director for Italy of the European Master in Human Rights and Democratisation (E.MA).

Ino Kehrer, PhD candidate in Human Rights, Society and Multi-Level Governance, University of Padova Human Rights Centre. LLM, University of Bologna.

Marco Mascia, Associate Professor of International Relations, UNESCO Chair "Human Rights, Democracy and Peace", Director of the Master's Degree Programme in Human Rights and Multi-Level Governance, University of Padova.

Fabia Mellina Bares, Former Ombudsperson for children of the Region Friuli-Venezia Giulia. Expert in institutions and techniques of human rights protection.

Index

D

E

F

G

Table of Cases

Court of Cassation, Criminal Division

Administrative Courts

Territorial Courts

European Court of Human Rights (in alphabetical order)

Court of Justice of the European Union

European Committee of Social Rights, decisions on collective complaints

Peter Lang – Italian Yearbook of Human Rights Series

The legal and political significance of human rights has increased enormously at the international and European levels. Awareness has risen that the respect and the promotion of human rights must be at the centre of States and local communities' public policies and that human rights are at the basis of civil society initiatives and movements. There is a large machinery monitoring, at all the levels of governance, the way in which States implement the obligations assumed toward each person under their sovereignty.

The **Italian Yearbook of Human Rights Series** provides year by year, a dynamic and up-to date overview of the measures Italy has taken to adapt its legislation and policies to international human rights law and to comply with commitments voluntarily assumed by the Italian Government at the international level. The Series thus intends to contribute to the continuous monitoring activity on the situation of human rights in Italy undertaken at the local, national and international levels by relevant intergovernmental and civil society actors.

Each volume of this series surveys the activities carried out, during the year of reference, by the relevant national and local Italian actors, including governmental bodies, civil society organisations and universities. It also presents reports and recommendations that have been addressed to Italy by international monitoring bodies within the framework of the United Nations, the Council of Europe and the European Union. Finally, each Yearbook provides a selection of examples from international and national case-law which cast light on Italy's position vis-à-vis internationally recognised human rights.

The Yearbook is edited by the Human Rights Centre of the University of Padova, in cooperation with the UNESCO Chair in Human Rights, Democracy and Peace of the same University, and with the support of the Region of Veneto. The Centre, established in 1982, carries out research and education following a global and interdisciplinary approach. It hosts the Jean Monnet Centre of Excellence on intercultural dialogue, human rights and multi-level governance.

www.peterlang.com

www.ingramcontent.com/pod-product-compliance
Ingram Content Group UK Ltd.
Pitfield, Milton Keynes, MK11 3LW, UK
UKHW021847100926
8556IPUK00020B/1105

9 782807 617957